ON STOIC AND PERIPATETIC ETHICS

THE WORK OF ARIUS DIDYMUS

RUTGERS UNIVERSITY STUDIES IN CLASSICAL HUMANITIES

Volume I:

ON STOIC AND PERIPATETIC ETHICS
THE WORK OF ARIUS DIDYMUS

EDITOR: William W. Fortenbaugh

Transaction Books
New Brunswick (U.S.A.) and London (U.K.)

ISSN: 0732-9814
ISBN: 0-87855-462-9 (cloth)
Printed in the United States of America

Contents

PREFACE

This is the first volume of *Rutgers University Studies in Classical Humanities*. The second volume will follow in two years and subsequent publication will be biennial. Each volume will focus on a single author or theme. The language of publication will be English, but contributors will not be restricted to the English speaking world.

Earlier versions of the papers and comments collected within this volume were presented at a conference on Arius Didymus, held at Rutgers University on March 26–28, 1981. Many of the contributions have been considerably reworked; all have benefited from the discussion which followed their initial presentation. The contributors are to be thanked for meeting publication deadlines, and Phillip DeLacy merits special mention for an editorial assist.

The Rutgers conference on Arius Didymus was held in conjunction with a meeting of Project Theophrastus. This is an international undertaking, whose goal is to collect, edit, translate and comment on the fragments of Theophrastus, Peripatetic philosopher and successor to Aristotle as head of the Lyceum. The next major meeting of the project is scheduled for 1983 at the University of Liverpool, England. A conference is again planned, this time focusing on Theophrastus. The papers of the conference will form Volume II of this series.

The National Endowment for the Humanities, the Provost's Office of Rutgers University, the British Council, and University College, London, are to be thanked for financial assistance most generously provided to several persons participating in the Arius Didymus conference of 1981.

W.W.F.

List of Contributors

Phillip H. DE LACY, 14 West Eleventh, P.O. Box 64, Barnegat Light, New Jersey 08006, U.S.A.

William W. FORTENBAUGH, Project Theophrastus, Alexander Library, Rutgers University, New Brunswick, New Jersey 08903, U.S.A.

David J. FURLEY, Department of Classics, Princeton University, Princeton, New Jersey 08544, U.S.A.

Herwig GÖRGEMANNS, Seminar fur klassische Philologie, Universität Heidelberg, 69 Heidelberg 7, West Germany

Allan GOTTHELF, Department of Philosophy, Trenton State College, Trenton, New Jersey 08625, U.S.A.

David E. HAHM, Department of Classics, Ohio State University, Columbus, Ohio 43210, U.S.A.

Pamela M. HUBY, Department of Philosophy, The University of Liverpool, P.O. Box 147, Liverpool L69 3BX, England

Brad INWOOD, Department of Classics, Stanford University, Stanford, California 94305, U.S.A.

Charles H. KAHN, Department of Philosophy, University of Pennsylvania, Philadelphia, Pennsylvania 19104, U.S.A.

George B. KERFERD, School of Classical Studies, University of Manchester, Manchester M13 9PL, England

Ian G. KIDD, St. Salvator's College, St. Andrews, Fife KY16 9AL, Scotland

Anthony A. LONG, School of Classics, The University of Liverpool, P.O. Box 147, Liverpool L69 3BX, England

Anthony PREUS, Department of Philosophy, State University of New York, Binghamton, New York 13901, U.S.A.

Margaret E. REESOR, Department of Classics, Queen's University, Kingston K7L 3N6, Canada

Michael D. ROHR, Department of Philosophy, Rutgers University, Newark, New Jersey 07102, U.S.A.

David SEDLEY, Christ's College, Cambridge, CB2 3BU, England

Robert W. SHARPLES, Department of Greek, University College, Gower Street, London WCIE 6BT, England

Nicholas P. WHITE, Department of Philosophy, University of Michigan, Ann Arbor, Michigan 48109, U.S.A.

PART I
General Papers

CHAPTER 1

Arius as a Doxographer

Charles H. Kahn

Arius Didymus or the Warlike Twin (as his Greek name might be rendered) is not one of the more familiar figures in the history of ancient philosophy. When I was invited to contribute a paper on Arius, the only thing I knew about him was that some interesting fragments were collected under his name in Diels' *Doxographi Graeci* (1879), including the most authentic version of Heraclitus' famous remark about the river (fr. 12 D.-K.). I know a bit more now, though much less than one would like to know. Part of the difficulty lies in the inadequate nature of our information; but there is also a formidable, and, in principle, removable obstacle to our study, which consists in the fact that the surviving remnants of Arius' work have never been collected in one place. Diels edited in the *Doxographi* only what he regarded as "physical" fragments. For the texts on ethics, which are too extensive to count as fragments, there has never been any proper edition. We are still obliged to consult these texts in Wachsmuth's 1884 edition of Ioannes Stobaeus' *Eclogae* or *Anthology*. Perhaps one happy result of the present group of papers may be the realization that Arius deserves an edition of his own, even if such an edition is composed by photographic reprint of the relevant texts from Diels and Wachsmuth.

This curious neglect of Arius as an author must be due to the rather accidental way in which his work has been preserved—or, to put it from our point of view, the indirect way in which his work was discovered and reconstituted, largely from anonymous quotations in Stobaeus. It will be best to begin with a brief review of the detective work by which Diels (following Meineke) brought Arius Didymus to light. I do not propose to redo Diels' work, which still stands unrivalled and mostly unchallenged after a century of active scholarship in the field. But I do want to sketch some of the main lines of inference and reconstruction, and mention some of the questions that can be raised. You will not expect me to provide all the answers.

First of all, there is the problem which philosophers call "fixing the reference." Whom are we talking about? Since the papers brought together here focus on Stoic and Peripatetic ethics, I assume that the name "Arius" is used first of all as a rigid designator for whoever it was that wrote the two corresponding sections of Chapter 7 in Book 2 of Stobaeus' *Eclogae* (pp. 57–152 in Wachsmuth's edition). Wachsmuth has actually printed the title "from the epitome of Didymus" at the beginning of this long chapter (p. 37.16), although the name "Didymus" is not found in the MSS. here, and the title *Epitome* is not found in the first two books of the *Eclogae* at all. Both name and title are, however, confirmed for at least part of the Peripatetic section by a passage in Stobaeus 4.39.28 *(Florilegium* ed. Hense, Vol. 3, p. 918.15), a passage verbally identical with *Eclogae* 2.7.17, and where the text of Book 4 does contain the lemma "from the *Epitome* of Didymus." So it is reasonably well established that Stobaeus' source for Peripatetic ethics was an *Epitome* ascribed to someone named Didymus. Let us take the next step and assume (with nearly everyone since Meineke and Diels) that there is *one* source for all three sections of Chapter 7, including the discussion of Stoic ethics (pp. 57–116) as well as the long introductory section on ethics in general and its divisions. This means assuming that the "I" of the introduction (pp. 41.26–42.11, 45.9–10) refers to the same author as the "I" of the Stoic section (pp. 57.15–17, 116.15–18), namely, to our friend Didymus.[1] I do not intend to be sceptical on the unity of authorship here; but it is worth pointing out that the material is quite heterogeneous and occasionally contradictory, especially in the introductory part. Style and procedure are also rather different in the three sections. As just noted, the author speaks in the first person in the introduction, where he explains his choice of organizing scheme, and again in the first person in introducing and closing the section on the Stoics. The account of Aristotelian ethics, however, is presented passionately but impersonally. Furthermore, the introduction and conclusion to the Stoic section make it look entirely self-contained.

Not only are there no clear *external* signs of continuity between the three sections; according to Diels, they would in fact have been taken from three quite different parts of the *Epitome*. In Diels' view, the *Epitome* was organized by schools, not by topics, so that the two sections on ethics would have been separated by a treatment of Stoic logic and physics; while the introductory discussion of ethics and its divisions would have been separated from the account of Peripatetic ethics by three sections on Plato and two on Aristotle.[2] If Diels is even approximately correct on the general outline of the *Epitome,* Stobaeus has not only combined material from three widely separated sections of the work; he has also reversed the order of Stoics and Peripatetics, while omitting a section on Platonic ethics altogether. So even if Stobaeus has transcribed Didymus' text verbatim (as we might reasonably suppose, on the basis of the evidence for Plato and the poets, where Stobaeus' source has been independently preserved), he has been quite free in selecting and transposing his material. It is only by conjecture that we (following or modifying the conjectures of Diels) can reconstruct the outline of the lost *Epitome*.

That Didymus' first name was Arius, and that his work included a section on physics, we know not from Stobaeus at all but from two passages in Eusebius' *Praeparatio evangelica* (frs. 29 and 39 in Diels, *Dox.* 464f. and 470f.), where Stoic doctrines on god and the soul are cited "from the *Epitome* (or *Epitomai)* of Arius Didymus."[3] On the basis of these two references (and another passage from Eusebius, to be mentioned in a moment), Diels assigned to Didymus some thirty-eight passages on Aristotelian and Stoic physics from the *first* book of Stobaeus' *Eclogae*. One of these thirty-eight texts (Diels' fr. 1) is a passage on Plato's doctrine of Ideas that is found *both* in Stobaeus 1 and in Eusebius, who quotes this text "from Didymus' account of the doctrines of Plato" (*Dox.* 447). Now the evidence from Eusebius on frs. 29 and 39 gives us good reason for believing that the strictly physical fragments of Stobaeus 1 *also* come from Didymus, and from the same *Epitome* that is utilized for ethics in Stobaeus 2. But the passage on Platonic Ideas (Diels fr. 1) has a different status, and we may reasonably raise two questions here: (1) Is this passage also taken from the *Epitome,* despite the different form in which the title is cited? And (2) if so, does it belong to the section on *physics,* as Diels assumed? For the moment I leave the first question open, but I want to answer a hesitant "no" to the second question. In the chapter "On Ideas" in Stobaeus 1 (ch. 12), the passage on Plato is followed by one on Zeno, which tells us that the Stoics denied the existence of Ideas but referred instead to "concepts," *ennoēmata* (Stobaeus 1.12.3 = Ar. Did. fr. 40 in Diels, *Dox* . 472). Now this passage on Stoic "concepts" is verbally identical with the definition of the term *ennoēma* in Diogenes Laertius 7.61; but that definition occurs, naturally enough, in the section on Stoic "logic," not physics. So Diels' fr. 40 probably, and fr. 1 possibly, belonged not to physics at all but to Arius' treatment of the rational or "logical" branch of philosophy. Diels thought that nothing was preserved of Arius' account of the *logikon meros,* but he seems to have been mistaken. Besides these two texts on Ideas and concepts, we have another quotation that is even more likely to belong to an epistemological section of Didymus' work. The passage is at Stobaeus 2.2.17 (pp.6.13–18), the only place where Didymus' name actually appears in *Eclogae* 1–2. What we find there quoted "from Didymus' work *On the Schools"* is the statement that Xenophanes was the first to introduce to the Greeks "a *logos* worth mentioning; he attacked in a playful way the audacity of others and insisted on his own caution, admitting that god of course knows the truth but 'guesswork (*dokos*) is what we have on all things'" (D.-K.21.A24, including the last verse of B34). Now whatever *logos* means here, the quotation must come from a context where knowledge and certainty are under discussion. (Thus the title of this chapter in Stobaeus claims "that the truth of intelligible things is *akataleptos* for men.") So we have a third quotation from Didymus apparently pertaining to the *logikon meros* of philosophy.

This Xenophanes text is interesting for several reasons. Dealing as it does with a Presocratic doctrine it will not naturally fit into Diels' picture of Arius' *Epitome* as treating only Plato, Aristotle and the Stoics. On the other hand, Didymus is cited here not as author of the *Epitome* but of a work *On the (philosophic) Schools (Peri haireseōn).* This title is sometimes given by modern scholars as the name for the work on ethics preserved in Stobaeus 2.[4] But others have suggested that the *Epitome* represented Arius' own excerpts from a longer work *On the Schools* (or *On the Doctrines of Philosophers*), in which the Presocratic schools were treated as well.[5] The evidence is so slight, however, that it seems unprofitable to entertain the hypothesis of two distinct works. The most reasonable assumption is the one recently restated by Moraux,[6] in essential agreement with Diels: The title *Epitome* refers to Arius' original work, which was itself a compendium or compilation of doctrines from a variety of sources, a kind of résumé summarizing views on the principal topics, as he says in connection with the Stoic section (pp. 57.15–16, 116.15–18). The title *On the Schools* refers to the same work, described in terms of its contents. And the title *On the Doctrines of Plato* (*Dox.* 447n.) will refer to a section of that work.

These titles give some support to Diels' view that Arius' handbook was organized by schools rather than by topics. But not much can be inferred from such a title, as we see from Arius' own use of the phrase *ta peri tōn areskontōn* ("The account of the doctrines ") at p.41.28, where it simply refers to the doctrines reported in the body of the work. A similar title is attached to the Plutarchean *Placita,* which are organized by topics rather than by schools.[7] The beginning of the preserved Stoic section from Didymus does suggest that it treats ethics in the context of other Stoic doctrines: "*I shall next (hexēs) give the résumé of ethics*" (p. 57.15–16); so perhaps Diels was right after all in assuming that the work was organized by schools. But there is no trace of any systematic treatment of Platonic ethics or physics, and only very slight evidence for any treatment of logic.

So much for the inferences that take us back from Stobaeus to his source, Arius Didymus. If we can say no more about the format of the book, we can say more about the man. For there seems no reason to doubt that our author is identical with the Arius who was court philosopher to Augustus and whose consolation to Livia on the death of Drusus is so fervently praised (and apparently paraphrased) by Seneca. Seneca, referring to Livia, calls Arius "her husband's philosopher," *philosophus viri sui,* and has Arius say that he is such a close friend of Augustus that he is acquainted with the intimate thoughts of both husband and wife *(Consolatio ad Marciam* 4). The most famous of several stories concerning Arius shows him in Augustus' company when the latter captured Alexandria: Augustus entered the city arm-in-arm with Arius, in private conversation, and then announced to the terrified Alexandrians that he was going to spare their city and their lives for three reasons: for their god Serapis, for their founder Alexander, and for their countryman, his philosopher-companion Arius.[8]

Thus we have a clear picture of Arius as philosophic intimate and advisor to the unchallenged ruler of the Mediterranean world for more than twenty years, from the capture of Alexandria (30 B.C.) to the death of Drusus (9 B.C.). Arius seems to have actually played the role which Plato dreamed of and Kant recommended: the philosopher as intimate counsellor to a king or emperor. (There are of course Platonic and Hellenistic parallels of monarchs inviting philosophers to their courts, though perhaps none so dramatically documented and long sustained.) We would naturally like to know what kind of philosophy shaped Arius' advice and what kind of policy he recommended.[9]

The standard modern histories (such as Zeller and Pohlenz) represent Arius as an eclectic Stoic, on good terms with Academics and Peripatetics alike, and pursuing a comprehensive vision of philosophy inherited from Antiochus of Ascalon, in which the three schools give different versions of what is essentially a single doctrine of virtue as the intrinsic good of the soul and a conception of the universe as organized by divine providence. Thus Pohlenz sees Arius as dealing with "the three Socratic schools," essentially from the standpoint of Antiochus, a standpoint taken for granted by Cicero and by most educated men of this age, emphasizing the role of philosophy as a practical guide to life while neglecting the theoretical polemic on doctrinal differences that had loomed so large in the third and second centuries B.C.[10] Diels pointed out that the philosophical milieu of Arius is more literary (or historical) and rhetorical than rigorous or argumentative: It was in Alexandria first of all that, in Seneca's words, *quae philosophia fuit, philologia facta est* (*Dox.* p.81). The famous consolation to Livia suggests just how effective and practical this applied philosophy could be. Arius seems to have combined the "edifying turn" in the Stoic tradition, prepared by Panaetius, with the revisionist harmonizing history of the Socratic schools initiated by Antiochus.

Can we go beyond these generalities and say anything definite about Arius' own approach to philosophical issues or his method of dealing with his sources? The problem is painfully complicated. In the first place, we cannot know how far Stobaeus (and perhaps some unknown intermediate source between Arius and Stobaeus) has abridged or distorted Arius' text. What is worse, it seems clear that Arius' work was itself already a compilation or extract from a multitude of different sources, some (perhaps all) of which were in turn compiled from earlier works. Thus when we find a literal quotation from Plato or Aristotle, we cannot be sure whether (1) Arius has himself consulted the original text, or (2) he has copied the quotation from a major author, like Cleanthes or Chrysippus, or (3) he is relying on some earlier manual or compilation which may in turn have the quotation at second or third hand. This last alternative seems in general the more likely. Moraux concludes that *none* of the Aristotelian quotations is made at first hand; it is his judgment that Arius' immediate sources were predominantly "the school literature of the first half of the first century" (p.443). But of course this literature was itself not very original.

So what we have in Arius is a multilayered collage, built up over a period of three centuries, in which the earliest material (from Plato, Aristotle, and the poets) is preserved within a context that may itself date from the third or second century B.C. (as the Heraclitean quotation is preserved in a context from Cleanthes), but which may have been reworked more than once before being excerpted by Arius himself. The situation is clearest in the case of the physical fragments, which we can compare in detail with Aristotle's own text. The comparison shows that Arius' sections on meteorology and astronomy consist very largely of close paraphrase from Aristotle's *Meteorologica*, a paraphrase so faithful that it tends to literal quotation.[11] The technique is essentially the same as in the literal paraphrase of

Plato's *Timaeus* in Theophrastus' *De Sensibus*.[12] However, some passages in Arius' account are derived not from Aristotle at all but from Theophrastus or some later author, perhaps Posidonius; and his knowledge of the variable visibility of solar eclipse at different times and places (fr. 10, *Dox.* 451.17f.) definitely presupposes the work of Hipparchus in the second century B.C.[13] Thus even where Arius is reproducing the text of Aristotle with almost slavish fidelity, there are traces of one or more intermediaries, including an excellent late Hellenistic source who has brought the astronomy up to date. Or could this "source" be Arius himself, drawing upon his own erudition? I see no way to decide such a question.

Under these circumstances it is difficult to recognize Arius' own intellectual personality, much less his literary style. Still, we can do something to make more precise what is meant by Arius' eclecticism and his harmonizing tendencies. As I have mentioned, his presentations of Stoic and Peripatetic ethics are strikingly different from one another; each section has distinctive characteristics, some of which will be discussed by other contributors to this volume. The contrast between the two accounts suggests that Arius was not a very skillful harmonizer, if harmonizing was his goal. But perhaps he simply chose in each case the available version which seemed to him the best and most informative, just as he says he chose the arrangement of topics that he found to be the clearest (p.45.10). The quite unusual eloquence which readers have admired in his Peripatetic section may be his own: after all, the intellectual mentor of Augustus and consoler of Livia must have been a man of considerable verbal power. I am in no position to pass a stylistic judgment here. But I want to propose for your consideration the idea that the *Epitome* of Arius was a kind of loosely organized and heterogeneous scrapbook in which he sometimes copied more or less verbatim from an earlier source (as in the Aristotelian meteorology) and sometimes organized the material according to his own plan and very largely in his own words. This seems to be true for the section on Stoic ethics, which is carefully rounded off by opening and closing remarks in the first person. If it is true that this section is arranged according to the division borrowed from Eudorus, that tends to confirm my suggestion that we should recognize a good deal of Arius' own personal work here in the organizing of material. His presentation of Peripatetic ethics from a fundamentally Stoic point of view may again reflect the personal conviction of our author, who is no doubt drawing on some earlier source (Antiochus or the like) but a source selected for its moral truth rather than for its historical accuracy. Why he ascribes the doctrine of *oikeiōsis* to Aristotle and not to the Stoics is an interesting question to which I shall return.

First a word about historical accuracy. That is obviously not Arius' *primary* concern. His contamination of Aristotelian ethics is an extreme case; some anachronism of vocabulary, even of doctrine, can be illustrated from every page. As Moraux has emphasized, there is no trace of the kind of scholarly rigor introduced by Andronicus into the study of Aristotle. Nevertheless, Arius achieves a level of historical reliability that compares very favorably with other representatives of his own handbook tradition, like Diogenes Laertius or Aetius. Arius had access to good sources, and he used them intelligently. As we have seen, his résumé of Aristotelian physics is outstanding; among all extant doxographies its quality can be matched only by the work of Theophrastus himself. We are unable to check his report on Stoic physics against the original texts, but we can appreciate the care with which he distinguishes between views ascribed to Zeno, Chrysippus, Posidonius, and Panaetius. Similarly for Stoic ethics: Arius is the only author to point out that Zeno defined the *telos* simply as *to homologoumenōs zēn* whereas Cleanthes added *tēi physei* (p.75f.). In view of Arius' isolation on this point, most nineteenth century scholars preferred the testimony of Diogenes and Cicero;[14] but recent historians of Stoicism have accepted Arius' report as the more reliable.[15]

Similar care in drawing technical distinctions can be observed even where his general report is contaminated. Thus the definition of *pathos* ascribed to Aristotle as "irrational movement of the soul tending to excess (*pleonastikē*)" is certainly anachronistic (p.38.18); but Arius himself contrasts this with the Stoic definition of *pathos* as "impulse in excess" (*hormē pleonazousa*) and points out that whereas for Aristotle a *pathos* is only *potentially* excessive, since it may also be *deficient*, for the Stoics it is always excessive (pp. 38.22–39.7). Thus he has Aristotle's doctrine right, even where the formulation is misleading. Even at the level of terminology he can observe that "none of the ancients used the word *hypotelis*, although they knew the thing" (48.3–5).

I conclude that Arius was a very intelligent man with an intellectual conscience and the capacity to draw significant distinctions. This is not to say that he had a good historical sense or a taste for scholarship for its own sake. But it does mean that his "harmonizing" tendency should not be exaggerated. It may or may not be true that the motive behind the work was, in the spirit of Antiochus, to show that the three Socratic schools agreed upon essentials. That is certainly not his explicit project. What he set out to do was to report *what the schools said,* and that meant, in general, to report different things for different schools. What is genuinely Antiochean, perhaps, is his sympathetic attitude to all three schools. This openness of mind is most clearly displayed in the introductory section (Stobaeus 2, pp.37–57); and I will conclude with a brief analysis of this passage.

These twenty pages divide into three unequal parts: (1) a short section on terms,[16] specifically the terms *ēthikē, ēthos, pathos, and ēthikē aretē*; (2) a discussion of the divisions of philosophy, summarizing the schemes of Philo of Larisa and Eudorus of Alexandria, both Academics; and (3) a somewhat rambling account of definitions of *telos* and of goods and evils, beginning with the poets and with dialectal uses, including definitions from Stoics and Epicureans, but focussing on "the ancients": Socrates, Pythagoras, Democritus, and above all Plato and Aristotle. (Thus the view of Eudoxus on pleasure as the end is cited from "the tenth book of the *Nicomachean ⟨Ethics⟩*," p.52.10). There is certainly evidence for Stoic terminology here, and traces of Stoic doctrine both implicit and explicit. Still, the dominant coloring is Platonic or Academic throughout. Thus the opening (essentially Aristotelian) definitions of moral character are assigned to "those who philosophize according to Plato" (p.38.14); both of the authorities cited for divisions of philosophy are Academics; and in the discussion of *telos*, goods, and evils, quotations from or allusion to the Platonic dialogues abound: *Timaeus* and *Laws* are cited repeatedly, but also *Protagoras, Theaetetus, Republic*, and *Philebus*. (I am struck by the intelligent, if not necessarily correct, account of the five-fold hierarchy of goods from the end of the *Philebus*: p.55.13–21.) There is also an echo of an etymology of *kalon* from the *Cratylus* at p.57.3–4. Thus we have six or seven dialogues cited in nine pages (49–57), including a long passage on human and divine goods from the *Laws* (p.54f.), quoted "for the beauty of its language and for its clarity." This introductory section breaks off with a contrast between Platonic and Aristotelian views of happiness, based upon the distinction between the possession and exercise of virtue (p.57).

Why should Arius' introduction be so loaded with Platonic elements, taking "Platonic" in the broadest sense to include Aristotle as well as Philo and Eudorus? Two alternative explanations come to mind: (1) that Arius has borrowed his introduction, more or less as we have it, from an Academic source, say from the school of Antiochus, or (2) he has himself selected "ancient" material from a variety of sources, in an archaizing spirit, deliberately returning to the noble origins of that Socratic tradition that is best represented in the dialogues of Plato (and in the works of Aristotle), but which is still alive in the contemporary Academy. In this case the first alternative, the hypothesis of wholesale borrowing from an earlier source, can probably be ruled out. The extensive use of a minor Alexandrian Academic (Eudorus) is pretty clearly the work of our own Alexandrian philosopher. And the chronological indications point to Arius himself. On the one hand Philo is quoted as a figure of the past: "Philo was a Larissaean, an Academic philosopher" (p.39.20). As a *terminus post quem*, this brings us down well into the first century B.C., practically to Arius' own lifetime. On the other hand, Eudorus is cited as if he were a contemporary ("author of a book worth getting," p.42.9); and we have independent evidence for dating Eudorus in the period of Augustus.[17] But if Eudorus and Arius are contemporaries, and fellow citizens of Alexandria, it is surely gratuitous to posit an unknown "intermediary" between them. So the introductory section as such is vindicated as Arius' own composition, even if he has borrowed some of the contents from earlier authors (e.g., probably the philological material on *telos*, perhaps the references to Aristotle, possibly even the quotations from Plato—though I would prefer to believe that Arius was capable of reading Plato for himself). And if it is true that the section on Stoic ethics is also based on the scheme of Eudorus (as Anthony Long, Giusta, and others have argued), then we have conclusive evidence that the "I" of the introduction and the "I" of the Stoic section both refer directly to Arius.

The opening pages of Chapter 7 constitute an introduction to ethics alone, not to physics, much less to logic. I suspect the *Epitome* was more loosely structured than Diels believed; and I propose to leave completely open the question how material from the other two branches of philosophy was arranged. Let us imagine that Stobaeus has preserved the bulk of Arius' discussion of ethics, only changing the order for reasons of his own, to bring the Stoics before the Peripatetics. Then we might explain the preponderance of Platonic material in the introduction by assuming *that Arius never composed a separate section on Platonic ethics,* of which we have after all no trace. I do not mean to insist too heavily on this suggestion. I mention it as a possibility, in order to bring out more clearly whatever connections we can find between the three sections as we have them. To the emphasis on Aristotle's own works in the introduction ("the *Nicomachean* ⟨*Ethics*⟩" cited at 52.10, "the *Ethics*" at 57.12) would correspond to the shift to Theophrastus and much later Peripatetics (or crypto-Stoics) in the following account of Aristotelian doctrine. And if we think of these three sections as originally standing in close proximity, rather than in the widely separated positions assigned to them by Diels, we may be better able to understand one of the strangest features of our text: namely, that the Stoic doctrine of *oikeiōsis,* which is presented in the introduction (first verbally implied at pp.44.7–9, 13, then briefly sketched in the account of *hypotelis* at p.47f.), and which is developed at length and with great ardor in the Peripatetic section (pp.118–26), is scarcely mentioned in the account of Stoic ethics. Regardless of the historical facts concerning the origins of this theory (and I am willing to believe that it is essentially Stoic), it seems clear that for Arius the doctrine of *oikeiōsis* was *not* the property of a single school. It expressed a truth about human nature, and about nature generally. And this truth was (in his view) also recognized by the Aristotelians, who founded ethics on human nature; it was presumably recognized by the Platonists as well. (Hence the language of *oikeiōsis* can be used in describing Eudorus' division of philosophy, which is in any case heavily Stoicized.) As Arius himself says in reference to *hypotelis* (p.48.3–5), perhaps the ancients did not use the word *oikeiōsis,* but they knew the thing. And the fact that Theophrastus *did* use the term *oikeiotēs,* and that Plato in the *Lysis* describes the *oikeion* as what is naturally dear, or *philon,* to someone, these facts can only have confirmed Arius and his sources in their view that the doctrine was ancient and universal. So, having treated this theory briefly in his introduction and at length in his account of the Peripatetics, Arius saw no need to repeat it in the concluding section on Stoic ethics.[18]

NOTES

1. Following Diels, an argument for the unity of authorship for the three sections of Chapter 7 in Stobaeus 2 is given by M. Giusta, *I dossographi di etica* 1 (Turin 1964), p. 39. As far as I can see, the only recent scholar to challenge this unity is Anthony Kenny, *The Aristotelian Ethics* (Oxford 1978), p.21f. Kenny suggests that the introductory section was written by Stobaeus himself, not by Arius. But there seems to be no parallel passage where Stobaeus speaks in his own name, or even in his own words. (And we will find independent support below for the conclusion that the "I" of the introduction, who quotes from Eudorus, must be Arius himself.) Strictly speaking, Stobaeus is not so much an author as a selective copyist: his work consists wholly of quotations, for

which he has provided the titles, that is, the name of the author and, occasionally, of the work quoted. Hence it is misleading to describe Stobaeus as a *source* for any of the information under discussion here; his anthology is simply the container within which the sources have been preserved. (For a partial dissent on this point, see Diels, *Dox.* 75 with n.4.)

2. *Doxographi Graeci,* p.72f. I doubt whether Diels can be right in placing "logic" before physics and ethics, in view of the order cited from Eudorus at pp.42.12–13, but that need not concern us here. (See also J. Dillon, *The Middle Platonists* (London 1977), p.121 with n.1 for the order of subjects.) In any event, Diels' overall reconstruction of the *Epitome* is poorly substantiated and almost certainly too systematic.

3. Fr. 29 cites "*Epitome*" in the singular; the plural "*Epitomai*" occurs at the end of fr. 39.

4. See, e.g., M. Pohlenz *Die Stoa* 1.254.

5. This is the view defended by E. Howald in *Hermes* 55 (1920) 68–69, and developed at length by M. Giusta, *I dossografi di etica,* 2 vols. (Turin 1964 and 1967), who believes, however, that there were a number of Epitomes made by different authors. See especially Giusta, Vol 1, p.193ff. For a general critique of Giusta's reconstruction, see G. B. Kerferd's papers in *The Classical Review* 81 (1967) 156–58, and 85 (1971) 371–73. Cf. Paul Moraux *Der Aristotelismus bei den Griechen* Vol. 1 (Berlin 1973) 264–68.

   The hypothesis of a larger work by Didymus would be slightly more plausible if we could follow Meineke and Zeller (3rd ed. 3.615 n.3) in identifying our Arius with the Didymus cited by Clement as a source for the sayings of the Seven Sages (*Strom.* 1.14.61 = PG vol. 8 col. 760B) and for a study of Pythagorean philosophy (*Strom.* 1.16.80 = PG vol. 8 col. 795A). Diels rejected this identification. (See *Dox.* 79f.; Moraux *Der Aristotelismus* 260 n.6, cites the evidence from Clement and Diels' rejection of it without passing judgment.) But apparently Diels did not notice that the Xenophanes citation poses similar problems for his reconstruction of the *Epitome*. In his view of the work, the only place for a discussion of Xenophanes' initiative in epistemology would be in Arius' (lost) introductory section on the *logikon meros*. That is not an impossible suggestion; compare the references to Pythagoras, Democritus, and other "ancients" in the introduction to ethics (2, pp.49 and 52).

6. P. Moraux *Der Aristotelismus* 270f.

7. Diels, *Dox.* 268 (= Aetius). Note that this work is also entitled an *Epitome*. For Arius' nontechnical use of the phrase *en epitomais,* "in summary form," see 2, p.41.25.

8. Dio Cassius 51.16.3; a slightly different version in Plutarch (*Praec. ger. reip.* 18, p.814D; *Life of Antony* 80; cf. *Reg. apophth. Aug.3,* p.207A–B). Further references in Moraux, *Der Aristotelismus* 261 n.17.

9. According to Plutarch, Arius advised Augustus against making Caesarion king in Egypt with a witty adaptation of *Iliad* 2.204: *ouk agathon polykaisariē*—"too many Caesars is not a good thing" (*Anton.*81). From another anecdote in Plutarch (*Apophth. reg. Aug.,* 5, p. 207B–C) we learn that Augustus appointed Arius as his governor in Sicily.

10. Pohlenz *Die Stoa* 1.254; the influence of Antiochus on Arius is argued for in detail in Zeller 3.616f.

11. Compare, e.g., fr. 12 (*Dox.* 452f.) on whirlwinds, presters, and thunderbolts with *Meteor.* 3.1 370b3–371a29. The last expository sentence of fr. 12 is quoted verbatim from 371a28.

12. See my *Anaximander and the Origins of Greek Cosmology,* p.21, following G. M. Stratton.

13. See Moraux, *Der Aristotelismus* 288f. P. Steinmetz argues for the direct influence of Theophrastus on Arius, in *Die Physik des Theophrast,* (Palingenesia 1, Bad Homburg

1964) pp.196–211, 274–78, 291–94, 297–99, 356f. with Anhang 8. Steinmetz's views are criticized by Moraux, pp. 290–99.

14. See A. C. Pearson *The Fragments of Zeno and Cleanthes* (London 1891) p.163, citing Wellmann and Ueberweg. Cf. Zeller 3.211n.

15. Pohlenz *Die Stoa* 1.116f.; F. H. Sandbach *The Stoics* (London 1975) p.53f.

16. *Peri tōn horōn* p.39.15. Cf. *to horikon meros* in D. L. 7.41–42, *peri horōn* in 7.44.

17. See Zeller 3.611, n.3, citing Strabo 17.1.5 (C.790). Compare Moraux *Der Aristotelismus* 261f. For the connection with Eudorus see H. Dörrie, "Der Platoniker Eudorus von Alexandreia" *Hermes* 79 (1944) 25–39, esp. pp.26 and 32 (where Dörrie suggests that Arius in pp.49–50 is following Eudorus' reading of Plato). See also John Dillon, *The Middle Platonists*, p.115ff. on Eudorus, especially p.122f. on Eudorus' views in Arius.

18. I am grateful to my colleagues in the Rutgers conference for a number of helpful suggestions and corrections, and especially to R. W. Sharples for references on Eudorus. My comments on Arius' treatment of Stoic ethics are directly influenced by Tony Long's contribution, which I had the opportunity to read before my own paper was complete.

CHAPTER 2

The Diaeretic Method and the Purpose of Arius' Doxography

David E. Hahm

The ethical doxography attributed to Arius Didymus raises many baffling questions about Arius' sources, method, and purpose as a doxographer.[1] Not the least of these is the question of Arius' personal role in the process that produced the text recorded by Stobaeus.[2] As a contribution toward the solution of some of these longstanding problems, I would like to investigate one of the prominent features of Arius' doxography, the use of the technique of division. By an analysis of the use of this technique in the Stoic and Peripatetic doxographies and a comparison with the use of division and the discussion of method in the introductory segment, I hope to be able to shed new light on Arius' personal contribution to the creation of the doxographies and his purpose and method as a doxographer.

I. THE STOIC DOXOGRAPHY

The divisions used in the Stoic doxography are of several different types. Some distinguish the different senses of a word, such as "goal" (*telos,* p. 76.16–23). Others divide the species (*eidē*) of a genus (e.g., p.87.14–16). The overwhelming majority, however, are expressed by the formula, "Of *x*, some are *a* and some are *b*" (*tōn. . .ta men. . ., ta de. . . .*), followed by a description of each category or by a specification of some or all of the members of each category. A good example is found at the very beginning of the Stoic doxography: "Of beings (*onta*) some are goods, some evils, and some adiaphora, etc." (57.19–20).

Divisions of this third type abound throughout the first two-thirds of the doxography (pp.57.19–99.5).[3] Though interspersed with other nondiaeretic material, they are so frequently and so consistently cited that they give every indication of constituting a single, coherent *diaeresis*. The series begins in the second line of the doxography with the division of beings (*onta*) into goods, evils, and adiaphora (pp.57.19–58.4). From here the doxographer progresses through a lengthy series of subdivisions of the category of goods. In the course of these subdivisions care is taken first of all to locate the virtues (p.58.5–9, cf. 58.9–62.6);[4] then the *diaeresis* proceeds to divide goods on a variety of grounds, such as universality, location and other attributes (pp.68.24–69.10; 70.8–72.18; 73.1–6, 16–19; 74.15–20; 77.6–15).[5] After the series of subdivisions of goods, the doxographer continues with a series of subdivisions of adiaphora (pp.79.18–80.6; 80.14–81.18; 82.5–19; 82.21–83.9; 84.18–20), in which care is taken to locate the preferred adiaphora (pp.80.16–81.18).

At this point the division of beings (*onta*) is complete and the doxographer turns to a series of divisions of actions, including divisions of appropriate acts (*kathēkonta*, pp. 85.18–86.4), moral acts (*katorthōmata*, p.86.5–8), inappropriate acts (p.86.8–9), passions (*pathē*, p.88.12–15; cf. 90.19–92.20), and finally the primary division of actions (*energēmata*) into moral acts, sins, and neutral acts (pp.96.18–97.5).[6] As this list shows, the surviving divisions of actions are fewer and seem to have been rearranged, with the primary division relegated to a position after the subdivisions; but the original unity of the series is easily recognized by the manner of specification. Whereas all the divisions of goods and adiaphora were specified by lists of nouns or substantival adjectives, the divisions beginning at p.85.12 are specified by verbs in the infinitive mood. The completeness of the divisions, combined with a uniformity of expression that extends to the linguistic form of the examples, strongly suggests that behind all these divisions was a coherent, extended *diaeresis,* dividing first "things," then "actions."

In the light of this pattern the one remaining division, that of men into wise (*spoudaios*) and foolish (*phaulos,* p.99.4–5), looks like a third unit of the original *diaeresis,* namely, a division of people. We may conclude, then, that among the sources for Arius' Stoic doxography there was a coherent division of everything—things, actions, and people,—and that the doxographer incorporated this division, not necessarily in full or continuously, but abridged and distributed throughout the doxography.

If we now disregard the divisions just examined, we see that the remainder of the doxography, though appearing fragmented and discontinuous, for the most part constitutes a series of typical Stoic topics: (1) virtues and vices (pp.60.7–9; 62.7–68.23), (2) goods and evils (pp.69.11–70.7), (3) the goal (pp.75.7–77.5; 77.16–78.6), (4) adiaphora (pp.79.1–17; 80.6–13; 81.19–82.4; 82.20–21; 83.10–84.17; 84.21–85.11), (5) appropriate acts (pp.85.12–86.4; 86.10–16), (6) impulses (pp.86.17–88.6), (7) passions (pp.88.6–93.13), (8) moral acts (93.14–18; 97.5–98.13), and the wise man (98.14–116.10).[7] To be sure, not every topic is discussed in full detail and the first five are interrupted by the interpolation of divisions from the previously sketched series; but on the whole this material gives the impression of having been drawn from a doxographic source similar to the kind preserved in Diogenes Laertius 7.[8] In fact, Diogenes' doxography contains an almost identical series of topics: (1) the goal (7.85–88); (2) virtues and vices (89–93); (3) goods and evils (94–101); (4) adiaphora (102–107); (5) appropriate acts (108–110); (6) the soul and the origin of the passions (110); (7) passions (111–116); and (8) the wise man (117–125 [or 131]).

This leads to the conclusion that the doxographer who originally composed the Stoic doxography has combined two sources: a typical doxographic survey and a separate coherent *diaeresis* of things, actions, and men. The synthesis has been skillfully arranged so that the divisions and the topics of the survey are interwoven with each other as follows:

Divisions	*Survey Topics*
I. Things	⎧ *1. Virtue*
A. Goods and Evils	⎨ *2. Goods and Evils*
	⎩ *3. The Goal*
B. Adiaphora	*4. Adiaphora*
	⎧ *5. Appropriate Acts*
II. Actions	⎪ *6. Impulses*
	⎨ *7. Passions*
	⎩ *8. Moral Acts*
III. Men	*9. The Wise Man and the Fool*

This approach to the creation of a Stoic doxography is unique with Arius, as a comparison with the Stoic doxographies of Diogenes Laertius and Cicero brings out.[9] Both Diogenes Laertius and Cicero *De finibus* in some way incorporate the divisions found in Arius' doxography, but these divisions are presented as topics in series with the other topics. The division of goods and evils presents the most striking contrast. In both Diogenes and Cicero the entire division of goods and evils is presented as a unit under the topic of goods and evils (D. L. 7.95–8; Cic., *Fin.* 3.55). Arius' doxography, in contrast, enlarges this set of divisions to surround and encompass the topics of virtue and the goal, as well as the topic of goods and evils. The division has provided the framework; the topics of the survey have been interpolated into the division as appropriate.[10] Though the contrast between Arius' procedure and that of Diogenes and Cicero in the use of the divisions of adiaphora and appropriate acts is less striking, the difference is similar (D. L. 7.105–7; Cic., *Fin.* 3.56).

The role of division in the Stoic doxography thus begins to become clear: it provides the fundamental structure for the presentation of Stoic ethics, a structure that is implicitly tripartite, proceeding from things to actions to men.[11] But the *diaeresis* does more than provide an orderly arrangement of the subject matter; it shapes the reader's entire approach to the question of ethics. The Stoic doxography in its present state provides an elaborate map of the moral universe.[12] The predominant function of this map, which is primarily the result of the elaborate *diaeresis* that surrounds and permeates the discussion, is the location of the constituents of the moral universe on the scale of moral value. This is evident from the categories chosen for the divisions. The primary divisions are all made into positive and negative categories. Things are divided into goods, evils, and adiaphora (p.57.19–20). Actions are divided into moral acts (*katorthōmata*), sins (*hamartēmata*) and neutral acts (*oudetera*, p.96.18–19). Men are divided into wise men (*spoudaioi*) and fools (*phauloi*, p.99.3–5).

Among the subsequent subdivisions, classification into positive and negative categories also predominates. Adiaphora are divided into natural, unnatural, and neutral (p.79.18–19) or into those possessing more worth and those possesing less worth (p.80.14–15) or, again, into preferred (*proēgmena*), rejected, and neutral (p.80.16–21). Appropriate acts (*kathēkonta*) are divided into perfect appropriate acts (i.e., moral acts) and imperfect, or intermediate (*mesa*), appropriate acts (pp.85.18–86.4). In fact, virtually every division is made in terms of categories that at least possess a positive or negative connotation.[13] Even what might have been a non-evaluative division, the division of preferred adiaphora on the basis of location (p.80.22–3), is explicitly transformed into a comparative division: "Since the soul is more important (*kyriōteras*) than the body also for living in accord with nature, they say that the natural and preferred [adiaphora] pertaining to the soul have more worth than those pertaining to the body or those that are external" (pp.81.19–82.2).[14]

Arius' complex map of the Stoic system of values is rooted in the Stoic doctrine of nature. Though the Stoic doxography nowhere provides an extended discussion of the doctrine of *oikeiōsis* and the first natural impulse, as do the doxographies of Diogenes and Cicero, it is clear that this theory provides the theoretical basis for an evaluation of moral worth in the world. From the outset the doxographer simply assumes that virtue is natural. Twice he reminds his readers that the impulse (*aphormē*) to virtue comes from nature (62.9–14; 65.8–9). Then when he comes to discuss the doctrine of the goal at the end of his division of goods and evils, he concludes with the claim that life according to nature is synonymous with the good (*kalon k'agathon*) and with virtue (p.78.1–3).

In his subsequent division and discussion of adiaphora, the role of nature becomes even more prominent, because it is the only grounds for differentiating value among the adiaphora. The first division of adiaphora is into natural, unnatural, and neutral (p.79.18–19); and the doxographer explicitly adds that the Stoics base their entire doctrine of adiaphora on what is primary by nature (p.80.6–8). Conformity with nature is what determines the value of adiaphora and their ability to motivate men to action (cf. p.80.9–13). Hence the doxography goes on to divide adiaphora in such a way that some have worth, are preferred, and motivate to action, whereas others have no value, are rejected, and motivate men to avoidance (p.80.14–21; 82.5–10). Finally, among the preferred adiaphora the ones pertaining to the soul are shown to have the most value because "the soul is more important (*kyriōteras*) than the body for living according to nature" (p.81.19–82.4).

When Arius turns to the subject of actions, he similarly maintains that the value of human actions is rooted in nature; but he is quick to add that the goods and preferred adiaphora provide the measure of that value. He identifies perfect, appropriate acts with the moral acts (*katorthōmata*) and defines them as "actions in accord with virtue" (p.85.18–21). Their basis in nature is thus due to the fact that virtue is natural. Intermediate acts (*mesa*), he claims, take as their standard of value the adiaphora, which are selected on the basis of their conformity with nature (p.86.12–14). In short, he makes it perfectly clear that the entire system of value is based on nature and that it is the natural value of "things," the goods, evils, and adiaphora, that determines the natural value of human actions.

There is still one subject left, the classification of men and their lives. Here the doxographer indicates that the value of men is determined by their actions, which, in turn, are determined in the case of wise men by the virtues. This way of looking at the wise man's value is apparent from the explanation of the division of men into wise men and fools: "Wise men use virtues throughout their life. . . .Hence, they always act morally (*katorthoun*) among all with whom they associate;. . .and the wise man, using the experiences of life, in his actions does all things well, that is wisely, moderately, and in accord with the other virtues" (p.99.5–12).

From this it would appear that in the Stoic doxography the technique of division has been used to generate an evaluative guide to the moral universe by classifying, in sequence, (a) the physical, psychological, moral, and social conditions in which people might find themselves; (b) the actions they perform; and, (c) the life-styles that such actions constitute. The reader is thereby led through the entire range of moral alternatives that he might face in life, applying the principle of evaluation that nature herself provides and proceeding in the order that nature dictates. In other words, the order of the *diaeresis* (things, actions, and men) seems to be much more than a convenient scheme for classifying moral alternatives; it has a logical and psychological basis that is rooted in nature. Though the wise man may be the Stoic ideal, no one can choose by a simple act of choice the life of the wise man. The life of the wise man is composed of a multitude of actions, each of which involves a human decision. Nor can these individual actions themselves be chosen. Actions result from the choice of some objective. A person does not choose an action, but a condition (whether moral, physical, or environmental) in which goods (or preferred adiaphora) are present. As Arius says: "We choose to have intelligence (*phronēsin*) and moderation (*sōphrosynēn*); we do not choose to think (*phronein*) and act moderately (*sōphronein*), since these are incorporeal predicates" (p.98.3–6). The only possible objects of choice are the real things in the real world, not the actions which are mere predicates of real things and results of choices. Thus the diaeretic structure that the author of the Stoic doxography has chosen as his framework appears to be of far-reaching significance not only as an organizational principle, but as a philosophical tool to help readers to penetrate to the principles that govern their moral decisions.

A crucial question now is who was responsible for the synthesis of the *diaeresis* with the topical survey, and so for the distinctive use of the technique of division that we have been investigating. Was it Arius himself? Or was it some predecessor, another doxographer perhaps, or a Stoic philosopher, whose name Arius has quietly ignored? The only way to establish any claim of originality on behalf of Arius is by a comparison of the use of division in the other major doxography attributed to him.

II. THE PERIPATETIC DOXOGRAPHY

Arius' Peripatetic doxography, like the Stoic doxography, abounds in division, but in contrast it uses a variety of formats. In addition to the form that predominates in the Stoic doxography (*tōn. . .ta men. . .,ta de. . . .*) the Peripatetic divisions are expressed in different ways, as the following examples show: "Of the soul part is rational and part is irrational" (p.117.11–12). "The three classes (*genē*) of goods choiceworthy in themselves are. . ." (125.10). "The good is divided into the beautiful, the beneficial, and the pleasurable" (p.130.15–16). "The form (*eidos*) of the virtues is twofold. . ." (p.117.18–118.1). "There are four differences (*diaphorai*) of friendship. . ." (p.143.1). "There are three forms (*ideai*) of lives. . ." (p.144.16). "Cities must be ruled either by one, or by a few, or by all" (p.150.17–18). "Favor is used in three senses" (*legesthai trichōs*, p.143.18). To be sure some of these, notably the last, occurred in the Stoic doxography; but they were overshadowed by the standard pattern. In the Peripatetic doxography there is no single predominant pattern.

Nor is there a discernible unity or coherent arrangement of the divisions or even a substantial number of them. Among the Peripatetic divisions of the good there are, at most, several series of continuous subdivisions.[15] This suggests that at some point an effort was made to integrate the Peripatetic divisions into a larger unity; but there is nothing resembling the elaborate, unified set of divisions we have found in the Stoic section. In fact, the impression left by the Peripatetic divisions is of a miscellaneous collection, culled from various Peripatetic sources of various periods.[16]

Though there is no evidence of a unified Peripatetic *diaeresis* serving as a doxographic framework, as there was in the Stoic doxography, we cannot conclude that there are no similarities between the Peripatetic and the Stoic doxographies in their use of *division*. As soon as we turn to the actual text of the Peripatetic doxography, we begin to see a familiar use of diaeretic patterns. The very first section of the doxography, the account of *oikeiōsis*, which is noted for its continuous, coherent exposition, is used by the Peripatetic doxographer to account for the choiceworthiness of three divisions of goods. After a general introduction, it is divided into three sections, one devoted to each class of things choiceworthy in themselves: external things (pp.119.22–122.10), things pertaining to the body (pp.122.11–123.20), and things pertaining to the soul (pp.123.21–124.13). Moreover, the account explicitly uses this tripartite division to demarcate a scale of value among things choiceworthy in themselves and culminates in an eloquent statement of the superiority of the virtues of the soul (p.123.21–7).

In addition to presenting the *oikeiōsis* theory in support of a comparative division of three classes of goods, the doxographer introduces material from other sources to accentuate the comparative division of his subject matter. After the account of the natural choiceworthiness of the three classes of goods, Arius adds two additional summaries of the hierarchical ordering of these three classes (pp.124.1–14; 124.18–

125.13). Likewise the concluding paragraph of the *oikeiōsis* account (pp.127.3–128.9), which included a list of the virtuous qualities that reason introduces into a man's life on the basis of the *oikeiōsis* concept, is broken up by the introduction of the distinction between moral and immoral actions and a description of the three ways in which immoral acts may occur.[17] Thus it would appear that Arius Didymus has presented the theory of *oikeiōsis* in such a way that it supports the comparative evaluation of goods and actions.

A little later the Aristotelian theory of the mean is introduced in a similar fashion as grounds for a comparative evaluation of the dispositions and affections of the soul (pp.137.14–142.13). In this account quantities are divided into excess, deficiency, and mean; and these, in turn, are divided into "relative-to-each-other" and "relative-to-us" (p.139.20–23). Then, after citing Aristotle and Theophrastus to support the claim that in every disposition the mean relative-to-us is best (pp.139.23–140.14), the doxographer classifies the dispositions to show that the excesses and deficiencies are bad (*phaulai*), whereas the mean dispositions are good (*spoudaiai*) and constitutive of virtue (pp.140.15–142.13).[18] This account of the mean, in turn, is followed by a tripartite division of passions into good, mediocre, and bad (*asteia, mesa, phaula*), again as a basis for a comparative evaluation (142.15–19). Thus, the two most extensively developed theories in the doxography, the theory of *oikeiōsis* and the theory of the mean, are used to account for the comparative value of a tripartite classification, in one case, of goods, in the other, of "psychic occurrences" (*ta peri psychēn ginomena*), including both affections and virtues.[19] In each case, further divisions from different sources are appended to extend the primary evaluative division.[20]

Finally, if we examine the sections on lives (pp.143.24–145.10), economics (pp.147.26–149.24), and politics (pp.150.1–152.25), we find them riddled with divisions;[21] and like the discussion of goods and of virtues and affections, these divisions are aimed at comparative evaluations wherever possible.[22] From this evidence we may conclude that the Peripatetic doxography shares with the Stoic doxography a pervasive use of the technique of division to demarcate evaluative classifications. Even if the Peripatetic doxography cannot be shown to parallel the Stoic in being based on a coherent diaeretic framework, the two doxographies share the same methodological perspective.

This still leaves the question of the structure of the Peripatetic doxography; for if both doxographies sought to use division for the same ultimate purpose, we might expect to find in them a similar overall structure. The structure of the Peripatetic doxography has always presented problems. The contemporary consensus of opinion is that it is a typical doxography with no real logic of continuous presentation: after an initial systematic account of *oikeiōsis* (pp.116.21–128.9) there are, at best, groups of thematically related divisions, propositions, or doctrinal summaries.[23] In this respect it is not unlike the Stoic doxography, which also gives the impression of containing clusters of thematically related fragments without explicit logical links. Now that we have found the Stoic doxography to be built on a coherent framework, an evaluative division of things, actions, and people, we cannot avoid looking for a similar or analogous framework in the Peripatetic doxography.

A clue to the doxographer's orientation in compiling the Peripatetic doxography may be found in his introduction of the theory of *oikeiōsis*. In justifying his account of this theory he remarks that it is in an attempt to preserve what is naturally *oikeion* that impulse (*hormē*), appropriate action (*kathēkon*), and virtue arise (p.119.2–4). He concludes his introduction by saying: "It happens that actions (*praxeis*) and the so-called appropriate acts (*kathēkonta*) take their origin from the choice of natural things (*tēs tōn kata physin eklogēs*) and the rejection of unnatural things. Therefore, both moral acts (*katorthōseis*) and sins (*hamartias*) occur in and concerning these [natural and unnatural] things. For nearly their whole ethical philosophy is based on these things, as I shall soon show" (p.119.15–21). With these words the doxographer announces his purpose: to show that the moral differences in human action are rooted in what is natural and what is unnatural. This assertion not only echoes Stoic vocabulary and conforms to Stoic theory,[24] but proposes the same doxographic program as the Stoic doxography, namely, to approach ethics by proceeding from a classification of things with respect to their natural value to a classification of human actions with respect to their moral worth.

The actual practice of the Peripatetic doxography shows evidence of the application of this program. After an account of the division of goods as things naturally worthy of choice (pp.119.22–126.11), the doxographer proceeds to discuss and classify the actions that result from such choices.[25] The conclusion of the account of *oikeiōsis* with an interpolation of a classification of sins from some other source serves as the springboard for his classification of actions (pp.127.3–128.9).[26] The vocabulary and thought of this passage echo his earlier announcement of his program (p.119.15–21) and show that the doxographer thought of himself as here fulfilling the promise he had made to demonstrate that the naturally *oikeion* is the basis for moral action.[27] In this passage he does not actually give an explicit division of actions, but he introduces the distinction between moral and immoral actions (pp.127.25–128.1), using the traditional Stoic terms *hamartanein* and *kathorthein*, the nominal forms of which served as the primary categories in the Stoic division of actions (cf. p.96.19–20). He only gives an explicit division of immoral actions (p.127.9–25) and then presents the division of moral acts as the converse (pp.127.25–128.2). The effect of his procedure, however, is to suggest a division of actions into moral acts and sins, with a further subdivision of each category.

The subsequent section continues the task of classifying actions on the basis of their morality (pp.128.10–143.23). It is somewhat fragmented and its chain of thought cannot be pursued here,[28] but we can look briefly at some passages that would seem to be inappropriate in a unit emphasizing the classification of actions, namely, the classifications of goods at pp.129.6–17, 130.15–16, and 134.8–137.12. In the Stoic doxography the classification of goods constituted the framework for the division of things and, therefore, was in principle excluded from the division of actions. In the light of this principle the appearance of the Peripatetic divisions of goods intermingled in a section of the doxography that seems directed toward actions is indeed a surprise, but not a fatal one.

One of the chief differences between the Stoic and Peripatetic philosophies from the point of view of the two doxographies was in the understanding of virtue. For both Stoics and Peripatetics virtue was a disposition of the soul,[29] but the Stoics made a great effort to distinguish virtue as a standard from the actions measured by it. Hence moral acts were defined as acts in accord with virtue (p.85.20–21), and sin as an act performed contrary to right reason (p.93.16–17). To emphasize this distinction the Stoic *diaeresis* used nouns for the virtues and the standards by which actions are measured, whereas it used verbs for the actions. The Peripatetic doxography not only ignores this distinction, but deliberately obscures it. Virtue is categorized as belonging to "things done" (*prakta*, p.139.19). In the first division of goods (p.129.6–17) the class of beautiful goods (*kala*) is specified as virtues and the activities (*energeias*) arising from them. The subsequent examples include both the noun and the verb forms: intelligence (*phronēsis*) and being intelligent (*phronein*), justice (*dikaiosynē*) and being just (*dikaiopragmein*, p.129.9–11). From this it would appear that the Peripatetic sources were not conducive to the isolation of things from actions in the manner of the Stoic doxography.[30] In recognition of this fact the doxographer sums up his division of moral and immoral acts with the picture of intelligence as the leader of a chorus of virtues taking charge of "things chosen and avoided, things done (*praktōn*) and not done, and things more and less."[31] In the absence of separate classifications of standards of morality and moral actions themselves in his Peripatetic sources, the doxographer has done his best to create such a division by attending first to the naturally *oikeion* goods and then to the virtues, affections, and activities that constituted the core of Peripatetic ethics.[32]

If the Peripatetic doxography resembles the Stoic in its progression from the things whereby morality is measured to the actions that constitute morality, it also parallels the Stoic doxography in concluding with a consideration of the people whose value is determined by the morality of their actions. In the Stoic doxography this took the form of an account of the Stoic wise man (*spoudaios*) and his contrary the fool (*phaulos*). The Peripatetic counterpart begins at p.143.24 with a passage that is usually titled "On Lives."[33] In the Stoic doxography the discussion of "lives" occurred as part of the account of the wise man (pp.109.10–110.8). The introductory statement of the Peripatetic passage on lives reflects a similar point of view: "The good man (*spoudaios*) will choose a life of virtue" (*bion ton met' aretēs*, p.143.24). Then, after introducing several kinds of lives, the account goes on to describe the life of the good man: "He will choose, do, and examine noble things. . . .He will marry, beget children, participate in public life, love with restraint, and drink freely at parties, though not as a primary activity. In sum, practicing virtue, he will both remain alive, and, if necessity dictates, depart life, having made provision for his burial, etc." (p.144.4–5, 8–15; cf. 19–20). The discussion of the best kind of life, then, becomes an aspect of the characterization of the life of the good man (*spoudaios*).

The doxography continues with an enumeration of the virtues and their defini-tions.[34] At first sight this may seem to have little to do with a description of the *spoudaios,* but we must remember that the Stoic description of the *spoudaios* began with the claim that the wise man displays all the virtues throughout life (p.99.5–6, 9–12). The Stoic account also contained a section specifically on virtue, enum-erating what Arius calls its various "names," but which we may better describe as its attributes (pp.100.15–101.4). The relevance of this passage on virtue to an account of the wise man seems to derive from the fact that virtue is included among the goods in which wise men participate (cf. p.101.5–9). Similarly, the enumeration of virtues in the Peripatetic doxography seems to be linked to the good man's pursuit of virtue, a theme that ran through the previous section (cf. pp.144.11–12, 21–22; 145.8–9). More specifically, the list of virtues is introduced by several definitions of virtue in general, one of which is "a disposition to examine, choose, and do (*theōrētikē, proairētikē, praktikē*) the *kalon* in actions" (p.145.15–16). This def-inition incorporates one of the summary descriptions of the ideal life of the good man that occurred in the previous section: "He will choose, do, and examine (*proairēsesthai, prattein, theōrein*) the *kala*" (p.144.4–5). In effect, then, the list of virtues with their definitions serves to characterize and describe the life of the virtuous man.

Finally, the doxography concludes with an account of economics and politics, again subjects that in the Stoic doxography were treated only in the context of descriptions of the wise man.[35] In the Peripatetic doxography the topic is introduced on the grounds that man is a "political animal" (p.148.3–4); and, though much of the summary is abstract, there are enough statements to show that the doxog-rapher's objective is to describe the *activity* of the economic and the political man. So the account of the origin of the *oikos* serves to support the claim that "man has the origin of his *oikos* by nature" (p.149.5–6), and economic intelligence (*oikon-omikē phronēsis*) is one of the things that is proper (*oikeian*) to man (p.149.8–10). On the basis of this application of the *oikeiōsis* doctrine the account proceeds to spell out the specific skills of the economic man (*oikonomikon,* p.149.15–21). Similarly the city is shown to arise by nature (p.150.1–3), and the remainder of the account describes, divides, and evaluates the various activities in which citizens participate, e.g., governing, revolution, offices, etc. Finally, the doxographer sums up the work (*ergon*) of the political man as governing the state and assigning the people their respective tasks to ensure the survival and virtue of the city (pp.151.23–152.10). With this description of the natural activities of man in community, the survey of the actions of the good man, and the doxography as a whole, concludes.[36]

From this investigation of the role of division in the Peripatetic doxography it is evident that this doxography is not simply a compilation of ethical information drawn from a variety of sources and arranged in clusters around various ethical topics, as is usually believed. The unifying perspective of the Peripatetic doxography seems to be a comparative evaluation of all the constituents of the moral universe. The doxographer's chief tool in this endeavor is division (*diaeresis*) and, in particular, division on the basis of categories of value, like positive and negative, or mean and extreme. In line with this goal, the doxographer not only incorporates divisions from a variety of Peripatetic sources, but selects and interprets his non-diaeretic doxographic material to support his evaluative divisions. Furthermore, he seems to have worked his way through the objects of the moral universe in the order that we previously found in the Stoic doxography. Beginning with the objects of choice and the external, corporeal, and psychic conditions provided by nature, the writer proceeds to the individual dispositions, affections, and activities of men, and then concludes with the constellation of dispositions and activities that characterize the life and death of the ideal man and which, by implication, differentiate people in moral worth.

The result of this procedure was a doxography that is not particularly unified, consistent, or even clear, except perhaps to one who knew and sympathized with the doxographer's intention. Coherent accounts are interrupted to introduce a division from another source or to accentuate a division implicit in the account. Important subjects like *oikeiōsis*, virtue, happiness, and the goal come up on more than one occasion, sometimes inconsistently. Terms are used in different senses. Philosophical propositions and related and unrelated divisions are strung together often without explicit logical connection, like so many colored beads on a string. All these are the results of an approach that has sifted through a mass of doxographical material with a view to preserving divisions, particularly those capable of dividing the field of ethics into positive and negative categories.

When we compare the method of the Peripatetic doxography to that of the Stoic doxography, we cannot fail to notice the resemblance. In both doxographies the individual units, whether divisions or short summaries of doctrines, are similar in scope and subject matter, even if the Stoic units are on the average somewhat shorter. Neither doxography provides enough explicit links between units to prevent the impression of being a fragmented and discontinuous scrapbook.[37] Yet both show the same preoccupation with evaluative division and both proceed through the evaluation of the constituents of the moral universe along the same logical path. Moreover, no other extant doxography pursues this diaeretic method with equal thoroughness. This can lead to only one conclusion: that the two doxographies were created by the same person.

The diaeretic method also gives us a clue to the philosophical position of that person. Since the comparative evaluation is best exemplified in the Stoic *diaeresis* and the diaeretic method fits the Stoic doxography more naturally than it does the Peripatetic, we may conclude that it was devised in the process of creating the Stoic doxography and subsequently applied to Peripatetic material. This may explain the presence of some of the Stoic features of the Peripatetic doxography. Though the later Peripatos (and hence later Peripatetic doxography) was no doubt influenced by Stoicism to some degree, it is possible that some of the Stoic terminology and method is the effect of the doxographer's attempt to fit the Peripatetic material into a basically Stoic mold.[38] At any rate, it is clear that there is more Stoicism in the

Peripatetic doxography than there is Peripateticism in the Stoic. If the two doxo-graphies were composed by a doxographer with Stoic propensities, and if their composition may be dated to the first century B.C. on internal grounds,[39] it is hard to deny Arius himself the credit for their composition, for he is the only doxographer known from that period who was considered a Stoic.[40]

III. THE ROLE OF DOXOGRAPHY IN ARIUS' ETHICAL PHILOSOPHY

The particular use of division found in the Stoic and Peripatetic doxographies also sheds new light on Arius' purpose as a doxographer and on the role of these doxographies in his ethical philosophy. To discover his purpose requires a careful analysis of the practice and incidental comments on method in the first segment of Stobaeus' excerpt.

At first sight the style and organization of the introductory segment seem to have little point of contact with the two doxographies we have been examining. The structure of the passage, unlike that of the Stoic and Peripatetic doxographies, is transparently clear. Beginning with a discussion of the definition of ethics and related terms (pp.37.18–39.18), it proceeds to a division of the subject matter of ethics (pp.39.19–45.10) before finally undertaking the actual discussion of the subject. The discussion itself is topical, beginning with the goal (pp.45.11–53.20) and moving on to goods and evils (pp.53.21–57.12). Each of these topics, in turn, is presented following the same outline as the introductory segment as a whole: first a definition, then a division, and finally a discussion.[41] If we compare this procedure with that of the Stoic and Peripatetic doxographies as we have them, we find little in common. Rather, it turns out to be the procedure used in the doxographic survey that served as one of the sources of the Stoic doxography. Not only was that survey arranged by topics, no doubt in the same order,[42] but each individual topic seems to have contained a definition, a division, and a brief discussion, including the relation of the concept in question to other relevant concepts.[43] Thus it would appear that the arrangement of the survey of ethics whose beginning Stobaeus has preserved for us followed the same arrangement that was to be partially obscured and transformed by the synthesis that produced the Stoic doxography.

This does not mean that there is no significant common ground between Stobaeus' first segment and the Stoic and Peripatetic doxographies. To understand the relation correctly we must look at the introductory segment's statement on method in ethics and in particular on the diaeretic method. In his account of the division of ethics Arius described at length the divisions used by the Academic philosophers, Philo of Larissa and Eudorus of Alexandria (pp.39.19–45.10).[44] An influence of these philosophers on Arius has long been sought in the structure and organization of Arius' doxographies. This line of investigation has had only moderate success;[45] for Arius does not claim to follow either Philo or Eudorus, but rather the arrangement of topics that seems best to him.[46] Moreover, even if Arius did follow Eudorus' arrangement, he did so only in the introductory survey, and indirectly in the Stoic doxography through the effect of a doxographic source that generally followed Eudorus' arrangement. In the more significant structure of the doxography his practice is quite different.

Arius' claim of independence in arrangement and the limited degree to which he uses the divisions he describes at such length raises the question why Arius quoted the divisions of Philo and Eudorus at all, and why he so admired Eudorus' work, calling it "a book worth buying" (p.42.8–9). The answer, I suggest, lies not in the divisions *per se,* but rather in the method and perspective that Eudorus' division entails.

Philo's division, as Arius takes great pains to make clear, depended on the analogy between philosophy and medicine (pp.39.20–41.25). It began with "Protreptic," in which the philosopher attempts to persuade people to submit to the healing powers of his art. Then came "On Goods and Evils," in which the philosopher attempts to cure a diseased state of the soul by replacing false concepts of good and evil with true ones. "On the Goal" followed as the objective and result of an introduction of correct notions of good and evil, just as health is related to the healing of the body. Three more divisions continued in the same vein. Arius rejects these divisions in favor of what he characterizes as a more ambitious program, namely an examination of (a) the substance (*ousia*) of the subject, then (b) its quality (*poiotēs*) and quantity (*posotēs*), and finally (c) the relation (*to pros ti,* pp.41.26–42.4). There is much that is obscure in this passage, but one thing seems clear. Arius regards it as a statement both of his own program in writing on ethics and at the same time as a description of a way in which Eudorus surpassed Philo.

Immediately thereafter, in introducing the division of Eudorus, Arius describes Eudorus' valuable book as one "in which Eudorus treats the entire field of knowledge on the basis of problems" (*problematikōs,* p.42.9–10). He again emphasizes the role of problems in his final assessment of Eudorus. There, without commiting himself to Eudorus' division, he asserts that "the investigation of the problems must begin with a treatment of the general topics" (*arkteon de tōn problematōn protattonta ta genē,* p.45.8–9). Like the previous description of his program in writing philosophy, the "problematic" approach is left unexplained; but it is obviously meant to describe both his own practice and the characteristic of Eudorus' practice that distinguishes him from Philo.

In the absence of a more detailed description of the methodology implied by these descriptions, the best we can do is speculate on the basis of Arius' comparison of the divisions of Philo and Eudorus. Most instructive is a comparison of each philosopher's approach to the topic of goods and evils. Philo described this division of ethics as analogous to therapeutics. Through this branch of ethics the philosopher attempts to remove false opinions, which are the cause of unhealthy decisions in the soul, and to introduce healthy opinions, thereby developing rationality in the student of philosophy (p.40.9–22). There is no discussion how the validity of true opinion is established. The philosopher who serves as mental therapist simply seems to know; his student simply accepts the true opinions that are placed into him (*enthetikon*, p.40.20).[47] From Arius' summary one could expect Philo's presentation to have taken the form of a dogmatic statement of what truly constitutes good and evil.

In contrast, Eudorus' discussion of goods and evils does not stand on its own, but comes as part of his "theoretic" section, which is devoted to the examination (*theōria*) of the value (*axia*) of objects of choice.[48] Throughout his account the emphasis is on examination and on value.[49] A special point is made of the fact that without *theōria,* there can be no rational impulse (p.42.13–18). *Theōria* is then summed up as both an investigation (*periskepsis*) of a subject and a kind of calculated decision about it (*hoion epikrisis kata ton peri autou logismon*, p.42.18–20). The subsequent divisions (*hormētikon* and *praktikon*), in turn, deal not with *theōria* or scientific investigation of the subjects of impulse and action, but with the actual implementation of the value judgments arrived at by *theōria*.[50] They seem to be related to the *theōrētikon* as clinical psychology is related to theoretical psychology.

The importance Arius attaches to *theōria* in Eudorus and the contrast with Philo on this point suggests that what appealed to Arius in Eudorus' division of ethics was not so much the division itself as the "theoretic" method that it implied. This method, in which ethics is based upon a scientific investigation (*theōria*) of the comparative value (*axia*) of the possible objects of choice, is probably also what Arius meant by the "problematic" method. In contrast to the prescriptive, therapeutic approach of Philo, the "problematic" approach would treat ethics or at least the theoretical foundations of ethics, as a series of problems or questions subject to scientific investigation (*theōria*). The questions would be those involved in determining what is choiceworthy and would therefore deal at least with the goal and everything that contributes to the attainment of the goal, such as goods, virtues, etc.[51] The heart of this endeavor, we may surmise, was the investigation (*episkopein*) of the three questions Arius considered essential to a serious treatment of ethics, (1) the substance, (2) the quality and quantity, and (3) the relations of each subject under consideration (p.42.1–4).

If this reconstruction of Eudorus' method is even approximately correct, we can see that Arius not only gave his formal stamp of approval to it, but used it in the opening segment of his comprehensive doxography. His initial topics, "On the Goal" (pp.45.11–53.20) and "On Goods and Evils" (pp.53.21–57.12), are the same topics with which Eudorus began his theoretical section of ethics, but more importantly, Arius approached these subjects in conformity with the method outlined above.

Under each topic Arius treated first the definition, then the division.[52] This practice takes on special significance in the light of Arius' methodological intent to treat first the substance, then the quality and quantity of each subject (p.42.1–4). The definition answers the question of substance, what the thing under consideration actually is. The division answers the questions of quality and quantity, how many there are, and of what sort each is.[53] The third question, the question of relation receives no attention in the section devoted to the goal, which breaks off in midsentence in the discussion of the division;[54] but the section devoted to goods and evils ends with a brief discussion as to whether every beautiful thing (*kalon*) is choiceworthy for its own sake (pp.56.23–57.12). This would be an appropriate element in a discussion of the relation between the good, the beautiful, and the choiceworthy, and could once have been part of Arius' treatment of the relation (*pros ti*) of goods and evils. Apart from this possible relic we must assume that the accounts of "relation" have been lost in transmission.[55]

In addition to the format, Arius' purpose and perspective conform to the "theoretic" method of Eudorus.[56] Eudorus' purpose in the "theoretic" section of his ethics was to examine the comparative value (*axia*) of objects of choice (p.42.16–17). That Arius had precisely the same purpose is glaringly obvious in his account of goods and evils.[57] There, after a brief discussion of the definition of good, Arius began to cite the divisions of good from Plato. The first division was quoted *verbatim* "on account of the beauty of its expression and its clarity" (54.10–13). It was Plato's *tour de force* of comparative classification from *Laws* 1 (631B–D). In it Plato divided goods into the divine, or greater, goods which comprise the virtues of the soul (intelligence, temperance, justice, and courage), and the human, or lesser, goods which comprise the virtues of the body (health, beauty, motive strength, and visual acuity). The constituents of each of these classes, in turn, were ranked in order of value and their ranks numbered. Arius concluded his quotation from Plato with Plato's assertion that this entire hierarchy of goods has been established by nature. After having given unusual prominence to this particular division, Arius proceeded to report other divisions from Plato (p.55.5–21), hastening to point out that they differ from the first only in expression, not in content (p.55.5–7). Thus Arius could have left no doubt in any reader's mind that he intended to use the process of division to evaluate the comparative worth of goods.[58]

In the face of the "theoretic" method that Arius credited to Eudorus and used in his discussion of the goal and goods and evils we have to see the technique of comparative division in the Stoic and Peripatetic doxographies as somehow related to the "theoretic" component of Arius' philosophical endeavor. In other words, it would be a mistake not only to regard the Stoic and Peripatetic doxographies as simple surveys of the complete ethical teachings of these schools, but also to consider them to be examples of Eudorus' overall scheme applied to Stoic and Peripatetic ethics. The practical implementation of ethics that occupied Eudorus'second and third divisions is nowhere in view. The Stoic and Peripatetic doxographies *in their entirety* appear to be part of Arius' attempt to evaluate the worth of all possible objects of choice or to provide for others the grounds for such evaluation. One might even be tempted to see them as a continuation of the discussion of goods and evils that breaks off on p.57.12. This would give that discussion a doxographic breadth comparable to that of the discussion of the goal.[59]

To suggest that the Stoic and Peripatetic doxographies were composed as components of the topic "On Goods and Evils" may seem absurd in the light of their style, which is totally different from the preceding segment. We might have expected some of their divisions to have been selected and recorded like those of Plato. We might not even have been surprised if the entire Stoic *diaeresis* and the entire Peripatetic collection of divisions had been presented. But it seems remarkable that Arius would have first synthesized the convenient divisions found in his sources with other types of doxographic material and then attempted to use the composite as a division of goods. What is more, the Stoic and Peripatetic doxographies are presented as summaries of ethics, not as divisions or surveys of goods and evils (pp.57.15–17;116.15–18;116.21–117.10; cf. 57.13–14; 116.19–20); and both doxographies are quite explicit about the fact that they go beyond goods and evils in the strict sense, to other subjects, like actions, virtues, and lives. Yet their preoccupation with evaluative classification, also in these areas, gives them the same function as the preceding division of goods and evils, namely as grounds for a "theoretic" investigation of the value of objects of choice.[60]

Though we may now feel somewhat more secure that the Stoic and Peripatetic doxographies with their method of comparative evaluation are from the same author who promoted and practiced Eudorus' "theoretic" approach to ethics, we can only speculate on the relationship between the two doxographies and the introductory segment. Were they preliminary compilations of evaluative divisions on the order of Aristotle's collections of constitutions? Or had Arius perhaps been following Eudorus slavishly from p.45.11 to 57.12,[61] and was he now beginning to introduce his own more elaborate syntheses to continue the process of providing evaluative classifications? Or should we see the Stoic and Peripatetic doxographies as different aspects of Arius' philosophical endeavor?

In the final analysis this may be the only way to "save the phenomena." If Arius Didymus was so committed to the method he found in Eudorus that he permitted himself the freedom to change, at most, only the order of the topics, he may have felt obligated in his capacity as a practicing philosopher to go beyond the doxographic survey whose beginning we have preserved by Stobaeus to create further "theoretic" materials that might serve as the foundation for practical moral decisions. We might conjecture that Arius chose the Stoa and Peripatos for special attention, because they were living schools of philosophy in the first century B.C. and could therefore provide currently acceptable ethical concepts and theories on which to base a system of moral values.

Whatever the exact relationship between the three segments may have been, the use of the *diaeretic* method shows that the Stoic and Peripatetic doxographies must be viewed as an aspect of the "theoretic" investigation of ethics, that is, as grounds for the evaluation of the value of objects of moral choice. Arius was, therefore, not obligated to discuss in them every ethical concept at length, nor to present concepts in the traditional doxographic order. Like the author of any other doxography, he drew his material from the handbooks and original sources available at the time, but his purpose now was not to produce another historical survey. It was rather to provide a guidebook or map of the array of moral choices he and others were facing in their personal lives. The Stoic and Peripatetic doxographies with their "theoretic" method were, therefore, practical doxographies, full of the raw material from which a rational man by investigation, comparison, and calculation might derive guidance in his own daily life. Once when Seneca described the "theoretic" method of Eudorus and Arius in a letter, he concluded with the advice: "Study not to know more, but to know better." (*Stude, non ut plus aliquid scias, sed melius, Ep.* 89.23). Arius would no doubt have agreed.

NOTES

1. The basis for the attribution to Arius Didymus, which, though speculative, has never been called into question, is discussed by C. H. Kahn, "Arius as a Doxographer" (this volume). Kahn also surveys the major issues dealing with Arius' sources and method. Cf. also H. von Arnim *Stoicorum Veterum Fragmenta,* (Leipzig 1905) vol. 1, pages xl–xliii; P. Moraux *Der Aristotelismus bei den Griechen von Andronikos bis Alexander von Aphrodisias,* (Berlin-New York 1973) vol. 1, 259–444, esp. 259–76, 435–43; and A. A. Long, "Arius Didymus and the Exposition of Stoic Ethics" (this volume) for further views on Arius' sources and method. M. Giusta *I dossografi di etica,* 2 vols. (Turin 1964–67) has attempted to prove that Arius composed a *Vetusta Placita* that was the basis for the excerpts in Stobaeus, as well as for all the other ethical doxographies. Though I cannot agree with his conclusions, Giusta's work is important for elucidating many aspects of the text and of the problem of Arius' relationship with other doxographic sources. Cf. the reviews of G. Kerferd, *CR* 17 (1967) 156–58 and 21(1971) 371–73 and P. Boyancé, *Latomus* 26 (1967) 246–49 as well as the comments of Moraux (above) 264–68.

2. The text consists of three segments: (1) a general introduction to ethical philosophy and the beginning of a topical survey (pp.37.16–57.12); (2) a survey (*hypomnēmatismon*) of the chief points (*kephalaia*) of Stoic ethics (pp.57.13–116.18); (3) a comparable survey of Peripatetic ethics (pp.116.19–152.25). At issue are (a) whether all three segments are the work of Arius Didymus (only the third is actually linked to his name by Stobaeus [4.39.28 p. 918.15]), (b) whether Arius' work was arranged by schools or by topics, and (c) whether he merely copied his sources or made substantial contributions himself to the content or arrangement of the work. For further discussion and bibliography see Kahn (above, n.1); cf. also Long (above, n.1).

3. There is one final division of sins introduced on p.113.21–23 as part of the lengthy account of the Stoic wise man and fool, but its isolation from the rest of the divisions of this type (to which it probably belongs in spite of its slight expansion of the standard wording) suggests that the main series of divisions of this type ended with the division of men on p.99.4–5.

4. Only the definition of virtue on p. 60.7–8 seems out of place in this set of subdivisions. As a definition of virtue it ought to have come in the division of goods into virtues and nonvirtues (p.58.5–9). I suspect it has been interpolated from another source.

5. It should be noted that evils are divided analogously along with the goods (cf., e.g., pp.58.14–59.3; 69.5–10).

6. The division of sins at p.113.21–23 also belongs to this group.

7. From a superficial reading it is not at all clear that item 8 (moral acts) is a separate topic from item 9 (the wise man); and some, such as von Arnim (above, n.1) vol. 1,

p. xl, and Long (above, n.1) have taken the discussion of the wise man to begin at p. 93.14. Diogenes Laertius' doxography provides a parallel for beginning the topic of the wise man immediately after the topic of passions (D. L. 7.117). Without getting into the knotty question of the subject matter and organization of 93.14–99.2, I will tentatively consider moral acts as a separate topic in order to bring out the relationship between this material and the *diaeresis* outlined above. There are a few additional statements whose relationship to this set of doxographic topics is not immediately clear (i.e., pp.73.7–15; 73.19–74.14; 75.1–6; 78.7–17; 93.19–96.17). One of these (pp.93.19–96.17) will be part of the discussion of the wise man, if item 8 is not a separate topic. For the present we shall leave these out of account.

8. Cf. von Arnim (above, n.1) vol. 1, pages xl–xli. The similarity to the topics of Eudorus' division of ethics suggests an influence of Eudorus on the arrangement of Arius' doxography; cf. Long (above, n.1). I shall return to this subject in Section III.

9. The uniqueness and advantages of Arius over the doxographies of Diogenes and Cicero are discussed by Long (above, n.1).

10. Since Diogenes presents these topics in the more logical order (the goal, virtues and vices, goods and evils), we may see Arius' postponement of the goal to a position after virtues and vices and goods and evils as a result of the synthesis.

11. The doxographer himself demarcates only the individual topics and makes no explicit mention of any general outline.

12. For this concept I am indebted to Long (above, n.1), who demonstrates in detail its role in the Stoic doxography.

13. E.g. primary and subordinate (pp.60.9–15; 88.12–15), universal and non-universal (pp.68.24–69.10), ends and means (pp.71.15–72.18; 80.15–16; 82.21–83.9), unmixed and mixed (p.74.15–20), necessary and non-necessary (p.86.5–8). Even sins are ranked when divided into sins that arise from a hardened disposition and sins that do not (p.113.21–23).

14. Only a few divisions show no superficial evidence of comparative evaluation; but these are divisions *within* the categories of highest worth (e.g., the classification of virtues into sciences and non-sciences [p.58.9–14], or the classification of goods pertaining to the soul into *diatheseis* and *hexeis* [pp.70.21–71.6]), and even they may entail some implicit evaluation in their examples, which set the four standard virtues in opposition to other virtuous qualities or actions.

15. Cf. R. Sharples, "The Peripatetic Classification of Goods" (this volume). The most notable examples are pp.129.6–9, 134.9–19, 134.20–136.8. Sharples called this practice "chaining."

16. Moraux (above, n.1) 377, 438, postulates a handbook collection of Peripatetic divisions.

17. Cf. Moraux (above, n.1) 329–32 for a full analysis of this section. Moraux has shown that the classification of sins (p.127.9–128.5) is from a different source.

18. For a more detailed analysis of this passage and its sources see Moraux (above, n.1) 379–390 and W. W. Fortenbaugh, "Arius, Theophrastus, and the Eudemian Ethics" (this volume).

19. The division of "psychic occurrences" into affections or passions, capacities, and dispositions (*pathē, dynameis, hexeis*) on p.139.1–18 seems to be introduced to link the mean to the virtues, which are dispositions (*hexeis,* cf. p.139.16–17; 140.12–14), as well as to the passions (*pathē*).

20. One of the added divisions of goods (p.124.18–125.12) is paralleled in [Arist.] *Div.* 56 (Rose 691) and must be from a compilation of Peripatetic divisions. The other (p.124.1–14) had to be modified to fit the scheme (see H. Görgemanns, "*Oikeiōsis* in Arius Didymus" [this volume]). The classification of passions and impulses on pp.142.15–143.23 makes use of a tripartite division (positive, negative, and mean, p.142.15–16,

25–26) that is totally incompatible with the division into excess, deficiency, and mean, in which the mean has the highest value. The only link tying this division to the division of the previous discussion is the use of the concept of the mean in reference to passion. On the isolation of p.142.15–143.23 from the preceding see Moraux (above, n.1) 396–97. For the thematic unity of a discussion of passion with ethical virtue see H. von Arnim, "Arius Didymus' Abriss der peripatetischen Ethik," *SBWien* 204 (1926) 69 and Giusta (above, n.1) 1.61–62.

21. The division take various shapes, but they may clearly be recognized as divisions; cf., e.g, p.144.2–4, 16–17; 148.15–16; 149.10–11; 14–15, 21–22, 150.17–19; 151.9–14, 20–22; 152.1–2, 6–8.

22. Cf. esp. pp. 144.4–8, 16–19; 144.21–145.2; 149.6–8, 21–23; 150.18–23, 151.3–5. For an analysis of the combination of conflicting schemes of division and evaluation in the discussion of lives see Moraux (above, n.1) 403–410.

23. Moraux (above, n.1) 349–53. Giusta (above, n.1) 1.61–62, 151–188 attempts to fit these groups into Eudorus' scheme, but finds only the most general correspondence.

24. Cf. F. Dirlmeier *Die Oikeiosis-Lehre Theophrasts*, Philol. Suppl. 30.1 (Leipzig 1937) 83–86, and M. Pholenz, "Grundfragen der stoischen Philosophie," *Abh. Göttingen* Ser. 3, No. 26 (1940) 26–30.

25. The transition to the subject of action is not clearly demarcated, but a superficial clue to its location is the increase in references to actualization (*energeia*) and action (*praxeis*), beginning with the discussion of the goal and happiness on p.126.12 and continuing through the passage on ethical virtue (pp.137.14–142.13). Actions are also mentioned in the preceding paragraph in a discussion of the utility of the goods for various types of lives (p.125.20) and in a discussion of the grounds for choosing between life and suicide (p.126.5); but the point of view in this paragraph still seems to be that of the objects of choice and has not shifted to the actions that result from choice. In contrast, the central portion of the doxography (pp.126.11–142.13) deals with topics that entail action, including (a) the goal, defined as "life in accord with virtue" (p.126.12–18) or as the actualization (*energeia*) of complete virtue (p.131.18–19); (b) happiness, defined as "an activity (*energeia*) in accord with virtue in actions (*en praxesi*) that are desirably equipped" (p.126.18–20, cf. p. 126.24–127.2; 129.19–20) or as the "use" (*chrēsis*) or "actualization (*energeia*) of complete virtue" (p.130.18–21; cf. 132.8–10); and finally, (c) virtue, which is characterized as a disposition from which praise devolves on the "actualizations (*energeias*) in the affections" (*pathē*, p.139.16–18), or as one of "the things done" (*praktōn*, p.139.19).

26. Cf. Moraux (above, n.1) 329–32. The original account of the conclusion has survived on pp.127.3–9 and 128.5–9. The intervening division of sins (pp.127.9–128.5), written in a different style and using Stoic terminology, has no point of contact with the conclusion of the *oikeiōsis* account beyond the mere mention of virtue and the concept of virtue (or one of the virtues) serving as leader (compare p. 128.1–2 and 5–6).

27. Compare esp. pp.127.25–128.8 with 119.2–19, with their common emphasis on choice and avoidance (*haireta, pheukta, haireseis, phygai*), decision (*krinein, epikrisis*), intelligence (*phronēsis, eidēsis*), virtue, moral actions and sins.

28. Moraux (above, n.1) 350–402 distinguishes the following thematic groups: happiness (pp.129.19–130.12, [130.18–21]; 132.19–134.6), goal (pp.130.15–132.18), goods (pp.134.8–137.12), virtue (p.128.11–25; 137.14–142.13), and affections (p.142.15–143.23). As one can easily see, these themes are intermingled in Arius' presentation.

29. For the Stoic definition see pp.60.7–8; 70.21–71.2; for the Peripatetic, see pp. 128.11–12; 139.16–17. The Stoics used the term *diathesis*, which they carefully distinguished from *hexis* (cf. pp. 70.21–71.14); the Peripatetics used either *diathesis* or *hexis* (which they distinguished from *dynamis* and *pathos*, cf. p. 139.3–18).

30. The Stoic division of "things" twice includes activities (*energeias*) along with virtues (pp.70.10–11; 77.7–8; cf. 70.16–18; 77.12–13). In the first case, activities are then divided off from the virtues in the next division (p.71.1–6; cf. 71.8–14). This practice, however, is rare.

31. Page 128.4–8; cf. 127.3–9 and Moraux (above, n.1) 331–32. The reference to more and less takes notice of the importance of the mean in determining the moral value of actions (cf. *ametrōs, eph' hoson, symmetrōs*, p. 127.19, 20, 24).

32. From this perspective the theme of virtues might be taken to begin as early as p.123.21, but at least the first few lines (p.123.21–27) are needed to complete the three classes of choiceworthy things (119.22–123.27).

33. There is also a description of the Peripatetic man of virtue earlier in the doxography in the discussion of ethical virtue (pp.141.5–142.5), but this cannot be taken as part of the classification of men. The Stoic doxography displays a similar procedure. In addition to the primary discussion at the end of the doxography the wise man is described in the discussion of virtue, which is part of the division of goods (pp.65.12–68.23), and again (I believe) in the discussion of moral acts, which is part of the division of actions (pp.93.19–96.17).

34. Included in the enumeration is a division of virtues in terms of genus and species with strong Stoic overtones (pp.146.15–147.21). This parallels pp.60.9–62.6 in the Stoic doxography. Cf. von Arnim (above, n.20) 98–119 and Moraux (above, n.1) 390–96 for detailed analysis of this text and its sources.

35. In the Stoic account economics is mentioned in support of the claim that only the *spoudaios* is an economic man (*oikonomikos*, p.95.9–14). A discussion of the definition of "city" occurs in justification of the claim that the fool (the contrary of the wise man) has no city (p.103.9–23). The wise man himself is described as both *politikos* and *oikonomikos* (p.100.5). Business (*chrēmastikē*), which is part of Peripatetic economics (p.149.21–24), is a subject the Stoic doxographer also treats (with economics) under the wise man (pp.95.9–24; 100.5–6).

36. Unlike the Stoic doxography, there is no account of the contrary, the *phaulos*. The closest thing to such a subject is the parenthetical remark after the first general definition of virtue that vice is the opposite (p.145.14). This is reminiscent of the frequent practice in the Stoic doxography to note that evil or the fool is "the opposite."

37. It seems impossible to decide to what degree the fragmentary nature is the result of the original composition and to what degree it is due to Stobaeus' abridgment. Evidence of Stobaeus' abridgment can be found in the introductory segment where the discussion of the three theories of the goal announced on p. 48.12–22 has clearly been abridged (cf. Giusta [above, n.1]1.141–42, 218–19). The account of the third type ends in mid-sentence (p.53.19). Of the second theory, that of the corporeal goal, only a small scrap survives (p.52.10–13) and even this may, in reality, be an interpolation by Stobaeus himself (cf. A. Kenny *The Aristotelian Ethics* [Oxford 1978] 21–22). On the other hand, Stobaeus evidently copied some of the linking material in the Stoic doxography (e.g., pp.79.1–4; 84.12–13). My own feeling is that Stobaeus did do some abridging of the Stoic and Peripatetic doxographies, but he did not do enough to account for their fragmentary nature. Even his abridged version of the introductory discussions of the goal and goods and evils is more coherent than the Stoic and Peripatetic doxographies. I suspect we can account for the difference only by assuming the original versions differed significantly in coherence.

38. Moraux (above, n.1) 440–42 has distinguished three areas of Stoic influence: (1) terminology, (2) method (notably definition, classification, and division) and (3) issues and answers. The first two areas are most likely to show the influence of the doxographer himself.

39. The date is based on the fact that the Stoic doxography shows an acquaintance with Panaetius (pp.63.25–64.12), Hecaton (p.62.15–20 compared with D. L. 7.90; cf. von Arnim [above, n.1] vol. 1, pages xlii–xliii), and possibly also Posidonius (cf. I. Kidd's article in this volume), while the Peripatetic doxography shows an acquaintance with Polybius and Critolaos (cf. Moraux [above, n.1] 328, 335, 412–13, 425–26).

40. Arius was listed among the philosophers of the Stoa in the lost portion of Diogenes Laertius 7 (cf. Diogenes Laertius, *Vitae Philosophorum*, ed. H. S. Long [Oxford 1964] p. 392: critical apparatus). The only other person fitting this description is Posidonius, but Kidd (above, n.39) has shown that his influence is surprisingly slim, chiefly one vivid metaphor. If he had had a role in the creation of the doxography, we would expect his influence to have been more pronounced (cf. von Arnim [above, n.1] vol. 1, page xliii). We must also mention here the name of Eudorus, the Platonic philosopher whom Arius admired and whom both Giusta and Long (above, n.1) see as the source of the structure of the Stoic doxography. Though Eudorus certainly exerted an influence on Arius, we shall see below (Section III) that it is impossible to credit him with the creation of the Stoic and Peripatetic doxographies as we have them.

41. The discussion of the goal consists of an elaborated discussion of the definition (pp.45.12–48.11), followed by a division of the subject (pp.48.12–53.20). Each part is further subdivided. The discusion of the definition consists of (a) the definition proper according to different authorities (p.45.12–46.22), (b) the first use of the term (p.47.1–6), and (c) the distinction between the proper term *telos* and other related terms, like *skopos, hypotelis,* and *eudaimonia* (p.47.7–48.11). The division of the goal (pp.48.12–53.20) is treated as a division of theories about the goal of life (p.48.12–22), each of which is exemplified by several proponents (psychic goals, p.48.23–52.9; corporeal goals, p.52.10–12; mixed goals, p.52.13–20 [cf. above, n.37]). The discussion of goods and evils is more perspicaciously divided into a discussion of definition (pp.53.22–54.9) and a division (pp.54.10–57.12). The latter appears to be incomplete (see below, n.54). Unfortunately all that survives of the formal discussion of either topic is a brief consideration of the question whether every *kalon* is choiceworthy for its own sake (pp.56.24–57.12), unless we wish to take the attempt to distinguish the term *telos* from related terms and concepts (pp.47.7–48.11) as a misplaced relic of the discussion of the concept of the goal.

42. See above, Section I. The order of the first few topics (including those of the goal and of goods and evils) in the Stoic survey is problematic. Since these are the only topics contained in the introductory segment, the similarity of order remains conjectural.

43. The pattern of definition, division, and discussion is most obvious in the discussion of the goal (pp.75.11–77.5; 77.16–78.6); appropriate acts (pp.85.13–86.16), impulse (pp.86.19–88.7), and passion (pp.88.8–90.6); but it can also be found in the account of virtue (pp.60.7–64.12), and adiaphora (pp.79.4–80.13). The pattern has been somewhat obscured by the interweaving of the *diaeresis* with the survey (see above, Section I).

44. On Philo see K. von Fritz, "Philon (40)," *RE* 19 (Stuttgart 1938) 2535–44. For Eudorus see W. Dörrie, "Der Platoniker Eudoros von Alexandreia," *Hermes* 79(1944) 25–39 (= *Platonica Minora,* Studia et Testimonia Antiqua 8 [Munich 1979] 297–309) and J. Dillon, *The Middle Platonists: 80 B.C. to A.D. 220* (Ithaca, N.Y. 1977) 115–35.

45. In the wake of the attempt of Giusta (above, n.1) to reconstruct an original version of the Stoic and Peripatetic doxographies on a completely Eudoran model, Moraux (above, n.1) 265–68, following H. Diels *Doxographi Graeci* (Berlin 1879) 70, has shown how independent of Eudorus' division the Peripatetic doxography really is. Long (above, n.1) has shown that Eudorus' three primary divisions (*theōrētikon, hormētikon,* and

praktikon) are applicable to the content of the Stoic doxography, but makes no claim that Eudorus' extensive set of subdivisions can be found in the Stoic doxography.

46. Arius rejected Philo's division (pp.41.26–42.6) and cited Eudorus' divisions as a superior alternative. After Eudorus' division he says, "The account of ethics *might* be divided (*temoit' an*) into these divisions; but the investigation of the problems *must* begin (*arkteon*) by treating first the primary topics (*genē; cf. topous genikous*, p.43.16) in the order that seems best to me and which I am persuaded produces a clearer division" (p.45.7–10). This statement is hopelessly ambiguous. If the "possible divisions" of p.45.7–8 refers to all the divisions quoted (i.e., both the divisions of Philo and those of Eudorus), the "order that seems best and clearest to me" may refer specifically to the divisions of Eudorus. On the other hand, the "possible divisions" may refer only to the divisions of Eudorus. Then Arius' claim to follow the best and clearest arrangement may be either Arius' way of putting his stamp of approval on Eudorus' division (So Giusta [above, n.1] 1.197–98), or an assertion of independence of arrangement in spite of an adherence to Eudorus' "problematic" approach (So Diels [above, n.45] 70 and Moraux [above, n.1] 267–68).

47. On Philo's method in ethics and its relation to his theory of knowledge see von Fritz (above, n.44) 2540–41.

48. See Giusta (above, n.1) 1.151–56, 160–70 for the reconstruction of Eudorus' outline and for a plausible reconstruction of the lacuna after 43.4. Wachsmuths' reconstruction (43.4–7) is almost certainly wrong in making "On Goods and Evils" part of "On the Goal." As Giusta, 1.153–56, has shown, "On Goods and Evils" must be part of "On Things that Contribute to the Attainment of the Goal."

49. Note the frequency of words derived from *the-* and *skep-*. "Worth" (*axia*) is mentioned four times (p.42.14, 16; 43.2, 15).

50. Cf. p.42.20–22. The second part of ethics is described as "the successful generation of an impulse with respect to the result of examination" (*to tēn hormēn tōi perinoēthenti kalōs epibalein*) and the third as "the attachment of action to the [previous two] things" (*to tēn praxin autois episynapsai*). The subdivisions of the third part (*praktikon*), including such subjects as protreptic, pathology, the causes of behavior, and ethical training, also portray this part as practical application. The same distinction between theory and implementation in impulse and action can be seen in Seneca's parallel description of the Eudoran division of ethics (*Ep.* 89.14–15).

51. Cf. p.43.1–10 and above, n.48. I do not agree with Moraux (above, n.1) 268 that "problems" simply implies a topical arrangement rather than by schools. It does, indeed, imply a topical arrangement, but, I believe, also an investigative, rather than dogmatic approach.

52. See above, n.41.

53. The division of goals, or more accurately, theories of the goal, introduces a discussion of the first division with the words: "Let us say. . .of what sort (*hopoioi*) those are who. . ." (p.48.23–24). The division of ethics is concluded with the words: "Ethics might be divided into these and this many [divisions]" (*tauta kai tosauta*, p.45.7–8).

54. On the abridgment of the account of the goal see above, n.37. The division of goods and evils is even shorter in length than the abridged account of the division of the goal. Moreover, it cites only Plato and Aristotle, whereas the division of the goal included Homer and the Presocratics before it broke off, and probably originally included discussion of the Stoics and Epicureans as well, since they were included in a catalog of definitions of the goal (p.46.5–10, 17–22). The Epicureans, it should be noted, would have been discussed under the second division (cf. p.48.12–16), which has been almost completely eliminated in the abridgment.

55. An additional clue to the nature of the third question, that of "relation," may be Arius' practice in the Stoic doxography. There the definition and division of a concept was apparently accompanied by an account of the relation between the concept in question and other philosophical concepts. In the discussions of appropriate acts, impulse and passions (pp.85.12–93.13), the passages (a) p.86.10–16; (b) p. 86.17–18 and 88.1–6; and (c) p.88.22–90.18 may be construed as abridgments of the "relational" discussion of the topics of appropriate act, impulse and passion respectively. Giusta (above, n.1) 1.196–97, 2.12–13, interprets Arius' statement (p.42.1–4) as a proposal to organize his discussion of each topic on the basis of Aristotle's ten categories and he devotes much of vol. 2 to demonstrating this thesis. I am not convinced that the categories play as large a role in the doxographies as he supposes, nor do I believe Arius' statement can be construed as an abbreviated list of the ten categories. Arius is clear that the four categories he gives constitute only three subjects for discussion (cf. *pro pantos. . .*, *k'apeita. . .*, *kai toutois ephexēs*) and he gives no hint that this is merely a sample of the possible subjects. Moreover, even Giusta 2.81–83, 95, cannot find evidence for the use of any other categories in the introductory segment.

56. Since the Stoic Seneca, *Ep.* 89.14–15, recounts the "theoretic" method, there is a question whether Eudorus derived it from the Stoa or whether Seneca obtained his account from Arius and hence indirectly from Eudorus. I leave this question open. Cf. Dörrie (above, n.44) *Hermes* 31. n.1 (= Studia 303, n.1).

57. It is not so obvious in the divisions of the goal, though it would certanly be appropriate in a comparison of the three kinds of theories. The incompleteness of the discussion, however, precludes any conclusions from silence. It should be noted that Dillon (above, n.44) 122–26 takes Arius' entire account of the goal and goods and evils to be derived from Eudorus and uses it, without discussion, as evidence for Eudorus. This is an unsupported hypothesis.

58. Though it is not made explicit, the comparative perspective may be seen also in the subsequent Aristotelian division of goods into "choiceworthy through themselves" and "choiceworthy through other things" (p.56.9–23).

59. That discussion, as we noted included Presocratics, Stoics, Epicureans, and late Peripatetics, as well as Plato and Aristotle.

60. On actions as objects of choice in the Stoic doxography see p.97.15–98.6. Men, in turn, are defined by their actions (p.99.3–8), and the list of actions of the Stoic wise man is the closest the doxographies come to providing concrete guidance in specific actions. The Peripatetic analog to the account of the wise man's actions is introduced as a *choice* of lives (p.143.24); cf. also the subsequent list of virtues in which virtue is defined as "a state of choosing the mean" (p.145.12–13) or "choosing the *kala di' hauta*" (p.147.22–25).

61. This is the assumption of Dillon (above, n.44) 122–26; see above, n.57.

PART II
Papers on Arius' Treatment of Stoic Ethics

CHAPTER 3

Arius Didymus and the Exposition of Stoic Ethics

Anthony A. Long

The second book of Stobaeus' *Anthology* contains the longest and most detailed surviving account of Stoic ethics (2, pp. 57–116 Wachsmuth). Much of this corresponds closely to Cicero *De finibus* 3 and Diogenes Laertius 7. These are the fullest parallel accounts, and there is every reason to think that all three derive ultimately from Stoic sources of unimpeachable orthodoxy. In some places Cicero, Diogenes, and Stobaeus are so close to one another that they appear like variant copies of a single tradition.[1] Their common features have been most thoroughly assembled and discussed by Michelangelo Giusta in his *I dossografi di etica*.[2] That work is packed with valuable material and insights. But it suffers, as reviewers have pointed out, from unitarian zeal.[3] Giusta was too ready to turn Eudorus of Alexandria (see n.4 below) into the mind and method latent in *all* summary accounts of later Greek ethical philosophy. There are important differences between Cicero, Diogenes, and Stobaeus which his book tends to obscure. In this paper I want to focus attention on some of the idiosyncratic features of the Stoic material in Stobaeus. This may put us in a better position to assess the method and purposes of its compilation, and its philosophical relationship with the accounts of Stoic ethics in Cicero and Diogenes.

I. ARIUS DIDYMUS' AUTHORSHIP

A preliminary point needs clarification—the authorship of the material in Stobaeus. It is quite certain that this Byzantine scholar produced his anthology from previous compendia, and thus the determination of his sources is crucially important for evaluating the material he transmits. An unchallenged answer to this question was advanced in the nineteenth century by a series of German scholars–*Arius Didymus*. The significance of Arius was considerable. He was active at the time of the Roman emperor Augustus, and well known as a philosophical encyclopaedist of higher repute than most.[4] If he could be proved to be Stobaeus' author or principal source, that was a conclusion greatly to be wished.

His name was first advanced on the grounds of general probabilities, but it was given evidentiary support by Meineke in 1859.[5] He pointed out that a short paragraph in Stobaeus 2 (pp. 129–30 W.) is repeated exactly in Stobaeus 4 (pp. 918–19

Hense): "the sources of happiness." According to one, but only one, of the manuscripts which records this second occurrence of the passage, Stobaeus prefaced it with the heading: "from the epitome of Didymus."[6] This was taken to show, in Zeller's words, that "not only the whole Peripatetic section," where the first passage on the "sources of happiness" occurs, "but also the corresponding section on Stoic ethics was derived from Arius' epitome; and that Stobaeus probably also took from Arius the four preceding sections which begin at 2, p. 37 W."[7] Wachsmuth himself supplied the words "from the epitome of Didymus" at this place in his edition of Stobaeus, supported (as he says) by Diels.

Arius is known from Eusebius to have written a handbook which contained Stoic physics, and Eusebius also included extracts from a work by Arius on Platonism.[8] It is entirely plausible that he should have written or compiled accounts of Stoic and Peripatetic ethics. But it is not certain that he did so, nor can the solitary reference to his epitome in Stobaeus 4, p.918.15 conclusively establish the hand of Arius in the *whole* of the Peripatetic section, much less the whole of the Stoic section and all of vol. 2, pp.37–152. Superficial impressions of the style perhaps suggest a single source, and the personal tone of pp.41–45 can hardly point to Stobaeus himself. It is also most appropriate for Arius Didymus to have an interest in Philo of Larisa and Eudorus of Alexandria, as he does in these pages. So there is good reason to speak of Arius as if he were the direct or indirect source of Stobaeus' material. But that should be done in full awareness that it is a conjecture, a good conjecture certainly, but not a fact, as the incautious reader of Wachsmuth or Diels might readily suppose.

If Stobaeus' Stoic, Peripatetic and preceding ethical material were presented on unitary organizational principles this could seem a pedantic recommendation. Arius' authorship would satisfy economy of explanation as well as historical plausibility. But Stobaeus' text, as will be shown towards the end of this paper, shows considerable internal discrepancies. One of these is so important that it can bear repetition. The Peripatetic section, as has long been recognized, is heavily contaminated with Stoicism, and this points to the eclecticism associated particularly with Antiochus of Ascalon.[9] But the Stoic section appears to be as accurate a summary of Stoic doctrine in Stoic diction as we possess. It does not seem therefore as if "Arius" has presented the two schools according to a common eclectic viewpoint. Yet eclecticism is strongly present in the preliminary definitions of terms (2, pp.37–39, 45–57) with more explicit interest being taken in Plato and Aristotle than in the Stoics.

If such points are not sufficient to disturb the conjecture of Arius' principal authorship throughout, they certainly raise questions about his methods of work and doxographical intentions. For the purpose of this paper I will assume that he is the main source for both ethical sections in Stobaeus, together with the preliminary material, and I will suggest a hypothesis to reconcile the discrepancies without abandoning Arius or carving him up into two or more people. Any methodological contribution of his own is likely to have consisted in the framework he adopts for presenting the first part of his Stoic section. For that, as will be seen, has some interesting features which are without parallel in Cicero or Diogenes Laertius. As for the Peripatetic section, such few traces as we may conjecture concerning Arius' trademark seem still harder to detect. I would hazard the guess that he has taken over a Stoicizing account, like that of Antiochus, without attempting to make it more than loosely similar in structure to his cast of the Stoic material.

II. THE "DIVISION" PROCEDURE AND SUBJECT HEADINGS

Arius' presentation of Stoic ethics is best known through the many passages excerpted from it by von Arnim for his *Stoicorum Veterum Fragmenta*. Placed, as they are, alongside a mass of parallel texts these excerpts from Stobaeus give few indications of any organizational principles in Arius' work, and even those who have studied his entire exposition find nothing to praise in its procedure. Diels, following Madvig, complained about the lack of order and apparently random juxtaposition of subjects; and he noted fifteen topics as the headings for discussion between pages 57 and 93 after which repetitions and inconsequentialities seem to become still greater.[10] Unfortunately Diels' censure was quite inadequately grounded. There are certainly a good many inconcinnities in this section of Stobaeus, taking it as a whole. But they coexist within a pattern of exposition which shows a definite system of arrangement. This deserves careful detection and analysis.

Arius himself promises a coherent procedure: he says that he will make an orderly shopping list of the headings of the essential doctrines of Zeno and the other Stoics (p. 57.15). In order to assess his fulfillment of this promise we may best begin by studying the opening sections (pp.57–79).

The first and most important step is to follow the guidance of his first two sentences: "Zeno says that these are the things which participate in existence; and of existing things some are good, others bad, and others indifferent" (p.57.18–20). The first sentence refers to something said by Zeno outside the context reported by Stobaeus, presumably to the effect that only corporeal things exist. In the second sentence Arius divides the class of existing things into the three specified subclasses. This division, and subdivisions dependent upon it, provide the main framework for his exposition. That this is so can be seen particularly clearly on pages 79 and 85 where he gives explicit instructions to his reader:

> Having dealt adequately with goods and evils and things to be chosen and avoided, and with the goal and happiness, we think we should expound in proper order the doctrines on indifferents (p.79).[11]

His treatment of "indifferents" includes, as it should in Stoic ethics, an account of "preferred things" (*proēgmena*). Having completed that he writes:

> The subject of the appropriate (*kathēkon*) follows on from the doctrine concerning preferred things (p.85).

Arius can expect his attentive reader to observe that everything from pp.57–85 has been developed out of his opening division into goods, evils, and indifferents: pp.57–79 handle goods and evils, while pp.79–85 deal with indifferents. *All* that material, including much detail on virtue and the goal, prepares the ground for a new topic, the "appropriate."

Diels (above, n.10) proposed that the material down to "indifferents" covers nine topics, but that suggestion completely distorts Arius' procedure. He thinks of himself as having handled two principal topics—goods and evils, and the goal— and that is a just statement of what he has done. For analytical purposes, however, it is better to distinguish three topics which govern the organization of his opening material: goods and evils, virtues and vices (strictly a subdivision of goods and evils), and the goal. It will be helpful to exhibit and label these divisions (down to p.85) in a table.

A Existing things consist of Goods, Evils, and Indifferents p. 57

B1	Goods and evils	pp. 57–58
	C1–6 Virtues and Vices	pp. 58–64
B2	Goods	p. 64
	C7–8 Virtues and Vices	pp. 64–68
B3–13	Goods and Evils	pp. 68–75
	D1–5 Goal and Happiness	pp. 75–78
E1–11	Indifferents	pp. 79–85

In what follows reference will be made to a more fully detailed "Table of Ethical Theses in Stobaeus" (appended to this chapter), which sets out all the principal theses of these pages using the same system of lettering and numeration.

As these tables show, Arius uses his division procedure in order to isolate one species of good, viz. virtues which are "sciences and skills" (Cl.i.1, pp.58–59). These are in turn divided into "primary" (the four cardinal virtues) and "subordinate", which comprise further similarly describable virtues falling under the cardinal ones. He next (p.62.7–14) appends a brief argument, the significance of which can be easily overlooked. First the conclusion is stated:

> All these virtues have life in accordance with nature as their goal, and they make man possess this goal through their own characteristics.[12]

This claim is justified by what follows:

> For he has from nature impulses for discovering what is appropriate, for the stable condition of his impulses, for acts of endurance, and for acts of distribution. Each virtue, by harmoniously performing its own function, makes man live in accordance with nature.[13]

If it were not for this important section, Arius' opening material would be radically different from Cicero *De finibus* 3 and Diogenes Laertius 7. In both of these accounts the discussion of Stoic ethics starts from *oikeiōsis*, a consideration of an animal's *natural impulse* to pursue what is appropriate to its constitution and to avoid the opposite. There is every reason to suppose that this was standard Stoic practice. Arius, as we have seen, begins his account quite differently. But in the brief argument translated above, together with his preceding material, he has provided the means of formulating the following thesis:

1. One of the constituents of reality is goods.
2. Goods include all the virtues.
3. Some virtues are sciences and skills.
4. Four of these virtues are primary: wisdom, moderation, courage, justice.
5. Man is impelled by nature to attain these virtues, and he lives in accordance with nature by each of these virtues performing its function harmoniously.
6. The goal of these virtues is life in accordance with nature.

The last two propositions in this thesis correspond very closely with Diogenes Laertius 7.87: "Zeno. . .said that the goal is life in agreement with nature, that is life in accordance with virtue; for nature directs us towards virtue." But Diogenes arrives at this specification of the goal by a different route. Unlike Arius his starting point is impulse (*hormē*), common to all animals, and he then marks out rationality (impulse shaped by reason) as the distinctive characteristic of human nature. In his opening procedures (and the same holds for Cicero) no general claims about goods and virtues are involved. Arius on the other hand has told us nothing at this stage about the relationship between rationality and human nature or virtue. These points will only emerge much later, when he has concluded his analysis of goods and evils, and passes on to consider the goal in detail (D1, D2, D5).

We should probably suppose then that Arius' brief remarks about the goal and human nature, at this early stage, are an interim conclusion which anticipates later sections but fits well into a detailed account of the cardinal virtues, where it is placed. Possibly he knows that Stoics regularly began their ethical disquisitions with an account of the primary impulse and human nature. For reasons we have yet to consider he is proceeding differently, providing a taxonomy of goods and virtues, evils and vices, before treating of the goal. But he is familiar enough with other procedures to give some satisfaction to readers who want to be told, pretty early, about the connection between goods, virtues, impulses, and the goal.

His main focus at this stage, however, is on the virtues. Having indicated that the cardinal virtues have life in accordance with nature as their goal, Arius amplifies their teleological significance from several points of view. Taking up what I have called his interim conclusion he repeats the claim that the cardinal virtues (and here he includes their subordinates too) are "constitutive of life's goal," and adds the new point that they consist of "rational principles" (*theōrēmata*, p.62.15 = C5). Lest, however, we should think that this holds for all virtues, he explains the different status of the "nontechnical virtues" such as mental health, which are "powers acquired by practice" and supervenient on the others (C1.i.2). Then, with a backward reference to his "interim conclusion" (p.63.7), he shows how the cardinal virtues are both inseparable, owing to their *common* principles and goals, and at the same time distinguishable through their specific targets and subject matter (C6.1, C6.2).

So far, it should now be plain, Arius has proceeded clearly and coherently. The virtues have been firmly located within the class of goods, their specific differentiae have been stated, and we are well informed about their relationship to the goal of life. Formally speaking the *telos* or goal has yet to be treated in its own right, but given Arius' division procedure, or any other procedure for that matter, he cannot deal with everything at once. If he is responsible for the next four theses in their present position—B2 and C7.1–7.3—his credit for orderliness goes down. B2 seems out of place,[14] C7.1 repeats C1.1; and C7.2 and C7.3 read like afterthoughts, albeit legitimate ones. There is little point in speculating about the history of these passages. Worse incongruities and repetitions occur later. But even if Arius himself let them pass, they do not do much to disturb his exposition, and all are germane to an account of the Stoic virtues.

There follow four pages (65–69) which, according to Diels, present a quite new subject: "the character of the wise man."[15] That is certainly an accurate description of their contents, but it misrepresents the coherence of Arius' exposition by implying that he has anticipated the subject of his final section. What he actually does here is to set out a series of theses concerning *virtuous and vicious dispositions* which simply continues his treatment of virtues and vices. The wise and the inferior man enter his discussion at this point because they illustrate a new and fundamental claim: "There is nothing intermediate between virtue and vice" (C8.1). This thesis helps to sanction C8.2: "The inferior are imperfect, and the good are perfected," and it prepares for C8.3: "The wise man always acts according to all the virtues." That proposition is inferred from the fact that "his every action is perfect, and so he falls short in no virtue" (p.65.13–14). The adverbs which now follow are no random description of the wise man's actions (C8.4). They are explicitly stated to "follow from" C8.1–8.3 (p.65.15). "The wise man does everything well," (C8.5) is partly based on his doing everything in accordance with virtue (cf. C8.3).[16] So, contrary to Diels, these pages continue and conclude the development of the virtues, which have been consistently classified as a subdivision of goods.

They provide, indeed, more than a catalogue. The wise man's sympotic and erotic activities are not merely asserted to be virtuous, but defined as instances of "understanding" (*epistēmē,* p.66.3–9). His "doing everything well" (C8.5), though related to C8.3, is clarified by the assertion that "virtue is an art embracing the whole of life" (p.66.20–67.2). Arius does include, to be sure, certain "professional skills" of the wise man (the so-called *epitēdeumata*) which are not, strictly speaking, virtues. They are "goods," defined by reference to virtue (p.67.12), and wholly appropriate to be mentioned here as being present in "good tenors," i.e. virtuous dispositions (p. 67.8). They are followed, moreover, by piety, which is a virtue (pp.67–68).

After briefly applying the same procedures to the inferior man (p.68) Arius (B3.i) returns in effect to his initial general thesis concerning all goods (B1.i): "Goods comprise virtues and not-virtues." That is the neatest explanation of the sequence of B theses which he now provides down to p.74. Nor is it difficult to justify his procedure for ourselves, as readers and students. Having exhaustively treated the most important species of goods, the virtues, he can now assume an understanding of virtue and particular virtues in these subsequent classifications. Having also introduced the wise and the inferior man he can refer to these without further explanation, as he does in his first new B theses (B3.i and B3.ii). Other concepts which have been briefly mentioned hitherto, e.g. nonessential goods and "professional skills" (*epitēdeumata*), are also taken up and amplified. Thus these further B theses provide us with both fuller understanding of anything good, and more particularly, a framework to classify types of good and specific goods. By the end of p.74 we can answer such questions as "What is courage?" or "What is joy?" and supply very detailed answers.

Regarding joy (*chara*) we can say that it is:

1. A good of the species not-virtue (B1.i.2).
2. It does not belong to all wise men, or to any of them all the time (B3.i).
3. It is beneficial, etc. (B4.i).
4. It is a final good (B7.i.1).
5. It is in motion (B10.1).

Or, regarding "musicality," we can say that it is:

1. A good of the species not-virtue (B10.2.b).
2. It does belong to all wise men (C8.5).
3. It is beneficial, etc. (B4.i).
4. It is a psychic good of the type "tenor" (*hexis*) (B6.i.1.2).
5. It is at rest (B10.2.b).

The traditional moral virtues, together with a vast range of other "good" qualities and skills, have now been suitably mapped. A quick glance at Diogenes Laertius (7.89–101) will be sufficient to show how much more minutely and methodically Arius has done his Stoic cartography.

Now at last he turns to a new topic, the goal (pp.75–78). Its relatively late appearance can be justified by at least two reasons. First, there is good evidence that the Stoics regularly discussed the goal (*telos*) after their treatment of virtue.[17] Secondly, according to Arius (p.76.17–18), the first sense of the term *telos* which they distinguished was "the final good," following "philological practice," and this makes it appropriate to expound the goal after a full exposition of "goods." In Diogenes Laertius 7 and in Cicero *De finibus* 3 the main treatment of the goal arises early, in connection with the doctrines of *oikeiōsis* and *primary* impulse. Arius, as we have seen, is anomalous in paying no attention to these. But he may reflect Stoic practice accurately in the fact that he reserves his detailed discussion of the goal to these later pages, while anticipating it in his brief remarks at C4 (cf. C8.1) on the relationship between living in accordance with nature, virtue, impulse, and the goal.

The Stoic goal is happiness (*eudaimonia*), and it is the elucidation of this newly mentioned concept with which he is chiefly concerned in D1–5. This accounts for two theses concerning goods and evils (D3, D4) which would seem out of place if Arius were thought to be merely wandering back to his earlier topic (B). But they are placed here because he is concerned with distinguishing between those goods and evils which are necessary to happiness and unhappiness and those which are not.

D6 concludes with the sentence: "And so the Stoic goal is equivalent to life in accordance with virtue" (p.78.5). That would be a fitting end to the whole treatment of goods and the goal, which is formally concluded half a page later (p.79.1–2). In between, our text continues inconsequentially with B14, a thesis about goods as "choiceworthy" and their difference from "benefits" (*ōphelēmata*) as "things to be chosen." As Wachsmuth noted, B14 seems quite out of order, and would fit better along with B13 which in turn interrupts the transition from goods in general to the goal. I doubt whether either of these theses can be confidently assumed to fit Arius' original design. But they are a small blemish in an otherwise coherent account.

Of the next four sections:

E theses	Indifferents (*adiaphora*)	pp.79–85
F theses	Appropriate acts (*kathēkonta*)	pp.85–86
G theses	Impulse (*hormē*)	pp.86–93
H theses	Lives (*bioi*)	pp.93–116

The first three need little discussion for the purpose of elucidating the structure of Arius' presentation. His E section was promised by his opening division (A) of existing things into goods, evils and indifferents. We have already seen how he announces his progression to the third of these. The substance and order of his treatment of indifferents agrees closely with Diogenes Laertius (7.104–7). But Arius is much the fuller, and there are differences over details.

Both doxographers conclude their treatment of indifferents with an account of those important *adiaphora* which have nonmoral value and disvalue, the so-called "preferred and rejected things" (*proēgmena* and *apoproēgmena*). The "preferred" indifferents form the material of "appropriate acts" (*kathēkonta*), and an understanding of the connection between the two concepts is vital to a rudimentary grasp of Stoic ethics.[18] It is therefore helpful for Arius to preface his treatment of "appropriate acts"(F) by observing that this topic follows on from the doctrine of preferred things (p.85.12–13). Diogenes Laertius fails to bring out that link, which is further elucidated in Arius by his noting that "appropriate acts" have "certain indifferents'' as their measuring stick (p.86.12–13). Cicero makes the same point at greater length (*Fin.* 3.58ff.).

"What sets impulse in motion is nothing else, they say, than an impression which directly impels the appropriate act" (p.86.17–18). This is the first sentence of Arius' section G on "impulse," and it is clearly intended to indicate the doctrinal connection between "appropriate acts" (F) and "impulse." That connection emerges in Cicero explicitly and in Diogenes implicitly in their opening accounts of the natural objects to which animals are attracted from their birth onwards.[19] Arius, as we have already noted, has dispensed with their material on *oikeiōsis*, and impulse has previously figured only briefly in his comments on the cardinal virtues and their goal (C4).[20] What the present section offers is a set of definitions, by genus and species, of impulse considered normatively, concentrating on the species of "practical impulse," and then passing to the deviant species, "passion" (*pathos*). Arius' procedure is utterly methodical, but it raises interesting questions about his difference from Cicero *De finibus* 3 and Diogenes Laertius 7. On "passion" Diogenes corresponds to Arius closely,[21] but the little that he says on normative impulse is stated quite differently: only traces of Arius' opening matter are included, and they are placed as an appendix to "passion" in a discussion of "good emotional states" (*eupatheiai*), a term completely absent from Arius.[22] Cicero has just one short paragraph on "passion" (*Fin.* 3.35), and does not connect it at all with any discussion of "impulse."[23] But both these writers show an interest, not shared by Arius, in connecting the concept of impulse with an animal's primary consciousness of values and the development of moral awareness.

It seems likely that Arius (or his sources) is more concerned with the systematic classification of concepts than with such questions as the justification or grounding of Stoic ethics. He has given a detailed account of impulse. But he has not made it primary, as appears to have been the Stoic practice. This then, as was noted above, is a problem demanding elucidation. It may be postponed until our general survey of his material has been completed.

The case for a coherent plan concerning section H in Stobaeus (pp. 93.14–116.10) is harder to make. As Wachsmuth notes (p.93), this section presents miscellaneous material and considerable repetition. Yet, as he also points out, one theme does predominate, "the character of the wise man."

Section H starts abruptly with a thesis concerning "perfectly appropriate acts" (*katorthōmata*) and "faults" (*hamartēmata,* p.93.14–18). It is given a cross reference to the previous discussion of "appropriate acts" (p.85.19). So either Arius or Stobaeus or an intermediary is aware of the position of this material. Next, linked on by "and" (*te*), comes a thesis concerning the community of goods possessed by good men, and the mutual hostility of inferior men (p.93.19–94.6). The next three pages seem to follow on quite coherently, dealing as they do with the social and political characteristics of the two classes of men. If this is their theme, there is good reason for them to juxtapose treatments of justice, politics, education, friendship, business activities, forgiveness, punishment, law—and to amplify the thesis concerning the community of goods (p.95.3–8). The opening thesis of the section, on "perfectly appropriate acts" and "faults," gains point as the preface to this list of actions, presented normatively as characteristic of the wise or inferior man. Some actions, however, such as talking and walking, are morally neutral taken by themselves, so Arius suitably rounds off this passage by a three part classification of actions (energēmata): "perfectly appropriate acts," "faults," and "neither" (pp.96.18–97.14).

The remainder of the whole piece continues the description of the two classes of men. Principal differences between them are outlined (pp.98.14–100.14). Then, after paragraphs on the different predicates applicable to virtue (p.100.15–101.4) and a reminder concerning the exclusive possession by good men of goods and by inferior men of evils (pp.101.4–102.3), we get a lengthy description of the epithets and actions which characterize the two classes of men, punctuated by occasional irrelevant paragraphs in the manner of the earlier sections.[24] The main intention, if marred at times by inept execution, is plain. On the basis of the ethical concepts outlined in the previous sections Arius is indicating that this is what a good man is like in Stoicism and how an inferior man differs. As before, he offers us a map which will enable us to locate the principal concepts of Greek social life and moral character on a Stoic interpretation of them.

Arius' treatment of Stoic ethics appears then to be based upon the following plan:

A   Goods, evils, and indifferents
B/C Goods and evils: virtues and vices
B   Goods and evils more generally
D   Goal
E   Indifferents
F   Appropriate acts
G   Impulse
H   Lives (good and inferior men)

How does this scheme compare with the accounts of Diogenes Laertius and Cicero? Like Arius, Diogenes passes from G (restricted by him to "passion") to H. At 7.117 he begins a characterization of the wise man which persists up to 124 with an interruption in 120 concerned mainly with the equality of all faults.[25] His final chapters (129–31) are a sketchy collection of material on the wise man's social behavior which corresponds broadly to Arius' treatment. These are preceded by a lengthy and ill placed discussion of virtue (125–29) which handles points presented by Arius within his discussion of goods.[26]

Minor differences apart, Arius and Diogenes agree in moving from the exposition of ethical concepts to a characterization of the wise man and the good life, focusing particularly on social behavior. Cicero's treatment in De finibus is similar. He too deals in his final chapters (from 3.62) with social conduct and the wise man. Like Arius and Diogenes he includes within this material a section on ethical concepts, justifying mention of them at this place by their relevance to "the preservation of human society'' (3.69).[27] We may conclude therefore that Arius' procedure in his final section had the authority of the sources used by Diogenes and Cicero.

As for the earlier sections of Arius, Diogenes agrees with him in the order of treating virtues and vices, goods and evils, indifferents, appropriate acts, and passions (C, B, E, F, G). The main procedural differences between them have already been mentioned: Diogenes begins with impulse and goal; Arius handles these later, and starts from the division into goods, evils and indifferents. Diogenes, it should be noted, knows of this division, but uses it only to conclude his discussion of goods and evils and to introduce indifferents.[28] It plays no structural part in his narrative, and its presence in Cicero is even more tenuous (*Fin.* 3.50).

Cicero proceeds less systematically than Arius or Diogenes. He agrees with Diogenes against Arius in starting with impulse, and this determines his early treatment of the goal and virtue (3.12–26). But his manner of presenting goods and evils, indifferents, and appropriate acts is sufficiently similar to theirs to indicate a common background. One oddity is the brevity and placing of his section on passions (see n.23 above).

The distinctive features of Arius' exposition appear to be:

1. His opening division into goods, evils, and indifferents.
2. His lack of interest in "impulse" as a primary ethical concept.
3. The amplitude, coherence, and exhaustive nature of his mapping of ethical concepts.

Would we be justified in attributing any of these characteristics to his own initiative rather than to Stoic or other sources?

III. THE BACKGROUND AND FUNCTION OF ARIUS' EXPOSITION

Diogenes Laertius reports a division of the topics of ethics which was adopted, he says, by all the leading Stoics from Chrysippus down to Posidonius (7.84): "They divide the ethical part of philosophy into: (1) the topic of impulse, (2) that of goods and evils, (3) that of passions, (4) of virtue, (5) of the goal, (6) of primary value and actions, (7) of appropriate acts, (8) of suasions and dissuasions." The interpretation of these headings is an unsolved problem. Most of them are familiar enough, and fit Arius' exposition with minor adjustments: 1 and 3 = G, 2 = B, 4 = C, 5 = D, 6 = E (in part), 7 = F. If "suasions and dissuasions" (8) corresponds to his final section "Lives (good and bad men)" (H), which seems plausible, the only misfit (and the same holds good for Cicero and Diogenes Laertius) is "actions" (the second part of 6). What seems to be needed in place of "actions" is a reference to "indifferents" (*adiaphora*).

More problematical is the ordering of the topics. Why are "passions" placed so early in the list? They are treated relatively late in all three of our authors, and that seems obviously where they should come. It has been suggested that the first three topics are generic; and if this is right, it would allow topics 4 to 7 to be treated under 2, (or 1 and 2), leaving "passions" till later.[29] But that solution is rather forced, since 6 and 7 are regularly expounded after the discussion of goods and evils has been completed. Rather than offering a general interpretation of the division, I propose to consider what light it may shed on the special features of Arius' exposition.

The first and basic observation is the support it gives to the opening procedures of Cicero and Diogenes against Arius. They both begin their treatment of Stoic ethics with "impulse," the first topic of the division. In Arius "impulse" plays a modest part in the treatment of C, D, E, and F, but it is not discussed in its own right until he reaches G, his seventh topic. There, moreover, as we saw, it subsumes the treatment of "passions," yet these are treated independently by Cicero and Diogenes, and their methodology has the support of the division attributed to Chrysippus and his successors. Arius' different procedure is much too sharp to be accounted for by disturbance to his text in the transmission to Stobaeus.[30] Otherwise, however, he agrees so closely with Cicero and Diogenes in his ordering of subjects that a common Stoic tradition appears to be at work.

Stoic interest in the systematic exposition of ethics received its chief stimulus from Chrysippus.[31] In the list of his ethical writings, partially preserved in Diogenes Laertius (7.199–202), several works are mentioned which may bear directly or indirectly on Arius' account. In his final words Arius notes that "Chrysippus has discussed all the paradoxical doctrines in many different works" and he singles out two of these: "On doctrines" and "Outline of the theory." The second of these is probably the first item listed in Diogenes' catalogue of Chrysippus' ethical books (7.199); and the first section of the catalogue includes other works whose titles recall material in Arius and the other summary treatments of Stoic ethics: "Ethical theses," "Definitions of the good man," "Definitions of the inferior man," "On the qualities of the virtues," etc.

From a comparison of Arius, Cicero, and Diogenes, von Arnim concluded that there existed a standard compendium of Stoic ethics, going back to Chrysippus, which was revised by later generations of Stoics.[32] What was common to all three authors, he suggested, could be explained by their recourse to this book by Chrysippus. Their deviations were due to "a later time"—by which I take von Arnim to mean differently annotated later editions of the book, or different use of the annotations it contained. This is an economical and plausible suggestion. But its plausibility is compatible with a different explanation of the principal differences between Arius and the others; it does not readily explain those differences, which are matters of procedure rather than details of doctrine.[33]

Cicero is distinctive in devoting the greatest space to *oikeiōsis* and the acquisition of moral understanding. Diogenes actually quotes Chrysippus on this subject (7.85), but his own exposition is more perfunctory than Cicero's. Arius, if he is the author of Stobaeus pp.47–48 and the Peripatetic section (pp.118–23), knows all about *oikeiōsis*, but omits it completely from his Stoic section. Cicero and Arius agree against Diogenes in presenting the main doctrines as a derived sequence of theses, coherently related together; but Cicero makes no use of the division into goods, evils, and indifferents. Arius is distinctive in the sheer quantity of information he provides, his systematic use of the division procedure, and his very sparse references to the attested views of individual Stoic philosophers. His theses are frequently presented in the form of arguments, unlike the bald summaries of Diogenes. But they are not arguments which carry the reader forward in an evolving progression, which Cicero attempts to do.

How much can we learn about the basis of Arius' procedure by considering further material in Stobaeus?

If it is correct to supply his name before the definitions of ethical terms given on pp.37–39, he was strongly influenced in these by Peripatetic and later Platonic theory. An orthodox Stoic would not define "moral character" (*ēthos*) by reference to "training the irrational part of the soul to be subordinate to reason" (p.38.3–4), and Arius attributes this and his other opening definitions to "the Platonists." An interest in "the irrational" is the dominant factor in this set of definitions, which continues with "passion" (*pathos*), "defined by Aristotle as irrational excessive motion of soul" (p.38.19–20). The material attributed to Aristotle is in fact contaminated with Stoicism, an indication of the eclecticism we could expect from Arius. He does make explicit reference to Stoic definitions in this section, but they are subordinate to the purportedly Platonic and Aristotelian doctrines.

Next we are given the divisions of ethics worked out by Philo of Larisa and Eudorus of Alexandria (pp.39–45). The Philonian division appears to have had no influence on Arius' presentation of Stoic and Peripatetic ethics. After expounding it, he says: "If I were lazier, I should be content with it and now unfold the doctrines, supported by his six-part outline. But since I think I should above all study the substance (*ousia*) of a subject, and then its quality and quantity, and following these, its relation, I believe I must make the further effort of studying some other people's views as well, not all of them, but those which differ on these points" (pp.41.26–42.6).[34] So he now outlines Eudorus' division of ethics. Following that he says he must "start with the main topics (*problēmata*), prefacing them with the headings (*genē*) according to my own arrangement, which I am convinced is conducive to clarity in division" (p.45.8–10).

These elaborate statements of procedure are peculiar and interesting. It sounds as if Arius is setting out acknowledged methods of division before settling upon a practice of his own. "My own arrangement" may refer both to the summary analysis of terms and topics which precedes the exposition of Stoic ethics (pp.45–57), and to that exposition itself. But first we have to ask how Arius stands in regard to Eudorus' division.

That scheme had three principal sections (p.42.13–15):(1) study of the value of each thing, (2) impulse, (3) action. The second section, impulse, is subdivided into (a) the species of impulse, (b) passion (p.44.3–4). Here at last we have found authority for Arius' idiosyncratic handling of impulse in his Stoic exposition. Both

Eudorus and Arius agree in removing impulse from the primary position for ethical topics. They also agree in dividing the topic of impulse, so that it includes both a list of its species and a treatment of passion. That too has no support in Chrysippus' division or in the accounts of Cicero and Diogenes.

Eudorus' third section, action, matches Arius less well (pp.44.6–45.6). It includes "appropriate acts" (kathēkonta); but these were treated by Arius in their own right according to regular Stoic practice. Material in Arius' own final section (H) on lives and social behavior found its place in Eudorus here, but under "action." Eudorus also treated moralizing advice and other topics which appear in Arius, if at all, only by implication from his descriptions of the wise and inferior man.[35]

Eudorus' first section is difficult to ascertain in detail owing to the defective state of Stobaeus' text.[36] From a summary it would appear that "goods and evils" served as a generic heading for the whole section (p.43.15–17, 44.1–2), which treated of goals, virtues, and also "the so-called preferred things" (proegmēna), such as fame and good appearance. If that is correct, this section of Eudorus will have embraced the material located by Arius in his sections B, C, and D, but it will also have been extended to take in the treatment of "indifferents" (Arius' section E), which falls outside Arius' sections on goods and evils.

That conclusion should not surprise us. Eudorus must have intended his division to cover the exposition of all ethical systems. His terminology and practice were influenced, as they were bound to be in the mid first century B.C., by the dominant place of Stoicism. But if he wanted his division to fit all ethical systems of the time, it had to be flexible enough to accommodate divergent doctrines. The Stoics were out on a limb in confining goods and evils to virtues and vices. Other schools were happy enough to treat the Stoics' "so-called preferred things" as goods of a certain kind.[37] Anyone like Arius, intent on expounding Stoic ethics per se, would have to make a sharp break between goods and indifferents, of which the "preferred things" are a species.

Given the general suitability of Eudorus' first section, the precise agreement between him and Arius on impulse, and the loose compatibility between them in regard to Eudorus' third section, it seems probable that Arius used Eudorus in working out his own division of Stoic ethics. But he used him discriminatingly, drawing also upon the standard divisions of Stoic philosophers, and contributing something of his own.

Before attempting to finalize this last point, I must say a word about two other passages of Stobaeus: the summary analysis of terms and doctrines which comes between Eudorus and the Stoic section (pp.45–57), and the Peripatetic section.

The summary analysis comes immediately after Arius' remarks on his "own arrangement of division." It appears to be an elucidation of the key terms which would figure in the first section of a Eudorean division: goal and target (cf. Eudorus p.43.2–3), subordinate goal (hupotelis), happiness, virtue, goods and evils. The sources of the material, acknowledged or unacknowledged, are eclectic in the highest degree. As in the introductory pages of definitions (37–39), the supposed views of

Plato and Aristotle have pride of place. But Stoics, and even Epicureans, get a mention. The most curious feature of this summary analysis is the treatment of "subordinate goal," *hupotelis*, a term which seems to originate with the early Stoic, Herillus.[38] No school of philosophy is mentioned in the account of "subordinate goal." But the doctrine reported, and nearly all the terminology, are pure Stoicism. We are given an entirely clear and accurate account of the Stoic doctrine of *oikeiōsis*, with reference to the primary impulse of living creatures and a list of "the primary things in accordance with nature" (pp.47.12–48.5). The purpose of the passage however is not to expound Stoicism as such, but to show that "the subordinate goal" accommodates all possible candidates, taking in all philosophical positions, for the object of the primary impulse. That catholic procedure is well known for its use by Carneades and Antiochus.[39] It suits our expectations of Eudorus or Arius very well.[40]

But if Arius is the author of this material he has behaved very curiously in excluding it from his treatment of Stoic ethics. All the more so, if he is the author of the Peripatetic section. For that presents a most detailed exposition of this very doctrine in its opening (pp.118.5–123.27). Other problems about Arius come to the surface once the Stoic and Peripatetic sections are compared. If he had the eclectic interests which are manifest in Stobaeus' introductory sections, we should expect these to be reflected in like manner in his expositions of the two ethical systems. We should also expect that his methods of dividing the topics of ethics would be similar in these two sections. Yet neither of these expectations is satisfied. The division procedure of Eudorus has only the loosest approximation to the methodology of the Peripatetic section, but it fits the Stoic section fairly closely. The Peripatetic section offers a glaring contamination of Stoic and Peripatetic material.[41] But the account of Stoic ethics, if largely unhistorical in its assimilation of material from different periods, does not appear to be infected with doctrines from any other school.

At this point it would be prudent to drop any pretense that we know Arius as the author of the Stoic section, especially when our sole *evidence* for his presence in Stobaeus comes from the treatment of Peripatetic ethics. But it may just be possible to devise an hypothesis to salvage his joint authorship, though its lack of economy will reveal its frailty.

We have to assume, I think, that Arius was largely content to transmit the principal sources he used without intruding his own contributions. In the case of the Peripatetic section he followed a handbook by Antiochus, or someone like him, which viewed Aristotelian doctrines through the strongly tinted glasses of Stoicism. For the Stoics Arius used a reliable Stoic compendium of the kind suggested by von Arnim. For his introductory sections he compiled material from standard handbooks so as to give a representative account of basic terms in common use in the different schools. But this unoriginal man had one or two ideas of his own about the right way to present summaries of doctrine. He tells us as much (p.45.8), and his greatest idea was to structure his division of Stoic philosophy around the stock classification:

goods, evils, indifferents. There is no evidence that Eudorus did this, and Arius did not do it for the Peripatetics but it seemed to him right for the Stoics.

The division had to be bought at a price, and the price was high. Arius decided he would have to jettison the Stoics' standard practice of beginning their ethics with the "primary impulse" and *oikeiōsis*. But he paid that price, justifying himself by Eudorus' division in which impulse arises second to goods and evils. He attempted, with only moderate success, to graft brief mentions of impulse onto his treatment of the goal. Fortunately, for our understanding of Stoicism, Cicero, and Diogenes Laertius were unaffected by Arius' procedure. But it may have been influential. Sextus Empiricus regards the division into goods, evils, and indifferents as characteristic of the Old Academy, Peripatetics, and Stoics,[42] and by beginning his ethical discussion with it he implies its logical priority. The division itself of course was utterly hackneyed. But Arius may have been original in using it as the structure for classifying the first topics of Stoic ethics.

If all this turns Arius into something of a hack, we should not complain. His detailed material in the Stoic section is probably more accurate and certainly fuller than anything else we possess. He could have followed the substance, if not the order, of a Chrysippean handbook very closely. Unlike Diogenes Laertius, he rarely names individual Stoics, and of those whom he does, he stops at Panaetius.[43] Unlike Diogenes again, he refers only once to specific books by Stoics, and those are the works of Chrysippus mentioned in his conclusion. Their titles suggest the sobering reflection that we may be reading a good deal of Chrysippus in Arius Didymus, or whoever he is.

APPENDIX

Table of Ethical Theses in Stobaeus 2 p. 57–85

A Existing things comprise: 1. goods 2. evils 3. indifferents	p. 57.19–58.4	D.L.7.101 (cf. Cic.*Fin*.3.50)
B1.i Goods (A1) comprise: 1. virtues 2. not-virtues, e.g. joy	p. 58.5–9	D.L.7.102
B1.ii Evils (A2) comprise: 1. vices 2. not-vices	p. 58.14–18	D.L.7.102
C1.i Virtues (B1.i.1) comprise: 1. sciences and skills 2. not-sciences or not-skills	p. 58.9–14	(cf. D.L.7.93)
C1.ii Vices (B1.ii.1) comprise: 1. ignorances and lacks of skills 2. not-ignorances or not-lacks of skills	p. 58.18–59.3	(cf. D.L.7.93)
C1.i.1 are cardinally exemplified	p. 59.4–11	
C1.ii.1 are cardinally exemplified	p. 59.11–60.5	
C2 virtue generically defined	p. 60.7–8	D.L.7.89
C3 virtues comprise: 1. primary (= C1.i.1) 2. subordinate (= C1.i.1)	p. 60.9–62.6	D.L.7.92,126

C4	The goal of all C1.i.1 virtues is life in accordance with nature	p. 62.7-14	(cf. D.L.7.87, Cic.*Fin*.3.22)
C5	All C1.i.1 virtues are constitutive of life's goals and consist of rational principles	p. 62.15-17	
	All C1.i.2 virtues are supervenient on them and acquired by practice	p. 62.17–63.5	D.L.7.90
C6.1	All C1.i.1 virtues have common rational principles and goal; inseparable	p. 63.6–64.12	D.L.7.125-26
C6.2	All C1.i.1 virtues differ in their subject matter		
C6.3	All C1.i.1 virtues view their subordinate and each other's subject matter		
B2	⟨goods as⟩ choiceworthy for their own sake comprise: 1. virtues = C1.i.1 (choiceworthy as goals) 2. all goods (intrinsically choiceworthy)	p. 64.13-17	D.L.7.127
C7.1	Virtues are plural and inseparable (cf. C6.1, C.6.2)	p. 64.18-20	
C7.2	Virtue is corporeal	p. 64.20-23	
C7.3	Virtue is a living thing	p. 65.1-6	
C8.1	Nothing between virtue and vice	p. 65.7	D.L.7.127
C8.2	Inferior are imperfect, good are perfect	p. 65.8-11	(cf.D.L.7.128)
C8.3	Wise man always acts in accordance with all the virtues	p. 65.12-14	

C8.4 Wise man's loving etc. is acting in accordance with virtue	p. 65.15–66.13	
C8.5 Wise man does everything well	p. 66.14–68.3	D.L.7.125
C8.6 Contrary theses concerning the inferior man	p. 68.3-23	
B3.i Goods comprise: 1. those which always belong to all wise men 2. those which do not	p. 68.24–69.4	
B3.ii Evils comprise: 1. those which always belong to all fools 2. those which do not	p. 69.5-10	
B4.i All goods are beneficial, etc.	p. 69.11-14	D.L.7.98 (cf.Cic.*Fin*.3.33)
B4.ii All evils are harmful, etc.		
B5.i 3 senses of the good	p. 69.17–70.3	D.L.7.94
B5.ii 3 senses of the evil	p. 70.3-7	
B6.i Goods comprise: 1. psychic 2. external 3. neither	p. 70.8-14	D.L.7.95
B6.ii Evils comprise: same division	p. 70.14-21	
B6.i.1 Goods comprise: 1. "invariant conditions" (*diatheseis*)—virtues 2. "tenors" (*hexeis*)—e.g. prophecy 3. neither	p. 70.21–71.6	D.L.7.98

B6.ii.1 Evils comprise: same division	p. 71.6-14	
B7.i Goods comprise: 1. final—e.g. joy (cf.B1.i.2) 2. efficient 3. both—virtues	p. 71.15–72.6	D.L.97,Cic.*Fin*.3.55
B7.ii Evils comprise: same division	p. 72.6-13	
B8 Goods comprise: 1. intrinsically choiceworthy 2. efficient	p. 72.14-18	
B9.i Every good is choiceworthy (cf. B2)	p. 72.19-25	D.L.7.98
B9.ii Every evil is to be avoided		
B10 Goods comprise: 1. moving—e.g. joy 2. stationary: a. in disposition (*schesis*) only b. also in tenor (*hexis*)	p. 73.1-15	
B11 Goods comprise: 1. absolute 2. relative	p. 73.16–74.14	
B12 Goods comprise: 1. unmixed 2. mixed	p. 74.15-20	
(theses B10 = 12 apply similarly to vices	p. 74.21-2)	
B13 ⟨good as⟩ choiceworthy distinguished from "takeable"	p. 75.1-6	
D1 Virtue and happiness described	p. 75.7-10	Cic.*Fin*.3.28
D2 Definitions and senses of goal	p. 75.11–77.5	D.L.7.87-8, Cic.*Fin*. 3.21,26

D3	Goods comprise:	1. necessary to happiness 2. not necessary to happiness	p. 77.6-15	
D4	Evils comprise:	1. necessary to unhappiness 2. not necessary to unhappiness	p. 77.10-15	
D5	Happiness as goal		p. 77.16-27	D.L.7.88
D6	Equivalence of goal to life in accordance with virtue		p. 78.1-6	D.L.7.87, Cic.*Fin.*3.21
B14	⟨good as⟩ "choiceworthy" distinguished from benefit "to be chosen"		p. 78.7-12	
E1	Indifferents defined in reference to:	1. good and evil 2. impulse	p. 79.1-17	D.L.7.104-5
E2	Indifferents (E1.1) comprise:	1. in accordance with nature 2. contrary to nature 3. neither 1 nor 2		cf. D.L.7.107, Cic.*Fin.*3.20,51
E3	Indifferents (E1.1) comprise:	1. small/great worth 2. intrinsic/efficient 3. preferred/rejected/neither	p. 80.14-21	Cic.*Fin.*3.56, D.L.7.107, D.L.7.105, Cic.*Fin.*3.51
E4	"Preferred" indifferents comprise:	1. psychic 2. corporeal 3. external	p. 80.22–81.6	D.L.7.106
(E4 classifications applied to "rejected" & "neither" indifferents			p. 81.7-18	D.L.7.106)

E5	E4.1 "preferred indifferents" of more worth than E4.2 & 3	p. 81.19-82.4	
E6	Indifferents (E1) comprise: 1. rousing impulse towards 2. rousing impulse away from 3. neither 1 or 2	p.82.5-10	
E7	Indifferents (E2.1) comprise: 1. primary 2. by participation	p. 82.11-19	
	(similarly applied to E2.2 indifferents)		
E8	All indifferents (E2.1, E2.2) are takeable/not-takeable	p. 82.20-83.9	
E9	3 senses of worth/non-worth	p. 83.10-84.17	D.L.7.105
	(E10 repetition of E3.1, E3.3 etc.)	p. 84.18-85.3)	
E11	Clarification of the term "preferred"	p. 85.3-11	Cic.*Fin.*3.52

NOTES

1. Cf. A. Covotti, "Quibus libris vitarum in libro septimo scribendo Laertius usus fuerit" *SIFC* (1897); H. von Arnim, *Stoicorum Veterum Fragmenta* 1.xxx–xliii.
2. 2 vols. Turin 1964, 1967.
3. Cf. G. B. Kerferd, *CR* n.s. 17 (1967) 156–58; P. Boyancé in *Latomus* 26 (1967) 246–49.
4. On Arius Didymus and what is known about him cf. H. Diels, *Doxographi Graeci* (Berlin 1879) 69–88, P. Fraser, *Ptolemaic Alexandria* (Oxford 1972) 1.489–91; J. Glucker, *Antiochus and the late Academy* (Göttingen 1978) 94–97. Fraser and Glucker should also be consulted on Eudorus, and cf. J. Dillon, *The Middle Platonists* (London 1977)114–35.
5. *Mützells Zeitschrift* 13 (1859) 564. Cf. Diels, *Dox graec.* 69 for the earlier references.
6. According to Hense's critical apparatus the lemma is included in S but omitted by M and A. S is a Viennese MS (Hunger I, 184 [0412.41.47]) dated to the 10th/11th centuries, see Wachsmuth's *Prolegomena to Stobaeus* 1 p.xiii. Wachsmuth himself, however (2 pp.129.19 ap. crit.), writes *inscriptum in T* where T = Trincavelli's ed. princeps (Venice 1536). Since the editors of Stobaeus treat T as having the status of a MS the discrepancy between their reports is unfortunate.
7. *Philosophie der Griechen* 4th ed. (Leipzig 1909) 3.1, 637 n.1.
8. *Praep. ev.* 15.15.9 (p.380 vol.2 Mras), 11.23.2 (p.51 vol. 2 Mras). The work *On Pythagorean Philosophy* is also attributed to Arius by Clem. Alex. *Strom.* 1.16.80.4 (p.52 vol.2 Stählin).
9. In his edition of Cicero *De finibus* Madvig was so impressed by the similarities between Stobaeus' section on Peripatetic ethics and the Antiochean material in *Fin.* 5 that he proposed Antiochus as their author (Excur. 7.838). Zeller accepted the point, regarding Arius as intermediary between Antiochus and Stobaeus, *Phil. d. Gr.* 3.1.637–3. Hirzel affirmed the link between Antiochus and Stobaeus without committing himself to Arius' transmission of the material, *Untersuch. zu Ciceros Phil. Schriften* (Leipzig 1882) 2.694ff. But Diels, with a strong interest in resuscitating Arius, insisted that Stobaeus' material showed too much difference from Antiochus to support an Antiochean compendium as Arius' source, *Dox. Graec.* 72. See further n.40 below.
10. *Dox. Graec.* 71.
11. I take "things to be chosen and avoided" and "happiness" as amplifications respectively of "goods and evils" and "goal," not as independent subjects. See pp.72.19–21, 77.16. Wachsmuth (ad loc.) suggests that "things to be chosen and avoided" are a spurious addition, or alternatively, that p.75.1–6 = B3 is a correctly placed fragment of a missing section on this theme: see n.14 below.
12. It may seem odd to write of "the goal of the virtues." Usener proposed to delete *to* before *telos,* and it would be possible, as Gisela Striker suggested to me, to take *telos* to mean "result" here. But I take the point to be that life in accordance with nature is brought about or realized by the cardinal virtues. The chief ethical problem facing the Stoics was to show why living virtuously is the human goal. Their answer, as suggested here and at p.65.8–9 (cf. Diog. Laert. 7.87), is that virtue gives the content of man's natural life, that to which he is impelled by his nature as a man. I fully agree with my commentator's stress on the importance of this point, and cf. my discussion in "The logical basis of Stoic ethics," *PAS* (1970/71), 96–103.
13. Wachsmuth follows Usener in adding *kata* before *to sumphōnon,* but there is no reason to change the text. Take *to sumphōnon* and *to heautēs* as compound objects of *prattousa.* The meaning is hardly affected.

14. B2 = p.64.13–17 explains Diogenes of Babylon's two senses of the phrase "intrinsically choiceworthy." I include this as a B thesis because it applies to goods in general and not only to the virtues. But it does refer to those virtues which are "choiceworthy in relation to the goal" (*telikōs haireta*), with a backward note to pp.62–63; and the virtues are being presented as a subdivision of goods. The position of B2 moreover is paralleled in the Antiochean section of Cicero *Fin*. 5.67–8 where it also follows C6.1–6.3. Stobaeus has three further sections on "choiceworthy," all of which are oddly placed: pp.75.1, 78.7, 97.15. Cf. Giusta *I dossografi* 1.43ff. for suggestions about their original position.

15. *Dox. Graec.* 71.

16. It is also based upon his acting in accordance with "right reason" (*orthos logos*), p.66.19–20. The justification and importance of this fundamental concept are not made clear by Arius, though he later gives a brief account of it in the context of "law" (p.96.10–12, repeated at p.102.4–6). On this point Diog. Laert. 7.86–8 is much superior, bringing "right reason" into an analysis of virtue and the goal.

17. Cf. Diog. Laert. 7.84 which is discussed below.

18. Cf. I. G. Kidd, "Stoic Intermediates and the End for Man," A. A. Long ed., *Problems in Stoicism* (London 1971) 150–72, esp. 155. A curious omission in Diog. Laert.'s treatment of "appropriate acts" is all reference to their "perfect" form, *katorthōmata*. He does however have one paragraph (7.108) which includes matter absent from Arius.

19. *Fin*. 3.20–25; Diog. Laert. 7.85–6.

20. It also plays a part in his account of indifferents, pp.79.8, 82.5.

21. Cf. his 7.110–15 with Arius, p.88.8–93.13.

22. At 7.116 Diog. Laert. lists joy (*chara*), watchfulness (*eulabeia*), and wishing (*boulēsis*) as the three *eupatheiai*. That list is standard, cf. *SVF* 3.431–442, but there is no trace of it in Stobaeus. Arius includes "wishing" as one of the species of "practical impulse" (p.87.16ff.), but "joy" is treated by him under "goods," and he has nothing to say about "watchfulness." Cicero knows of the *eupatheiai*, citing them in *Tusc. disp.* 4.12–14, but not in the *De finibus*.

23. His cursory treatment of "passion" may be due to his having already dealt with it fully in *Tusc. disp.* 4.10–32.

24. E.g. p.113.18–23 where a short account of the equality of all faults has no connection with its surrounding contexts on the behavior of wise men.

25. So too Stobaeus; see previous note.

26. But Stobaeus himself has a paragraph on the predicates of virtue, p.100.15ff., within his final section which corresponds to an early part of Diogenes' exposition on the predicates of good, 7.99. Such common disorder suggests confusion probably subsequent to Arius in the transmission of the material.

27. *Ut vero conservetur omnis homini erga hominem societas, coniunctio, caritas, et emolumenta et detrimenta* (quae *ōphelēmata et* blammata *appellant*), *communia esse voluerunt*. Similarly Arius, p.101.5–13 within his last section.

28. 7.101. As Charles Kahn pointed out in the discussion of the paper, this sentence of Diogenes is wrongly printed in the modern editions. It goes with what follows, and should thus begin a new paragraph.

29. This was argued by A. Dyroff, *Die Ethik der alten Stoa* (Berlin 1897) 4–7. Zeller accepted the generic interpretation of the first three topics, but he rejected Dyroff's attempt to classify the remainder accordingly, *Phil. d. Griechen* (4th ed.) 3.1.210–12.

30. I do not exclude considerable tampering with Arius' text to account for minor displacements and incongruities, see Giusta, *I dossografi* 1.43–5 for suggestions about some of these.

31. In his catalogue of Chrysippus' works Diog. Laert. gives a whole section to "the articulation of ethical conceptions" (7.199); the earlier Stoic Sphaerus wrote a book *On the arrangement of ethics* (ibid. 7.177).

32. *SVF* 1 p. xli.
33. For a good account of significant differences between Cicero and Diogenes cf. Hirzel, *Untersuchungen* 2.2.574ff.
34. This showy parade of Aristotle's "categories" plays no apparent part in the succeeding exposition, though Giusta has maintained otherwise.
35. But the 8th Stoic topic in Diog. Laert. 7.84, "suasions and dissuasions," well describes much of Eudorus' subject-matter.
36. I must briefly indicate that Wachsmuth's understanding of this passage, and the supplement he prints, seem to me quite mistaken. He takes it that "goods and evils" and "virtues and vices" were treated as quite distinct topics. That seems to be due to a misreading of p.43.1–4. The conclusion of the passage makes the "most generic" status of "goods and evils" perspicuous, and it need be no objection that virtues and vices are not restated as an example of "the many divisions" of goods and evils, p.43.17ff.
37. Cf. the Peripatetic section, p.124.15ff.
38. *SVF* 1.411. Cf. Dyroff (above, n.29) 49ff.
39. Cf. Cic. *Fin.* 5.16ff., and Zeller *Phil. d. Gr.* 4.635 n.1.
40. John Dillon, *The Middle Platonists,* 116, thinks Arius' list of *problēmata* (pp.45–57) is taken from Eudorus. That may well be so, although the preface to these (p.45.8–10) seems to refer in the first person to Arius himself.
41. See n.9 above. This assessment of the Peripatetic section is not intended to cast doubt on the genuinely Aristotelian/Theophrastean thrust of the work as a whole. But Diels' comment is valid: *"Stoicae disciplinae non guttae sed flumina immissa sunt,"* *Dox. Graec.* 71. Wachsmuth's critical apparatus collects the obvious references to Stoic doctrine. Antiochus of course maintained that those doctrines were largely derived from the Platonic/Peripatetic tradition, so that their presence does not represent "contamination" in his eyes. The evidence for Stoic material in this section is not restricted to the occurrence of terminology (e.g. *kathekōnta*), and the opening interest in *oikeiōsis* (for which a Peripatetic origin has sometimes been claimed). Quite distinctively Stoic doctrines are frequently included: e.g., selection of natural advantages, p.119.16; justified suicide, p.126.6; moral progress (*prokopē*) p.131.17.
42. *Adv. math.* 11.3ff.
43. The complete absence of "good emotional states" (*eupatheiai*) from Arius' treatment of impulse (see n.22 above) may suggest that this doctrine was posterior to Chrysippus.

Comments on Professor Long's Paper

Nicholas P. White

It would take several essays fully to develop the interesting issues that Professor Long has raised. I shall confine ·myself to the following points.[1] (1) I find the Stobaean account of Stoic ethics less well organized than Professor Long suggests, but his discussion raises the more important question *what sort* of organization it has or lacks. (2) In general, it dispenses with Stoic arguments for their views, and is not organized on any argumentative plan. (3) This is true of the treatment of *hormai*, particularly by contrast with Cicero's discussion in *De finibus* 3. (4) Instead, its organization is like that of a glossary—not a good organization, even if well carried out, for the exposition of Stoic ethics. (5) Given the difference in organization between the Stobaean account and the accounts in Cicero and Diogenes Laertius, we should feel little confidence in von Arnim's hypothesis of a common source for parts of all three. (6) In addition, there are important differences in organization between the Stobaean account of Stoic ethics and the Stobaean account of Peripatetic ethics, and they seem to be stitched together from different kinds of expositions. I would remain quite agnostic on conjectures about any role of Eudorus. (7) Whether the account of Peripatetic ethics is contaminated with Stoic material is a complex question requiring further investigation.

1. Judgments about degree of coherence are subjective and difficult to assess. Professor Long's description and table are very helpful for seeing how the account is laid out, however coherent or incoherent it may be. But contrary to Professor Long, the author of the Stoic section does not actually *say* that his account will be coherent or orderly (p.57.15–17; cf. 116.15–18), and whatever his aim, I am not especially struck by his orderliness.

Rather than bickering about whether the account is or is not orderly, let us ask the more important and tractable question what the principle of organization is. I am not sure what Professor Long's answer to this question is. He thinks that the division of existents into goods, evils, and indifferents is a notable part of it, but the section dealing with this division (to p. 85) is broken up in many other ways, and the rest of the account (pp. 85–116) is organized around different topics. At one point, Professor Long may be suggesting an order determined by the idea that the notions explained earlier should be those required for understanding those explained later. Clearly, however, this idea does not operate most of the time, nor does Professor Long say that it does. Elsewhere, he speaks of the account as presenting, in common with Cicero, a "derived sequence of theses," but it is not made clear what sort of "derivation" is involved or how the sequence is to be thought of as generated. At another point, Professor Long compares a section to a "map." Often he seems to mean merely that the account tends (with some lapses) to take up one notion first and then another, or that it is not totally chaotic.

I press these points because they seem to me to show how very difficult it has been, understandably, for Professor Long to spell out any clear principle or principles governing the organization of the account. It shows some major topic headings, but we do not pass from primitive to defined notions, or from axioms to theorems, or from infancy to later stages of life, or in pedagogical fashion from what is easier to understand to what is harder, or indeed in any other way at all that one could put one's finger on.

Sometimes even the main topic headings become garbled, as Professor Long recognizes. Contrary to Diels, who thought that p.65 marked a sudden shift from the topic of virtue to the topic of the wise man, Professor Long urges that pp.65–69 actually continue the former topic. Here it seems fair to say that even if this is right, the author of the account has by his phraseology much obscured the continuity (see esp. 66.14ff).

2. If we are hard put to say what plan the account follows, we can at least identify readily one plan that it does not follow, namely, a plan under which systematic argument would be given for Stoic ethics as a whole and for its major parts. At one point Professor Long seems to agree, when he says, "It seems likely that [the author is] more concerned with the systematic classification of concepts than with such questions as the justification or grounding of Stoic ethics." At another point, however, he says that its "theses are frequently presented in the form of arguments, unlike the bald summaries of Diogenes." Here he perhaps has in mind such fragmentary bits of inferring as, for example, these: pp.62.9–10, 63.8–19 and 24–25, 64.6, 65.13, 66.19. My impression, however, is that many of the uses of *gar*, in particular, are rather epexegetic than inferential (e.g., pp.63.8–9, 64.6, 65.13), and that the amount of argumentation is extremely small. This is not to say that there is much argument in Diogenes Laertius either. Closer research on both texts is needed to yield comparisons that are more than merely impressionistic. The main point, however, is that the Stobaean account is not constructed on anything that could be called an argumentative plan.

3. A good illustration of this point arises from matters, to which Professor Long gives much attention, concerning *hormai, oikeiōsis*, and the like. Here there is an obvious contrast with Cicero's account. Much of the early part of *De finibus* 3 is an attempt to explain how a human being can by a natural development from infancy come to pursue what the Stoics identify as the *telos*. This explanation served argumentative purposes important to the Stoics.[2] For one thing, they had to show that the process of coming to aim at living according to nature, as they construed this, was itself a natural process—something that they could not legitimately take

for granted. For another thing, they needed to defend themselves against the charge, evident in *De finibus* 4.26ff, that their *telos* was so very peculiar that nobody could have the motivation to adopt it. It is difficult to be sure just when these argumentative needs arose and were answered, but there is good reason to hold with Pohlenz that, like Epicurus, the earliest Stoics actively discussed such questions about human motivational development.[3] But whatever the chronology, Cicero gives an important and ample place in his account to an extensive line of argument that was vital to Stoic purposes. This is not true of the Stobaean account. Pages 86–88 contain, as Professor Long makes clear, quite a lot about *hormai,* but as he also recognizes they are not introduced in the particular way in which they are in Cicero's account, as part of an extensive argument for the Stoic view of the *telos.* In both the Stobaean account (p. 62.9–10) and that of Diogenes there is a very brief allusion to the argument for their *telos*-thesis that the Stoics based on *hormai,* but it is tangential and insignificant for the organization. (Notice that the issue has to do not simply with *where* a treatment of *hormai* is placed, but with whether it plays a role in any expressed argument.)

4. Surely the predominant impression one has of the organization of the account is that much (not all) of it is a sort of glossary or lexicon, often arranged in divisions of one concept into several that fall under it (e.g., pp.57.18ff, 58.5ff, 60.9ff, 73.16ff). The problem with which Professor Long is grappling concerns how these explanations are arranged, but it is at least as important to notice what this arrangement, or lack of it, is of. Once we do, it occurs to us that Chrysippus is reported by Diogenes Laertius to have written several books of *Horoi* on ethical topics (7.199). We therefore can say that this manner of presentation of Stoic ethics has a venerable history. On the other hand, we cannot think that this manner is well suited to its subject. Though we know that the Stoics prided themselves on the coherence of their system (Cic. *De fin.* 3.74), a lexicographical presentation tends by its episodic character to minimize the relevant sort of coherence. That sort of coherence had to do with what we have observed lacking in the Stobaean account: arguments, and the fact that each part of the Stoic system seemed to help to support the other parts (*ibid.*). When Chrysippus wrote his books of *Horoi,* he can hardly have meant them to stand on their own as expositions of Stoic ethics. Nor does the Stobaean account do so, even though it contains much enormously valuable information for checking or elaborating our other smoother but often more superficial or simplified accounts.

5. Von Arnim developed a complex hypothesis about the sources of various parts of our accounts of Stoic ethics, including the supposition that the first parts of the accounts in Stobaeus and Diogenes go back in different ways to a compendium due to Chrysippus.[4] Professor Long follows von Arnim to some extent, at least in thinking that the author of the Stobaean account "could have followed the substance, if not the order, of a Chrysippean handbook very closely," and thinks that much in Stobaeus, Cicero, and Diogenes indicates "that a common Stoic tradition appears to be at work." Although I have no space to treat this matter at all adequately here,

I must say that I do not think that either von Arnim or Professor Long has given us any solid reason for tracing these accounts to any single work. That they contain much Chrysippean material need not be doubted, but I believe that all of the correspondences in doctrine and terminology noted by scholars can be explained in other ways than by a single compendium. It is particularly important to realize that if we are presented with several accounts of Stoic ethics with similar content but different organization, we have no stronger right to assume that they go back to a single work by an early Stoic that has been variously reorganized by later figures, than we have to assume that they go back to different works by one early Stoic (or different similarly-minded early Stoics) who wrote various differently organized accounts of his selfsame Stoic ethical doctrine. We know from Diogenes Laertius that Chrysippus expounded ethics in different forms (cf. esp. 7.199 and 202), and we have absolutely no reason whatsoever to assume that there was any such thing as "*the* standard Stoic practice" (my emphasis) in the ordering of their presentation of ethics, though there was *a* standard division of topics (D. L. 7.84). Before we jump to conclusions about a single common source, we have to reckon with other possibilities, such as that —*just* for example—the Stobaean account may derive largely from Chrysippus' books of *Horoi* (as may Diogenes' account as well, since parts of it, too, are lexicographical), whereas Cicero's account descends from something else, equally Chrysippean perhaps, but differently organized at the very beginning. Obviously this matter needs much further exploration, as does the whole question of the various styles of organization that the Stoics adopted for the exposition of their views. I simply leave off here with this question: Is it entirely accidental that the Stobaean account is partly governed by the division of goods, evils, and indifferents, while three of the books of *Horoi* attributed to Chrysippus are about the *asteios,* the *phaulos,* and *ta anamesa?*

6. Professor Long suggests that the author of the Stobaean account may have been taught something by Eudorus of Alexandria about how to organize a treatment of ethics, though he rightly says that he cannot have applied the lesson too strictly to the Stoic account. This is helpful, for our attention is drawn to just how shaky the attribution of the account to Arius Didymus is, and that only through the Peripatetic account, at best, can the connection be made. By Professor Long's own reckoning, however, Eudoran ideas about organization find "only the loosest approximation" in the Peripatetic section, though a better one in the Stoic section. All of this seems to leave us with perhaps some evidence—though not at all strong evidence—for Eudoran influence on the Stoic account. (It seems clear, though, that Eudorus' apparent *rationale* for his style of organization—that we need *theōria* about value before our *hormai* can be reasonable [p. 42.17–20]—has no impact on the account.) But it leaves precious little evidence for Eudoran influence on *Arius Didymus,* unless we assume that Eudorus influenced him alone. Professor Long clearly recognizes the difficulty, and his final paragraph seems to be intended simply as a suggestion about how we might save the attribution of the Stoic section to Arius in spite of it.

There are some further facts to be noted about the setting of the Stoic account in its context and its relation to the Peripatetic section. These facts tend to make the connection between Arius and the Stoic account still weaker. Though this is a partly subjective matter, my impression is that the Peripatetic account is not only smoother and more continuous than the Stoic account, but also contains much more in the way of argument for the theses it contains, and more explicit indication of the logical relations among them. It contains plenty of definitions and divisions (see esp. pp.134–37), but it also contains more extensive pieces of argumentative exposition than anything in the Stoic section (esp. pp. 116–128). This consideration suggests that the Stoic section was put together with different intentions from those governing the Peripatetic section, and this suspicion is perhaps confirmed by the fact that at both the beginning and the end of the former, the author of it describes it as a *hypomnematismos* (pp.57.15–16 and 116.18), a word not used for the Peripatetic section. The usage of this word does not allow us any rigid conclusions, but it certainly suggests the notion of a kind of reference work or notebook. As I have said, this seems to me what the account is, not so much an exposition of Stoic ethics as a catalogue of its major concepts and theses—as Professor Long puts it, a "map." There is even reason to believe that it was part of a longer reference work on the whole of Stoic doctrine. The beginning of the account, on p. 57.15, reads much more like the continuation of a work that has just finished with some other part of Stoicism—"Next I shall give a *hypomnematismos* concerning ethics"—than like a work that has just finished with other views about ethics. Moreover, some of the subsequent discussion of ethics seems to presuppose familiarity with Stoic logical notions, like that of *katēgorēma* on p. 98.3–6; the distinction between *haireton* and *haireteon*, etc., on p.78.7–17; and the ontological point on p.64.19–23. We are probably best off supposing that someone took two sections from two sources with somewhat different aims and stitched them together—adding *phēsi*, for example, on p.116.21, which does not go at all well with "Aristotle and the other Peripatetics" in line 19, which must have a different origin.

My own conclusion is, following what I take to be the thrust of the evidence that Professor Long presents, to refrain from attributing to Arius Didymus either the Stoic section or the linking of it to the Peripatetic section, though of course I have no definite reason positively to deny the attribution. This is why I have called the section "the Stobaean account."

7. Finally, I have another brief and programmatic remark, about the matter of alleged Stoic "contamination" of the Peripatetic account. One must distinguish different sorts of cases in which an exposition of the ideas of a school is "contaminated" by ideas of another school. In one case, theses of the one are simply dropped and replaced by theses of the other that directly conflict with them. In another case, terminology of the one is replaced by terminology of the other without change in doctrine. In a third case, terminology of a school may be used where the other school lacked a convenient term, but again without change of doctrine. In a fourth case, School A may be presented as taking a position on an *issue raised*

by School B but not earlier pronounced upon by School A at all; here one has subtypes, depending on whether the position ascribed to A is the same as that of B or not. This last sort of case is particularly interesting historically, since an important way in which a philosophical movement can have influence is not merely by persuading people that its views are correct, but by raising new issues and problems and inducing older movements to respond to them.

There is no space here to take up all putative cases of Stoic "contamination" in the Peripatetic section, so let me briefly mention just those that Professor Long cites (n.40). I doubt that there are any instances at all of the first type that I mentioned, or of the second type. The reference to *prokopē* (p.131.17) is of the third type. The case on p.119.15–21 is of the same type, because it involves some Stoic terminology, but is primarily of the fourth type. It is also closely linked with the one involving *oikeiōsis*. Here there is need for much careful work, and I can only sketch the line of thought that seems to me right. I have argued elsewhere[5] that the accounts of human motivational development presented in Books 3 and 5 of Cicero's *De finibus* as, respectively, Stoic and Academic-Peripatetic are not simply wavering forms of the same account, but are really quite distinct, and that each is fairly well adapted to its own school. Without being able to argue the point here, I suggest that the Peripatetic account in Stobaeus is essentially the same as the one in *De finibus* 5 and essentially different from the one in Book 3, so that it is, after all, Peripatetic and not Stoic. This *is* "contamination" of a sort, the fourth sort, because it shows us Peripatetics feeling forced to take a position on a question raised actively by the Stoics (and also the Epicureans) after having been treated only sketchily by Aristotle (much less sketchily by Plato), namely, the question how moral motivation developed from infancy on.[6] The fourth sort also covers the treatment of justified suicide (p.126.5–11), because the Stoics forced others to take a position on the issue of suicide, which had not seemed central to Aristotle and had been only touched on by Plato in the *Phaedo*.

These distinctions are important in the present discussion because they provide evidence about the construction of the Peripatetic account in Stobaeus. If the Stoic "contamination" is of the fourth sort, as I have suggested, then it involves some real thinking-out of the doctrine being expounded, rather than crude doxographical splicing. There are of course intermediate points between these extremes, but I think that we are dealing here with a philosophical more than a doxographical development. Scholars, including Professor Long, have suspected that Antiochus of Ascalon was at work here. That seems likely enough, if he was also at work in *De finibus* 5. What sort of role that leaves for Eudorus or Arius seems to me unclear.[7]

NOTES

1. I have taken the liberty of adding to what I said in the original oral comments on Professor Long's paper, not only to respond to changes made by him in the published version but also to add some further observations.

2. Professor Long has discussed the argument of *De finibus* 3 in his papers, "The Stoic Concept of Evil," *Philosophical Quarterly* 18 (1968) 329–43, esp. 335f, and "The Logical Basis of Stoic Ethics," *Proceedings of the Aristotelian Society* 92 (1970–71) 85–104, esp. 90f. I have discussed the same matter in my paper, "The Basis of Stoic Ethics," *Harvard Studies in Classical Philology* 83 (1979) 143–78, with different conclusions, largely because of a study of the differences between it and the argument of *De fin.* 5.

3. Max Pohlenz *Die Stoa*, 4th ed. (Göttingen 1970–72) 1.111ff, and White *op. cit.*, pp.144–47.

4. H. J. von Arnim *Stoicorum Veterum Fragmenta* (Stuttgart 1905) 1.xxxviii–xliii.

5. White, *op. cit.*, esp. p. 149–59.

6. One must also reckon with the view of von Arnim and Dirlmeier that both Stoic interest in this issue and their position on it are due to Theophrastus. See von Arnim *Arius Didymus' Abriss der peripatetischen Ethik* (Vienna 1926), esp. pp.131–37, and F. Dirlmeier, "Die Oikeiosislehre Theophrasts," *Philologus* suppl. 30 (1937). The claim that their position went back to Theophrastus was rebutted by Pohlenz *Grundfragen der Stoischen Philosophie*, Abh. d. Gött. Ges., phil.-hist. Kl., 3. Folge 26 (Göttingen 1940) 1–81; but it may well be that interest in the issue was alive before the Stoic position developed in response to it.

7. I am indebted to discussion with Professor David Hahm at the conference, many of whose views on the Stobaean account developed in parallel with my own and helped them.

CHAPTER 4

On The Stoic Goods in Stobaeus, *Eclogae 2*

Margaret E. Reesor

I

The basis for our discussion in Part I is to be found in three passages:
1. Sextus Empiricus, *Against the Ethicists* 25–27 (= *Math*. 11.25–7):

> "Good" has three descriptions, they say. . . .In one sense, "Good" is said
> to be that by which (*hyph'hou*) or from which (*aph'hou*) it is possible to be
> benefitted. This is the principal good and virtue. For from this, as from
> 26 some spring, every benefit naturally arises. And in another sense, it is that
> according to which "being benefitted" results (*to kath'ho sumbainei ōphel-*
> *eisthai*). In this way not only the virtues will be described as good but also
> the actions according to them, if "being benefitted" results according to
> 27 these also. In the third and last sense, "that which is able to benefit" is
> said to be good, this description embracing the virtues and the virtuous
> actions and friends and good men, and both gods and good daemons.

2. Stobaeus, *Eclogae* 2.7.5d (p.69.17–70.3):

> They say that the Good is described in several ways, the first is such that
> it has the role of a spring and it is defined in this way: that from which
> (*aph'hou*) "being benefitted" results or by which (*hyph'hou*), (for this is
> p.70 the primary cause); the second is that according to which "being benefitted"
> results; the phrase "such as to benefit" is of more general application and
> covers what was said previously.

3. Diogenes Laertius, *Lives of the Philosophers* 7.94:

> Consequently, virtue and the Good that participates in it are said to be of
> three kinds as I shall point out: for example, the Good is that from which
> (*aph'hou*) results [. . .] as, for instance, the action according to virtue; by
> which (*hyph'hou*), as, for example, the good man who participates in virtue.

This last passage has a lacuna, which Long fills with *ōpheleisthai, to de kath'ho*
sumbainei, words which may be translated as "being benefitted, and that according
to which it results."[1] He made this restoration on the basis of von Arnim, *Stoicorum*
Veterum Fragmenta 3.76.[2]

The first description of the Good: "that by which or from which it is possible to be benefitted" (S. E.), or "that from which (aph'hou, Stobaeus and D. L.), or by which (hyph'hou, Stobaeus) 'being benefitted' results" seems to refer to sōma (body). We have a passage in Stobaeus (1.13.1c p.138.14–17 = SVF 1.89) which reads: "Zeno says that an explanatory factor is that 'because of which'; and that that for which there is an explanatory factor is an attribute (sumbebēkos). And that the explanatory factor is a sōma, and that that for which there is an explanatory factor is a predicate (kategorēma)."[3]

The second definition of the Good: "that according to which 'being benefitted' results," is more difficult to interpret. The first problem is the meaning of the word sumbainei. Diogenes Laertius defines the Good as expedient, and writes: "Expedient because it brings such things that from their happening (hōn sumbainontōn) we are benefitted" (7.99 = SVF 3.87). "Those things that happen" result from the Good. The meaning "result" is brought out more clearly in a passage in Plutarch based on Chrysippus: "Furthermore, I believe," he says, "that we shall be alienated from praise for those things that result (tōn sumbainontōn) from virtue in such matters as, for example, abstaining from an old woman who has one foot in the grave and enduring steadfastly the bite of a fly" (De Stoic. repugn. 1039A = SVF 3.212). This is clearly in line with Aristotelian usage. Referring to Gen. an. 766b28, Senn comments: "So haben . . . die sumbainonta die Bedeutung eines im Zusammenhang mit einem andern Vorgang erfolgenden Geschehens."[4]

Here I want to anticipate an objection—namely, that the word kata in Sextus Empiricus' second definition of the Stoic Good should be translated by the English word "by" on the analogy of such phrases as "by chance" (kata tychēn). I am not convinced by this interpretation for several reasons. First, the word kata occurs in the following sentence twice with the meaning "according to." Secondly, the word kata is used in Sextus Empiricus' definition of the lekton with the meaning "according to" (Math. 8.70 = SVF 2.187, cf. D. L. 7.63 = SVF 2.181). The passage reads: "A lekton is that which subsists according to a rational presentation." Similarly, a perceptible may be said to subsist according to a perceptive presentation. If the word kata denotes the relation between that which subsists and a presentation, it must also denote the relation between that quality or expressible which is said to subsist, and the content of the presentation.

To continue my investigation I turn to a diaeresis of kathēkonta and katorthōmata in Ecl. 2.7.8 p.85.12–86.16. Stobaeus defines the kathēkon (appropriate act) as: "That which is in conformity with (sc. logos) in one's way of life, for which, when done, a reasonable account can be given" (p. 85.14–5). The katorthōma is a fully constituted (teleion) appropriate act (kathēkon p. 93.15–16).

```
                    kathēkonta
                (appropriate acts)
teleia kathēkonta or              mesa kathēkonta
katorthōmata                      (intermediate appropriate acts, as,
(fully constituted appropriate    for example, to marry, to serve as
acts)                             an ambassador)
hōn chrē                          ta d'ou, i.e. ouch hōn chrē
(belonging to those that          (not belonging to those that
necessarily are)                  necessarily are)
```

Stobaeus describes *katorthōmata* in the following way: "Some belong to those that necessarily are, others do not (*ta d'ou*). Those that belong to those that necessarily are, are benefits (*ōphelēmata*) in predicate form, as, for example, the exercise of practical wisdom, and the use of moderation; those that are not so do not belong to those that necessarily are" (p. 86.5–8 = *SVF* 3.503).[5]

Dr. David Sedley has pointed out to me that *hōn chrē* is equivalent to *toutōn ha chrē*. He translates this as "belonging to the things that are required." Although the Greek word *chrē* does correspond to the Latin *oportet* ("it is required that"), it also has the meaning "it is determined that." Italie, in his *Index Aeschyleus*, indicates this meaning by *in fatis est*.[6] There is a correspondence between some of the terms used by Aeschylus and similar terms in the Stoics.[7] I have used Dr. Sedley's phrase "belonging to" to translate the genitive, and have supplied the infinitive *einai* with *chrē*. Accordingly, I have translated *hōn chrē* as "belonging to those that necessarily are," that is, "belonging to those that are by necessity." I have translated *ouch hōn chrē* as "not belonging to those that necessarily are." With this we may compare *Ecl.* 2.7.11i, p.101,9–10, where we read: "Just as those things that correspond to the bad, that belong to those that cannot be by necessity (*haper estin hōn ou chrē*), happen to the bad alone." If *chrē* has the meaning "must," then *ou chrē* should be translated "cannot."

Stobaeus specifies *hōn chrē* (belonging to those that necessarily are) by *to phronein* (the exercise of practical wisdom) and *to sōphronein* (the use of moderation). A passage in Stobaeus that relates these terms to the corresponding quality may shed some light on why these terms "necessarily are." It reads: "For it is impossible, if there is *sōphrosynē* (moderation) in regard to some things, that there should not be *to sōphronein* (the use of moderation), or, if there is *psychē* (soul), that there should not be *to zēn* (living), or, if there is *phronēsis* (practical wisdom), that there should not be *to phronein* (the exercise of practical wisdom)" (1.13.1c, p.138.21–22 = *SVF* 1.89). In all these specifications, the predicate follows from the quality. The term "belonging to those that necessarily are" (*hōn chrē*) denoted not only predicates formed from the virtues, but predicates formed from other goods as well. Stobaeus specifies *katorthōmata* by *phronein* (to exercise practical wisdom), *sōphronein* (to use moderation), *dikaiopragein* (to act honestly), *chairein* (to rejoice), *euergetein* (to show kindness), *euphrainesthai* (to be glad), *phronimōs per-ipatein* (to walk sensibly, 2.7.11e, p.96.18–22 = *SVF* 3.501). He describes all of these terms as "all those things which are done according to right reason" (p. 96.22 = *SVF* 3.501). In *Ecl.* 2.7.5b p.58.5–14, we find that *chara* (joy) and *euphrosynē* (gladness) are listed as Stoic goods.

In the passage quoted above (2.7.8, p.86.5–8), Stobaeus described *hōn chrē* as "predicated benefits" (*katēgoroumena ōphelēmata*). Our evidence for the *ōphe-lēmata* is found in Stobaeus. The Stoics distinguished between *orekton* and *orekteon* (the desirable and that which ought to be desired), *boulēton* and *boulēteon* (the reasonably desirable and that which ought to be reasonably desired), *haireton* and *haireteon* (the choiceworthy and that which ought to be chosen).[8] Stobaeus adds to this list the *apodekton* and the *apodekteon* (the receivable and that which ought to be received). He writes: "*Haireta* and *boulēta* and *orekta* ⟨and *apodekta* are the goods, but the *ōphelēmata* (benefits) are *hairetea* and *boulētea* and *orektea*⟩ and *apodektea,* since they are predicates, and are closely connected with the goods" (2.7.11f. p. 97.18–21 = *SVF* 3.91).

The act of choosing (*hairesis*) is directed towards "that which ought to be chosen," the *ōphelēmata* (benefits), or towards the possession of the good. Stobaeus indicates this in the following passage:

> The "choiceworthy" is everything ⟨good⟩ and "that which ought to be chosen" is every benefit (*ōphelēma*), which is recognized as equivalent to
> p. 78.10   the possession of the good. Because of this we choose "that which ought to be chosen," as, for example, "being wise" (*to phronein*) which is rec-ognized as equivalent to the possession of practical wisdom (*phronēsis*); the "choiceworthy" we do not choose but, if it is present, we choose to have it. In the same way, all good things are "sustainable" (*hypomeneta*) and "maintainable" (*emmeneta*), and this applies to all the virtues generally,
> .15   even if they have not been given names; but all the benefits (*ōphelēmata*) are such that they "ought to be sustained" and "ought to be maintained" (2.7.6f, p.78.8–16 = *SVF* 3.89).

The words *ho theōreitai para to echein to agathon,* which I have translated as "which is recognized as equivalent to the possession of the good" have been translated by Long as "which is understood to depend upon the possession of the good." Long comments upon the passage as follows: "When Stobaeus says that 'what has to be chosen is understood to depend upon the possesion of the good' I take him to mean that the possession of the good is regarded as a necessary and sufficient condition of choosing what has to be chosen."[9] The interpretation of the passage cannot be determined by a study of the use of *para* in the Greek language. The translation of *para* as "equivalent to" is attested by the tragedians Isocrates and Xenophon. On the other hand, the word *para* has the meaning "thanks to" or "because of" in a sentence in Plato's *Laws* which reads: "Safety for the city and its contrary arise thanks to this" (715D). It is this second usage which justifies Long in translating *para* as "depends upon."

My interpretation may receive some support from another passage in Stobaeus:

> The *haireseis* (acts of choosing), *orexeis* (desires), and *bouleseis* (reasonable
> p. 98.1 desires) are directed towards predicates, just as the *hormai* (impulses) are
> also. Moreover, we choose to have and we reasonably desire to have, and
> in the same way, we desire to have the goods, wherefore the goods are
> "choiceworthy," and "reasonably desirable" and "desirable." For we choose
> to have *phronesis* (practical wisdom) and *sophrosyne* (moderation) but not
> .5 (sc. to have) *to phronein* (the exercise of practical wisdom) and *to sophronein*
> (the use of moderation) (2.7.11f, p. 97.23–98.5 = *SVF* 3.91).

Stobaeus states that the good is "choiceworthy" in so far as it moves a rational
choice (*hairesin eulogon*, 2.7.5i) p.72.19–22 = *SVF* 3.88). He makes the same
point when he describes the *haireton* (choiceworthy) as "capable of moving a
complete impulse" (*hormes autotelous kinetikon*, 2.7.5o p.75.2 = *SVF* 3.131).
Long has suggested that *autotelous* is simply a corruption of the adverb *autotelos*.
He points out that *autoteles* was used to describe a complete or principal cause.[10]
Stobaeus also states that every *agathon* (good) is a *haireton* (choiceworthy), and
that the good, insofar as it moves a rational choice, is choiceworthy (2.7.5i, p.72.21–
22 = *SVF* 3.88). He places *ta agatha* (the goods), however, in all three groups:
haireta (choiceworthy), *bouleta* (reasonably desirable) and *orekta* (desirable, 2.7.11f,
p.97.15–98.6 = *SVF* 3.91). The *haireton* (choiceworthy) as a cognitive presentation
moves the *horme* (impulse) which is assent and movement (2.7.9b, p.88.1–6 =
SVF 3.171).

"Action according to virtue" is an action which has its source in an individual
horme. In a passage in which he discusses three Stoic classifications of activity
and movement, Simplicius writes: "What is more important, however, is *to
aph'heautou poiein* (acting on one's own account), which is, generally speaking,
acting in consequence of one's individual *horme* and something different from
acting in consequence of a rational impulse which is described by the term 'imag-
ining.' Further, acting in accordance with virtue is a particular species of this"
(*SVF* 2.499 = Simpl. *In Arist. Cat.* 306.24–7).

We are now in a position to make some observations regarding Sextus Empiricus'
second definition of the Stoic good: "And in another sense, it is that according to
which 'being benefitted' results. In this way, not only the virtues will be described
as good but also the actions according to them" (*Against the Ethicists*, 26). The
predicate "being benefitted" (*opheleisthai*) seems to be equivalent to "having
benefit," and consequently seems to denote a *haireteon* (that which ought to be
chosen), and an *ophelema* (benefit). If this is the case, the good according to which
"being benefitted" results is the *haireton* (choiceworthy). The words "action according to virtue" describe the movement of the impulse which has been moved
by the Good, that is, by the *haireton* (choiceworthy).

I argued above that the *katorthomata* "belonging to those that necessarily are"
are formed from an individual quality, such as *phronesis* (practical wisdom) and
chara (joy). Practical wisdom and the virtues are permanent dispositions of the

soul. They are the antecedent causes of *boulēsis* (reasonable desire, Sen. *Ep.* 95.57 = *SVF* 3.517) and of the *ōphelēmata* (benefits). Predicates, such as *akolastainein* (to be licentious), and *aphrainein* (to be foolish) are *hōn ou chrē* (belonging to those that cannot "be by necessity").

How, then, shall we specify *ouch hōn chrē*, (not belonging to those that necessarily are)? A clue may be found in Diogenes Laertius, who offers the following threefold classification: appropriate acts, those which are contrary to the appropriate act, those which are neither appropriate acts nor contrary to the appropriate act. The appropriate acts are defined as what the *logos* chooses and are specified by such terms as "honoring one's parents," and "honoring one's fatherland"; those which are contrary to the appropriate act are defined as what the *logos* chooses not to do, and they are specified by "neglecting one's parents" and "disregarding one's fatherland"; the third class, those which are neither appropriate acts nor contrary to the appropriate act, are defined as what the *logos* neither chooses to do nor chooses not to do, and are specified by such terms as picking up twigs or using a writing tablet or a scraper (D. L. 7.108–9 = *SVF* 3.495).[11] I suggest that Stobaeus' term *ouch hōn chrē* (not belonging to those that necessarily are) should be specified by "honoring one's parents" and "honoring one's fatherland." These acts do not follow by necessity from the fixed disposition of the soul, and they have contradictories.

II

In Part II, I want to consider a very puzzling passage in Stobaeus 2.7.18 (p.130.21–131.13). It may be translated as follows:

> (A) If then to be happy (*to eudaimonein*) is an end (*telos*), and happiness is said to be a goal (*skopos*), and wealth a good, and being wealthy (*to ploutein*) belongs to those that necessarily are (*hōn chrē*), for the sake of
>
> p.131.1 accuracy in names we must . . . to those who draw such distinctions. (B) Yet we must follow the custom of the ancients (*archaioi*) and say that the end is "that for the sake of which we do everything, while we do not do this for the sake of anything else," or "the ultimate of the desirables," [or,
>
> .5 "living according to virtue in those goods that pertain to the body and external goods, either all or most of them and the most important."] Since this is the greatest of the goods and the most perfect, it is served by all the others. (C) We must say admittedly that those things which contribute to it
>
> .10 are good, and that those things which hinder ⟨it are bad, and that those things which neither contribute to it nor hinder it⟩ are neither good nor bad, but "indifferents." For not every fine action contributes to happiness.[12]

The clause, "If then to be happy (*to eudaimonein*) is an end (*telos*), and happiness is said to be a goal (*skopos*)," may represent the views of Panaetius. In a passage in which he discusses Zeno's definition of *eudaimonia* (happiness) as *euroia biou* (the easy flow of life), Stobaeus (2.7.6e, p.77.21–7) writes:

Cleanthes has used this definition in his writings and Chrysippus and all those after him, saying that *eudaimonia* is not any different from *ho eudaimōn*
p.77.25 *bios* (a happy life) and yet saying that *eudaimonia* is a *skopos* (goal) and that attaining *eudaimonia* is a *telos* (end), for this is the same as *to eudaimonein* (being happy).

Since Stobaeus states that Panaetius regarded the end (*telos*) as "attaining the goal" (*to tuchein tou skopou*), and identifies this with "being happy" (*to eudaimonein*, 2.7.565, p. 63.25–64.12), Hirzel argued that the passage translated above should be attributed to Panaetius.[13] Similarly, Wiersma argued that Stobaeus was using a later Stoic source, such as Panaetius, in this passage.[14] Recently, Alpers-Gölz asserted on the basis of a passage in Plutarch (*De Stoic. repugn.* 1040F = *SVF* 3.24) that Chrysippus used the words *hypokeimenos skopos* (underlying goal) in a technical sense and that there was no good reason not to attribute the whole passage in Stobaeus to the older Stoics.[15] In these passages Stobaeus connects the term *skopos* (goal) with *tychein* (attaining): 2.7.3c (p.47.7–10), 2.7.6c (p.77.1–5), and 2.7.6e (p.77.20–27). In the last two passages, he specifies it by *eudaimonia*. Since Antipater of Tarsus was the first Stoic, so far as we know, who introduced *tychein* (attaining) into his definition of the *telos* (end), we should assume that Stobaeus' source for these passages was later than Antipater, and that it was probably Panaetius.

The words *to de ploutein hōn chrē* ("to be wealthy belongs to those that necessarily are," p.130.23–131.1) cannot be reconciled with the diaeresis of the *kathēkonta* (appropriate acts) which I considered in Part I. Since no Stoic held that wealth was good, we have to assume either that the writer of this passage was misrepresenting Stoic teachings, or that the philosopher whom he was attacking was a Peripatetic. According to Diogenes Laertius, Panaetius held that virtue was not sufficient (i.e., for happiness), but that there was need of wealth, external means, and strength.[16] Moreover, Stobaeus refers to mixed goods, as, for example, the blessing of children, a green old age, living well (p.74.15–20 = *SVF* 3.101, cf. D. L. 7.98 = *SVF* 3.102). A critic of this kind of Stoicism might misrepresent Stoic teachings by saying that wealth was regarded as a good. Von Arnim describes the spirit of the passage when he writes: "Diese Bezugnahme ist aber keine Entlehnung, sondern eine Polemik: mit ironischem Lobe der Ausdrucksgenauigkeit, die in der stoischen Unterscheidung zwischen *telos* und *skopos,* zwischen *agathon* und *hōn chrē* angestrebt wird (der *skopos* ist als *agathon* ein *sōma*, das *telos* zu den *hōn chrē* gehörig, ein *kategorēma*), wird diese Unterscheidung doch abgelehnt und der einfachere Sprachgebrauch der *archaioi* beibehalten."[17] If wealth was a good, "being wealthy" which followed from it, might be described as "belonging to those that necessarily are."

Philippson, Dirlmeier, and Wehrli argued that the criticism was directed against the Peripatetic philosopher Critolaus.[18] Stobaeus refers to the younger Peripatetics who belonged to the school of Critolaus, and assigns to them the following definition of the *telos* (2.7.3b, p.46.10–13): "that which is composed from all the goods (that is, from the three classes)." These three classes, as Stobaeus states in the sentence which follows, are the goods of the body, external goods, and the goods of the soul. Critolaus' definition of the *telos* is criticized at 2.7.14 (p.126.12–18), a passage in which it is argued that the *telos* is not composed of corporeal or external goods. If Critolaus is the object of the criticism on pp.130.21–131.2, we have an explanation for the statement "wealth is a good." We have to assume, however, that Critolaus or a member of his school had adopted the Stoic distinction between *skopos* and *telos,* and the use of the Stoic *hōn chrē* to describe a predicate. For this there is no evidence.

If the third definition of the *telos* in B—"living according to virtue in those goods that pertain to the body and external goods, either all or most of them and the most important,"—is not excised, we have to conclude that all the definitions of the *telos* in B are Peripatetic in origin. The first definition of the *telos*—"that for the sake of which we do everything, while we do not do this for the sake of anything else"—is similar to a statement in Aristotle's *Metaphysics* 994b9–16. The second definition—"the ultimate of the desirables"—is not found in Aristotle but adequately represents his views. Because, however, the words "since this is the greatest of the goods" seem to be related to "the ultimate of the desirables" rather than to the third definition of the *telos,* I have followed von Arnim in excising them.[19] The word *archaioi* (p.131.2) does not indicate that B is Peripatetic. In 2.7.3c (p.48.4) and 2.7.16 (p.129.4) Stobaeus uses the word to refer to the older Stoics.

The first definition of the *telos* in B—"that for the sake of which we do everything, while we do not do this for the sake of anything else"—is found with the addition of the adverb "appropriately" in Stobaeus 2.7.3b (p.46.5–7), and attributed to the Stoics. It appears again without the word "appropriately" in 2.7.6e (p.77.16–17). The second definition—"the ultimate of the desirables"—was attributed to the Stoics by Stobaeus 2.7.6b (p.76.16–23 = *SVF* 3.3). Stobaeus writes:

> 76.16   The telos is said to be of three kinds by those of this persuasion: the *telikon agathon* (final good) is said to be an end in verbal usage, just as they say that *homologia* (agreement) is an end. And they say that the *skopos* (goal) is an end, as, for example, they call "the life in agreement" (*ho homologoumenos bios*) an end by reference to the predicate which is connected
> .20   with it. According to the third signification, they say that "the ultimate of the desirables" is an end, because to this all the others refer.

The source of this passage recognized "the life in agreement," a *skopos* (goal), as a *telos* (end) only because it was connected with the corresponding predicate, that is, with "living in agreement." In 2.7.6e (p. 77.21–7)—the passage that I attributed to Panaetius—*eudaimonia* was a *skopos* and the object of *to tychein* (attaining). In 2.7.6b (p. 76.22) *eudaimonia* appears to be "the ultimate of the desirables" mentioned as the third *telos*. When, however, Stobaeus writes on p. 77.21–27, "Cleanthes and Chrysippus and all those after him, saying that *eudaimonia* is not any different from *ho eudaimōn bios* (the happy life)," he appears to be contradicting the earlier passage. On p.76.16–23, Stobaeus presented a Stoic interpretation of the *telos* which is an alternative to Panaetius' *skopos* (goal) and *telos* (end). It is, I believe, this alternative which is suggested by the definition of the *telos* as "the ultimate of the desirables" (p. 131.4).

Meineke indicated a lacuna after the phrase *tois men houtō diorizousi tēs akribeias tōn onomatōn charin* (p. 131.1–2), words which may be translated as: "For the sake of accuracy in names we must [* * *] to those who draw such distinctions." The words *tēs akribeias tōn onomatōn charin* may mean "accuracy of names," that is, "accuracy of terminological niceties," or "accuracy of terms." By the latter I am suggesting that the critic who was discussing the *telos* was saying that, if he was to provide an accurate account of the word *telos,* he had to take into account the views of those philosophers who regarded *eudaimonia* as a *skopos* and *eudaimonein* as a *telos,* although he must follow those of the older philosophers.

But why should we find a criticism of the ethics of the Middle Stoa and an expression of preference for the older Stoics in the midst of a discussion of Peripatetic ethics? The passage, pp. 130.21–131.13, is, I believe, a digression. The definition of *eudaimonia* as *teleias aretēs chrēsin* (the use of complete virtue) on p. 131.14–15 is a continuation from p. 130.18–19. Pages 130.21–131.13 make much greater sense viewed as a commentary on 2.7.6b (p.76.21–3), 2.7.6e (p.77.16–27), and 2.7.7 (p. 79.12–17). Indeed the puzzling sentence, "For not every fine action contributes to *eudaimonia*" (p. 131.12–13), becomes clear when it is read in conjunction with the account of indifferents on p. 79.12–17:

> According to the former, we must say that those between virtue and vice are called "indifferents" according to those of this persuasion, yet not with
> **p. 79.15** a view to selection and rejection; therefore, some have selective value, others disvalue fit for rejection, being in no way contributory to the happy life.

Is it possible that the passage on pp. 130.21–131.13 belongs at the end of p.79.17, and that in the process of transmission it was incorrectly inserted in the later section? We may conjecture further that it was some scribe, believing that the passage was Peripatetic, who added the third definition of the *telos,* "living according to virtue in those goods that pertain to the body and external goods, either all of them or most of them, and the most important" (p. 131.5–8). An affirmative answer is tempting but by no means certain. I rest content to have raised a question for consideration by other scholars.

NOTES

I would like to thank Dr. David Sedley of Christ's College, Cambridge University for his most helpful comments on an earlier version of my paper. His keen analysis of the material has helped me to avoid many errors, and has opened up new avenues of interpretation.

1. H. S. Long, *Diogenis Laertii Vitae Philosophorum* (Oxford 1964) 337.
2. H. von Arnim, *Stoicorum Veterum Fragmenta* 3 (Stuttgart 1964) 19.

3. For "explanation" as a translation of *aition* see G. E. L. Owen, "Aristotle on the Snares of Ontology," published in *New Essays on Plato and Aristotle,* edited by R. Bambrough (London 1965) 82. For further discussion of *SVF* 1.89 see A. Graeser, *Zenon von Kition: Positionen und Probleme* (Berlin 1975) 82–89.

4. G. Senn, *Die Entwicklung der biologischen Forschungsmethode in der Antike und ihre grundsätzliche Förderung durch Theophrast von Eresos* (Basel 1933) 227.

5. For a discussion of *katorthōma* see D. Tsekourakis, *Studies in the Terminology of Early Stoic Ethics* (Wiesbaden 1974) 114–23; G. B. Kerferd, "What does the Wise Man Know?" published in *The Stoics,* edited by J. M. Rist (University of California Press 1978) 125–36.

6. G. Italie, *Index Aeschyleus* (Leiden 1964).

7. See W. Burkert, "La Genèse des choses et des mots. Le papyrus de Derveni entre Anaxagore et Cratyle," Les Études philosophiques (1970) 448, n. 3.

8. For a discussion of *haireton* and *haireteon* see A. A. Long, "The Early Stoic Concept of Moral Choice," published in *Images of Man in Ancient and Medieval Thought. Studia Gerardo Verbeke* (Leiden University Press 1976) 77–92; Tsekourakis (above, note 5) pp. 101–23.

9. Long (above, note 8) 87.

10. Long (above, note 8) 82–83.

11. For a discussion of the term *kathēkon* see I. G. Kidd, "Stoic Intermediates and the End for Man," published in *Problems in Stoicism,* edited by A. A. Long (London 1971) 150–72; and I. G. Kidd, "Moral Actions and Rules in Stoic Ethics," published in *The Stoics* (above, note 5) 247–58.

12. Just before section B, I have marked a lacuna in the text. Meineke indicated a lacuna at this point. The words in brackets in C are an addition by Spengel.

13. R. Hirzel, *Untersuchungen zu Ciceros philosophischen Schriften,* (Leipzig 1882) 554–57.

14. W. Wiersma, "Telos und Kathekōn in der alten Stoa," *Mnemosyne* 3 (1937) 219–28.

15. R. Alpers-Gölz, *Der Begriff Skopos in der Stoa und seine Vorgeschichte* (Hildesheim 1976) 65–66.

16. *Panaetii Rhodii Fragmenta,* edited by M. van Straaten (Leiden 1946, 1962) F 110 = D.L. 7.128.

17. H. von Arnim, *Arius Didymus' Abriss der peripatetischen Ethik* SB Wien 204.3 (1926) 24.

18. R. Philippson, "Das erste Naturgemässe," *Philologus* 87, n.s. 41 (1932) 464; F. Dirlmeier, "Die Oikeiosis-Lehre Theophrasts," *Philologus* Suppl. 30, Heft 1 (1937) 13; F. Wehrli *Die Schule des Aristoteles* Heft 10, *Kritolaos und seine Schüler* (Basel-Stuttgart 1969) 68.

19. See von Arnim (above, note 17) 26.

Comments on Professor Reesor's Paper

David Sedley

This stimulating paper invites comment on every page, but in an effort to keep the spotlight on the eponymous hero of this volume I shall limit my own discussion to the passage *Ecl.* 2.7.18 (pp.130.21–131.13), considered at some length in Part II of Miss Reesor's paper. Following the conventional identification of Stobaeus' source here as Arius Didymus, I shall suggest that these lines might be made to yield valuable clues about his view of the doxographer's methods.

I am impressed but not persuaded by Miss Reesor's attempt to conjure up a Stoic target for the passage. It fits comfortably into its immediate context, an epitome of Peripatetic views on *eudaimonia* and the *telos,* and to prize it away involves either the supposition of an unsignalled and bafflingly irrelevant digression, or editorial reorganization of the text. Moreover, the people under discussion are ''the ancients''(p. 131.2), a term which in Hellenistic and later philosophical usage standardly signifies pre-Stoic philosophers, especially the early Platonists and Peripatetics. The practice is followed elsewhere in Stobaeus' text, and pp.48.4 and 129.4, cited by Miss Reesor as exceptions, are in my opinion no such thing: on the former see Hirzel, *Untersuchungen zu Cicero's philosophischen Schriften* 2.834, n.1, and on the latter von Arnim (article cited by Miss Reesor in note 17) pp.18–19. Indeed, the people in question are saddled with two thoroughly un-Stoic doctrines: (a) that wealth is a good, (p.130.23), and (b) the definition of the *telos* as ''living according to virtue in those goods that pertain to the body and external goods, either all or most of them and the most important'' (p.131.5–6). I can see no good reason for excising the latter. In fact both (a) and (b) are elsewhere represented by Arius as standard Peripatetic doctrines ((a) passim; (b) p.126.16–18), and both are so alien to Stoicism that it takes very special pleading to envisage how anyone could hope to pass them off as Stoic.

What is interesting here, then, is the concession which Arius or his source makes, in passing, to Stoic terminological niceties in his report of Peripatetic doctrine: Strictly, the sticklers for accuracy will say, it is not *eudaimonia* that should be called the *telos,* but the predicate *eudaimonein,* while *eudaimonia,* being a thing, is the *skopos* (p.130.21–131.2). This is not, I think Stoic *doctrine,* but the imposition on Peripatetic doctrine of a standard Stoic terminological distinction. Targets are corporeal things (cf. p.77.1–2), while goals are predicates (cf. ''The target of the fund is a million pounds; its goal is to rebuild the church steeple''). Similarly, the author goes on, when the Peripatetics call wealth a good they should strictly add that the corresponding predicate ''to be wealthy'' is not a good but ''behoven'' (*hōn chrē*, cf. p.86.6–7; 101.7–9), and this, incidentally, seems to confirm Professor Kerferd's interpretation of the latter expression elsewhere in this volume. Things being designated by nouns, are most appropriately recommended by the adjective ''good,'' but predicates are expressed by infinitives and hence should be recommended by a word like *chrē*, ''it behoves'' (one *to do* something).

This use of philosophical anachronisms in the interpretation of ancient thinkers is of course what we ourselves practice under the title ''analytic technique.'' It would be most interesting to know whether Arius, or his source, regards it with approval or contempt. The difficulty here is that at p.131.2 a second gerund seems to have fallen out alongside *akolouthēteon*. Strache conjectured *hekteon* immediately before *akolouthēteon*, presumably meaning ''one must pay attention to. . .'' (*prosekteon* might have been better). The point will then be that we should pay due attention to Stoic terminological niceties, that is, we should listen to them politely, but nevertheless in practice we should follow the older usages when speaking about the Peripatetic *telos*. This may well be right. But since the likelihood is that the missing gerund fell out through *homoioteleuton,* one might expect it to be the second gerund that is lost. In that case pp.130.21–131.6 will translate as follows:

> But if to be happy is called the goal, while happiness is called the target, and wealth is called a good while to be wealthy is called ''behoven,'' we
>
> p. 131.1 ought to follow those who make these distinctions in the interests of terminological accuracy. But even so, we should pay due heed to the usage of the ancients and say that ''that for the sake of which we do everything but which we do not do for the sake of anything else'' is the goal, or ''the
>
> .5 ultimate of the desirables,'' or ''to live virtuously in the bodily and external goods, either all of them or most of them and the chief ones.''

The advice is now reversed: we should follow the Stoic terminological distinction, while paying due heed to the older, less exact ways of talking about the *telos*. In other words, the doxographer should employ the latest philosophical tools, but at the same time should put on record the original formulations of the doctrines. This would be closer to modern practice. Could it be considered a proper description of Arius' own methods?

CHAPTER 5

Two Problems Concerning Impulses

George B. Kerferd

I. INTRODUCTION

I take it as common ground, and so not here in need of demonstration, that for the Stoics the whole of reality is to be understood as the product of two material principles, the Active and the Passive. All states and conditions, all activities and changes are manifestations of the Active Principle, and the Active Principle, or Logos, is divine, rational, and good. So Chrysippus could say (*SVF* 2.937): "No particular thing, not even the slightest, can come about otherwise than in conformity with universal nature and its reason." This means that to account for evil is more difficult for Stoics than is the case for at least some non-Stoic thinkers. If the Active Principle is the source of all change and of all states and conditions, and there is no other source for any change or condition, then any dualism of good and evil is automatically excluded. It would still be theoretically possible for matter, as the Passive Principle, to act as a principle of inertia, and so, by functioning as a source of frustration in relation to the Active Principle, to provide in effect a source of evil. But even this is excluded when we realize that for the Stoics the Passive Principle as such lacks all qualities; any qualities it receives come to it from the Active Principle. Consequently when, three years ago, I was concerned to consider the origin of evil in Stoic thought, I concluded that there was only one line of explanation available to Stoics, and I argued that the sources for early Stoicism made it abundantly clear that this was, in fact, the path that they followed (see my article "The Origin of Evil in Stoic Thought," *Bulletin of the John Rylands University Library of Manchester* 60 [1977/8] 482–94).

On this view the situation can be briefly described as follows: In the physical world around us the Active Principle is in operation at various levels. In inanimate objects it is responsible for the *hexis,* or way in which they are held together, e.g., the structure of a stone; in plants and animals it is responsible also for (or perhaps better: is also) the principle of growth (*physis*), and in animals it functions also through *hormai,* impulses to action. If a *hormē* is entirely rational it is of course good. But when a *hormē* is not in accordance with reason or is not completely so, then it constitutes a *pathos,* and *pathē* are bad. The problem of evil in human actions is accordingly the problem how *pathē* can arise out of *hormai* which are

87

expressions of the Active Principle which is itself inherently good. The answer given by the Stoics was that a *pathos* was an impulse or *hormē* that "went too far" and their name for this principle of "going too far" was *pleonasmos*. The evidence is overwhelming that when an impulse which was itself good went too far or became pleonastic, it then became bad. The Stoics seem to have regarded impulses as functioning in a way that we might describe as analogous to the movements in a watch or clock. An escapement mechanism is necessary to restrain the impulse derived from weights or the spring to an appropriate degree; if the escapement mechanism fails, then the impulse becomes pleonastic—the clock races, and bad things inevitably result for our pattern of living. A further modern analogy can be found in the physiological doctrine according to which the vagus nerve is understood as restraining the rate of heart beat, preventing damaging "racing." In the case of *hormai* it is a weakness or failure of *tonos* or tension in the soul which enables them to "go too far."

This way of looking at things provides an intellectually satisfying explanation of the way a *hormē* comes to function as a *pathos*. But I want now to pick just one out of a number of questions that such a view may seem to pose. Aristotle in his doctrine of the mean in actions, expounded in the *Nicomachean Ethics*, had argued that in addition to failing by overshooting the mark it was also possible to fail by undershooting. So in the case of courage; if one overshoots, the result is foolhardy rashness and if one undershoots the result is cowardice. Ought not the Stoics to have made provision in their analyses not merely for an impulse for going too far but also for an impulse that fails or falls short, thus constituting a *pathos* because it does not go far enough? It would then be not pleonastic but meiotic, even though this second term was not so used by Stoic writers. What I want to suggest is that the Stoics did possess just such an analysis, though it seems not to have attracted very much attention. This is the Stoic doctrine of *arrōstēmata*.

II. THE PROBLEM OF *ARRŌSTĒMATA*

The Evidence Found in Stobaeus

In the first of the three ethical epitomes which Stobaeus appears to have complied or extracted from Arius Didymus (2.7.1–4b, pp. 37.18–57.12 W.) the material is arranged not by schools but by topics. In the course of his division of the ethical section, in 2.7.2 (p.44.3–6, not in *SVF*) we read:

> Now in the case of the discussion of the *hormē* one part is concerned with *hormē* as a species (sc. of movement in the soul), and the other is concerned with *pathē*. For either every *pathos* is a *hormē* carried to excess, or at least the majority of them . . .

After the words "the majority of them" there follow in the manuscripts five Greek words *meth' hormēs kai ta arrōstēmata*. Meineke punctuated the sentence with a comma after *hormēs*, apparently giving the meaning "or at least the majority of them (? are) accompanied by *hormē*, and (? there are also) the *arrōstēmata*." The resulting sense is however puzzling, as it would seem to imply that some *pathē* are not *hormai* at all, and Wachsmuth followed Usener in deleting *ta*. But the meaning is still unsatisfactory as the text would then appear to say, "or at least the majority of them are accompanied by *hormē* and are *arrōstēmata*." The puzzle arises because all *pathē* are unquestionably *hormai*. What is accordingly wanted is that the text should be kept unchanged, and a full-stop or colon placed after *pleista*. We then read, "For either every *pathos* is a *hormē* carried to excess, or at least the majority of them are; *arrōstēmata* also involve a *hormē*," and the meaning will be as follows: either all *pathē* involve impulses carried to excess or at least the majority do. In the latter case *pathē* which do not involve impulses carried to excess, i.e., *pathē* which are *arrōstēmata* still involve a *hormē* though in such cases one which is deficient rather than excessive.

I believe that this solves the problem of the reading in this sentence of Stobaeus. But whether it does so or not, it surely points to the importance of attempting to secure a precise understanding of the Stoic doctrine of the *arrōstēma*.

Both Cicero (*SVF* 3.424) and Galen (*SVF* 3.471, p. 120.21ff.) tell us that Chrysippus was very fond of comparing diseases of the body with diseases of the mind. The primary term he uses for disorders of the mind is *nosēma*, and a mental *nosēma* consists in persistently judging that something is highly desirable when it is only mildly desirable or not desirable at all (*SVF* 3.422, 428). A similar account is found in the second, or Stoic, ethical epitome in Stobaeus (2.7.10e p. 93.6–9 = *SVF* 3.421). Examples of such *nosēmata* are given by Stobaeus as (1) *philogynia* (or *mulierositas*) elsewhere called *gynaikomania*; (2) *philoinia* (or *vinulentia*); and (3) *philargyria* (or *avaritia*). To this list Cicero (*SVF* 3.427) adds *ambitio, pervicacia, ligurritio* (gluttony), *cuppedia* and similar unpleasant habits. It is clear that the list was in no sense a closed list, but could be extended more or less indefinitely.

A special case under the general heading of *nosēmata* was the class of *arrōstēmata*, a term translated in Cicero by *aegrotationes*. These are regularly defined as "*nosēmata* accompanied by weakness" (*SVF* 3.421, 422, 424, 425). There is perhaps no reason to be surprised by this since the word *arrōstēma* itself means "weakness" or "lack of strength." But considerable difficulty does arise when we ask what is the nature of the weakness involved in an *arrōstēma*. Strictly speaking neither a *nosēma* nor an *arrōstēma* should be identified outright with a *pathos* despite the implication of the statement in Stobaeus discussed above. Rather, each of them should be seen as the result of repeated *pathē;* as Stobaeus says (2.7. 10e p.93.6–8) this result is the establishment of a *hexis* which has become deep-rooted. So it should be regarded as the *ekgonon* or offspring of the original *pathē* which have produced it (Philo *De post. Caini* 46 and 74, not in *SVF*). Nonetheless the relationship with *pathē* is clear and we would expect *nosēmata* and *arrōstēmata* to reflect appropriate characteristics from their parent *pathē*.

Now there are texts which associate weakness in the soul with *atonia* or lack of tension (*SVF* 3 p. 120.31–121.3 and p. 123.1–2). *Pleonasmos* is associated with the *apostrophē* or turning aside of reason in the soul (*SVF* 3.479, 475, 476), and this also seems to imply a lack of restraining tension and so of weakness in the soul. Conversely, strength in the soul is equated with *tonos* or tension in Stobaeus (2.7.5b4 p.62.25–63.1 = *SVF* 3.278). This led Bonhöffer to suppose that the weakness in the soul which permits *pleonasmos* is the same weakness which constitutes the weakness in the *arrōstēma* (*Epiktet und die Stoa* 1890, 275–76). Others seem to have supposed that the weakness in question is not so much the weakness which permits *pleonasmos* as the weakness which results from prolonged *pathē* which then produce the corresponding *arrōstēmata*. But both these explanations must be rejected as they fail to survive an overwhelming objection: All such weaknesses are necessarily nondiscriminatory between *nosēmata* in general and *arrōstēmata*. Yet we are told quite clearly that it is the association with weakness which is the *distinguishing* mark of *arrōstēmata* in relation to other *nosēmata*. In fact we seem to be told in Stobaeus (2.7.10e p. 93.10) that *arrōstēmata* are actually opposed to (*enantia*) the (other) *nosēmata*. It follows that what is needed is a full investigation into the nature and range of *arrōstēmata*.

Stobaeus, as we have seen, lists *philogynia* and *philoinia* as typical *nosēmata*. As examples of the opposite *arrōstēmata* he gives *misogynia* or *odium mulierum* and *misoinia* and he adds a third, namely, *misanthrōpia,* translated by Cicero as *odium in hominum universum genus* or hatred of the whole human race. (This last might seem to imply that philanthropy was a *nosēma,* but in fact the word *philanthrōpia* is not used, it would seem, in Stoic contexts in any unfavourable or for that matter favourable sense—apart from *SVF* 3.292 it is apparently simply not used at all.) In relation to the corresponding *nosēmata* these *arrōstēmata,* we are told by Stobaeus (p. 93.10), arise *kata proskopēn,* a strange expression, translated by R. Anastasi by "*nate da un senso di repulsione*" (*I frammenti degli stoici antichi* vol. 3 Padua 1962, p. 121). Even in the text of Stobaeus the expression clearly seemed obscure to scribes and in manuscript P the word *proskopēn* has become *prokopēn,* presumably in the sense of "growing progressively."

The term *proskopē,* however, occurs once elsewhere in Greek in a passage dealing with the same Stoic doctrine, namely, in Diogenes Laertius 7.113 (= *SVF* 3.396) where we read, "Hatred is a desire that it should go ill with someone, accompanied by *proskopē* and *prostasis*"; Here also some manuscripts correct *proskopē* to *prokopē* and this seems to have been adopted by all modern editors. The passage is then interpreted as meaning "Hatred is a growing and lasting desire" (Hicks) or "desire for an evil that is growing and lasting to happen to someone" (Anastasi). But the correctness of the reading *proskopēs* in Diogenes Laertius is, I think, established: First, because it appears to be the original, i.e. uncorrected, manuscript reading in the texts of Diogenes; secondly, because it is confirmed by its citation in the definition of hatred found in the *Suda* (s.v. *epithymia*); thirdly, because it is also found in the description of *arrōstēmata* in Stobaeus, and finally, as we shall see, because it is found also in Cicero where *proskopē* is translated into Latin as *offensio*. All of the difficulty both in ancient and in modern times has arisen from a failure to understand that we are here dealing with a technical Stoic doctrine— the doctrine of the *proskopē* or collision leading to repulsion. To anticipate, the passage in Diogenes Laertius should be translated, "hatred is a desire that it should go badly for someone, when this desire is accompanied by a repulsion and [?] an imperative." (Both the text and the interpretation of the term *prostasis* are also difficult, but to save space I forbear discussion of this second problem here.)

The Evidence Found in Cicero

Further evidence, of considerable importance, is to be found in Cicero, *Tusculan Disputations* 4.23–31 (see *SVF* 3.423–427). The close relationship between this passage and the source or sources used by Arius in Stobaeus has already been noticed by Zeller (*Ph. d. Gr.* 3.1 p. 237 n.2 init.). Despite this, the difficulties in Cicero's account are usually regarded as considerable, and as a result little use seems to have been made of it in the interpretation of Stoic ethics (for a statement of the traditional view of these difficulties see A. Bonhöffer *Epiktet und die Stoa* 276 n.1). Two views have commonly been taken by editors of Cicero's text. The commonest is that found in Dougan's commentary (Vol. 2 p. 131) according to which Cicero has become muddled and confused in his use of Stoic terminology. More elaborate was the view of Mario Sansone in his edition of Book 4 of the *Tusculan Disputations* (Milan 1933) according to which Cicero is in effect combining two different accounts, one of which is "empirical"and the other "gnoseological" or analytic in character.

All such views, I want to argue, are both unfair to Cicero, and unhelpful to us as well. Once we recognize one fact, everything else falls into place, and Cicero's account is consistent throughout, being indeed precise, coherent and carefully articulated. As we have seen, Stobaeus contrasted *arrōstēmata* with *nosēmata* in a particular way. Cicero tells us that he is translating *nosēma* by *morbus,* and *arrōstēma* by *aegrotatio.* But when he goes on to offer a definition *of aergrotatio* and to give examples of it, the definition is the definition found in Stobaeus for *nosēma* and so also with Cicero's examples—in Stobaeus these are given as examples, not of *arrōstēmata,* but of *nosēmata.* Hence the charge that Cicero has fallen into confusion. But the simple answer is that in Cicero Stobaeus' *arrōstēmata* are referred to by a different term, *offensiones,* or more strictly are classed as the consequences of *offensiones,* whereas *morbi* and *aegrotationes* are linked together in such a way that they are virtually equivalent to *nosēmata* in Stobaeus. Nor is this usage a sign of confusion in Cicero, or a tiresome change on his part in the use of technical terms. His usage follows standard medical terminology, for in medical writers we often find no distinction drawn between a *nosēma* and *arrōstēma* (see e.g. ps. Hipp. *De flatibus* 9, Galen in *SVF* 3 p. 120.34, *Anon. Londinensis* 3.44–4.5). When a distinction is drawn at all, an *arrōstēma* tends to mean the weakened condition of the body resulting from the *nosēma* (Anon. *Lond.* 3.16–17, 29–32, cf. Aristotle, *PA* 671b9). When such a weakened condition has arisen it is likely to take a considerable time before disappearing, if it does so at all. Cicero has just such cases in mind when he used the terms *morbus* and *aegrotatio* (see above, the beginning of *Tusc. Disp.* 4.24), and this same nontechnical use of *arrōstēma* seems to occur once in Diogenes Laertius (7.115 = *SVF* 3.422) though it is followed immediately by the correct definition of the term when used in contrast with *nosēma*.

Once this point has been grasped about Cicero's terminology our difficulties in following his argument virtually disappear. More than this, we can use some of the extra things that he has to say to supplement and extend our basic understanding of the doctrine found in Stobaeus. What Cicero says may be summarized (in a kind of free and curtailed translation) as follows:

> There is a parallelism between soul and body in that disturbances in each can arise from internal conflict. In the case of the body when the blood has been impaired there is an overflow of one of the humors involved, i.e., phlegm or bile. In the same way the soul is disturbed with diseases and robbed of its health through the confusion brought about by wrongful opinions and their conflict with each other. The first consequence of these disturbances is the *morbi* which Cicero tells us the Stoics call *nosēmata*, and also things which are the contraries of these *morbi* and involve collision with and aversion from certain objects. The second product is *aegrotationes*, called *arrōstēmata* by the Stoics, and the contrary collisions which confront them likewise. To sum up we may say that it is as a result of the chronic disturbance induced by the conflict of opinions that we have *morbi* and *aegrotationes*, and the collisions which are contaries of these *morbi* and *aegrotationes*.
>
> All of these conditions (i.e. *morbi, aegrotationes* and their *offensiones*, and not merely the first two as most editors have supposed) are in practice found joined together, and they arise from desire and from pleasure. On the one hand we have for example avarice, desire for renown, and *mulierositas (philogynia)*. Their contraries include hatred of women, misanthropy and hatred of strangers. These last arise from a kind of fear of the things which they shun and hate, and they are included by Cicero correctly in the class of mental disorders or *aegrotationes* (though they constitute only one group of the members of that class). In another sense they are to be classed as (the product of) collisions or *offensiones* which are the contraries of (the remaining) *morbi* and *aegrotationes*. But even while being their contraries they are also in the widest sense themselves mental disorders or diseases. [In just the same way, in Stobaeus 2.7.10e p.93.9–13 = *SVF* 3.421 while *arrōstēmata* are the contraries of *nosēmata*, they nonetheless themselves are *nosēmata*, namely *nosēmata met' astheneias*.] Finally Cicero makes it clear that what we might call the primary disorder involves a persistent strong opinion that something is desirable when it is not. The secondary disorder, arising through *offensio* is a similar opinion, but to the effect that something is to be shunned when it should not be shunned.

The Evidence in Combination

So much for what Cicero actually says. I now want to venture on an overall interpretation, attempting to draw together the evidence from all sources, but above all the evidence of Stobaeus and Cicero. What I want to suggest is that we have here in front of us the remains of a doctrine of very considerable interest. The basic doctrine is that a *pathos* is an impulse that has gone wrong, and the typical example of an impulse that has gone wrong is an impulse that has gone too far because it has not been restrained by reason to keep its function in accord with reason. This arises most commonly not through the complete absence of reason (indeed children not yet possessed of reason are exempt from *pathē—SVF* 3.477), but through a mistaken judgment as to the desirability of the objects of the impulse, so that reason is not so much inoperative as failing to operate adequately or correctly in the given circumstances. The result is an impulse that is pleonastic and is allowed to go too far.

But the situation is not nearly as simple as this might suggest. For we are subject not to one impulse only, but to many, and this raises the surely alarming possibility of subjection to a plurality of pleonastic impulses. Pleonastic impulses constitute *pathē*, and all *pathē* can be reduced, Stobaeus tells us (2.7.10 p.88.12–19 = *SVF* 3.378) to four that are primary—desire, fear, pain and pleasure. Among these, pain and pleasure are secondary in relation to desire and fear. Desire is directed towards what appears to be good, and fear is concerned with what appears to be bad. If we apply this to some of the examples already mentioned we arrive at the following analysis. An excessive desire for wine can *conflict* with an excessive fear of wine. Indeed all fear and all desire is pleonastic; the wise man never experiences fear, though he does exercise caution (D. L. 7.115 = *SVF* 3.431) and he does not experience desire, though his impulse towards what is good proceeds "to the right extent" (*hoson chrē—SVF* 3.441). The confrontation between desire and fear involves a collision—*proskopē, offensio*. This is the internal conflict of wrongful opinions called by Cicero an *inter se repugnantia* (Tusc. Disp. 4.23 = *SVF* 3.424). If fear prevails the original impulses become weakened (the *arrōstēmata* as defined in Stobaeus 2.7.10e p.93.11–13 = *SVF* 3.421) and we become victims of the opposite *pathē*, e.g., we become temperance fanatics in our hatred of wine. But hatred is itself a desire (Diogenes Laertius 7.113 = *SVF* 3.396) and as such is pleonastic. So one pleonastic impulse when blocked and frustrated by collision with fear leads by counterreaction to another pleonastic impulse, namely hatred. *Mulierositas* or *gynaikomania* leads by counterreaction to misogyny, but the wise man is of course immune both to love and hate (cf. *SVF* 3.396). The intimate relationship of love, fear and hate is a theme not neglected in modern psychology, and it is of some interest to see them already so closely linked in the psychopathology of the Stoics.

III. *HORMAI* IN RELATION TO *KATĒGORĒMATA*

A *hormē* or impulse is "a movement of the soul towards something according to its kind" (Stobaeus 2.7.9 p.86.19 = *SVF* 3.169), and four lines later in the same passage we are told that a "rational impulse is a movement of the mind (*dianoia*) towards something that belongs in the class of actions." Now for the Stoics the soul is a body (*sōma*—cf. *SVF* 2.781). In fact, it is *pneuma,* as we are told in innumerable passages, and the same is true of the *dianoia* in the human soul (Stobaeus 2.7.5b7 p.64.21 = *SVF* 3.305). It follows that a movement of the soul, like any other movement, is itself both a movement of something that is material, and is also spoken of as itself being bodily and material (see e.g. *SVF* 2.385). None of this is likely to cause us any particular difficulties—given the materialist bases of the Stoic system it all seems straightforward enough. Nor are we likely to be disturbed when we are told that impulses to action require acts of assent in living creatures (*SVF* 2.980), and we can also understand Stobaeus when he says that all *hormai* are acts of assent (2.7.9b p. 88.1 = *SVF* 3.171) since acts of assent are changes in the rational part of the soul, the *hēgēmonikon* (cf. *SVF* 2.836) and as such are also classed as bodies by the Stoics (*SVF* 2.848). One of the causes of acts of assent are *phantasiai,* and this also is easy to understand since a *phantasia* is itself a kind of physical movement, described as an imprinting or *typōsis* in the soul (I have tried to discuss some of the problems raised by the doctrine of assent to *phantasiai* in *Les Stoiciens et leur logique,* Actes du Colloque de Chantilly (Paris 1978) 251–272). So far everything that has been said gives the appearance of an essentially straightforward mechanistic materialism, albeit of a dynamic kind, in that it proceeds on the basis of its own built-in material source of motion, the Active Principle.

But further statements in ancient texts raise considerable difficulties and may seem to suggest at first sight that we have an alternative, nonmaterialistic analysis inconsistent with the basic doctrine of Stoic materialism. Our starting point must be Stobaeus 2.7.9b p.88.1–6 = *SVF* 3.171. Here we are told first that all *hormai* are acts of assent, but that the objects of acts of assent and of impulses are different, in that acts of assent belong to certain *axiōmata* or statements, while impulses are directed towards *katēgorēmata* or predicates which are in a sense contained within the *axiōmata.* Now both *katēgorēmata* and *axiōmata* are for the Stoics *lekta* and as such are incorporeal (see e.g. *SVF* 2.132, 170, 331). The doctrine that *hormai* are directed towards *kategorēmata* is found also in Cicero (*Tusc. Disp.* 4.21 = *SVF* 3.398) and it occurs in Stobaeus at 2.7.11f. p.97.22–98.1 = *SVF* 3.91. This had led Victor Goldschmidt, in commenting on the passage in Cicero, to write "*La logique stoicienne classe les 'prēdicats' parmi les choses 'incorporelles,' c'est-à-dire n'existant que dans la pensée. L'emploi, ici, de ce terme fait ressortir l'irréalité et la vanité de l'objet que se propose le désir.*" (*Les Stoiciens,* texts trans. by E. Bréhier Paris 1962, p. 1282).

Such a conclusion would be surprising indeed, and clearly the whole matter requires further investigation. First some definitions. An *axiōma* is a proposition that makes an assertion or denial; a *lekton* is complete or self-sufficient so far as concerns itself (D. L. 7.65 = *SVF* 2.193); a *katēgorēma* is a predicate; an incomplete *lekton* combines with a subject to form an *axiōma* (D. L. 7.64 = *SVF* 2.183). It follows that a verb is always involved, and when examples are given (e.g. D. L. 7.58 = *SVF* 3.22) they are, in fact, frequently simply verbs, often in the infinitive mood. This makes acceptable sense in relation to *hormai* if we reflect that a *hormē* (impulse) is necessarily an impulse to do something, and "to do something" already involves what is expressed by a verb in the infinitive. But the impulse "to do something" is an impulse to do something in the real world, and is not easily understood as a movement of the mind towards a *lekton*. Consequently, it is probable that most scholars would agree with Zeller when he said that, strictly speaking, the object of the impulse is not the *katēgorēma* but rather the activity referred to by it (*Ph. d. Gr.* 3.1 228 n.2). But if this is so, why did Arius Didymus not simply say so outright? The answer is probably to be found in a further Stoic doctrine concerning *axiōmata* which is preserved in a remarkable passage not included in *SVF*, but which should unquestionably be added in any future revision of that work.

The passage in question is to be found in a scholium on Lucian's satire *Philosophers for Sale* (*Scholia in Lucianum* ed. H. Rabe, Teubner Series 1906, reprinted Stuttgart 1971) 128.18–129.16. Lucian has been making fun of the Stoic fondness for technical terms, and in particular of the term *symbama* meaning in ordinary language an accident or casualty, and in Stoic technical terminology a complete predicate or *katēgorēma*. The first part of the scholiast's comment is as follows:

> May you be damned, accursed fellow, for twisting everything round as you speak to make it ridiculous, and putting all things that are wise in the class of things that are comic. For the other dialecticians say that propositions consist of a noun and a verb combined without further residue to produce an assertoric sentence, for example "Socrates walks," "Dion discusses," and they call subject the noun or something from the class of the things that fulfil the function of a noun, and they say that the verb is predicated. But the Stoics, being people who make a display of accuracy and who like to use strange words, for their part say that a complete proposition such as "Socrates walks" is an occurrence (*symbama*) or a predicate (*katēgorēma*). For "walking" is something that has happened to Socrates.

There follow a further fourteen lines of the scholiast's commentary, in which he gives the fullest and clearest exposition that we have of a series of Stoic technical terms—*parasymbama, parakatēgorēma,* and the contrast between a complete *katēgorēma* and what is "less than a *katēgorēma*." These, I believe, enable us to clear up a series of puzzles and uncertainties raised, e.g., by *SVF* 2.183 and 184, and they also show that von Arnim (followed also by K. Hülser in the new edition of R. T. Schmidt *Die Grammatik der Stoiker* Wiesbaden 1979, 153–55) was wrong to condemn as false two further passages, one in the Suda, and one in Priscian (cf.

SVF 2 p.60.16–17). But all this is by the way. What is important for my present purposes is that at the end of the passage translated above we have a clear statement to the effect that for the Stoics there was a sense in which a whole statement could be regarded as predicated of the situation in the real world. In this sense a *katēgorēma* is not a grammatical phenomenon within a sentence, referring to the grammatical predicate which in turn is to be related to the grammatical subject. Instead it possesses an extralinguistic reference to what is the case. This means that it is possible to say that *katēgorēma* and *symbama* both mean the same thing (so Porphyry, *SVF* 2.184, p. 59.32). Alongside this way of looking at things, however, there was also the view that a *katēgorēma* was best treated as a purely grammatical term—as a "defective *lekton* joined to a nominative case in order to yield a statement" (D. L. 7.64 = *SVF* 2.183). As a grammatical phenomenon *katēgorēmata* would then be isomorphic, rather than identical, with what we find in the physical world.

I believe that this Janus-faced characteristic of the *katēgorēma* can be of considerable help in our attempts to understand another important but difficult and obscure Stoic doctrine, for which our main source is, in fact, Stobaeus. This is the distinction between that which is *haireton* and that which is *haireteon,* terms which may for convenience be translated by "choiceworthy" (*haireton*) and "has to be chosen" (*haireteon*). On this whole question we should start with the excellent discussion by A. A. Long, "The Early Stoic Concept of Moral Choice" in *Images of Man, Studia G. Verbeke Dedicata* (Leuven 1976) 77–92. According to this doctrine we are concerned with two distinct classes (see Stobaeus 2.7.6f. p. 78.7–12 = *SVF* 3.89, and 2.7.11f. p.97.15–98.6 = *SVF* 3.91) which are as follows: (I) Things beneficial, which have to be chosen, which are *katēgorēmata,* which are connected with things that are good (*parakeimena*), which are incorporeal, which we choose. As examples we have two infinitives, *phronein,* "to be wise" and *sōphronein,* "to be prudent." (II) Good things, which are choiceworthy, which are corporeal, which are virtues (see Stobaeus 2.7.11h p.100.15ff. = *SVF* 3.208), which we do not choose, but which we choose to have. As examples we have two abstract nouns, *phronēsis,* "wisdom" and *sōphrosynē,* "prudence."

There is much that is obscure here and indeed that is likely to remain so. But the basic opposition or distinction seems to be between (II) states or dispositions which are corporeal, and (I) actions which are incorporeal and which are described as *kategorēmata.* The Stoics saw the relationship in causal terms, as expounded in a passage in Sextus Empiricus (*Adv. math.* 9.211 = *SVF* 2.341):

> Every cause is a body which is the cause to a body of something incorporeal; for example, the lancet is a body and the flesh is a body, and the *katēgorēma* "being cut" is incorporeal; and again fire is a body, and the wood is a body, and the *katēgorēma* "being burnt" is incorporeal.

The relation between cause and effect is however so intimate that they amount to two aspects of the same thing. We are fortunate to have a passage from Arius

Didymus' physical epitome (Stobaeus 1. 13.1c p.138.14 = *SVF* 1.89) which actually applies this analysis to "wisdom" and "to be wise."

> Zeno says that cause is that through which, and that of which, it is the cause is what occurs. And the cause is a body, while that of which it is a cause is a *katēgorēma*. And it is impossible for the cause to be present, and for that of which it is the cause not to be there also. What is being said has the following significance: a cause is that by which something comes to be, for example through wisdom there comes about being wise, and through the soul there comes about living, and through prudence there comes about being prudent. For it is impossible when there is prudence concerning certain things not then to be prudent, or when the soul is present not to live, or when wisdom is present not to be wise.

This makes clear the Janus-faced function of the *katēgorēma*—while it is caused by the corporeal situation there is no chronological sequence involved—where there is soul there is life, where there is wisdom there is "being wise." It is in this sense that we must understand that a *hormē* is directed towards a *katēgorēma*.

When we are told that benefits are connected (*parakeimena*) with things that are good, we would be well advised to regard such benefits not as consequences which are unimportant because immaterial (as Goldschmidt, quoted above), but rather as things that are good *seen as* benefits, in the same way as that in which the soul is, and is seen as, life. It may be noted that the causal relationship here involved between goods and benefits will be that of the *synektikon aition* or *causa continens* rather than the *prokatarktikon* or antecedent cause, while the *hormē* will be *prokatarktikon* in relation to the resultant physical state and also to the *katēgorēma* associated with the resultant physical state in question. For an excellent account of the different kinds of causes distinguished by the Stoics, see M. Frede, "The Original Notion of Cause" in *Doubt and Dogmatism, Studies in Hellenistic Epistemology*, ed. M. Schofield, M. Burnyeat and J. Barnes (Oxford 1980) p. 217ff.

Finally I want to suggest that this interpretation may shed some light on another obscure passage in Arius Didymus, namely Stobaeus 2.7.8a p.86.5–9 = *SVF* 3.503, where we are told:

> There are two classes of *katorthōmata* or "right actions," namely those which are of things which are right (*hōn chrē*) and those which are not of things which are right. Things which are right possess the *katēgorēma* benefit [keeping the manuscript reading here], for example being wise, being prudent, and things which are not of the class of things which are right, are things which are not so. The same technical explanation applies to things which are *para to kathēkon*.

At first sight this may seem merely to be introducing a new heading, that of "negative *katorthōmata*" or cases where it is a "right action" for the wise man *not* to do something. This involves taking the expression "do not belong to the class of things which is right to do" as the equivalent of "belong to the class of things which it is not right to do, and so belong to the class of things which it is right not to do.'' But I see two objections to this interpretation: To begin with, it involves a transition from contradictory to contrary (''not right to do'' = ''right not to do'') which is perhaps not fatal by itself. But the expression ''the things which are not so'' must mean ''things which do not have the *katēgorēma* 'benefit' '' and this suggests that perhaps we are concerned with the contrast between the two cases which we have previously labeled (I) and (II). On this view *katorthōmata* which have the *katēgorēma* ''benefit,'' and are exemplified by being wise and being prudent, are cases falling under class (I). These are said to be connected with things that are good (*parakeimena*) in Stobaeus 2.7.11i p.101.5–9 = *SVF* 3.587. Those that lack this *katēgorēma* would then be class (II) corporeal entities such as wisdom and prudence. This adventurous hypothesis might seem to fail when confronted with the fact that nowhere else are virtues classed as *katorthōmata*. All *katorthōmata* would seem to be activities and thus class (I) entities (See, e.g., Stobaeus 2.7.11e p.96.18–22 = *SVF* 3.501; cf.p.97.5–12 = *SVF* 3.502.) But then nowhere else are we invited to contemplate two different *kinds* of *katorthōmata*. What we are told is that the activities of which *katorthōmata* are (usually) said to consist are activities in accord with virtue (Stobaeus 2.7.8 p.85.20–86.1 = *SVF* 3.494).

Comments on Professor Kerferd's Paper
Possible Stoic Methods of Impulses

Anthony Preus

My starting point is this passage in Professor Kerferd's paper:

> The Stoics seem to have regarded impulses as functioning in a way that we might describe as analogous to the movements in a watch or clock. An escapement mechanism is necessary to restrain the impulse derived from weights or the spring to an appropriate degree—if the escapement mechanism fails then the impulse becomes pleonastic, the clock races, and bad things inevitably result for our pattern of living. A further modern example or analogy can be found in the physiological doctrine according to which the vagus nerve is understood as restraining the rate of heart beat and so preventing damaging "racing." In the case of *hormai* it is a weakness or failure of *tonos* or tension in the soul which enables them to "go too far."

As Professor Kerferd indicates, both models postdate the ancient Stoic school, and thus could not have been the mechanical or physiological models upon which their account was based. Since I am in substantial agreement with Professor Kerferd's explanation of *arrostēmata* and *proskopē* (and, for that matter, with what he says about *katēgorēma*), I take this occasion to investigate some models of the impulses which the Stoics could have (might have) had in mind as they developed their moral psychology.

Professor Kerferd is surely right in arguing that the *arrōstēmata* involve pathologically deficient *hormai*; his reading of Stobaeus 2.7.2, and of the related passages in Cicero and elsewhere, makes this abundantly clear, since the *arrōstēmata* and the "pleonastic" *pathē* are contrasted in a way which inevitably remind us of Aristotle's doctrine of the mean. Indeed, it is the very Aristotelianism of the contrast which would, if anything could, call into question this part of Professor Kerferd's analysis. Perhaps Arius Didymus, and Cicero, here reproduce a feature of a post-Chrysippean Stoic account of the *hormai*, a syncretism of Posidonius or Panaetius. However that may be, a more difficult part of Professor Kerferd's analysis centers on the interpretation of the word *proskopē*, particularly to the extent that it depends on the (modern) models introduced in the passage quoted above.

The simplest way of applying the "clock" model to what the Stoics say about *hormē* would make *hormē* the mainspring, or the tension in the mainspring, or the weight which drives the main cogwheel, if that is the motive force of the clock.

Two such mechanical sources of energy, widely used in the time of the Stoics, were the windlass, cranked up and then driven by a falling weight, and twisted cords, whose tension provides the power. Aristotle suggests the application of a related model in the *Movement of Animals* 7.701b1ff: He says that animals may be described as moving like the marvelous automatic puppets, *hōsper de ta automata kineitai mikras kinēseōs ginomenēs, lyomenōn tōn streblōn kai krouontōn allēla,* "as the automata move when a small movement has occurred, the *streblai* being loosened and striking each other." The work *streblai* may mean "windlasses," around which cords are wound; releasing weights at the ends of the cords, motive power may be supplied to the puppet. Martha Nussbaum and I[1] understand the passage thus. Alternatively, LSJ and the older translators understand *streblai* as cords twisted together to give motive power upon release, as in a catapult. Either way, a wound-up *streblē* is a good model for a *hormē,* and it gives us a first step toward Professor Kerferd's clock model. What it lacks is any clear escapement mechanism—Aristotle's puppet lacks any internal regulatory device. There is only the release, which allows the weight to fall or the cords to unwind. Something (cords, pieces of wood) "strike each other" in the activity, suggesting *some* interpretion of *proskopē* perhaps, but not Professor Kerferd's regulative interpretation.

One way of taking what Professor Kerferd says about the escapement would be that reason regulates the escapement in the well-ordered man; if reason relaxes its hold on the escapement, the *hormē* races, and a *pathos* of excess results. This would be an attractive interpretation if all *pathē* were of excess, as is often suggested by writers on the Stoics. It has the further virtue of similarity to mechanisms which existed in antiquity—the windlass used for pulling ships out of the water has cogs and a trigger-lever to keep the windlass from unwinding until one wants the ship to roll back into the water. In the pseudo-Aristotelian *De mundo* ch. 6 (a rather Stoic document, by the way), God is compared to the engineer who, in releasing a trigger mechanism of this sort, called a *schastēria,* causes many multifarious movements. This account does not, however, fit what Professor Kerferd says about *arrostēmata,* since they would then be vices caused by too strong an application of reason, not a plausible Stoic theory.

A more complex mechanism has a spring, or some other power source, holding down the trigger; this is a necessary condition for a true escapement mechanism. If we take this additional source of power as another, and different, *hormē,* then we can apply Professor Kerferd's model thus: if the main *hormē* is too strong, the trigger *hormē* too weak, or the teeth worn down, the main wheel races, and thus there is a *pathos* of excess; if the trigger *hormē* is too strong, the main *hormē* too weak, there is no action. We may interpret what Kerferd says about *proskopē* according to this model thus: if the main *hormē* is desire, the trigger *hormē* fear, then *proskopē* may be the clicking into place of the trigger when a strong desire for female companionship is checked by a strong fear of the consequences, and misogyny results. There are fundamentally two difficulties with this interpretation: one, that the Stoics probably did not have in mind a mechanism of this complexity;

the other, that classic or old Stoicism seems to assert the existence of just one fundamental *hormē*, and not two or more potentially conflicting *hormai*. These difficulties are perhaps not insurmountable, but we do need to look at the evidence in more detail.

Although all the earlier Stoics wrote books entitled "Concerning *Hormē*,"[2] the remaining fragments do not encourage the construction of precise models. One of the better sources of useful fragments is Galen's *Doctrines of Hippocrates and Plato,* in which long sections of Chrysippus are quoted and paraphrased. On Galen's showing, the model is very simple; he quotes Chrysippus comparing *hormē* to the momentum of a moving person: "When he is walking *kath' hormēn* the movement of his legs is not excessive, but is in a way commensurate with his *hormē,* so that he can stop when he wants to, or change his pace. But when he runs *kath' hormēn.* . . the movement of the legs exceeds *para hormēn* so that they are carried away and cannot easily change their pace."[3] That is one explanation of a *pathos* of excess: when a man walks, his movements are all under control and readily altered instantly; when a man runs, many of his movements are not readily altered. So the man who indulges his appetites immoderately cannot easily alter his behavior. If we try to interpret *arrōstēma* according to this model, we might compare it to the movement of a person dragging himself along, unable to change pace because this is the only one he can manage, but all too able to stop completely. No ready interpretation of *proskopē* appears in this model, and indeed everything Galen says in his *Doctrines of Hippocrates and Plato* 4 and the beginning of 5 indicates that Chrysippus, at least, had a very hard time accounting for conflicts in the soul. Galen's account suggests very strongly, to me at least, that Chrysippus could not have developed, as a prominent part of his psychological theory, the sort of model of psychological conflict which Professor Kerferd proposes as an interpretation of the word *proskopē*. Of course it is possible that Galen, quarrelsome as he is, did not see the evidence in Chrysippus for some sort of model which could account for conflict in the soul.

One of the constant themes of Galen's *Doctrines of Hippocrates and Plato* is that the Stoics, and in particular Chrysippus, failed to develop or use the insights of Plato in their psychological theory. Galen aptly quotes *Republic* 4.439e2–440a7, where Socrates tells of Leontius of Aglaion, who, happening upon some corpses at the place of public execution, both wanted and did not want to look at them; this Socrates (Plato) took as evidence that *orgē* might be in conflict with *epithymia*. Plato's theory of contrary impulses is developed in *Politicus* 305ff, where the political art weaves together the moderate and the courageous. The courageous tend to be "hybristic and maniacal" when they go to excess; the moderate tend to be heavy, slow, soft, to the point of cowardice and indolence. Although these two sorts of characters may be in conflict, the kingly art weaves them together as warp and woof. Plato's theories of the soul allow readily for explanations in terms of opposing impulses, both through excess, and through defect; Galen is right about that. It is something of a difficulty for Professor Kerferd's interpretation of *arrōs-*

tēma and *proskopē* that Galen thought there was nothing of the sort in Chrysippus, and perhaps consequently not in any of the older Stoics.

We have already mentioned Aristotle's mechanical model of human action closest to Kerferd's clock model, the automata of *MA* 7. That passage, and indeed the *MA* as a whole, does not have much to say about the problem of conflicting impulses. Much closer to Kerferd's account of *proskopē* would be *Nicomachean Ethics* I.13, where Aristotle says that rational and irrational principles in the soul may be in opposition: "As when we intend to move a paralysed limb to the right it turns to the left instead, so in the soul; the impulses of incontinent people move in contrary directions." This is, incidentally, one of the few places in which Aristotle uses the word *hormē* in the explanation of action, so it is very possible, indeed likely, that this passage influenced Stoic writers, or Arius Didymus, or Cicero and his sources, in their discussion of conflicting impulses.

Although Plato and Aristotle do not have Professor Kerferd's clock model, I think that it is clear enough that they could readily accept it —the impulses of *epithymia* or the sensitive-locomotive soul are regulated by the rational faculty, describable as an opposing impulse. The earlier Stoics would have found it more difficult to accept because they were attempting to give a reduced (unitary) psychological theory, in which all motivation would be explicable in terms of one fundamental *hormē* in a unified soul. The basic difficulty in Kerferd's interpretation, as applied to the earlier Stoics, is that *proskopē* as he describes it requires a division in the soul, of the Platonic or Aristotelian variety, and it is just that division of the soul which the earlier Stoics deny. This does not at all prevent the post-Chrysippean Stoics from holding a theory which allows for Kerferdian *proskopē*, however, and that is sufficient to allow for his being right about the passages in Arius Didymus and Cicero.

Several mechanical models for the impulses may be discerned from various sources in post-Aristotelian philosophy. In the *De mundo* we find not only the trigger mechanism, mentioned earlier, but also another kind of puppet, the marionette (at 6.398b1ff.) moved at the end of strings held by God in his role of first cause. Here, however, the source of movement is from outside, so this is not a model for the innate *hormē*. (Compare Plato *Pol* 269C, where God periodically winds up the universe, then releases it.)

Hero of Alexandria describes various mechanisms in the greatest detail of any ancient writer; some of his mechanisms have features which bring them close to the features of the mechanical clock, and consequently provide analogues which could have been used by at least the later Stoics. The closest approach to a true escapement mechanism which I have been able to find in ancient sources is in Hero's description of the control mechanism of the arms of the workmen in the first scene of the *Nauplius*.[4] A weight-driven windlass with pegs in it moves a lever, also counterbalanced by a weight. Depending upon the exact way in which the windlass and the lever are mechanically interrelated, the lever may operate as a true escapement. It is drawn as an escapement by Prou, but Schmidt makes it look much more like part of an Aristotelian puppet. This lever is called a *hysplēggion* or "little pig whip" in this passage. The normal form of the word, *hysplēx* ("pig whip"), is used elsewhere in Hero (2.8) of the twisted cords which are used to power an automaton, and thus as equivalent to one of the senses of *streblē* which we distinguished earlier. It is not immediately obvious what, if any, relation there may be between the motive power *hysplēx* and the quasi-escapement *hysplēggion*. The tightly-wound cord is undoubtedly the primary application of the term "pig whip"; perhaps an escapement-like mechanism was sometimes powered by a small "pig whip," so by extension the lever which could be thus controlled may have taken on the name.

The *hysplēx* is used as a model of human impulses in Plutarch's "On the Sign of Socrates" (*Moralia* 588–89). In the passage, Simmias (of *Phaedo* fame) is explaining that a human being whose soul is in exceptionally fine tune may respond directly to the activity of the intelligences of higher powers: "The soul of man, stretched tight with myriad *hormai*-like *hyspleges*, is, when touched according to reason, by far the most sensitive of instruments, tending to move toward the object of thought. For the origins of *pathē* and *hormai* are stretched to the mind, but when it is shaken, they are pulled, and in turn they pull and give tension to the man." The model is a hybrid of the Aristotelian automaton and the musical instrument suggested by Simmias in the *Phaedo*; without much effort it could be made to accomodate all parts of Professor Kerferd's account, including *arrostēmata* and *proskopē*. The major difficulty would be that Plutarch is explicitly a Platonist, above all in this essay, and the idea that men have *countless* competing impulses is hardly orthodox Stoicism. Still, some such image might have been used by a platonizing Stoic. In this passage, Plutarch is not attempting to explain the various ways in which someone may go wrong, but how it is that someone may be in such good condition (tune) that the gods may communicate directly to one's mind. Simmias is represented as developing a somewhat materialistic interpretation of an undoubtedly Platonic notion.

The essential point of contact between this passage in Plutarch and the Stoic theory of the impulses may be in the shared notion of the stringiness of the soul. The Stoics thought of *pneuma* as stringy in character, stretched from the central and governing organ (the heart) to the various sensory and motor parts.[5] The *tonos* of the *pneuma* holds living things together, and indeed stretches throughout the cosmos.[6] Chalcidius seems to ascribe to Chrysippus an image of the soul as a spider in its web,[7] with pneumatic strands in the web. For Chalcidius, this model explains sensation rather than impulse, but that is not at all an insurmountable difficulty. In view of the pneumatic theory of the soul, the tension in the strands in the web is the analogue of the *tonos* of the *pneuma*, so it is not only the case that movements in the web are transmitted to the spider, but movements of the spider may result in movements farther out in the web. Working out the physiological details of a Chrysippean theory may turn out to be quite difficult, and perhaps Chrysippus did not have a consistent interpretation of his model; we may, however, remember that the heart was the center for both sensation and movement, and the system of *neuroi* (sinews, nerves) was stringy and associated with *pneuma,* whose tension is necessary for appropriate action. In a puppet, the first mover of the strings, the *hegemonikon,* is ultimately outside the puppet, but the first mover of the animal is inside. Interpretations for *eutonia,* right tension, and *atonia,* wrong tension, appear immediately in the model.

Galen's account of Stoic theory does not include the "spider" image, but he does preserve evidence which is consonant with a "neurospastic" Stoic soul:[8] he says that Zeno held that the *pathē* are "certain *systolas* and *chyseis, eparseis* and *tapeinoseis."* The "contractions" and "expansions," or at least the contractions, are explicitly present in Chrysippus' account of *hormai* and *pathē,* as reported by Galen: for example, a *systolē* occasions a *hormē,* but if the *systolē* is weaker, the *hormē* does not occur; it is also possible, says Chrysippus, that there will be an *epiginomenē diathesis,* translated by De Lacy as "supervening disposition."[9] This "supervening disposition" can, for example, prevent weeping when there is otherwise an impulse to weep, prevent laughing when there is an impulse to laugh.[10]

We can, I believe, interpret the three sorts of pathological conditions, which Professor Kerferd finds in Stobaeus plus Cicero, in terms of the "spider web" model. Chrysippus distinguishes several sorts of *pneuma,* at least the auditory, optic, vocal, generative, and governing,[11] and surely more. These may be taken as separate strands of the internal web. If the generative *pneuma* is hypertonic, and the governing pneuma is dystonic in this respect, then the way is clear for the *pathos* of *gynaikomania;* if the vocal *pneuma* is hypotonic, then we may have a pathological weakness of an inability to speak. But besides strength and weakness absolutely and in comparison with the *hegēmonikon,* which account for morbid excess and defect, there is also the fact that the strands of the web cross, so that the *tonos* of one strand may interfere with the operation of another. Thus the "supervening diathesis" occurs, describable as an "interference," a *proskopē* or an *offensio* or even a *"repugnatia inter se"* as in Cicero (*Tusc.* 4.10.23).

Returning to Professor Kerferd's analogies, quoted at the beginning of this essay, we should say a bit about the vagus nerve. I am not entirely sure just what Professor Kerferd means—the rate of heart beat is regulated by a very complex interaction between the heart and the rest of the body, including but not limited to stimuli carried by the vagus nerve. In the context of a discussion of *Stoic* ideas, the analogy is more bewildering, since the Stoics believed the heart to be the location of the governing power, the first impulse, and they did not believe the brain and nervous system to regulate the heart. Galen makes a great deal of this Stoic (and Aristotelian) misunderstanding of physiology; the regulation of heart-beat by the vagus nerve would accord with Galenic ideas, and for that matter with those of Hippocrates and Plato. However, a Stoic might prefer to point to another of the functions of the vagus nerve, the regulation of the activities of the stomach and digestive system; if the vagus nerve is hyperactive, too much digestive acid is produced in the stomach, and ulcers result. Inactivity of the vagus is medically more manageable, but untreated results in chronic indigestion.

Let us return to the passages in which *proskopē* and *arrostēma* occur. If we read the text of Diogenes Laertius 7.113 as Professor Kerferd does, "hatred" is defined as "desire that it should go badly for someone, when this desire is accompanied by interference (K:collision) and is long-lasting." At Cicero *Tusc.* 4.10.23, I would take *offensio* as "interference" again, for the same reasons. At the end of the first paragraph of his paraphrase of this passage, Professor Kerferd leaves out a comment: there is a chronic disturbance induced by the conflict of opinions—"When this boiling and excitement become established in the soul, and as it were taken up residence in the veins and marrow," there are illness, weakness, and the interferences (collisions) which are the contraries of these illnesses and weaknesses. The comment is interesting in this context because the veins and marrow are plausible locations for finding strands of instrumental pneuma, prior to the more accurate determination of the nervous system, as described, for example, by Galen. When the boiling and excitement take up residence in the vagus nerve, peptic ulcers commonly result.

Finally, turning to Stobaeus 2.7,10e: there are three *kinds* of sickness of the soul: (1) tending to take more than one ought; e.g., love of women, love of wine, love of money; (2) illnesses which occur with interference, e.g., hatred of women, or of wine, or of mankind; (3) illnesses of weakness, or *arrōstēmata*, not exemplified in the passage. Total disinterest in wine, women, and song would count.

On another matter entirely, Professor Kerferd parenthetically remarks that *philanthropia* might by implication be thought a disease of excess, judging from the passage in Stobaeus. In fact, though the Stoics seem not to use the word, the favorable sense was so developed by their time that it surely could not have been understood as something negative. Two inscriptions, translated by A. R. Hands,[12] use the word for acts of generosity; Socrates in Plato's *Euthyphro,* the Hippocratic writer in *Precepts,* and Xenophon in the *Cyropaedia,* all suppose "philanthropy" to be an admirable condition (cf. LSJ). Perhaps the closest approach to an excessive vice opposed to the defect of "misanthropy" would be *kolakeia* as described in Aristotle and Theophrastus,[13] as the *kolax* is typified by an excessive desire to please other people.

I have little to say about Professor Kerferd's second problem, concerning *katēgorēmata.* His treatment of this concept as it occurs in the Stobaeus passage seems consonant with discussions of Stoic theory of language by A. A. Long, Michael Frede, and Andreas Graeser.[14] I am also reminded of the sign a colleague has posted on his door: "NO LOITERING. Persons who loiter are subject to the predicate 'to loiter.' "

Cicero found it necessary to quote the Greek term in *Tusc.* 4.9.21, where he says that the Stoics define *desiderium* as "a desire of seeing someone who is not present." He continues, "They also define it as a desire of those things which are said of one or more persons, which the logicians call *katēgorēmata,* e.g., to have wealth, to gain honors, while *indigentia* is of the things themselves, the honor or the money.'' Obviously the distinction is made between wanting to be wealthy and wanting (some particular) money. A similar distinction may be made between wanting sexual activity and wanting a particular person as a sex partner.

Cicero's distinction overlaps, and is not identical with, the distinction made in the Arius Didymus passage, Stobaeus 2.7, 11f., where the distinction is between two ways of wanting a predicate, one possible, the other nonsensical; we choose ''to have wisdom or temperance'' but we do not choose the (incorporeal) predicates themselves, the ''to-be-wise,'' the ''to-be-temperate.''

Putting Cicero and Stobaeus together, it appears that you may want Bo Derek for sexual purposes (all right if you're Tarzan), or you may want to have sexual activity (*aphrodisiazein*) (cf. Plato *Rep.* 4.426a), but you cannot want the ''to-have-sex'' itself. The first want is of a presumably physical entity, or a conjuction of such entities. The second is of a predicate—Tarzan wants that the sentence ''Tarzan is having sex'' be true. The third want is nonsensical, of the predicate itself. Only a misguided Platonist could even dream of wanting that.

NOTES

1. Martha Nussbaum, ''The Text of Aristotle's *De Motu Animalium*,'' *Harvard Studies in Classical Philology* 80 (1976) 111–59; A. Preus *Aristotle and Michael of Ephesus on the Movement and Progression of Animals* (Olms, Hildesheim, 1981) pp. 84–85.
2. A. Preus, ''Intention and Impulse in Aristotle and the Stoics,'' *Apeiron*, 1981.
3. *Doctrines of Hippocrates and Plato* 4.2, DeLacy ed. and trans. (Berlin, Akademie Verlag, 1978) 240–42.
4. Hero, *Automatopoiētikēs* 24, Schmidt ed. (Leipzig 1899) p. 424, illustration p. 425; cf. V. Prou, *Les Théatres d'Automates en Grèce*, (Académie des Inscriptions et Belles Lettres, Paris, n.d.) p. 176.
5. *SVF* 2.449, cf. 379, 389; see also David Hahm, *The Origins of Stoic Cosmology*, (Columbus, Ohio, 1977) pp. 165ff.
6. This point is made clearly by Hahm in *Origins* and by Michael Lapidge in ''Stoic Cosmology,'' in J. Rist, ed., *The Stoics* (Berkeley, California, 1978).
7. Chalcidius, *Commentary on the Timaeus*, p. 220, *SVF* 2.879.
8. See, for example, *Doct. of Hipp. and Plato* 5.1, DeLacy p. 293.
9. *Doct. of Hipp. and Plato* 4.7, DeL. 284; there are plenty of other passages of the same general tenor. This Chrysippean version of the theory was criticized by Posidonius, as described at *Doct. of Hipp. and Plato* 4.7, DeL. 288. I am not sure what that would do to the hypothesis that Posidonius originated the theory found in Arius Didymus.
10. *Doct. of Hipp. and Plato* 4.7, DeL. 284.
11. *Doct. of Hipp. and Plato* 5.3, DeL. 306.
12. A. R. Hands, *Charities and Social Aid in Greece and Rome* (Cornell, 1968) pp. 199, 200.
13. Aristotle, *Nicomachean Ethics* 4.6; Theophrastus, *Characters* 2.1.
14. A. A. Long, ''Language and Thought in Stoicism,'' in Long, ed., *Problems in Stoicism* (London, 1971); Michael Frede, ''Principles of Stoic Grammar,'' and Andreas Graeser, ''The Stoic Theory of Meaning,'' in J. Rist, ed., *The Stoics*.

CHAPTER 6

Euemptōsia-Proneness to Disease

Ian G. Kidd

The important and obvious contributions of Arius Didymus to Posidonian studies lie in natural philosophy. They occur in Book 1 of Stobaeus' *Eclogae* and refer to substance and matter (F92 E.-K.; F20 Diels *Dox.Gr.*); cause (F95 E.-K.; F18 Diels); generation and corruption (F96 E.-K.; F27 Diels); time (F98 E.-K.; F26 Diels); and star (F127 E.-K.; F32 Diels). All these fragments are named; in all except the last the evidence is crucial, informed, and highly important. In contrast, in the excerpt on Stoic ethics in Stobaeus, Book 2.7.5–12 (p.57–116 W.), Posidonius is never mentioned. This is hardly surprising. The approach of the two accounts is quite different. In the Physics section (*vid.*, e.g., the fragments in Diels *Dox.Gr.*) Arius is concerned with individual differences of opinion, both between Schools and within Schools. The ethical extract, on the other hand, is a plain, straightforward School summary of "the doctrines of Zeno and the rest of the Stoics" (p. 57.13W.), packed to a great extent with a catalogue of definitions which are common currency. We have the accepted slogans, without the individual interpretation or argument. If it is a common core, "the main points of the fundamental doctrines" (p.57.16W.), it is likely to be basically Chrysippean, which is indeed the impression gained on reading it, seemingly confirmed by the subscript, which mentions only Chrysippus (p. 116.11–18W.).

The question remains whether in this *mélange* of commonly accepted and acceptable Stoic ethical doctrine of the time, there intrudes any sign at all of the individuality of Posidonius, whose work Arius must have known. A good test case would be the section on emotion (*pathos*) (p. 88.8–93.13W.), for it is well known from Galen that Posidonius differed strongly in approach from Chrysippus on this topic. In general (again, as one would expect) the section seems to be rather from Chrysippus' angle than from that of Posidonius, but in two places there seem to me to be curious Posidonian echoes. The first is at p. 89.8, *ekpheromenous kathaper hupo tinos apeithous hippou,* "swept away as if by a disobedient horse," and the second at p. 93.1, the single word *euemptōsia,* "proneness to disease," accompanied by definition and examples. I want to suggest that these are not simply verbal echoes, but derive from peculiarly distinctive Posidonian positions. None of this can be shown from the bleak account of Arius, of course; one must go where the evidence is more ample, embedded in context and accompanied by argument and criticism: Galen, *De placitis*.

In *De plac.* 296.6f DeLacy (F163.18f E.-K.), Galen specifically says that *to euemptōton eis noson* was Posidonius' nomenclature (*houtō gar ōnomasen ho Poseidōnios*); indeed the quotation confirming this is reproduced literally (*kata lexin*) immediately below (F163.27f. E.-K.; 296.14f. DeL.), and also has the noun *euemptōsia* (F163.30 E.-K.), which reappears in another quotation, F164.35 E.-K. No earlier occurrence is known to me. But the expression seems to become current in the 1st c. B.C. Cicero's *proclivitas* (*Tusc.* 4.27-28) may translate it. Philodemus, *De ira* 97.15–18 Wilke has " . . . and so one must accept that the wise man is more prone (*euemptōteron*) than some irrational men to fall into fits of anger. . . ." Galen's phrase is insufficient to conclude that Posidonius coined the term; but we know other examples where Posidonius coined a phrase for a certain context in ethics: e.g., *hē pathētikē holkē*, "the emotional pull" (F169.80, 84 E.-K.); *proendēmein* "to live with beforehand" (F165.28ff E.-K.). The phrase is not Chrysippean, which in itself shows that we are not dealing with a verbal preference, but with a technical label encapsulating critical argument. To substantiate this it is necessary to analyze the argument of F163 E.-K. (*De plac.* 294.32–296.36 DeLacy), of which a translation follows.

> But on the subject of what sort of thing the mind of imperfect men is, both in respect to emotions and before emotions, the accounts (of Chrysippus and the old philosophers) are no longer similar. Chrysippus you see says
> 5   that it is comparable to bodies apt to fall into fevers, attacks of diarrhoea or something else like that, on a small or chance cause. Posidonius criticizes his comparison; the mind of imperfect men, says he, should not be compared to that, but to bodies that are healthy simply; for whether you run a fever
> 10   from big causes or little makes no difference in relation to being affected by it and being brought into an affected state in any way at all; no, bodies differ from each other by falling into disease easily or with difficulty. So he says Chrysippus is not correct in comparing on the one hand the health of the mind with physical health, and on the other comparing the disease of the mind to that condition of the body that falls easily into sickness;
> 15   because the mind of the wise man is immune to affection obviously, but no body can exist immune to disease. No, he said it was more correct to liken the minds of imperfect men "either to physical health with its 'proneness to disease' " (that was Posidonius' nomenclature), "or to disease itself," for he said that it was either a kind of sickly state, or already sick.
>
> 20   But he himself agrees with Chrysippus to the extent of saying that all imperfect men are sick in mind and that their sickness is like the stated conditions of the body.
>
> At least he says the following, to quote him: "For this reason too sickness of mind is not like, as Chrysippus had assumed, that sickly bad condition
> 25   of body by which the body is swept off to fall into random irregular fevers; mental sickness is rather like either physical health with its proneness to disease, or disease itself. For physical disease is a state already sick, whereas Chrysippus' so called disease is more like proneness to fevers."

30   This much I approve of Posidonius in that he says that the minds of imperfect
     men, whenever their condition is apart from emotions, are similar to bodies
     that are healthy, but I do not approve of him giving the name disease to
     conditions of that sort. If he were making a correct comparison he should
35   say that the minds of good men are in similar state to bodies immune to
     disease, whether or not there are any such bodies, for the investigation of
     that question is superfluous to our proposed image; the minds of progressors
     in virtue are like robust bodies, the minds of average men like healthy bodies
     without being robust, those of the majority of imperfect men like bodies
40   sick at a slight cause, minds of men enraged or in a temper or completely
     settled in some emotion like bodies already sick. But you see, I think he is
     careful not to be caught disagreeing with Chrysippus in everything. What
     other explanation could one give for him likening the disease of the mind
45   to the condition *both* of healthy bodies *and* of bodies already sick? Minds
     that are sick were better compared not with both, but with sick bodies only;
     for it is impossible that a single thing, disease of mind, be likened to two
     opposite things, health and sickness at the same time. For if you actually
50   grant that, health too will necessarily be basically similar to disease, if it is
     true that each of the two is like disease of the mind; for things which are
     similar to the same thing are certainly, I imagine, similar also to each other.

In this passage Galen tells us that Posidonius criticized Chrysippus for using the
medical metaphor of sickness and health to illustrate the condition of mind (*psychē*)
of *phauloi*, or imperfect men. Context (298ff. DeLacy; *SVF* 3.471) makes clear
that the background to the controversy over the analogy between mental and physical
health and sickness is related to the *therapeia* or cure of sickness and emotions.
The fragment itself falls into three main sections: (i) 7–20, a report by Galen of
Posidonius' criticism of the analogy, expressed in indirect speech, apart from a
snatch of quotation taken from the second section; (ii) 23–30, a literal quotation
from Posidonius; (iii) 30–52, some criticism from Galen of Posidonius' position.
    Part at least of the passage in Chrysippus which provoked attack is given at *De
plac.* 298.3–7 DeLacy (*SVF* 3.465): "We must suppose that sickness of mind is
very similar to that feverish state of the body in accordance with which fevers and
shivering fits occur not at regular intervals but without any order and at random
from the condition of the body and at the onset of small causes." At least that
sentence is clearly corrected in Posidonius' quotation (23–30), and alluded to in
Galen's introduction (4–6). Galen gives Posidonius two criticisms which are wider
than the quotation at 23–30, and therefore Galen had more of Posidonius before
him: (i) The magnitude, and presumably the chance nature of the external cause is
irrelevant (7–12); this is where Posidonius substituted in the place of the external
cause, *euemptōsia*—proneness to disease (9–11). (ii) The straight analogy of physical and mental health is impossible, because the wise man is absolutely healthy
in mind, and there is no such thing as absolute physical health; so physical health,
which is always prone to disease, if applied at all, would apply to a *phaulos* (12–
18). The conclusion comes in the quotation (23–30): if we talk about *phauloi* being
sick in mind, it is not in the straight physical sense of sickness and health, but

more like saying *phauloi*, or imperfect humans, are *either*, as it were, physically healthy (i.e. *prone* to disease) *or* just sick.

It is at this point (30ff.) that Galen himself becomes a little confused, and while he approves Posidonius' ascription of physical health to the *phaulos*, he accuses him of committing a logical contradiction by likening sickness of soul both to healthy bodies and to sick bodies. Things that are like the same thing, he says rather pedantically, are also like each other. So health would be like disease (33, 43–52). That Galen, who tends to be over-laudatory of Posidonius, criticises him at all is a kind of guarantee of the fidelity of his report. And his misconception actually clarifies Posidonius' position. If the term ''healthy'' is used metaphorically in an absolute sense of the wise man, then all *phauloi*, imperfect men, will be sick. But if, like Chrysippus, an exact analogy is to be made with physical health, then physical health, with its proneness to disease, is inapplicable to the wise or perfect man; all relative degrees of health and sickness relate to *phauloi*. Still—and this is emphasized in Posidonius' use of *ētoi* . . . *ē* (''either . . . or,'' 27f.)—a *phaulos* will not be both ''healthy'' and ''sick'' at the same time. Galen mistakenly applied a modification of the first of Euclid's Common Notions against the man he respected as the most ''geometrical'' of the Stoics (T83, T84E.-K.). Galen's own brief list of equivalences of mental is physical constitutions are in line with his classification of bodily states in *Ars med.* 4 (I. 317 K). The virtuous, the progressors in virtue (*hoi prokoptontes*), average men in the middle (*hoi metrioi*), the majority of *phauloi*, those in a state of emotion (*pathos*), are represented, in order, by immunity to disease, robust constitutions, healthy without being robust, bodies that become ill at a slight cause, sick bodies. This is hardly out of line with what we know of Posidonius, and a similar sort of Stoic progression appears in Seneca, *Ep.*72.6–11.

Posidonius was not quibbling over words. The very nature of the attack against misapplication of the medical metaphor shows that. The interplay of medicine and philosophy in the history of ideas in Greece was both beneficial and harmful to both sides, illustrated from *Ancient Medicine* onwards. The medical analogy, already strong in Plato, became more dominant, perhaps dangerously so, in Hellenistic philosophy and could distort. Posidonius was claiming that Chrysippus' confusion of health and sickness in the inexact application of the analogy confounded two main points, fundamental to Stoic philosophy: First, the absolute distinction between the ideal wise man and everyone else, the *phauloi*, which could not be represented accurately by health and sickness; secondly, a quite different problem, the very complex variation of condition within the range itself of imperfect humans which could not adequately be glossed as sick; and further, that the medical analogy used by Chrysippus actually misled the reader about the cause of moral sickness (i.e. *pathē*) and its cure, because his straight analogy between medicine and philosophy, health and moral sanity, suggested a comparison without qualification between physical and mental cures (Galen, *De plac.* 298.27ff, DeLacy, *SVF* 3.471).

In the first place, *phauloi* are not always sick, i.e. in an emotional state. So how do they become so? It is necessary to know that to effect a cure. From the analogy of disease, Chrysippus' metaphor suggested that it was due to the magnitude of some fortuitous irregular external cause (3–12; *De plac.* 298.5–7 DeLacy). Posidonius not only contests that here, but also strongly in a long excerpt in Galen *De plac.* (264.9ff, DeLacy, F164 E.-K.); although he thinks that Chrysippus' suggestion may follow from his unitary rational psychology, he maintains that it is countered in fact. Posidonius stoutly maintained that the cause of *pathos* and of vice lies within us, and is not external (vid. esp. F169; F35 E.-K.). Hence if we must have a medical metaphor, Posidonius characterizes it by *euemptōsia*, or proneness to disease. Nor can the situation be described simply by Chrysippus' "infirmity" or "weakness" of soul, *arrōstēma* (attacked also in F164 E.-K.), whether this means weakness of judgement (F164.59f. E.-K.), or described in terms of physical tension; because in the first place this is already sickness itself, secondly it is merely descriptive not explanatory, and thirdly, Posidonius cannot understand how "weakness" can be explained in the context of Chrysippus' single rational *hēgemonikon*, or how or why this can vary from one moment to another in an individual.

As is well known, Posidonius' own account of the internal cause is based on his assumption of plurality of *dunameis*, or powers in the soul, irrational as well as rational (F142–146, F31, F34, F169 E.-K.). It is precisely because the irrational *dunameis* have their own natural goals (*oikeiōseis*) and impulses (*hormai*) that we are by nature *euemptōtoi* to disease, through being liable to think mistakenly that relative goals are absolute (Frs. 158–162 E.-K.). Posidonius sees such false opinions (*pseudeis doxai*) as triggering off an impulse (*hormē*) of an irrational mental power (*dunamis*) to go too far (*pleonazousa*, the normal Stoic definition of *pathos*), which by its emotional pull (*pathētikē holkē*, a phrase coined by Posidonius, F169.91 E.-K.) countermands reason to demand an assent (*sunkatathesis*) and so affects a *krisis* or decision for a particular act (F169.78–84 E.-K.).

Now this leads us back to the first of two phrases from Arius mentioned earlier in this paper—namely, Stob.2, p. 89.7–9: "those in emotional states . . . carried away by the intensity as if by a disobedient horse" (*ekpheromenous kathaper hupo tinos apeithous hippou*). That is without doubt Posidonius' simile, for he used, with suitable Stoic modifications, the charioteer-and-two-horses simile of the soul from Pl. *Phdr.* 246a6ff (vid. F31.16–29 E.-K.). So his picture of the "going too far" (*pleonazousa*) aspect of the impulse (*hormē*) of emotion (*pathos*) (F166.11ff E.-K.) is that of a runaway horse (*ekphoros*) (F166.11,16; F31.22 E.-K.) disobediently (*duspeithōn*) (F31.22 E.-K.) carrying off its rider, reason, by force until brought under control (F166.10,13; *cf.* F165.139, F31.19 E.-K.). Chrysippus' image was different: that of runners carried on beyond the point they wish to stop (*De plac.* 240.35ff. DeLacy), an image again clearly suited to Chrysippus' monolithic psychology. It is explicitly attacked as Chrysippean by both Galen and Posidonius. Galen (*De. plac.* 244.14ff. DeLacy) argued that Chrysippus' image did not help him, for it already implied a duality between the rational and the irrational.

What carried the runner on after he wished to stop was the weight (*baros*) of the body. Posidonius (F34.15ff E.-K.) objected that reason could not be the cause of going too far, because reason (*logos*) itself cannot exceed (*pleonazein*) its own acts and measures.

All this lies behind Posidonius' proneness (*euemptōsia*) as propensity for ("easily swept down to") emotion (*eukataphoria eis pathos*, Stob. 2 p.93.1). The instances to which we are prone, as singled out by Arius, are interesting: vexation or grief (*epilupia*), irascibility (*orgilotēs*), enviousness (*phthoneria*), boiling temper (*akrocholia*), and the like. Of these terms, *akrocholia* and *orgiloi* are paired in Plato, *Rep.* 411c1 in a theory of natural and developed tendencies to anger and bad temper. The same pair of terms are analysed in Aristotle *EN* 1126a18f. The other two terms also have preechoes in *EN* and *MM*. For the term *eukataphoria* (propensity, "easily swept down to") compare Arist. *E.N.* 1109a14ff: "For instance we ourselves have rather a natural relationship towards pleasure, and so we are more easily carried down (away) (*eukataphorōteroi*) to intemperance than to moral discipline." Now Chrysippus was criticized for ignoring "the old philosophers" (*hoi palaioi*), by which Plato and Aristotle are usually meant, while Posidonius kept returning to them and referring to them (e.g. T101, T102, F34, F157 E-K.). Posidonius may have thought that he saw the seeds of *euemptōsia* in Plato and Aristotle.

There remains perhaps the most important aspect for Posidonius against Chrysippus in the medical metaphor, because the context of the analogy in Galen is geared to the cure of mental disturbance (*therapeia* and *iasis*). Chrysippus was blamed for being unable to explain how one can heal *pathē* when they occur, or prevent them from occurring (*cf. De plac.* 312.22–316.20 DeLacy; F167 E.-K.). Posidonius believed that his own emended medical analogy showed the way. For the *phaulos* healthy but prone to disease was in a different state from the *phaulos* when sick, and therefore at least two treatments different in kind were necessary. When sane, the *phaulos* was governed by the rational, but when carried away by sick emotion he was governed by the irrational; but "the irrational is helped and harmed by the irrational, the rational by knowledge and ignorance" (F168.16f; *cf.* F31.1–29, F169 *fin.*, F165, F164 E.-K.). So in his saner moments the *phaulos* is instructed in the *logos* philosophy and Stoic physics (e.g., F169.114f. E.-K.), and also no doubt by precepts and the *admonitio pars* of philosophy (F176 E.-K.); but when emotionally sick the method used is by habituation and training (F169.115ff.; F168; F166 E.-K.). Above all, the cure cannot be related to some external cause and the magnitude of its impression (F164 E.-K.). The cause is within us (F169 E.-K.). The inner reaction is more important than the outward experience. Our "proneness" requires study, both in general as a natural human condition, and also specifically as types and individuals. That is why Posidonius linked to this the investigation of *physiognōmonia* (F169.84ff. E.-K.).

The detailed investigation of all this is another story. It is time to return to Arius. If *euemptōsia* is Posidonian as it certainly is in the context of *pathos*, then it has crept into doxography by the first century B.C. The distinction between proneness to disease (*euemptōsia*) and disease (*nosos*) passes into general discussion at the same time, as in Philodemus and Cicero; but Cicero is talking only specifically of types with no trace of the deeper Posidonian arguments (*Tusc.* 4.27–28). In the doxographies (also in D.L. 7.115) *euemptōsia* becomes simply another technical term without Posidonian coloring. This is not unexpected. It is the physical doxographies, both in Arius and Diogenes Laertius which are strongly tinted with Posidonian idiosyncracy. The ethical extracts embody the common definitions which Posidonius also accepted. They are not the place for the individual arguments and interpretations. If so, *euemptōsia* has simply been accepted technically defined, drained of controversy. But the really odd, out-of-place phrase in Arius is that horse, the *apeithous hippou,* which can belong to no one but Posidonius. I do not know how it got there.

Comments on Professor Kidd's Paper

Phillip H. De Lacy

Professor Kidd's identification of Posidonian elements in Arius' account of Stoic ethics is persuasive. The case for *euemptōsia* (p.93.1 W.) is perhaps not so strong as that for the disobedient horse (p. 89.9), since, as he points out, the word *euemptōsia* had got into the doxographical tradition by the first century B.C. and the peculiarly Posidonian psychology associated with the term in Galen's account is nowhere explicit in Arius. But the simile of the disobedient horse is a clear vestige of Posidonian revisionism, and its presence in Stobaeus gives support to the supposition that *euemptōsia* is also Posidonian.

We are left, then, with Professor Kidd's concluding remark: "I don't know how it got there." Nor do I; but perhaps some reflections on the nature of Arius' account and on the Stoic background will make the presence of these Posidonian elements less perplexing.

I would suggest that the summary of Stoic ethics preserved by Stobaeus and generally assigned to Arius was compiled by a non-Stoic with the help of a Stoic informant. The compiler is commendably impartial, except perhaps at p.65.5–6, where he comments, "Accordingly they say also that prudence is prudent, for that way of speaking follows from their views." Again on p. 66.3–6 he includes among the Stoic virtues the science of conducting drinking parties. It appears that in these passages the Stoic informant was pressed to admit to positions that the compiler found amusing or absurd.

A conspicuous feature of the summary is the presentation of Stoic ethical concepts with relatively little attention to the theory behind them. There is a brief mention, introduced almost parenthetically, of the nature of the soul and of the doctrine that virtues are living things (p. 64.18–65.4), but the more extended review of psychological concepts is found in paragraphs that follow paratactically after the section on virtues and vices. The treatment of *pathos* is a case in point. For Chrysippus and for Posidonius the *pathē* are of central importance in ethical doctrine. Chrysippus wrote a treatise in four books on the *pathē,* and he held that it is *pathos* that causes us to reject the guidance of *logos* (SVF 3 pp. 94.44–95.13). Posidonius, while rejecting Chrysippus' view of the nature of the *pathē,* yet agrees with him about their importance: "In my view," he says, "the examination of things good and evil, of ends, and of virtues depends on a genuine examination of the *pathē* (F30.3–

5 E.K.), and "Not only those who have a vice that has gone to extremes and who, being in a slippery state, fall easily into affections, but all unwise men, so long as they have their vice, fall into affections both great and small" (F164.34–7 E.-K.).

By contrast, the word *pathos* does not even occur in the Stobaean account until p. 77.14, a third of the way through, and even there the epitomator's only concern is to point out a difference between *pathē*, 'affections,' and *kakiai*, 'vices.' In earlier passages *lupē*, 'distress,' and *phobos*, 'fear,' are mentioned (cf. pp. 58.17–18, 69.8–10, 72.9–11), but again only as differing from the vices. The fuller discussion of the *pathē* is on pages 88–93, and even here emphasis is placed on the difference between the irrationality of *pathos* and the irrationality of error (p. 89.4–90.6). Here and elsewhere in the account it is made quite clear that one may be irrational, and hence wretched, without experiencing a *pathos*, and indeed that it is the irrationality of vice rather than of *pathos* that causes unhappiness (cf. p. 69.6–10, 72.9–13).

What is noteworthy here is not the distinction between two kinds of irrationality—Chrysippus and Posidonius had recognized that there is more than one way to depart from right reason—but the emphasis on the vices at the expense of the *pathē*. Whether this emphasis results from the interests of the compiler or of his Stoic informant is not possible to say; but its significance for the problem before us is that it permitted the informant to avoid the controversy within the school about the nature of the *pathē* and thus to use both Chrysippean and Posidonian material without concerning himself with doctrinal differences.

Here it is relevant also to point out that it must have been much easier for a post-Posidonian Stoic to live with the differences between Posidonius and Chrysippus than would appear from Galen's anti-Chrysippean polemic. For one thing, Chrysippus presented his own teachings with remarkable restraint, as if he were expecting, even inviting, further discussion. Consider for example his use of the term *eulogon*, 'reasonable.' This term is appropriate for a Stoic, since it suggests conformity to *logos*, 'reason,' and *logos* has a very high position indeed in the Stoic scheme of things. But *eulogon* was also the term that Arcesilaus, the Academic skeptic, had used of a choice between alternatives when the alternatives themselves are matters on which one suspends judgment; cf. Robin *Pyrrhon et le scepticisme grec* (Paris 1944) pp. 61–64, and Sandbach *The Stoics* (London, 1975) p. 47. Chrysippus, presumably, defended Stoicism against Academic attack, so his use of the term *eulogon* has added significance. It suggests to a reader that in certain areas he is willing to suspend judgment; he may incline toward a view without firm commitment to it. Thus Chrysippus says that it is *eulogon* that the part of the soul to which meanings go and from which discourse comes is the ruling part (*SVF* 2 p. 244.9; cf. also p. 250.27). Since anger arises in the chest, it is *eulogon* that the other desires are there also (*SVF* 2 p. 241.2). In one passage we find the sequence, "One might inquire . . . it seems to me . . . it is *eulogon*" (*SVF* 3 p. 117.20, 26, 34). There is a tentative note also in Chrysippus' reflections on the nervous system, then a recent discovery: "Let us look into the matter," he says, and he qualifies the statement of his opinion with *schedon*, "surely" (*SVF* 2 p.246.39). The very use of *zētein*, inquire, and its compounds might be enough to remind the contemporary reader that one of the names for Pyrrhonic skeptics was zetetics, inquirers (Diog. Laer. 9.69).

Chrysippus' verbal restraint gave license to his followers to modify or reject his teaching without incurring the charge of parricide. The temptation must have been especially strong in the case of the Chrysippean theory of the soul. Galen has preserved for us a paragraph from Chrysippus' *De anima*, in which Chrysippus notes the disagreement among physicians and philosophers about the location of the soul's ruling part and mentions briefly Plato's view of the tripartite soul (*SVF* 2 pp. 238–39). Galen makes much of the fact that Chrysippus made no attempt to refute Plato's arguments but simply proceeded with his own inquiry (*zētēsomen*, *SVF* 2 p. 239.32). Whatever inferences we may wish to draw from this about Chrysippus' attitude toward Plato, it would seem that a follower of Chrysippus could easily take the non-refutation of Plato as an indication that the question of the nature of the soul has not yet been fully answered, and further inquiry is in order. Posidonius' further inquiries, then, could be viewed as quite proper responses to the spirit of inquiry that Chrysippus himself appeared to foster.

Finally, the differences between Posidonius and Chrysippus that Professor Kidd has pointed to in his paper are real enough, but they are somewhat disguised on the verbal level by the fact that Posidonius could still remain fairly close to Chrysippus' language. In "swept away as if by a disobedient horse" the word for "swept away", *ekpheresthai*, had been used by Chrysippus to describe persons affected by *pathos* (cf. *SVF* 3 pp. 127.4, 128.22, 130.9), and "disobedient to reason" also appears in Chrysippus' discussion of the *pathē* (*SVF* 3, pp. 113.24, 27; 126.28). The introduction of the horse thus appears to be no more than a modification of Chrysippean doctrine.

It is the same with "proneness to disease", *euemptōsia*. In his development of the analogy betwen health/disease of body and health/disease of soul, Chrysippus is characteristically undogmatic. He notes that in ordinary linguistic usage such terms as strong and weak, firm and soft, well and ill are used of both soul and body, and so, he says, there must be physicians of the soul as there are of the body. And as disease of the body is said to be a lack of balance in its constituents, so it will be said that disease of soul is a lack of balance in its parts. Zeno was right to compare disease of soul to an unsettled state of the body (*SVF* 3 pp. 120–21). In such an unsettled state of the body a slight cause will bring on fevers and chills (*SVF* 3 p. 117.1–4), and the ordinary person whose soul lacks strength will in many situations act shamefully (*SVF* 3 p. 123.28–33). One of the terms that Chrysippus uses for this abandonment of right action is *ekpiptein* (*SVF* 3 p. 130.22). Posidonius' criticisms of this Chrysippean scheme have been well stated in Professor Kidd's paper, but again, on the verbal level, Posidonius' term, *euemptōsia*, "easily falling," seems entirely appropriate to the condition of the ordinary soul as Chrysippus had portrayed it, and indeed Galen uses the terms *empiptein* and *euemptōtos* in his own restatements of Chrysippus' views (*De plac.* pp. 294.35 and 308.6).

In view of all this, the unheralded introduction of Posidonian doctrines and terms into an account of Stoic ethics that appears to be primarily Chrysippean is not surprising. It would be less surprising in a Stoic than a non-Stoic, since an outsider looking at Stoicism would be likely to make note of the disagreements within the school, whereas a Stoic informant presenting the doctrine to an outsider would avoid drawing attention to doctrinal differences. It took the sharp eyes of Professor Kidd to discover them in the Stobaean summary.

PART III
Papers on Arius' Treatment of Peripatetic Ethics

CHAPTER 7

Peripatetic Definitions of Happiness

Pamela M. Huby

The Peripatetic definitions of happiness which I wish to discuss occur in groups in Stobaeus' collection of ethical material.[1] These groups overlap, and each is surrounded by other matter which is relevant to our understanding of them. Many of the definitions come directly from Aristotle, but others differ from him in emphasis and expression, and may be supposed to originate with some of his successors. Further, between the originators of the definitions and the final putting together of the material by Ioannes Stobaeus nearly a millenium later, a number of other writers seem to have played a part and it is not an easy matter to disentangle their contributions. On many points certainty cannot be reached, but I hope at least to make some progress in understanding what the problems are.

In this volume it is appropriate to begin with Arius Didymus. It is now generally agreed that the Peripatetic epitome (p.116.19–152.25) is his work, though the possibility of later additions and rewriting must remain open. More problematic is the ethical "prolegomena," (p.37.15–57.12). The majority opinion seems to be that this too is the work of Arius, but Anthony Kenny has recently argued[2] that at least a part may be by Stobaeus himself, and, in particular, has suggested that the passage containing the set of definitions of happiness (p.50.11–51.17) was added by him, because it contains discrepancies from the other main set of definitions in the epitome. P. Moraux[3] on the other hand, accepted the view that Arius used two inconsistent sources.

This seems to me more probable. For there are in our material vivid traces of a character who can hardly be Stobaeus, but who can plausibly be identified with Arius. The prolegomena contains a section on the Division of Ethics (p.39.19–45.6) in which the author begins with Philo of Larisa's account of this division. He then goes on (p.41.26–42.6) in effect: "If I had been an idle fellow I would have been content with giving Philo's account, but since I consider it proper to myself to inquire first into the substance of whatever I am dealing with, then its quality and quantity, and after that its relations, I think I ought to consider the views of others too—not all, but the most outstanding." What he does is to give a puff for a work by Eudorus of Alexandria, the Academic—"a book worth having"—and quote at length from it, and that is all. Not one other "outstanding philosopher" is mentioned, and he goes straight on to individual topics. Unless

121

Stobaeus has left out a great deal, this is a bit of a joke. He really does seem to be an idle fellow, content to copy from just two books. Surely he could have done better. And what is the point of all this stuff about substance and quality and quantity and relation?[4] Is this the style of Augustus' court philosopher?

A clue to the date of the passage is given by the philosophers quoted. Philo of Larisa was the teacher of Cicero, and belongs to the first half of the first century B.C., and Eudorus was an almost exact contemporary of Arius, and they must have been in Alexandria together.[5] It seems then an acceptable view that the author of this section, and of at least the greater part of the prolegomena, is Arius.

I draw two conclusions: First, if Stobaeus bothered to copy out this personal passage, which has no philosophical importance, he cannot have been working very hard at excerpting, and may be supposed to be following his original in a straightforward way. Secondly, the man who wrote this passage originally is not likely to have been disturbed by discrepancies among his sources, so that I cannot agree with Kenny that such discrepancies indicate the hand of Stobaeus rather than Arius.

Before proceeding to the other writers who may be involved, I want to look at the definitions themselves. In the prolegomena there are three definitions of happiness, preceded by a closely related definition of *telos* (the goal of life): in the epitome there is an account of the "material" of happiness, followed by three definitions of happiness and three of *telos*. These sets of definitions are interrelated, and we must also bring in another short section of the epitome, Aristotle's two *Ethics*, his *Politics* and the *Magna Moralia*.

I will translate the relevant passages and number the definitions for future reference:

A (p.50.11–51.1 and 51.8–16)

> A1 Aristotle says that it (the *telos*) is the use of complete virtue in *prohē-goumenois*. "Use" is more than possession, for he wants happiness to be activity, and the goal . . .[6]

It is possible to define happiness in a number of ways according to him:

> A2 Activity in accordance with complete virtue in a complete life *prohē-goumenē*,

> A3 A noble (*kalos*) and complete life *prohēgoumenos*,

and, the clearest of all,

> A4 The use of complete virtue in a complete life *prohēgoumenē*.[7]

He says "a complete life" with respect to the duration (*diastasin*) of the use of good things, *prohēgoumenē* for the purpose of the use being among good things and not bad. This, then, is the *telos*.

B (p.130.15–21 and p.131.2–6)

The good is divided into the beautiful, the useful, and the pleasant: these are the targets of particular actions. But what comes from them all is happiness. Happiness is:

> Bi1 The use of complete virtue in a complete life *prohēgoumenē*, (or)
>
> Bi2 The activity of a complete life (here *zōē*, elsewhere *bios*) in accordance with virtue, (or)
>
> Bi3 The unimpeded use of virtue in things according to nature (*en tois kata physin*)
> But the same thing is also the *telos*. . . . .

We must follow the custom of the ancients and say that the *telos* is:

> Bii1 That for which we do everything, but which itself we do for nothing, (or)
> Bii2 The last of things desired, (or)
>
> Bii3 To live in accordance with virtue among goods both of the body and external, either all, or the majority and those most properly so-called. . . .

Of these, Bi2 is identical with *EE* 2.1 1219a39, except that the latter adds "complete" a second time—"the activity of a complete life in accordance with *complete* virtue."[8] Bi1 is found almost word-for-word at *Metaph.* 2.2 994b9–16, though in a metaphysical context where the idea of human action is absent. But it also occurs at *EN* 1.1 1094a18, and although there it is put hypothetically—"If there is any *telos* of the things we do . . ."—it is clear that Aristotle believes that there is such a *telos*.[9] Bii2 seems also to be derived from Aristotle. I do not think that he ever put it exactly this way, but it seems almost an accident that he did not.[10]

These three definitions are closely connected with Aristotle. The remainder contain elements that seem foreign to him. First let us look at the word *chrēsis*, "use," which appears several times. In Bi1 (which is identical with A4), Bi3, and A1, happiness (or in A1 the *telos*) is defined as the *use* of virtue. John Dillon has connected this emphasis on use with Cicero's teacher Antiochus of Ascalon, suggesting that he wanted to give ethics a practical slant.[11] Kenny[12] on the other hand, thinks that in Aristotle's works themselves there is a difference, and that there is a greater stress on *use* in the *EE* than in the *EN*. If so, the definitions could be much earlier than Antiochus.

Let us look at some facts: It seems to me that the *EN* and the *EE* are more similar than Kenny suggests, and that neither lays much stress on *use*. It is present in *EN* 1.8 1098b32, where the pair "possession or use" is followed by "state or activity," both referring to virtue and both marking the same contrast between having and using. Again, at *EN* 10.9 1179b3 Aristotle says that it is not enough to know about virtue; one must try to have and *use* it. The *EE* is not much better: at 2.1 1219b2, which immediately follows the definition of happiness quoted above as being similar to our Bi2, Aristotle defends his definition with reference to common opinions: "To fare well and to live well are the same as to be happy, each of which is use and activity," which contains the same close connection between use and activity as the *EN*. It is true that the *EE* refers to use in connection with a variety of things, and that there is a long discussion of it at the beginning of Book 8, which is in many respects a very strange book, but the idea that happiness is to be *defined* as the use of virtue is as foreign to the *EE* as it is to the *EN*.

It is therefore a little surprising to find that Aristotle himself says at *Politics* 7.13 1332a7–10 that he has defined happiness "in the *Ethics*" as "complete activity *and use* of virtue," because that is not so.[13] The nearest we get to such an expression is *MM* 1.4.3 1184b32–36: "Happiness then would be in some use and activity. For, for those things which have a state (*hexis*) and a use, use and activity are the *telos*."[14] The simplest explanation of all this seems to be that in all these works Aristotle treats "use" in this type of context, as almost a synonym for "activity." Thus at *EE* 2.1 1219a13 he distinguishes two kinds of *ergon*, *products* and *uses*, but then returns to speaking of *activity* of soul rather than *use* of soul. This would explain his casual use of "use" in his reference back to "the *Ethics*" in the *Politics*; it was the way he thought of the matter, and neither term was of fundamental importance to him. I conclude that for him "use" was an unemphatic term, marking the contrast with "possession," but not meaning more than that.

Michael Rohr has suggested in discussion that the terms "use" and "activity" are not interchangeable. This is certainly correct, for the noun attached to "use" will normally be the *object* which is used, while that attached to "activity" is normally the *subject* which carries out the activity. But the fact remains that Aristotle does use them casually in the examples I have given and was, I suggest, more interested in the similarities than in the differences. This is supported by the example I gave from the *Politics* where it seems naturally to take virtue as qualifying both *use* and *activity*.

If Aristotle's use of this word was unemphatic, it is legitimate to ask why it is so prominent in the definitions we are now discussing. John Dillon, in associating it with Antiochus of Ascalon, relies on Cicero, *Academici libri* 1.22–3, where Antiochus is credited with the view that both Academics and Peripatetics held that happiness lies in virtue, but that it needs, in addition, goods suitable for the employment of virtue (*ad virtutis usum idonea*, 1.22). Dillon suggests that Antiochus wanted virtue used positively in political life, and implies that he seized on the word *chrēsis* in Aristotle, and gave it a more emphatic meaning than it originally had.

Some caution is necessary here. The detailed steps of the argument are: In the course of setting out views supposed to be derived from Plato, Cicero says that the third element required for living well, after body and mind, is life, and that calls for adjuncts which are available for the *use* of virtue (1.21). He then turns particularly to the Peripatetics, saying that *vita beata* depends on virtue alone, but to be *beatissima* it needs also goods of the body and other things appropriate to the use of virtue. Now even if we grant that all this is Antiochus' novel interpretation of his predecessors, it does not seem to me that there is any great stress on a *positive* use of virtue, as distinct from the mere exercising of it, which is opposed, as in Aristotle, to simple possession. It also seems to me that this may itself be an interpretation of earlier discussions of *chrēsis*. I would therefore hesitate to accept the view that the actual definitions originated with Antiochus.[15]

To complete this discussion of "use," I must shortly refer to another possible player in the drama. It seems desirable to separate the definitions themselves from the comments on one of them, A4, which follow them at p.50.12–13. Here someone says: "Use is (finite verb) more than possession. For he (Aristotle) wants happiness to be activity." He immediately goes on to discuss other terms and seems, like Aristotle, to treat "use" as an unemphatic term. But we need not treat him as evidence for the intention of whoever it was who first formulated the definitions.

A final small puzzle is from Aristotle himself. In the book on justice he applies "the use of complete virtue" not to happiness but to justice (*EN* 5.1 1129b31). This is justice in its wider sense, which is equated with virtue as a whole. Here he stresses that virtue may be a mere *hexis*, or exercised only with regard to oneself, but justice is essentially related to other people. It might be said that here the notion of use is stressed, but there seems to be no connection between this passage and those later ones which connect the use of virtue with *happiness*. There remains a gap in our knowledge of later developments.

The other major notion that is absent or unemphatic in Aristotle is that expressed by *prohēgoumenē* or *en prohēgoumenois*. This is found in all four definitions in A, and in Bi1. It also occurs in the section preceding that where the B group is found, where it is said that "happiness arises from noble and *prohēgoumenōn* actions" (p.129.19–20), and a little further back again, "happiness is an activity in accordance with virtue in actions *prohēgoumenois* as one could wish" (p.126.19–20).

First, a textual matter. In practically every case, Wachsmuth saw fit to change *prohēgoumenē*, etc. into *khorēgoumenē*, etc. This is presumably a compromise. The form used by Aristotle in the relevant passages is *kekhorēgēmenos*, but the change from this to *prohēgoumenos*, etc. would have been difficult to account for palaeographically. Wachsmuth seems to be assuming that some Peripatetic took the step of substituting *khorēgoumenos* for *kekhorēgēmenos, passim*, and that a copyist then, also *passim*, wrote *prohēgoumenos*.[16] This is an unlikely story, though it might be acceptable if the word *prohēgoumenos* were completely unknown in this kind of context, or, alternatively, if it were so well known that it might naturally be substituted in error. Neither of these alternatives seems to me to be the case. In particular, the expression *en prohēgoumenois* is found elsewhere in connection with happiness. Alexander of Aphrodisias *Quaestiones* 4 (Ethical Problems) 25 (p.148.30–

4 Bruns) defines happiness as "an activity, in accordance with virtue, of the rational soul,"—with the addition of "in a complete life" and "*en prohēgoumenois*"— and Aspasius (*Comm. on Nicomachean Ethics* p.151.11 Heylbut) discussing 1153b8– 17, where Aristotle almost identifies pleasure and happiness, says: "If some activities of each *hexis* are unimpeded, like those of the best, when they occur *en prohēgoumenois* and chosen, with nothing impeding them. . ." These examples alone are sufficient to justify us in keeping *en prohēgoumenois* in Stobaeus.

The meaning of this and related expressions is, however, far from clear. It is not in fact found in Aristotle, though in several places it is attributed to him either implicitly or explicitly.[17] It appears in later works as an expression that is familiar enough to need no explanation, and we have no material that helps us to discover its origin. There are however several passages in which the context seems to give it a fairly clear meaning. First, pseudo-Alexander, *Mantissa* 160.31–161.3, in the section headed "That virtue is not sufficient for happiness," says, "Again since the activity connected with each skill is twofold, the one *en prohēgoumenois,* as in the case of the piper, if he is healthy in body, and has the pipes of his choice and nothing external troubles him, the other in circumstances he does not want, and the opposite of what we described before, just as in other skills the goal is in activities connected with what is wanted and *prohēgoumenais,* so with virtue, if at least that is a skill."

The first part of this seems almost to amount to a definition of *en prohēgoumenois*: it appears to mean "in favourable circumstances." If we take the text as it stands, the following expression, "in *prohēgoumenais* activities," must be taken as something like "in unhampered activities," bringing us near to Aristotle's "unimpeded." I would suggest, however, that perhaps we should read *en prohēgoumenois* which would indeed produce a better text, "*en tais peri ta boulēta kai en prohēgoumenois energeiais,*" and translate it as "activities in favourable circumstances," then having exactly the same usage as the one a few lines earlier.

A difficulty arises, however, if we turn to Aspasius. For in his commentary on the *EN* he uses various forms of this word, and another interpretation must be considered, namely the notion of what is most proper or important in a certain connection. Thus, at 3.7 the healing art *prohēgoumenōs* chooses health, and is related to disease only by having knowledge of it; at 52.34 the *prohēgoumenē* activity of the liberal man is giving, although he is also concerned with receiving (cf.96.14) and, similarly, at 98.8 the *prohēgoumenon ergon* of the liberal man is correct giving, and it is this by which he is defined (*eidopoieitai*); at 96.35 we most properly (*prohēgoumenōs*) say that *a man* uses something, though we can also say the soul uses it, and even virtue and vice; at 97.16 these things are called useful which the good man would use *prohēgoumenōs* (cf.97.29–30).

I note in particular that *prohēgoumenē* activity at 52.34 is the *proper* and *special activity* of the liberal man. On this view the plural of this, in *prohēgoumenais* activities, which is in Alexander's text above, should perhaps be kept, and could perhaps mean "activities proper to whatever it is that is engaged in them." This would certainly cover another example from Aspasius (30.11): How can a man be happy in great sorrows and hindered *epi tas prohēgoumenas energeias* (in doing his proper activities)?

We should therefore consider this as an alternative way of interpreting our definitions so that the notion involved would be that of living a life proper to man. In this case *prohēgoumenos* would introduce something new and not be a mere replacement for the two Aristotelian notions of "unimpeded" and "well-supplied."[18]

We cannot get much help from the comments on the definitions found in Stobaeus if they are, as I have suggested, quite independent of them. As comment on A2 and A4 we have: "(He says) '*prohēgoumenēn*', because the use (of virtue) occurs in good things . . .not in bad" (p.51.14–15); and, in the epitome: "The activity of virtue is *prohēgoumenē* because it is absolutely necessary for it to exist in things by nature good, since the good man would use virtue nobly even in bad (things), but he will not be blessed. . ."[19] (p.132.8–11). This, as it stands, is obscure, but seems to reflect the same line of thought as Alexander.

A further difficulty with this second passage, is that the words "activity of virtue is *prohēgoumenē*" are not in fact to be found in the set of definitions B, and the passage itself immediately follows the discussion of Bi1 in which happiness is defined as *use,* not activity, and the expression *en prohēgoumenois,* not *prohēgoumenē,* occurs. The only definition which exactly fits this discussion is A2. Since Bi1 is identical with A1, this section seems more like a comment on A than on B. This point confirms the close connection between A and B, and also the independence of the commentary.

The passage on the materials of happiness (p.129.19–130.12) needs separate discussion:

> Happiness arises from noble and *prohēgoumenōn* actions; hence it is noble overall (*di' holōn*), just as the activity of a player on the pipes is artistic overall. For it is not the employment of the materials of pure nobility that produces happiness, just as it is not the use of the instruments of medicine that produces the overall skilled activity of a doctor. Every action is some activity of the soul. Since he who acts uses some (actions) as means to the completion of his project, we must not regard these as parts of the activity, although each of the aforesaid requires the other, not however as a part, but as productive of the skill. For it is not correct to call those things without which it is impossible to do something, *parts* of the activity. For we must consider the part as being that which helps to complete the whole, but the things without which it cannot be done as that which brings it about, by bringing and cooperating towards the end.

p.130.1

.5

.10

This needs many comments. First, the text itself is uncertain: Trendelenburg thought there was a lacuna in the first sentence, before "just as"; the word I have translated "materials"—*hylikōn* (p.130.1)—is probably correct, but *holikōn* is an alternative reading; in addition, the word *arkhōn* (elements) is inserted after it in one branch of the tradition. These are only a selection of the textual variants. Further, the passage is made more difficult by having, for the most part, been put into *oratio obliqua*. This means that in the sentence translated "For. . . .doctor" (p.129.22–130.3), both subject and object occur in the accusative, so that it is not possible to tell which is which from its grammatical form. I postulate that we have here a chiastic construction, which would have been perfectly clear in the original *oratio recta*, but is by no means clear here.

One way of taking this is to say that we may only speak of happiness at a certain level of activity. There is a hierarchy of activities—a point already made by Aristotle himself (*EN* 1094a10ff.)—and it is only appropriate to speak of *happiness* at the highest level. Analogous cases are the level of activity which may be spoken of as, e.g., practicing medicine, as opposed to actions, like using a knife, and the making of music as opposed to playing individual notes. This is quite a sophisticated point, reminiscent of what Ryle called a category-distinction. So possibly in this case the word *prohēgoumenos* is used to describe actions that are at the highest level—those which can appropriately be described by terms like "making music," "practicing medicine" and the like.

Possibly the lines at p.130.15–18 are relevant here: "Good is divided into noble, expedient and pleasant,[20] and these are the targets of particular actions. But what arises from them all together is happiness." We may see this passage as implying that individual actions at a lower level than that appropriate to happiness may be described as noble, as expedient, or pleasant, and therefore good, but at the higher level they are all good in the sense of contributing to happiness.

Our passage continues (p. 130.4–8) with a distinction between tools and parts, which occupied philosophical thought for centuries. One major controversy in which it figured was that between Stoics and Peripatetics about how logic was related to philosophy, the Stoics saying that it was a part, the Peripatetics only a tool, of philosophy.[21] (This was not merely a verbal matter; the Peripatetics limited logic to what was useful in actual argument and proof, whereas the Stoics felt free to indulge in "pure" logic.) Many different arguments were deployed on this issue. The one relevant here was used by Alexander of Aphrodisias in the opening pages of his commentary on the *Prior Analytics* (2.20ff.): he is developing the point that some things can be both products *and* tools. Thus a hammer can be both the product and the tool of the blacksmith's art, and, generalizing, he says: "If some things connected with the same science or art have this relationship (*taxin*) to one another, the one of them will be the tool, the other the product for which the rest is done, and a part (*prohēgoumenon ergon te kai meros*)."

The next sentence in Arius Didymus (p.130.8–9) reflects a remark of Aristotle (*EE* 1214b26–27) that "some people" call the things which are *sine qua non* of happiness, "parts", a view which Aristotle himself seems to reject.

To clarify all this I think we must suppose that two kinds of tools are envisaged: on the one hand, objects, e.g., hammers or riches; on the other, actions. In some cases we can classify things and actions thus: The rider uses the reins as his tools, but the actions of the maker of the reins are also to be seen as tools. In other cases only one man is concerned, and he uses some of his actions as tools to produce others, e.g., the doctor uses his skill in mixing potions to treat his patient.

I am uncertain about the extent to which this distinction between actions as tools and actions as parts can be applied generally, but in any case we are left with the point that there are some other actions (or activities) which stand to these either as wholes to parts or as master-activities to slave-activities, and it is these which are *prohēgoumenoi*.

If this view is correct, we have here a use of *prohēgoumenos* which is clearly different from those discussed earlier.[22]

To complete the picture we must look at the Stoics. The most prominent Stoic term here is *proēgmenon* (preferred). But it has been argued that this is the passive term to which *prohēgoumenon* is related as the active. Arius Didymus (p.84.23) says that Zeno himself introduced *proēgmena* and *apoproēgmena,* and adds that "they" call *proēgmenon* that which, being indifferent, we choose according to *prohēgoumenos logos* (guiding reason, or principle).[23] The plural, "they say," however, takes us away from Zeno to Stoics in general, and a further difficulty is that the term *prohēgoumenon* is very rare among the fragments of the earlier Stoics.[24] It has alternatively been suggested that the term was taken over by the Stoics from the Peripatetics at a comparatively later date. In any case, most Stoic uses are either irrelevant or as difficult to interpret as the Peripatetic ones.[25]

Let us now turn to the definition of happiness Bi3. This brings in two new notions, "unimpeded" and "in natural matters." "Unimpeded" goes straight back to Aristotle. In him it is primarily associated with pleasure (*EN* 7.12 1153a15) but it is also connected with happiness at 1153b9–13: "But perhaps it is necessary, if there are unimpeded activities of every *hexis*, whether happiness is the activity of all or of some one of them, if it is unimpeded, that it is what should above all be chosen." And in the *Politics* (4.111295a36) Aristotle again claims to have said "in the *Ethics*" that the happy life is the unimpeded life in accordance with virtue.

The notion of *ta kata physin* (things in accordance with nature) is, however, not so prominent in Aristotle, though we do find, in the passage on pleasure mentioned above (1153a14), "pleasure is the unimpeded activity of the natural *(kata physin) hexis.*" It does however have a long history. Speusippus (fr.57 Lang, from Clement of Alexandria) said that happiness was a perfect *hexis en tois kata physin ekhousin* (in things according to nature), and Theophrastus, according to a scholion on Plato's *Laws* 631C, said that everything desires *tēs kata physin diatheseōs* (its natural state). Finally, Antiochus, if it is his view at Cicero, *Academici libri* 1.22–23, lays great stress on nature: the goal (*bonorum finis*) was to obtain *quae essent prima natura* (1.22).

These notions, then, have a respectable Peripatetic and Academic pedigree. But *ta kata physin* was also an important expression for the Stoics, and it might therefore be seen as an element which the Peripatetics took over from the Stoics. Thus at Stobaeus p.119.15–18, in Arius Didymus' Peripatetic section, the reference to the choice *tōn kata physin* has been seen as Stoicizing. But Plutarch (*Comm. not.*

23.1069E) claims that it was Zeno and the Stoics who have followed the Peripatetics and the Old Academy, and this seems equally probable.[26]

Bii3 is identical with a definition of *telos* at p.126.17–18. This is attributed to Antiochus by Wachsmuth, again referring to Cicero, *Academici libri* 1.22–3, discussed above. However on page 126 this is immediately followed by the definition of happiness as an activity in accordance with virtue in actions *prohēgoumenais* as one could wish, also discussed above. Both definitions surely have the same source; both or neither must be from Antiochus. If so, he must have given several alternative definitions. The date of this section may be deduced from the fact that the definitions are introduced in the course of a criticism of a different one, that the *telos* is a *symplērōma* of all goods, including those of the body and external, which is clearly the same as that attributed to Critolaus of Phaselis at p.46.10. He was head of the Peripatos after Aristo of Ceos, and died before 111 B.C. This discussion can therefore be dated to the late second or the first century B.C., which would suit the date of Antiochus. On the other hand John Dillon[27] thinks it possible that the criticism of Critolaus on p.46 is by Eudorus, and the discussion on p.125, which contains our two definitions is by Aristo of Alexandria, Eudorus' rival. In any case the date is near to that of Arius Didymus himself.

I have suggested that the section in which the definition of happiness Bi1 is discussed (p.131.14–132.18) is independent of the definitions themselves, that is that it is a commentary by someone who was not responsible for the formulation of the definitions. It contains a puzzling item: "They said that happiness was the use of perfect virtue because they used to say that some of the virtues are perfect but others imperfect. Perfect virtues are (i.e., include) justice and *kalokagathia*, imperfect *euphyia* and *prokopē*" (131.14–17). This raises the question of what is meant by *euphyia* and *prokopē*. Both terms are used by the Stoics: Diogenes Laertius 7.106 has a list of "preferred" (*proēgmena*) things which includes among the mental ones *euphyia*, *tekhnē*, *and prokopē*. But Aristotle used *euphyia* of both physical and moral dispositions (e.g., *EN* 1114b8 in connection with the ability to discern what is truly good), and, as a further complication, Diogenes Laertius 7.127 claims that for the Peripatics *prokopē* is intermediate between virtue and vice. So the treatment of *euphyia* and *prokopē* as virtues, even imperfect ones, is not entirely consistent with either Stoic or at least some Peripatetic views.[28]

The only closely related passages are from a period later than Arius Didymus, the second century A.D.. The closest is Albinus (chap.30), who distinguishes between perfect and natural virtue, using both Aristotelian and Stoic terms, and refers in the second class to *euphyiai* and *prokopai*. Apuleius, *De Plat.* 2.6 p.108.20 ff. has it that Plato "*inperfectos virtutes semet comitari negat*" (i.e., denies *antakolouthia*); and the Anonymous Commentator on the *Theaetetus* from the same period refers to *euphyia* in the same connection, and adds that "the ancients"—who are not Stoics—say that there is one *euphyia* for each virtue.

It is possible that all this reflects some earlier discussion, but we should also consider the possibility that the discussion of the definition Bil dates from a time after Arius Didymus. This would mean that Stobaeus or someone intermediate between Arius and him, added the discussion. Certainly the discussions of definitions do not seem to be either well put-together or well-informed. The very passage we are discussing, about imperfect virtues, does not agree very well with Aristotle's own view of perfect virtue, and what comes next also seems rather odd: "To the perfect the perfect is fitting. The *telos* of such (i.e., perfect) virtue, then, is activity, from which no part is missing." If this is more than a play on words its meaning is obscure. In addition it is not clear whether it is the activity or the virtue from which no part is missing. Grammatically it should be the former, but it would fit the play on words better if it were the latter.

The writer then comments on "in a complete life." The first lines seem to be no more than a rather woolly restatement of what is already in well-known Aristotelian material, but he goes on to add some new points: " 'Complete' is that which at its longest God has delimited for us. 'Delimited'—within loose limits, like the size of the body too. Just as one line would not constitute a part in a play, nor one extension of the hand a dance, nor one swallow a spring, so neither would a short time make happiness" (p.132.1–6). This looks like a conscious elaboration of what Aristotle says at *EN* 1098a18, where he refers only to a swallow and spring, not to a play or a dance. Possibly there is also here a hint of the kind of thinking I have already mentioned in connection with some uses of *en prohēgoumenois,* the idea that there are different levels of activity, but I am inclined to think it is mere embroidery.

The commentary continues: "For happiness must be complete, arising from a complete man (*andros*) and a complete time and a complete *daimōn.*"[29] Part of this last thought is to be found at *MM* 1.4.5 which indeed resembles the whole discussion of "complete" in a less flowery way. In particular, we have: "The complete must be both in complete time and in a complete man."

But the man here is *anthrōpos,*, not *anēr*, and there is no mention of a *daimōn.* What is this *daimōn?* Have we just another play on words, from *eudaimonia,* an external *daimōn,* or an internal one like that of Posidonius and other later Stoics? It is difficult to see what the perfect *daimōn* adds to the perfect man and the complete life. Is it fate?

The final section (p.132.8ff.) we have already considered: "The activity of virtue is *prohēgoumenē* because it is absolutely necessary for it to exist in things by nature good, etc." Not only is this not relevant to the B definitions but it is not entirely clear.

If this is a final layer in our material, I would suggest the following chronological development: the early Peripatetics produced a number of different definitions of happiness and the *telos.* These were later formed into collections, and these collections were used by Arius Didymus. The comments on the definitions may be later again, and in any case are quite independent of them.

A few puzzles remain:

There are a number of passages which seem to relate *prohēgoumenos* to something else:

a) Stobaeus p.134.17–19: "Of those things to be chosen for themselves, some are *telika*, some *poiētika* (productive). *Telika* are actions *prohēgoumenai* in accordance with virtue, productive are *ta hylika tōn hairetōn.*" The manuscripts F and P read '*hairetōn.*' Wachsmuth prints *aretōn,* following a conjecture found in a Vatican manuscript. This textual crux is difficult. I am inclined to support the reading *aretōn,*[30] but neither reading helps very much to understand the whole sentence. Little can be learned either from the Stoic passage on *telika* and *poiētika* goods at p.71.15–72.13 because that deals with people and emotions and virtues, not with actions.

b) Alexander, *Quaestiones* 4.25, mentioned above, is also difficult. He explains the addition of *en prohēgoumenois* thus: "because *prohēgoumenai* and *bouleutai*[31] activities need tools." He goes on to say that for the possession of happiness the virtues of the rational soul are needed, but it is not clear if this is a new point or a continuation of the point about tools. I am inclined to think it is a new one. If so, we are left with a single sentence of which the reading is doubtful and the meaning obscure.

To sum up, the definitions in Stobaeus are closely related to Aristotle's esoteric writings and the *MM*. Some are identical with some attributed in our sources to the Stoics; if these attributions are not mistaken, both schools may have derived them from Aristotle. A few departures from Aristotle, either in emphasis or in expression, have been noted: It has not been possible, for lack of evidence, to give a final account either of the emphasis on *use,* or of the reasons for introducing the word *prohēgoumenos* and related expressions. It has been argued that the discussions of the definitions are quite independent of the definitions themselves, and, tentatively, that part, at least, may be later than the time of Arius Didymus.

NOTES

1. References throughout are page and line numbers of Wachsmuth's edition of Book II.
2. *The Aristotelian Ethics* (Oxford 1978) p.21–2.
3. *Der Aristotelismus bei den Griechen* 1 (Berlin 1973) p.274.
4. It seems forced to relate this to the arrangement of the whole work, as does M. Giusta, *I dossografi di etica* (Turin 1964 and 1967). On detailed points, however, his book is valuable.
5. Alexandrian scholars of the period were interested in Aristotle's own esoteric works, and not merely in handbooks. According to Alexander of Aphrodisias, *In Aristotelis Metaphysica* 58.31–59.8, the Alexandrians Eudorus and Euharmostus made some changes in the text of *Metaph.* 988a 10–11.
6. After "goal" (*telos* p.51.1) the text is here corrupt. There follow 8 lines (p.51.1–8) which I do not translate.
7. Note the varying form of *prohēgoumenos*. Besides *en prohēgoumenois* in A1, *prohēgoumenē* qualifies "life" (*zōē*) in A4 and "activity" in A2, and *prohēgoumenos* qualifies "life" (*bios*) in A3.

8. *EN* 1102a5 has "an activity of *soul* in accordance with complete virtue "and 1098a16 (the good of man) is "the activity of soul in accordance with virtue."
9. At Stobaeus p.77.16, in the Stoic epitome, the same definition is found. Since it originates with Aristotle, we need not consider the suggestion that it was taken over by the Peripatetics from the Stoics. It may be behind Antiochus' *quo omnia referrentur* in Cicero, *Academici libri* 1.19, the Platonic discussion of the *telos*.
10. This, too, is attributed to the Stoics at Stobaeus p.76.22, and is also found in the passage from Cicero discussed in n.9 as *extremum. . .rerum expetendarum.*
11. *The Middle Platonists* (London 1977) p.75.
12. *The Aristotelian Ethics* p.7–8, 68.
13. See Newman, *Aristotle's Politics* p.341, 575. The same definition also occurs at *Pol.* 1328a37.
14. Since on most views the *MM* is later than *Pol.* 7, it is unlikely that the *Pol.* is referring back to the *MM* (See Kenny, op.cit., p.9–10 for a summary of recent views on the *MM*
15. Other similar definitions are given by Philo, *Quod det. pot. insid. sol.* (1.272 Cohn): "The use of complete virtue in a complete life." Cicero, *De finibus* 2.19 says that Aristotle "joined the use of virtue with the prosperity of a complete life." Alexander of Aphrodisias never refers to use in this connection.
16. Another copyist produced a different corruption by writing *proēgoroumenous* for *prohēgoumenous* at 109.10.
17. E.g., explicitly Aspasius, *In EN* p.22.23, unless this is a *summary* of Aristotle's views (cf. p.22.35) and in Stobaeus p.50–1, i.e., A1–4 above.
18. A similar use is found in many other places. Thus, as early as Theophrastus, *De igne* 14, we have, "Cold may have the same effect as heat in ripening fruits, but not *prohēgoumenōs,* only *kata symbebēkos.*" Alexander, *De mixtione* H226.26: "How would it not be unworthy for God to have as his *prohēgoumenon ergon* to be engaged permanently in creation. . .?" Again in the Alexander corpus we have (*Quaestiones* 3.4, p.87 Bruns) in a discussion of the sun's place in generation and destruction (I summarize): There are *prohēgoumena* among the things that come to be, and others opposed to them, and it is of the *prohēgoumenōs ginomena* that we speak primarily (*kyriōs*) when we use the words *genesis* and *phthora.* (The word "*prohēgoumenos*" occurs in various forms six times in this passage).
19. Here the text becomes uncertain, but it does not affect the present point. The reading *estai,* "will be," is Heeren's suggestion for *estō.* The manuscripts vary about *apodeixait'* etc. I suggest punctuating with a colon after *estai,* to give balancing clauses. Further the manuscript reading *eudaimonōs* is not impossible. Cf. Alex., *De anim. mantissa* 159a16.
20. These three are mentioned by Aristotle at *EN* 1104b30 as *ta eis tas haireseis* (with their opposites).
21. John of Italy, a very late authority, attributed some of these arguments to Aristotle and Theophrastus. Elsewhere only Peripatetics are mentioned.
22. Dr. Sharples has drawn my attention to 135.11–16, which contains the related notion of "sum-totals."
23. In this section (p.84–85) the manuscripts frequently confuse *prohēgoumenon* and *proēgmenon,* and in some places editors disagree about what should be read. Thus at 85.5–7, Wachsmuth, following Madvig, wants *proēgmenon* twice, but Festa (*Zeno* p.66) seems to want *prohēgoumenon* twice, though I do not follow his arguments fully.
24. In *SVF,* apart from Stobaeus passages, there is only No.1157, a passage from Origen about animals being for the use of man. A Stobaeus passage I have not discussed is p.76.13–15 from Antipater (of Tarsus?), who said that the *telos* is to do everything, to obtain *tōn prohēgoumenōn kata physin.* (Antipater was a contemporary of Carneades, mid–second century B.C.)

25. *Prohēgoumenos* raises problems wider than those discussed here. For literature see P. Moraux, op. cit., p.353 n.117 and R. W. Sharples in *BICS* 22 (1975) 49, 60–61.
26. Ian Kidd, "Stoic Intermediates and the End for Man" in *Problems in Stoicism* (ed. A. A. Long) 150–72, has shown that the picture we have of Stoic views is very confused.
27. *The Middle Platonists* p.124.
28. Eudorus' division of ethics, quoted by Arius (p.43.18) has a division of the things called *prohēgoumena (proēgmena,* Wachsmuth), which seems to include friendship, pleasure, good repute and *euphyia.*
29. "Perfect," as against "complete," would make better sense with "daimōn" but not with "time."
30. *MM* 1184b34 has both *haireton* and *areton* in the manuscripts.
31. The manuscripts have *bouletas.* The reading *bouleutas* is Spengel's correction. In *Quaest. 29 (p. 160 Bruns), boulēta* and *bouleuta* appear together and make sense as they stand, but Spengel wanted to read *bouleuta* in both cases.

Comments on Mrs. Huby's Paper

Michael D. Rohr

When Clym Yeobright, in *The Return of the Native*,[1] asks his mother, " . . . what is doing well?," Hardy assures us that "Mrs. Yeobright was far too thoughtful a woman to be content with ready definitions . . . ." It is much to our benefit that Mrs. Huby also has proved to be "far too thoughtful a woman to be content with ready definitions" of "doing well," of *eudaimonia* and *telos*; presented with a string of such pat definitions by the rather glib Arius, she has interrogated them, examined their pedigree, dragged their obscurities into the light of day, patched their texts, and cross-connected them with parallels in such a way as to make interpretation seem possible, if not certain. She has made useful comments on a considerable number of individual points and passages, of very varied sorts, and I could not hope here to offer a response to all of them even if I had some comment, criticism, or correction for each, which I do not. Instead, I offer a rather general observation of my own on one qualm I have about Arius's treatment of Aristotle, and then express some difficulties I felt in thinking about her discussion of two central notions in the texts she discusses, the notions of *chrēsis* and the *prohēgoumenon*. Since I am a philosopher, not a philologist, the issues I raise will be of a corresponding nature.

First, then, I note that what Arius mainly offers us in the texts under discussion are in fact definitions. Philosophers from Socrates to Ayer have thought that the central results, though not the only results, of the philosophical enterprise, are definitions; and Aristotle's theory and practice put him and the Peripatos squarely within this tradition. It is therefore no surprise that an epitomator like Arius should choose this form for chunks of his doxography. He doesn't label every definition explicitly as such; e.g., "The definition of *x* is *yz*"; but he drops clues and uses the appropriate technical terminology often enough to make his intentions clear. It's generally clear, too, when he's doing something else besides offering a definition, e.g., listing different classifications of goods or matching up virtues to their related vices (*vid.* the papers in this volume by Dr. Sharples and Professor Fortenbaugh). In the case of Mrs. Huby's definitions A1 through A4, for example, A1 was really meant by Arius to be a definition, as shown by the parallel in the Stoic summary (p.46.5); that the same holds for A2–4 Arius tells us when he's talking about how happiness was defined (*horizesthai*) by Aristotle (p.51.9). Throughout a doxography we should expect to find a variety of definitions of any particular important notion like happiness, since each new and original thinker, whether founding a new school or carrying on a research tradition in an old one, would wish to contribute his own revised and corrected formulation. Less obvious is why we should run across different definitions attributed to the same thinker. In the Aristotelian case, the problem is especially acute, for it is an explicit doctrine of Aristotle's that there cannot be more than one definition of the same thing.[2] Hence, when Arius says, "There are many ways it's possible for happiness to be defined, according to Aristotle" (p.51.8–9), and reels out A2 through A4, his doxographic impulse to collect strings of definitions itself compels a falsification of Aristotle's philosophy. We have grounds for thinking, then, that Arius's report is not a transcription of a single Peripatetic account setting forth an Aristotelian system. We should expect, further, that there will not be any proper one-to-one pairing of Arius's reports to Aristotelian definitions; the two are working at cross-purposes.

Mrs. Huby is reluctant to attach any great significance to the use of *chrēsis* rather than, or in addition to, *energeia* in some of Aristotle's statements about happiness. She suggests that Aristotle treats *chrēsis,* in this kind of context, as merely another term for *energeia,* and she concludes that for him the term was unemphatic. It is not clear to me, however, that this is correct, for *chrēsis* seems to me to associate with other words differently from the way in which *energeia* does, both in Aristotle and in Arius's definitions. What *chrēsis* is of—what gets used—is virtue, in the various definitions, while what *energeia* is of—what gets activated—is something else, soul or life. Happiness is, of course, activity of soul in accordance with virtue. Soul is not used, and virtue is not activated.[3] While the two conceptions are not necessarily incompatible, they will differ in emphasis; one emphasizes the psychological-metaphysical aspect of happiness, the other, the practical-behavioral aspect. Arius's carelessness in running them together bespeaks his insensitivity to the metaphysical side of Aristotle's ethics.

My last set of comments concerns the various forms of *prohēgoumenos* and their translation. The meaning of *prohēgoumenos, prohēgoumenē,* and so on, is always "primary," "ahead of the rest," or "first-rate" (as Professor Fortenbaugh translates its use at *Ecl.* p. 129.20 and 130.19). The application of this notion in any particular case will, of course, presuppose some scale or principle of ordering to answer the question, "Primary in respect of what?"; and an interpretation of a passage in which it is used will require determining what particular scale the author had in mind. Mrs. Huby considers three different principles of ordering as providing possible interpretations of *prohēgoumenos,* etc., in the definitions she discusses: (1) primary in respect of degree of favorableness to the use of virtue (or skill); (2) primary in respect of being proper to an agent; (3) primary in respect of being at the highest level of activity, i.e., as being a whole rather than a part, or a master-activity rather than a slave-activity. It seems to me probable that in all the passages in Stobaeus she discusses, (1) is correct. It is certainly possible in all the passages, and it is, I shall argue, preferable as well.

First, (1) is preferable to (2). The passage from pseudo-Alexander she cites to illustrate (1) is a much closer parallel to the definitions in Arius than are any of the passages from Aspasius she cites to illustrate (2). The passage from pseudo-Alexander concerns precisely those activities which are uses of a *state* and which constitute happiness; while the passages from Aspasius primarily concern activities of an *agent* which do not constitute happiness. From the logical point of view, we see that (1) requires mention of the state exercised in the activity but not of the agent, for the scale to be applied; while (2) requires mention of the agent but not of the state exercised. Now Mrs. Huby's definitions A1, A2, A4, and Bi1 mention the state exercised (as do also Bi2, Bi3, and Bii3, which do not use any form of *prohēgoumenos* although Bi3 and Bii3 seem to use parallel notions), while none of these definitions of happiness mentions the agent, with or without the state exercised.[4] I conclude that the sentence frames which the definitions in Arius exemplify make (1) more likely than (2). I refrain from drawing the philosophical implications of this.

Mrs. Huby proposes that we detect scale (3) behind the passage at p.129.19–130.12. She is right in seeing a notion of levels of activity at work in that passage, but this does not entail that we should interpret *prohēgoumenōn* at p.129.20 as presupposing scale (3). The lines at p.130.15–18, which mark a change of subject, are not much help, since they are incompatible with p.129.19ff; the latter says that happiness arises from noble actions and is noble as a whole, while the former says that happiness arises from noble actions plus other distinct kinds of actions and suggests that what is noble is just a part of happiness. The lines at p.129.19ff. seem to say that happiness arises from actions which are noble and *prohēgoumenai*. On Mrs. Huby's interpretation, this must mean not "from actions which are noble and also from actions which are *prohēgoumenai*," but rather "from actions each of which is both noble and *prohēgoumenē*." What does *prohēgoumenē* add to "noble?" Mrs. Huby suggests "at the highest level," and seems to take this to justify the inference that happiness is noble overall (p.129.20–1). But that is either not necessary or not sufficient to justify the inference. The most natural way of understanding the inference, I contend, is:

> I1. All the actions from which happiness arises are noble; therefore, happiness as a whole is noble.

This inference, which ignores *prohēgoumenōn,* is quite plausible. But if it does not work, taking *prohēgoumenēon* to mean "at the highest level" will not help it, since the new inference will fail if the other did:

> I2. All the actions from which happiness arises are noble and at the highest level; therefore, happiness is noble at the highest level.

I2 cannot be any more valid than I1. There seems even to be an inconsistency in Mrs. Huby's reading: If happiness is at the highest level, how can its components, actions from which it arises, be at the highest level also, i.e., at the same level as happiness. The right account of the passage in question seems rather to be this: It's *presupposed* that happiness is a highest level activity consisting of, and produced by, lower level activities. There must be actions which help to complete the whole (p.130.9–10) these must be noble, if the whole is to bé noble. There must be actions which carry towards and cooperate towards the whole i.e., goal (130.11–12); these must be done under circumstances favorable to the (noble) exercise of virtue. (The two sorts are not mutually exclusive, of course.) The two characteristics of the source of happiness mentioned in the first clause of the passage correspond, as they should, quite neatly to the dichotomy in the rest of the passage. Nobility carries over from the constituents to happiness itself as a whole, as stated. There is no hint, however, that whatever *prohēgoumenōn* stands for carries over to happiness itself; and indeed productiveness of the use of virtue does not so carry over. Hence, (1) rather than (3) is preferable here; and if here, then elsewhere *a fortiori*. I conclude that we should take scale (1) as lying behind *prohēgoumenos* in all its uses in Arius's report of Aristotle's account of happiness, and speculate about sources and parallels in light of this.

NOTES

1. Book 3, chapter 2.
2. *Top*. 141a31, 142b35, 148b14, 151a34, b17, 153a21, 154a10, *An. Post.* 91a14–33, *Metaph.* 998b12.
3. One might cite *EE* 1219a24f. and *Pol.* 1332a9 as counterexamples; but the text in the former is very uncertain (Wilson's *touto,* followed by Rackham, may eliminate the problem), and the latter is very loosely constructed, the construction for *chrēsis* being left ungrammatically to do duty for *energeia* as well.
4. A3, which mentions neither agent nor state exercised, is of no help in deciding between (1) and (2). I omit Bii1 and Bii2 from consideration entirely because they are definitions not of *eudaimonia* but of *telos*. Though the Peripatetics (and others) claimed that the *telos* is *eudaimonia*, the two notions have distinct definitions; thus the identification of *eudaimonia* (as defined) as the *telos* (as defined) is a substantive thesis. Once the identification has been made, of course, it is easy to offer carelessly a definition of *eudaimonia* in response to the question, "What is the *telos*?"; and this is what is done in Bii3.

CHAPTER 8

The Peripatetic Classification of Goods

Robert W. Sharples

Within Arius Didymus' account of Peripatetic ethics there occurs a section (p. 134.7–137.12 Wachsmuth) headed, "In how many ways the term 'good' is applied." It consists of a long series of classifications, of which only the first and, indirectly, the second are in fact concerned with different applications or *uses* of the term "good"; the others are rather classifications of *goods* (in the plural).[1] It is with this at-first-sight chaotic sequence of classifications that I shall chiefly be concerned. To facilitate discussion I offer at the outset a translation. Letters and numbers in the text, e.g. [A1], mark sections of divisions. A tabular presentation of these divisions will be found in an appendix.[2] Notes in parentheses, e.g. (80), refer to notes of this paper where textual points are discussed.

I. Translation of p. 134.7–137.12

p.134.7   [In how many ways "good" is applied.]

Since happiness is the greatest good for us, we must distinguish in how many ways "good" is applied. [A] Well, [the Peripatetics] say that it is
10   applied in three ways; for [it is] [A1] that which is the cause of preservation for all beings, and [A2] what is predicated of every good [thing], and [A3] what is choiceworthy for itself; and of these [the one, A1] is the first good (80), [the next, A2] the genus of goods, [the last, A3] the end, to which we refer everything, which is happiness. [B] And "choiceworthy for itself" is applied in three ways: it is either [B1] that for the sake of which, as
15   ultimate, we do certain things, or [B2] that for the sake of which we do all things, or [B3], thirdly, what is a part of these (48). [C] And of things that are choiceworthy for themselves, [C1] some are of the nature of ends (*telika*), [C2] others are productive. [C1] Of the nature of ends are primary (18) actions in accordance with virtue; [C2] productive are the materials of the virtues.
20   [D] And of good [things], [D1] some are deserving of honor, [D2] others are deserving of praise, [D3] others are potencies, [D4] others are beneficial. [D1] Deserving of honor are, for example, God, the ruler, one's father; [D2] deserving of praise are, for example, justice, practical wisdom; [D3] potencies are, for example, wealth, rule, authority; [D4] beneficial are the things that produce and preserve these, for example [those that produce and

139

p.135.1   preserve] health and good physical condition. [E] Moreover, of things that are choiceworthy (17) and good, [E1] some are [so] (17) in themselves, [E2] others for (on account of) other things (32). [E1] For the things that are deserving of honour and of praise, and potencies, [are good and choiceworthy] in themselves (for the potencies, too, are among things good in
5   themselves—for example, wealth and rule, which the good man would use well and would seek out; the things which a good man can use well are by nature good in themselves, just as [those things are] (35) healthy which the doctor would seek out and could use). [E2] But the beneficial things [are good and choiceworthy] for other things; for it is by producing and preserving
10   other things that they are among choiceworthy things. [F] Another division: of the things which are good in themselves, [F1] some are ends, [F2] others are not ends: for example, [F1] justice and virtue and health are ends, and in general all the sum totals resulting from individual occurrences—like
15   health, [F1′] but *not* [individual things that are] healthy, or the care of the sick. [F2] But good natural endowment, [acts of] remembering, and [acts of] learning are not ends. [G] Another division: of ends, [G1] some are good for everyone, [G2] others are not good for everyone. [G1] Virtue and practical wisdom are good for everyone, for they benefit whoever possesses
p.136.1   them; [G2] but wealth and rule and power (or: potencies (97)) are not good for everyone without any qualification, inasmuch as their being good is defined by the use the good man makes of them (for it is clear that ⟨good men⟩ (30) both seek out these things and benefit [others] by using them),
5   but the things that the good man uses well the bad man uses badly, just as the things that the musical man uses well the unmusical man uses badly. And in using [such things] badly [the bad man] is harmed, just as a horse which is a good [horse] benefits the man skilled in horsemanship, but does no little harm to the man who is not so skilled.

10   [H] Moreover, of good [things], [H1] some are concerned with the soul, [H2] others are concerned with the body, [H3] others are external. [H1] Concerned with the soul are, for example, good natural endowment, skill, virtue, wisdom, practical wisdom, pleasure; [H2] concerned with the body are health, keenness of perception, beauty, strength, soundness, and all the parts [of the body] with their powers and activities; [H3] external are wealth,
15   good reputation, good birth, political power, friends, relations, one's country. [I] And of the goods concerned with the soul, [I1] some are always present by nature, like sharpness and memory and, in general, good natural endowment; [I2] others come subsequently from practice (82), like the preliminary studies and liberal occupations; [I3] others exist as a result of
20   perfection, for example, practical wisdom, justice, and finally wisdom,

[J] Moreover, of good [things], [J1] some can be both acquired and lost, like wealth; [J2] others can be acquired but not lost, like good fortune and immortality (86); [J3] others can be lost but not acquired, like perception
p.137.1   and life; [J4] others can neither be acquired nor lost, like good birth.

5   [K] Moreover, of good [things], [K1] some are choiceworthy for themselves only, like pleasure and freedom from trouble; [K2] others are productive only, like wealth; [K3] others are both productive and choiceworthy for themselves, like virtue, friends, health.

10

[L] And good [things] are divided up in many other ways too, because there is no one genus of them, but rather they are spoken of in the ten categories; for "good" is an ambiguous expression, and all such things have only their name in common, the definition which corresponds to the name being different.

II. Commentary on p. 134.7–137.12

The Coherence of the Sequence of Divisions

There have been three major treatments of this series of classifications, by von Arnim,[3] by Giusta,[4] and by Moraux.[5] Von Arnim endeavoured to stress the unity and coherence of the sequence. He was compelled to admit the presence of certain inconsistencies, but held that the whole derives—as he held the whole of Arius' section on Peripatetic ethics to derive—from a single, authoritative early Peripatetic source, and that what is not Aristotelian in it reflects the views of Theophrastus.[6] But Philippson showed by the presence of a reference to the views of the second century B.C. philosopher Critolaus, that Arius' account of Peripatetic ethics cannot derive as a whole from an early Peripatetic source.[7] Giusta's treatment of our series of classifications is closely bound up with his attempt to discern a common scheme of treatment in a great part of ancient ethical doxography generally, a scheme which, he argues, is based to a large extent on the Aristotelian categories, and which he attributes to the influence of Arius himself.[8] He thus tries to relate a number of our divisions to the various Aristotelian categories.[9] But the identifications frequently seem unconvincing, and there is often not much correspondence between these divisions and others—in Arius' or Diogenes Laertius' account of Stoic ethics, for example—which Giusta argues are based on the same categories.[10] Moreover, Giusta's assignment of divisions to categories ignores the way in which some, but only some, groups of divisions seem to be arranged in deliberate sequences, as I shall be arguing later. Moraux stresses the difficulties and inconsistencies between the different divisions, arguing that we have to do with a heterogeneous collection taken from a multiplicity of sources,[11] not by Arius himself but by some intermediate source which he used.[12]

On the major issue, that of the unity or heterogeneity of the sequence of divisions as a whole, I do not think we can argue with Moraux's conclusion. But it is perhaps a result of the emphasis of his treatment that he stresses the divergencies and discrepancies. What I want to do in this paper is, while not challenging his main conclusions, to consider how far there are signs of a concern with system running through *some* groups of the divisions, and also to assess the extent to which there are indeed incompatibilities between them.

It is clear that "ends" has a wider application in the division I have labelled F than it does in C. However, it should be remembered that Aristotle himself, in *EN* 1.7, allows that there is a hierarchy among ends, and even speaks of some ends which are "more perfect," or "more final" (*teleiotera*) than others.[13] Further, it is common both to C and to F that things can be described as good or choiceworthy in themselves, even if they are simultaneously described as not being ends.[14] I will throughout be taking it that "good" and "choiceworthy" are equivalent expressions; this has been mentioned by Arius just before as the view of the "ancients,"[15] it is supported by the usage of Aspasius, the second century A.D. commentator on the *EN*,[16] and it means that F can be seen as a subdivision of the first class produced by the division of E (to which I will henceforth refer, for the sake of brevity, as "E1," and so in other cases).[17] Since it will be necessary to discuss whether anything turns on the difference between "choiceworthy *di' hauto*" (as in B and C) and "choiceworthy *kath' hauto*" (as in E1), I shall use "for itself," i.e., for its own sake, to render *di' hauto,* and "in itself" to render *kath' hauto.*

The application of "productive," too, is different in C (where it covers everthing except virtuous actions[18]), in D (where it is contrasted not only with virtues but also with some external goods) and in K (where it applies, either under K2 or under K3, to some goods at least of all three classes—virtues or goods of the soul, bodily goods, and external goods[19]). But, just as "ends" is a term admitting of degrees, so may "productive" be.[20]

In spite of these variations, however, there are certain points on which all the divisions are in agreement. Firstly, there is no suggestion in *any* of these divisions that bodily or external advantages are not *good*; the most that is ever at issue is whether or not certain external goods, in particular, are good or choiceworthy in or for *themselves*. In other words, the Stoic doctrine that *only* virtue is good is simply ignored.[21]

Furthermore, it is nowhere explicitly claimed in our divisions that *no* external goods are good and choiceworthy in and for themselves. That the major external goods, at least, are choiceworthy in themselves is clearly the view of DEFG.[22] The interpretation of C is more problematic, as no examples are given; but it seems probable that some bodily and external goods, at least, are included under C2 as productive, and hence are choiceworthy for themselves. (See further below.) K lists "friends" under things choiceworthy for themselves, and gives no indication that external goods in general are not choiceworthy for themselves, with the exception of wealth. (That some of the things that are choiceworthy for themselves are also productive—namely, those in K3—is of course irrelevant[23]). Possibly, however, it is not only wealth among external goods that is excluded from being choiceworthy for itself in K. Professor Görgemanns points out that external goods can be divided into those that are social—friends, fatherland, and the like—and those that are not, such as wealth and political power.[24] It is friends, an example of a social external good, that are included as choiceworthy for themselves in K3; and this suggests that the basic contrast underlying K where external goods are concerned is one between social external goods, which are choiceworthy for themselves, and nonsocial ones, which are not. Nonsocial external goods *are* clearly regarded as choiceworthy in themselves in E1, which picks up D3; indeed, D3 includes *only* the nonsocial external goods, which is natural enough, as D3 is a list of potencies (*dunameis*), and social external goods are hardly potencies. Similarly, it is *non*social external goods that are included in G2.

It is true that, on p.56.9ff., only *bodily* goods are included among things choiceworthy for themselves, external goods being conspicuous here by their absence.[25] However, this division comes not from the account of Peripatetic ethics, but from the ethical doxography, arranged by topics rather than by schools, earlier in this chapter of Stobaeus.[26] In G, on the other hand, where bodily goods are not explicitly mentioned at all, it seems that they should naturally be classed with external goods (G2) rather than with soul-goods (G1); for they can be misused, it would seem, as much as can external ones.[27] Moraux, indeed, finds it odd that things should be described as *ends* in G if they can be misused.[28] But, as he himself points out,[29] the point is made explicitly on p.135.3–8 that potencies, which can be used well or ill, are none the less good in themselves; the important point is that they can be used well by the good man, and it is he who should be taken as the standard of reference.[30]

A fortiori, it is nowhere suggested that only ends are choiceworthy for themselves, or that only virtues are. It is true that in an earlier passage (129.8ff.) only virtues and virtuous actions are "noble" (*kalon*); but "noble" is a narrower term than "good."[31]

Divisions DEFG

It was suggested above that some of these divisions, at least, form sequences, each in the group being a further subdivision of one of the products of the previous division. The most obvious case is that of DEFG—or perhaps, rather, DFG, for E is not so much an independent division, as a comment on D.[32] F takes E1 as its dividendum, and G takes F1. It is striking that each of the divisions D, F, and G has a close parallel in book 1, chapter 2 of the *MM*, attributed to Aristotle.[33] However, in the *MM* the order of the corresponding divisions is different (DGF), and they are all presented simply as divisions or classifications of goods, not as a chained sequence of successive subdivisions.[34]

It might at first sight seem that the chaining together of the divisions in Arius has produced a discrepancy which is not present in the *MM*. For F, which is in the latter simply a division of goods, is in Arius a division of things good *in themselves;* and at first sight it thus seems to be implied that healthy things and the care of the sick (p.135.15), though not ends, are good in themselves. This would conflict with DE, where things which produce health are classed under D4 and hence, by E, are *not* choiceworthy in themselves.[35]

Now in the *MM*, indeed, a contrast is drawn between health, which is an end, and the things we seek for the sake of it, which are not. But in Arius's F the situation is not so simple. There is in fact not one contrast there, but two. The main contrast is between items in F1, such as health, which are ends, and the items under F2—good natural endowment and acts of recollection or learning—which are not. But, before we even come to F2, F1 is clarified by a subordinate contrast between, on the one hand, (F1) health, for example, which is the sum total of many individual healthy actions, and, on the other, (F1′) the individual occurrences (such as, one may suppose, exercise or surgical operations) which produce and preserve health; the former is an end, the latter are not. (Although "sum total," *kekephalaiōmena,* might suggest that it is the relation between health as a whole and the individual parts that *constitute* a healthy life that Arius has in mind here, the emphasis seems rather to be on the contrast between health as a *result* and the individual actions that *produce* it; this is suggested by the reference to care of the sick under F1′.) Since division F is a division of things good in themselves, it certainly follows that items falling under F1 and F2 must be good in themselves; but as what is healthy, mentioned under F1′, does not form part of the main division at all, occurring simply in a comment on F1, it does not follow that it must be good in itself, and so there is no conflict with DE. In other words, the contrast in the *MM* between health, which is an end, and the things which produce health, which are not ends, is replaced in Arius's F by a contrast between ends, including health, on the one hand, and things such as acts of recollection which are good in themselves but not ends, on the other. The items in Arius's F2 are all, in fact, goods of the soul (for "good natural endowment" compare p.136.11); it is not immediately clear where they would fit into D, if indeed D is intended as an exhaustive classification, but it seems that they would most naturally be classed with the potencies in D3. There is certainly no implication that they fall under D4, and so are not good in themselves, which would imply a conflict.

A division corresponding to D occurs also in the commentary by Alexander of Aphrodisias on Aristotle's *Topics,* cited as occurring in (Aristotle's) "division of goods."[36] And von Arnim and Giusta have argued, by the occurrence of points in FG that do not occur in the *MM*, that Arius is probably drawing not on the *MM* directly, but rather on the Aristotelian "Divisions."[37]

There are two lists of these, with considerable overlap; one preserved in Diogenes Laertius's life of Plato,[38] and the other in a manuscript in Venice.[39] As it happens, our division D does not occur in either list. Mutschmann in fact suggested that Alexander's reference to the "division of goods" might simply indicate, not an item in any list of divisions, but *MM* 1.2 itself; though there are points in Alexander's account which do *not* appear in the *MM*, not explicitly, at any rate,[40] and Mutschmann also recognized the possibility that the *MM* and Alexander are both drawing on a common source.

However, the only division in our list that occurs in the surviving lists of Aristotelian divisions is H, the division into goods of the soul, bodily goods and external goods[41]; but this is a commonplace.[42] Nor is there much more correspondence between the "Aristotelian" lists and other places where Arius discusses Peripatetic views about goods.[43] And, further, there is little evidence in the surviving lists of Aristotelian divisions of the chaining together of divisions, or even—since the order might have been disturbed—of cases where what is a product of one division forms the dividendum of another, even if not of the immediately following one. If, then, a list of "Aristotelian" divisions did form Arius's ultimate source, and the surviving lists reflect its character at all accurately, it seems necessary to postulate an intermediate stage where the "chaining" could have occurred. It could of course have been Arius himself who introduced it; but in that case it is odd that only some of the divisions are chained together, and that, as will be argued in a moment, we have two distinct chains. It seems more plausible to suppose that Arius took these over from different sources. What does seem unlikely is that *MM* 1.2 could be based on a source which already displayed the "chaining" that we find in Arius. For it is not likely that a series of divisions, forming a chained sequence, should be broken up to form a series of merely coordinate divisions of goods, as in the *MM*.[44]

Divisions ABC

As DEFG form a chain, so, it would seem, do ABC. B appears to distinguish between different applications of "choiceworthy for itself," which was the last of the three senses of "good" distinguished in A; though, since *happiness* in A3 corresponds not to B as a whole but only to B2, we must either suppose, with Giusta, that the mention of *happiness* specifically in A3 is an error which has obscured an earlier coherent pattern, or else suppose that the chaining was not all that carefully done.[45] As for "end" in A3, whether this too conflicts with the linking of B to A3 depends on whether it is interpreted in a narrow sense, so as to apply only to the *supreme* end, happiness, or whether it is given a wider application.[46]

C, in turn, seems to be a classification of things described as choiceworthy in themselves, not in all the ways listed in B, but in the last, B3. For it is not the supreme end itself, happiness (B2) that can be classified under the two heads of "things that are ends" on the one hand and "things that are productive" on the other; if this applies to any of the things distinguished as choiceworthy for themselves in different ways in B, it applies to the *parts* of the end, B3.[47] However, there are difficulties here. Firstly, if A3 covers *all* applications of "choiceworthy for itself," and if "end" (taken in a broad sense) *is* in place there, it is clear that "end" in A3 has a wider sense than it does in C1. This however should not worry us unduly; it has been seen that the term "end" admits of degrees. A more serious difficulty is the following. If B is intended as an *exhaustive* classification of ways in which "choiceworthy for itself" is applied, it follows that the items in C2 must be included somewhere within it, and clearly, if they *are* included, it must be under B3. But items under B3 are described as parts of B2, the supreme end;[48] and so, by implication, the items in C2 are being described as parts of the supreme end. The difficulty here is that C2 is naturally taken as including goods other than those of the soul; and, earlier in Arius' epitome, it has been suggested that goods other than those of the soul are *not* parts of the end, this being directed against the view of

Critolaus that happiness is a complete realization of all three types of goods.[49]

There seem to be three possible ways out of this dilemma:

1. Deny that C2 includes goods other than those of the soul. This however seems implausible; that such goods *are* included is suggested both by the reference to the material of the virtues[50] and by the fact that Arius has recently described both bodily and external goods as "productive."[51] Furthermore, goods other than those of the soul are described as choiceworthy in or for themselves both in Arius's earlier discussion[52] and in the subsequent divisions E and K; which means that, if C as a classification of goods that are choiceworthy for themselves *is* confined to those of the soul, it either reflects a different doctrine from that found elsewhere in Arius, or else is incomplete.
2. Deny that B *is* intended by Arius as an *exhaustive* list of applications of "choiceworthy for itself;" or else suggest that it reflects a narrower view about what is choiceworthy for itself than does C, but that Arius or his source, in chaining the divisions together, failed to take account of this.[53]
3. Suggest that goods other than those of the soul *are* included in B3, and that the earlier passages, arguing against Critolaus that external and bodily goods are not parts of the end, are simply not relevant to the interpretation of the present passage; which might have implications for our view of the origin of this collection of divisions. It might be claimed against this that it is implausible that goods other than those of the soul should simultaneously be described as *productive* (in C2) and as *parts* of the end (in B3); however, in C itself, if they are included in C2, they are described both as productive and as choiceworthy for themselves.

In support of point 3, it may be urged that it is preferable to try to interpret the whole collection of divisions of goods as a unit, rather than bringing in an issue—the attack on Critolaus—from elsewhere. The difficulty with all this material, however, is the possibility of a difference between the intentions of the originators of the various divisions, and the understanding of their implications by those—ending with Arius?—who assembled them together at various stages in the tradition. So it is not clear that point 2 can be ruled out, either.

It is however stiking that B does approach the whole matter in terms of the relation of part to whole, rather than of that of means to end; for the whole-part relation is the better suited to express the relation of virtuous action to happiness.[54] And, *if* external goods are regarded as choiceworthy for themselves in B as they are elsewhere, the whole-part relation is also the better suited to express a view in which wealth, for example, is pursued for its own sake and not just for the use that can be made of it.[55]

Division K: "Choiceworthy in Itself" and "Choiceworthy for Itself"

In K, wealth and possibly other nonsocial external goods are described, by implication, as not being choiceworthy for themselves. This conflicts with E, which implies that wealth is choiceworthy in itself.[56] Von Arnim, indeed, argued that a distinction should be drawn between things choiceworthy *for* themselves and those choiceworthy *in* themselves; drawing attention to Aristotle, *Topics* 3.1 116a29ff., he argued that the natural antithesis to "choiceworthy *in* itself" is not "choiceworthy for something else" but "choiceworthy *per accidens.*" And, further, he claimed that "choiceworthy in itself" covers both things that are choiceworthy for themselves only (K1) *and* things that are choiceworthy both for themselves and for something else (K3); the only things that it excludes are those that are choiceworthy *only* for something else (K2).[57] As von Arnim recognized, however, this does not remove the discrepancy between E and K as far as wealth is concerned, for in E it is asserted that wealth is choiceworthy in itself (as is implied by G, too, in its context), while in K it is implied, not just that wealth is not choiceworthy for itself *alone,* but rather that it is not choiceworthy for itself *at all.*[58]

It seems appropriate, therefore, first to discuss the plausibility of von Arnim's point in general, and then to consider the problem that in any case remains concerning wealth (and, perhaps, nonsocial external goods in general). For, quite apart from its failure to resolve the latter issue, it may be doubted whether von Arnim's general distinction between "choiceworthy for itself" and "choiceworthy in itself" stands up. Aspasius and Heliodorus, commenting on the *EN,* seem to regard the two expressions as equivalent.[59] Alexander of Aphrodisias, commenting on the passage of the *Topics* cited by von Arnim, does indeed recognize a distinction between "choiceworthy for itself" as opposed to "choiceworthy for something else," on the one hand, and "choiceworthy in itself," as opposed to "choiceworthy *per accidens,*" on the other;[60] but he applies "choiceworthy *per accidens*" not just to things which are good only for the sake of something else, but to things which in themselves might seem positively *bad*—for example, hunger, disease, and death.[61] It is thus not ruled out for him, as it apparently is for von Arnim, that there might be things which are good entirely for the sake of something else, but are none the less choiceworthy in themselves, in their own nature, rather than *per accidens;* for example, clothing for one who is cold, or food for a hungry man.[62]

Moreover, even leaving aside the usage of the Aristotelian commentators, it does not seem natural for the distinction that von Arnim draws—between what is choiceworthy only for itself, and what is choiceworthy both for itself and for something else—to be expressed by the contrast between "for itself" and "in itself." Just as K1 and K3 are both choiceworthy *in* themselves, according to von Arnim, so too they are surely both choiceworthy *for* themselves. It is in fact the "only" that may be supplied from the context in K1 that is significant, rather than any contrast between "for" and "in."[63]

The contrast as drawn by Alexander, however, between things that are good *in* themselves though only *for* something else, and things that are only good *per accidens,* might seem to resolve the discrepancy over wealth in Arius. For if the items in Arius's D4 are good only *per accidens,* wealth might be placed in D3 as being good and choiceworthy *in its own nature,* even though—as is implied in K— it is only choiceworthy for something else. Aspasius, in *his* version of D, gives as examples of the fourth class things which are very definitely good only *per accidens:* medical treatment, cutting and burning.[64] Arius's reference merely to things that produce and preserve health and good bodily condition does not so obviously suggest things that in themselves might seem bad rather than good, though due allowance must be made for the nature of ancient medical treatments!

Unfortunately, such an interpretation of the contrast between D3 and D4 will not work. The fact that the combination of G with F indicates that wealth is an end is not the greatest problem; Aristotle is prepared to say that things are ends and in the same breath to allow that they are sought (entirely) for the sake of something else.[65] But a far more obvious difficulty is the fact that D1–3 are contrasted in E *not* with things that are choiceworthy *per accidens,* but with things that are choiceworthy for other things. This strongly suggests that Arius does not draw any distinction between "choiceworthy in itself" on the one hand, and "choiceworthy for itself" on the other; and this rules out the suggestion that he might not have intended, in DE, to assert that wealth was choiceworthy *for* itself, but only that it was choiceworthy in its own nature rather than *per accidens.* There is, then, a discrepancy over the status of wealth, and it is to this issue that we must turn.

The Status of Wealth

Aspasius seems in some perplexity over the status of wealth.[66] Commenting on *EN* 1.5 1096a7, he raises the question why Aristotle says there that wealth is choiceworthy for the sake of something else, but elsewhere that it is good and choiceworthy for itself.[67] His answer is that wealth is choiceworthy for itself for the good man, because he uses it well.[68] More interesting than this answer, however, is the question what passage he had in mind when he cites Aristotle as saying that wealth is choiceworthy for itself.[69] Von Arnim draws attention to a passage in the *Rhetoric* in which wealth is described not only as productive but also as the excellence of acquisition.[70] However, Aspasius is familiar not only with our division D, but also with the point that items in D4 are not choiceworthy for themselves— that is, with Arius's E,[71] so it may be the source of Arius's DE that he has in mind here too, in saying that Aristotle at times says that wealth is good and choiceworthy for itself. (As has been seen, Aspasius does not seem to distinguish between "in itself" and "for itself" in this connection.) There are two passages earlier in Arius in which external goods are said to be choiceworthy in themselves,[72] but *wealth* is not mentioned in either of them.

Although von Arnim refers to the *Rhetoric* passage concerning wealth as providing some basis for the view that wealth is choiceworthy not only for other things but also for itself, he holds that the position adopted in K, where wealth is *only* good in an instrumental way, for the sake of something else, is the more authentically Aristotelian one.[73] Holding that the whole of our Arius passage reflects a single, authoritative, and hence early Peripatetic source, he argues that the attitude to wealth adopted in DEFG, since it does not reflect the position of Aristotle, must reflect that of Theophrastus.[74] But, apart from the questionable assumptions involved in this argument, it may be noted that the general claim that potencies (D3) are choiceworthy in themselves, which von Arnim rightly sees as underlying the particular claim about wealth,[75] is present not only in Arius but also, by implication, in Aspasius.[76] If it derives from Theophrastus in Arius, it should presumably do so in Aspasius too; and, although arguments from silence are dangerous, there seems no particular reason to suppose that it does.

Divisions A, I, and J

A is closely parallel to passages in the *EE* and the *MM* which are concerned to establish which sense of "good" is relevant to ethical discussion.[77] In both these passages the Platonic Idea of the Good is attacked; and reference to the good as predicated in the ten categories, which may be compared with our divison L, occurs both in them and in *EN* 1.6, which, again, attacks the Platonic Idea.[78] In A, however, we have not a reference to the Platonic Idea, which would not be in place in what is a constructive, rather than a polemical context, but rather a reference to the "first god" as the cause of preservation to all things. Critics have attempted to link this with various Aristotelian texts;[79] however, the closest verbal parallel is in the pseudo-Platonic *Definitions,* and this has the additional feature that it clearly has an ethical reference, which is not obviously the case with the Aristotelian parallels.[80]

The closest parallel to division I is not in Aristotle but in Cicero,[81] although, as von Arnim points out, the ideas underlying it have an Aristotelian basis.[82] Moreover, although division I does not correspond in terminology to Aristotle's attribution of virtue to nature, teaching and habituation,[83] it is not that far removed from it in substance; for Arius does refer to "preliminary *studies*" under the heading of goods from practice, and the goods which he lists under "perfection" include righteousness or justice, which, for Aristotle, is the result of habituation.[84]

Division J seems to have no parallels in extant Aristotelian texts, though von Arnim suggests that it might have been derived from the Aristotelian "Divisions."[85] The problem here is raised by J2, the goods that can be gained but not lost. The manuscripts offer "good fortune" and "immortality"; various emendations have been offered,[86] but von Arnim and Moraux agree in finding none of them plausible, Von Arnim argues that there is *no* human good that can be gained but not lost, according to the Peripatetics, and suggests that this subdivision has been interpolated for the sake of completeness.[87] It might in fact be better to say "included," for we do not know that there was ever a stage in the history of this classification when it existed without the inclusion of J2. Moreover, the examples given by the manuscripts *could* perhaps be defended, *if* one were desperate enough to find *some* examples of goods that could be gained but not lost, in order to produce a neatly symmetrical classification. Immortality can be acquired, if we believe myths like that of Tithonus (although this is of course quite un-Aristotelian![88]), but it might be argued that, by definition, it cannot be lost, since if one loses it one never had it in the first place. The example of "good fortune," too, might be justified by the argument that no man enjoys good fortune unless his whole life is fortunate, although Aristotle himself conducts this argument in terms not of good fortune (*eutuchia*) but of happiness (*eudaimonia*)[89]

There is no overt allusion in J to the issue, debated among the Stoics, of whether *virtue* can be lost once it has been gained.[90] None the less, this issue may still be at the base of division J; for it may represent an attempt to adapt to a Peripatetic context a scheme of division which is naturally at home in a Stoic context, and to find more or less plausible examples to fit into the subdivisions which were designed with Stoic doctrines in mind; most obviously, for some Stoics at least, including Chrysippus, virtue would fall under J2.[91] But it should be stressed that it does not follow that it is Arius himself who has imposed a Stoic scheme of division on Peripatetic material; this might well have happened long before, and simply have been reflected in the source Arius was following at this point in his Peripatetic section.

Arius does, however, include a series of divisions of goods in his Stoic section too; and *if* there were basically similar patterns of division in the two accounts, *and* signs that a Peripatetic pattern had been forcibly imposed on Stoic material or vice versa, it might be plausible to suppose that it was Arius himself who was responsible for this.[92] This however does not seem to be the case. Some of the divisions in the Stoic section do correspond in a general way to some of those in the Peripatetic section (though of course, given the difference in doctrine, the *items* in the various subdivisions are different).[93] But many more of the Stoic divisions do not correspond to any of the Peripatetic ones.[94] And, in the Stoic section, each point that is made about goods is subsequently applied to evils too;[95] this does not occur in the Peripatetic section. There does not therefore seem to be any sign that Arius has in fact tried to harmonize the Stoic and the Peripatetic accounts.

Returning to the series of Peripatetic divisions, what conclusions can be drawn? It is clear that there are irremovable discrepancies between some of the divisions, and that they cannot all be reduced to a single overall coherent scheme. At the same time, there is a broad measure of agreement between them on many points, which should not be overlooked; and there are clear indications of connected sequences (DEFG, HI, and probably ABC) in which each division is presented as a subdivision taking further that which has preceded. Many of the divisions have clear Aristotelian parallels, especially with the *MM*; but it seems likely that some of the organization of the material took place at an intermediate stage, before it reached Arius himself.

APPENDIX

Peripatetic Classifications of Goods in Stobaeus Ecl. 2.7.19 (p. 134–37 Wachsmuth)

A. p. 134.9 GOOD:

1. Cause of preservation to all beings; the first god
2. Predicated of all goods; genus of goods
3. Choiceworthy for self; *telos*, happiness

EE 1.8 (esp. 1218b8ff.); *MM* 1.1 1182b2ff. [96]

B. p. 134.14 CHOICEWORTHY FOR ITSELF (= A3?):

1. Ultimate for sake of which we do certain things
2. That for sake of which we do all things
3. Part of these

MM 1.2 1184a8

C. p. 134.17 CHOICEWORTHY FOR THEMSELVES (= B3?):

1. *Telika: prohegoumenai* actions according to virtue
2. Productive; material of virtues

Cf. Cicero *De finibus* 5.68; Diogenes Babylonius ap. Stob. 2 p. 64.13

D. p. 134.20 GOODS:

1. Deserving honor: God, ruler, father
2. Deserving praise: justice, practical wisdom
3. Potencies: wealth, rule, authority
4. Producing & preserving—e.g. producing health

MM 1.2 1183b19; Alex. *In Top.* 242.4 (Arist. fr.113 Rose); Aspasius *In EN* 32.10

E. p. 135.1 CHOICEWORTHY AND GOOD (THINGS) (= D)

1. Choiceworthy and good in themselves (D1-3)
2. Choiceworthy and good for other things

EN 1.6 1096 b 8ff., 10.6 1176b3; *Topics* 3.1 116a29. Cf. K, and Stob. 2 p.56.9

F. p. 135.11 THINGS GOOD IN THEMSELVES (= E1?):

1. Ends: justice virtue, health (1' Not ends: healthy things, care of sick)
2. Not ends: good natural endowment, acts of recollection, acts of learning

MM 1.2 1184a3; cf. *Topics* 3.1 116b22

				References
G. p. 135.17 ENDS (= F1):	1. Good for everyone; virtue, practical wisdom	2. Not good for everyone: wealth, rule, powers[97]		MM 1.2 1183b8
H. p. 136.9 GOODS:	1. Soul-goods: good natural endowment, skill, virtue, wisdom, practical wisdom, pleasure	2. Bodily goods: health, perceptiveness, beauty, strength, soundness, all parts + potencies and activities	3. External goods: wealth, reputation, good birth, political power, friends, relations, country	EN 1.8 1098b12; MM 1.3 1184b1; Diog. Laert. 3.81, 5.30; Stob. 2 p. 56.8
I. p. 136.16 GOODS CONCERNING SOUL (= H1):	1. Always present by nature: sharpness, memory, good nature endowment	2. From practice: preliminary studies, liberal occupations	3. From perfection: practical wisdom, justice, wisdom	Cicero Ac. post. 1.20 (Antiochus)
J. p. 136.22 GOODS:	1. Acquired and lost: wealth	2. Acquired but not lost: good fortune, immortality	3. Lost but not acquired: perception, life	4. Neither acquired nor lost: good birth
K. p. 137.4 GOODS:	1. Choiceworthy for themselves only: pleasure, freedom from trouble	2. Productivity only: wealth	3. Both: virtue, friends, health	EN 1.6 1096b9-25,[98] 1.7 1097a25ff.; Aspasius In EN 15.14-16.5[99]; Alex. In Top. 229.1ff.
L. p. 137.8 GOODS: Ten categories				EN 1.6 1096a23; EE1.8 1217b26; MM 1.1 1183a9; cf. Topics 1.15 107a5ff. and Alex. ad loc.

NOTES

I am most grateful to Professor David Furley, the commentator on this paper, and to all those who participated in the discussion of an earlier version of it at the Arius Didymus conference; their observations and suggestions have enabled me to make a considerable number of improvements in the present version. I am also grateful to the British Council for a grant for the expenses of my travel to America.

1. "Choiceworthy for itself" appears in the singular at p.134.14, in the second division, but in the plural at p.134.17. Cf H. von Arnim, *Arius Didymus' Abriss der peripatetischen Ethik*, SitzB. Wien, phil.-hist. Kl., 204, no.3 (1926) 47ff. Cf. further below.
2. In the right-hand column of the table I have listed a number of passages, chiefly from Aristotle but in some cases from other authors, which correspond closely to Arius's divisions.
3. Above, n.1, especially 47–63.
4. M. Giusta, I dossografi di etica 1 (Turin 1964) and 2 (Turin 1967); especially 2.91–5 and 115–31.
5. P. Moraux, *Der Aristotelismus bei den Griechen* 1 (Berlin 1973) 259–443, especially 365–77.
6. Von Arnim, 12–14, 128f., 158; cf. Moraux, 247 n.56.
7. R. Philippson, "Das 'Erste Naturgemasse' " *Philologus* 87 (1932) 464. Cf. F. Dirlmeier, "Die Oikeiosis-Lehre Theophrasts," *Philologus* suppl. 30.1 (1937) 13f., 77ff.; O. Regenbogen, 'Theophrastos' *RE* suppl. 7 (1950) 1492–4; Moraux, 275f.
8. Cf. Moraux 264–68, and reviews of Giusta by G. B. Kerferd in *Class. Rev.* 17 (1967) 156–8 and 21 (1971) 371–73, and by P. Boyancé, *Latomus* 26 (1967) 246–49.
9. Viz. D (and the earlier division at 129.8) to the category of quality; E, F and G to that of relation; H to that of place; I and J of that of time; and K to that of action and passion (Giusta, 2.94f.).
10. Thus there seems little connection between Arius p. 73.16ff. (on the Stoics) and our divison E, both assigned by Giusta 2.119ff. to the category of relation; and Seneca *Ep.* 106.4ff., cited by Giusta 2.130f. in connection with our K, does not contain a classification of goods at all. While division J may well derive ultimately from the Stoic controversy over whether or not virtue, once achieved, can be lost (see further below), the contrast, in Stoic contexts, between goods, like virtue, that are always present to the wise and those, like joy, that are not (Arius p. 68.24ff., cf. Diogenes Laertius 7.98) is only comparable in a very general way to our I and J (cf. Giusta 2.127f.). Moreover, Giusta argues with reference to the category of relation that the two contrasts, "good for everyone or not good for everyone," and "always present or not always present," originally distinct, have been *conflated* in Arius p.68.24ff. and in Apuleius,*De Platone* 2.10 113.15–20 (but is the latter contrast really implied in this passage of Apuleius at all?), while an epitomator later than Arius has *omitted* the latter from its rightful place after G, to avoid repetition with I and J. (Giusta 2.123). Giusta's postulated original arrangement is thus not preserved in any extent text! The same epitomator is also blamed for the fact that the tripartition in H is not also stated immediately after C, as it should be according to Giusta's scheme (2.93f., cf. 115). But, as Boyancé (above, n.8) points out, the title "Didymus' Epitome" (Stobaeus 4.39.28, p. 918.15) is more naturally taken in the Greek to indicate a summary *by* Arius than a summary *of* Arius (against Giusta I.194). At 2.121 n.5 Giusta argues that the fact that two divisions are identical in their content is irrelevant if it can be shown by comparison with "corresponding" passages in other doxographies that they belong to different parts of the overall scheme; but there is a clear danger of *petitio principii* here.
11. Moraux, 368, 371, 377; cf. 315f., 438f. He points out that this was the general view before von Arnim (373 n.187).

12. Moraux, 273f., 377, 435ff., basing this on the remoteness of the arrangment of material in Arius here from that in the Aristotelian texts. Cf. further below.
13. *EN* 1.7 1097a25ff. Cf. J. L. Ackrill, "Aristotle on Eudaimonia," *Proc. Brit. Acad.* 60 (1974) 9; Aspasius *In EN, Comm. in Aristot. Graeca (CIAG)* 19.1 15.20ff.; Eustratius *In EN, CIAG* 20 61.5f. Indeed this passage in the *EN*, corresponding to Arius's K, is a classification of ends, *telē*; cf. Moraux, 372.
14. Von Arnim, 54.
15. Arius p.129.4. Cf. von Arnim, 18; Giusta, 2.91f.; Moraux, 366.
16. Aspasius, *In EN, CIAG* 19.1 13.27ff., 14.8, 14.12.
17. The connection is even closer if we follow Giusta, who argues (2.121n.4) that *hairetōn kai* in Arius p. 135.1 should be kept, but *haireta* on p.135.2 deleted, comparison with p.135.3, 4 and 7 showing that the reference on p.135.2 is to things *good* (or *good and* choiceworthy) in themselves.
18. *Prohēgoumenai* actions in accordance with virtue; on the force of *prohēgoumenai* compare Mrs. Huby's paper, and cf. the contrast between F1 and F1´ below.
19. Cf. also Arius p.126.21, 129.13, and 130.7; von Arnim, 50, 52; Moraux, 367 n.168, 374 n.189.
20. Giusta, 2.130, relates the differing uses of "productive" to his theory that the divisions are based on different Aristotelian categories; but the general point may stand even if his theory is not accepted as far as the categories are concerned.
21. Cf. Moraux, 377. At p.129.13ff. bodily and external goods are described as necessary; cf.p.130.8ff., 132.8ff. Von Arnim, 20; Moraux, 367f. Cf. also A. A. Long, "Aristotle's Legacy to Stoic Ethics," *BICS* 15 (1968) 83 n.10.
22. Moraux, 375, questions the inclusion of external goods in F1; but, *if* G is a subdivision of F1, the inclusion of external goods in F1 is implied by their presence in G2; though there is a difficulty here, of which more later.
23. Cf. Giusta, II.130.
24. Part III of his article in this volume.
25. Moraux, 314f., argues that external goods are here regarded as choiceworthy only for other things and not for themselves.
26. Moraux explains discrepancies between this earlier doxography and the account of Peripatetic ethics by suggesting that both are by Arius, but that he is using different sources in each case (Moraux, 310–14 and nn.; also 276). A. Kenny, *The Aristotelian Ethics* (Oxford 1978) 22 n.1, argues that it is more plausible to suppose that it is *Stobaeus* who has combined two sources, and that the earlier account is not from Arius at all. Cf. also Giusta, 1.145f. and 410f. It appears that 56.9ff. is in conflict with F over the status of learning; its presence in F implies that it is choiceworthy in itself, while in the earlier passage it is denied that it is choiceworthy for itself.
27. Strength is among the examples of things not choiceworthy in every circumstance in *MM* 1.2 1183b38ff. Cf. also Plato, *Meno* 87E ff. Moraux, 375, however, places bodily goods tentatively under G1.
28. Moraux, 371.
29. Moraux, 370; cf. von Arnim, 51.
30. Cf. *MM* 1.2 1183b28–30; *EE* 8.3 1248b27ff.; Aspasius *In EN, CIAG* 19.1 5.27ff., 6.7ff.; Alexander *In Top., CIAG* 2.2 242.1ff. Von Arnim, 51, 55, 60; Moraux, 371 n.179. It is true that, if something can be misused, there must be some further end in terms of which it can be judged whether it has been misused; indeed, it may seem odd to call anything that is *used* an end. But it has already been seen that one end may be subordinate to another (above, n.13). In the *MM* the division corresponding to Arius' G is only of goods, not of ends; below, n.34.

The *MM* however, refers to things good *in every way (pantōs)*, rather than *for everyone (panti)* as in Arius (*MM* 1183b38ff.). Meineke emended to *pantōs* in Arius too; von Arnim, conversely, argues that *panti* in Arius is supported by the parallel with 135.3–8, and proposes reading *panti* in the *MM* too, comparing *EN* 1.3 1094b18. Giusta 2.122 argues that the MSS readings should be kept in both texts, Arius having substituted *panti* for *pantōs* under the influence of the category of relation. In 136.3 one should read, with von Arnim 54f., *zētein ⟨tous spoudaious⟩ kai chrōmenous ōphelein:* "it seems that ⟨good men⟩ seek these and give benefit by using them."

31. Cf. Aristotle, *Top.* 3.1 116b37; Alexander *In Top.*, *CIAG* 2.2 242.3ff.

32. On p. 135.2 and 9 Spengel emended the MSS *di' heterōn* ("through other things") to *di' hetera* ("on account of other things"). Giusta 2.121 n.3 argues that the MSS text should be kept, on the grounds that it is unlikely to have been corrupted in both places. However, the accusative gives the better sense.

33. Von Arnim, 51; Moraux, 370, 372; R. Walzer, *Magna Moralia und Aristotelische Ethik* (Berlin 1929) 171f. and 270. Although E as a whole has no parallel in *MM* 1.2, its central section, p. 135.3–8, corresponds to 1183b28ff.

34. Von Arnim, 54; even though, as he points out, the sequence in the *MM* has the clear purpose of leading up to the *teleion telos* (1184a8ff.), in a way that the succession of divisions in Arius does not. The contrast between complete and partial ends in *MM* 1.2 1184a8ff. is however presented as a subdivision "chained" to the division that corresponds to Arius' F; compare the position of B in Arius.

35. It is not suggested in E1 that healthy things *are* choiceworthy in themselves—which would imply a conflict with D4. Rather, the point being made is an analogy; potencies are choiceworthy in themselves because the *good* man uses them well, just as surgical tools, for example, are health-giving because the *doctor* uses them to produce health, even though in unskilled hands they can do harm. We should not therefore punctuate after *hugieina* on p.135.7, and we should translate "just as ⟨*those things are*⟩ healthy which . . ." (I owe this point to Professor A. A. Long.) Von Arnim 52 points out that the things mentioned in D4 will include those which produce or preserve *any* of D1–D3; cf. also Alexander *In Top.*, *CIAG* 2.2 242.7. The translation of 134.24–5 (D4) follows Wachsmuth's correction: The manuscript text would give simply "for example, health and physical condition." But *health* appears as a good in itself in F1 which picks up D1–3; cf. *MM* 1.2 1183b pp. 35–37.

36. Alexander, *In Top.*, *CIAG* 2.2 242.4ff.; Aristotle fr.113 Rose. Von Arnim, 51; Moraux, 370 n.177. D1–D3 occur in *EN* 1.12 1101b11 (where V. Rose, *Aristoteles Pseudepigraphus*, Berlin 1863, 127f., points out that the classification is referred to as if it were an established one). *Top.* 4.5 126b4ff. contrasts what deserves honor, or is choiceworthy, for itself on the one hand, and potencies and what is productive on the other, describing *all* the latter as choiceworthy for something else; similarly Alexander ad loc., *In Top.*, *CIAG* 2.2.349.15ff. All four classes from D appear in Aspasius *In EN*, *CIAG* 19.1 32.10ff.; Aspasius makes the point that items in the fourth class are never choiceworthy for themselves, but always for something else, thus by implication agreeing with Arius that items in D1–D3 are choiceworthy for themselves.

37. Namely, the mention of "seeking" as well as of "using" on p.135.5 (contrast *MM* 1.2 1183b29f.); and the definition of ends on p.135.13f. Von Arnim, 54; Giusta, 2.121f.

38. 3.80ff.; Aristotle, fr.114 Rose. Cf. Rose, above n.36, 677; H Mutschmann, ed., *Divisiones Aristoteleae* (Leipzig, Teubner, 1906) v.

39. *Cod. Marc. Gr.* 257; Aristotle, fr.115 Rose.

40. Mutschmann, xxiv–xxv. Alexander includes "parents" and "happiness" among things honored; refers to the second class as "noble" as well as "praiseworthy"; and, like Arius and Aspasius (above, n.36), uses the term *ōphelima*, "beneficial," of the fourth class.

41. *Cod. Marc. Gr.* 257, division 44; Diogenes Laertius 3.81 (division 5).
42. Von Arnim, 56.
43. The analogies between goods of the soul, of the body, and external goods on p.124.19ff. also occur (with rather different examples) at *Cod. Marc. Gr.* 257, division 56; cf. Professor Görgemanns' paper, part III, and Mutschmann, xxviii–xxx. The division of "good" into noble, advantageous and pleasant on p.130.15 also occurs at *Cod. Marc. Gr.* 257, division 21; but this again is a commonplace (cf. Aristotle *EN* 2.3 1104b30 and von Arnim, 22). Cf. Mutschmann, xxviii, also comparing division 2 in Diogenes 3.81 (= *Cod. Marc. Gr.* 257, division 58) with the classification of types of friendship in Arius p.143.2ff.
44. It may be noted, too, that Arius shares with Aspasius. *In EN, CIAG* 19.1 132.16f., but *not* with the *MM*, the point that items in the fourth class in division D are not choiceworthy for themselves (above, n.36).
45. Giusta, 2.93. Cf. von Arnim, 49; Moraux, 369.
46. I am grateful to Professor Furley for drawing my attention to this point.
47. Von Arnim, 50, suggests that only C1, and not the whole of C, takes up B3; see further below.
48. Von Arnim, 49f., suggests that *toutōn*, "of these," in B3 (134.16) should be emended to *toutou*, "of this," so that the items in B3 will only be parts of the *supreme* end, in B2, and not also of the subordinate ends in B1. Moraux, 369 n.176, argues against this.
49. This is argued on p.46.10ff. (Critolaus fr.19 Wehrli), and again, without Critolaus being named, on p. 126.14. It is not indeed explicitly asserted in the latter passage that bodily and external goods are not parts of the end; but cf. 129.19ff. (von Arnim, 50). That "some people" hold that things necessary for happiness are parts of it is already indicated at Aristotle *EE* 1.2 1214b26; cf. Dirlmeier above, n.7, 13. There is a variation on Arius p.46.10ff. in Cicero *De finibus* 5.68 (Antiochus), where goods of the soul *and bodily goods* constitute the supreme good, external goods being choiceworthy in themselves, but not parts of the supreme good (Giusta 2.117).
50. Cf. p.130.1; von Arnim, 50. For external goods as the material of virtue in Stoic contexts cf. Plutarch, *Comm. not* 1069E and Cicero *De finibus* 3.61. Also see Long, above n.21, 75.
51. 126.20ff.; Giusta, 2.117.
52. 122.7ff., 20ff., 125.17. Moraux, 320ff.
53. Cf. von Arnim, above, n.47. Professor Furley suggests to me that *A* is not an exhaustive classification of applications of "good," since it fails to include instrumental goods that are not choiceworthy for themselves (D4, E2). But perhaps they, like all other goods, are covered by A2?
54. Cf. Ackrill, above n.13, especially 5, 10ff. Moraux 369 complains that, because of the lack of examples, it is not made clear whether the 'parts' referred to in B3 are parts of wholes or means to ends.
55. Compare (with regard to the virtues) Arius, p.71.15ff. = *SVF* 3.106.
56. That the case of *wealth* is problematic is pointed out by von Arnim, 59ff., and Moraux, 373. A classification corresponding to K is put forward by Alexander, *In Top., CIAG* 2.2 229.1ff., on Aristotle, *Topics* 3.1 116a29; but here the class corresponding to K1 includes happiness and things deserving honour (cf. D1), that corresponding to K2 exercise, money-making, and beneficial (*ōphelima*) things in general (cf. D4), and the third class, things choiceworthy both for themselves and for other things, includes virtues, health, *wealth* and potencies in general (cf. D3). 'Freedom from trouble,' *aochlēsia*, in Arius's K1 is an Epicurean term (Epicurus, *Letter to Menoeceus* 127), though used by other schools too (Sextus Empiricus, *Pyrrh. Hyp.* 1.10; cf. Posidonius in *SVF* 3.12. F. Dirlmeier, *"Die Zeit des Grossen Ethik,"* *RhMus.* 88 (1939) 242).

57. Von Arnim, 58f.
58. Von Arnim, 59–61; cf. Moraux, 374 n.190.
59. Aspasius, *In EN, CIAG* 19.1 13.24ff., 14.8, 12f., 15.27 (where '*in* itself' and '*for* something else' are treated as non-exclusive *alternatives*). The text in 13.27 seems difficult, and may be corrupt; there is a lacuna just before. Heliodorus, *In EN, CIAG* 19.2 10.9, 12.
60. Alexander, *In Top., CIAG* 2.2 229.19f. He does at first suggest that the two contrasts may be equivalent (230.6–17), but then comes down on the side of concluding that they are indeed distinct. Cf. also ibid. 242.14ff.
61. Ibid., 231.11.
62. Ibid., 230.20ff.
63. Thus von Arnim 58 comments that Arius, in his view, might have described the items falling under E2 as "choiceworthy *only* for something else" (my italics).
64. Aspasius, *In EN, CIAG* 19.1 32.17f. Cf. "are by nature (*pephykenai*) good in themselves" at Arius p. 135.7.
65. Above, n.13; though it may be doubted whether he would be prepared to do so while contrasting them with things that are not ends.
66. Cf. Aspasius *In EN, CIAG* 19.1 13.29; he seems in doubt over the status of health, too, here (even though its being good in itself, 14.1, does not *exclude* its *also* being good for, or on account of, something else; above, n.23). Moraux 371 n.180. At 26.15–24 Aspasius says that wealth, strength and reputation are not necessary for happiness, while health,perceptiveness and friends are.
67. Aspasius, *In EN, CIAG* 19.1 11.4ff.; cf. 162.5ff.
68. Ibid.; cf. above, n.30. At 15.20ff., however, Aspasius treats wealth only as choiceworthy for something else. Alexander, who, as has been seen, does draw a distinction between things choiceworthy *in* themselves and things choiceworthy *for* themselves, generally treats wealth as choiceworthy *in* itself (i.e., not *per accidens)* but only *for* something else; *In Top. CIAG* 2.2 231.4ff., 242.14ff., 26ff., 243.4ff. However, at *In Top.* 229.1ff. he regards wealth as choiceworthy for itself, although money-making is not; above, n.57.
69. Heylbut, the *CIAG* editor, suggests *EN* 4.1 1120a6. But all that this says is that the liberal man will use wealth well; this agrees with Aspasius's *explanation* of the alleged statement, but hardly goes as far as the alleged statement itself.
70. Aristotle *Rhet.* 1.6 1362b18; so too at *Pol.* 1.5 1259b20. Von Arnim, 61. It may be doubted, though, whether von Arnim is right in taking the distinction at *Rhet.* 1.5 1361a16, between wealth that yields interest and wealth from which nothing else comes except the use of it, as showing that the latter is good for its own sake.
71. Above, n.36.
72. 122.7ff., 125.17.
73. Von Arnim 59ff., citing *EN* 4.1 1120a4, where wealth is described as useful. However, *Top.* 3.1 116b37, which he also cites, states only that wealth is *honoured* and *praiseworthy* for something else rather than for itself, not that it is good and choiceworthy only for something else; cf. above, nn.31 and 68.
74. Von Arnim 63. He points to p.124.19ff. as evidence that Arius's source tended to treat soul-goods, bodily goods and external goods all on a level; ibid. 61. Cf. Professor Görgemanns's paper, Part III.
75. Von Arnim 60; he suggests that this reflects an emphasis on the claim that potencies are objects of natural impulse, rather than on the question whether they are good only as means to further ends.
76. *In EN, CIAG* 19.1 32.9ff.; above, n.36. Cf. also Alexander, *In Top., CIAG* 2.2 229.6; above, n.56.

77. I am grateful to Professor Furley for stressing this point. Cf. von Arnim, 47f.; Moraux, 368 and n.173.
78. Von Arnim, 62; Moraux, 376 n.194. The definition of ambiguous terms (*homōnyma*) at p.137.10–12 corresponds to Aristotle *Cat.* 1 1alf.; cf. von Arnim 63, Giusta 2.81 and n.2, Moraux 376 n.195.
79. Von Arnim 48f. cites *Metaph.*, Lambda 7 1072b14. Moraux 369 n.174 adds *De caelo* 1.9 279a28–30, but points out that the idea of preservation (*sōteria*) is not explicit in these texts, and compares rather [Aristotle] *De mundo* 397b16, 20, 398a4, b10, and 400a4 (ibid. n.175). Cf. also Giusta 2.92.
80. [Plato] *Definitions* 414E: "the good is the cause of preservation to the things that are; the cause of everything that relates to oneself(?), from which it comes about that one chooses what one ought." Giusta 2.92 also compares Plato, *Republic* 6.508E. On p.134.12 of Arius, von Arnim 47ff. retains the MSS *theon* and *ton prōton*, giving "of these, one (application of "good"; i.e., A1) is the first god," rather than, with Usener's and Heeren's emendations, "of these, the divine is the first (application of "good")"; accordingly he rejects Usener's additions of *to deuteron* and *triton to* ("the second," "the third") on p. 134.12 and 13. Cf. Giusta 2.91f.
81. *Ac. Post.* 1.20; Giusta 1.101ff., Moraux 376 nn.191f.
82. Von Arnim, 56f. For intellectual and ethical goods as present by nature he compares *EN* 3.5 1114b6, 6.13 1144b34; for the importance of practice in ethics, *Pol.* 7.13 1332a39; and for virtues as perfections (*teleiōseis*) *Phys.* 7.3 246b2, 247a2; *Metaph.*, Delta 16 1021b20. Accordingly he proposes reading *ek teleiōseōs* ("as a result of a process of perfection") rather than *ek teleiotētos* ("as a result of a state of perfection") on p. 136.19f., as being more to the point. On p. 136.18 Giusta 1.102 n.2 and 2.128 proposes *hexēs epimeleiāi* ("subsequently by practice") for the MSS *hexēs epimeleias*; Profesor De Lacy suggests to me *hexēs 〈ex〉 epimeleias* ("subsequently from practice").
83. *EN* 10.9 1179b20ff. and (on potencies) *Metaph.* Theta 5 1047b31–35. Cf. nature, habituation, and reason at *Pol.* 7.13 1332a40 (von Arnim 57).
84. *EN* 2.1 1103a24. It may be noted that I is a subdivision of H, taking up H1; so we here have another "chain," though a every short one.
85. Von Arnim, 57.
86. The MSS have *eutuchia* (good fortune) and *athanasia* (immortality). Spengel proposed *eupsuchia* (good courage), Trendelenburg *euboulia* (sound judgement), and Usener *athaumastia* (not wondering at anything); however, as von Arnim 57 points out, the last-mentioned is attested only for Democritus, in a secondary report (68A168 Diels-Kranz). Von Arnim himself tentatively suggests *euthanasia* (a good death); but cf. next note.
87. Von Arnim, 57, citing Simplicius *In Cat.*, *CIAG* 8.402.20–22. Moraux, 376.
88. Immortality is an example of the impossible (for man) at *EN* 3.2 1111b23; and for a mortal man to become immortal would conflict with the principle that a beginning in time implies an end and vice versa, which forms the subject of *De caelo* 1.12.
89. *EN* 1.10 1100a10ff. However, it has been pointed out to me that a type of god-given *eutuchia* which is "more continuous" than other good fortune is recognized in *EE* 8.2 (especially 1248b7).
90. Moraux, 376.
91. Cf. *SVF* 3. 237–44; J. M. Rist,*Stoic Philosophy* (Cambridge 1969) 16–19.
92. I am grateful to Dr. Inwood for drawing my attention to this point.
93. Compare p.71.15ff. with C and K; 72.14ff. with E and D4 (and also with p.56.9). P.68.24 has a certain affinity with J, though the pattern in J is more complex (cf. above, n.10). On p. 80.22ff. "things preferred" are classified in terms of soul, body, and what is external, as in H; but this is a commonplace.

94. P. 69.7; 70.8, 21; 73.1, 16; 74.15. There is little sign of "chaining" in the Stoic divisions, except for one sequence on p.73.1–15.
95. P. 69.5, 13; 70.3, 14; 71.6; 72.6; and as a general principle on p. 74.21.
(Notes to the Appendix)
96. I am grateful to Professor Furley for pointing out that it is from here that the parallel starts.
97. Or "potencies" in general (*dynameis*)—cf. D3? The corresponding passage of the *MM* has *dynamis* "power" in the singular (1184a3).
98. Cf. especially 18–19; Moraux 372.
99. Cf. also 14.11–13; and above, n.66.

Comments on Dr. Sharples' Paper
A Note on Arius and Magna Moralia 1.1–2

David J. Furley

It seems clear that Arius regards the first three items in the list beginning at p. 134.7 [translated in Section I of Dr. Sharples' paper and labelled A, B, C, by him] as forming a unit of some kind, although they are not united by progressive *diairesis*, as later groups are. The first move [A] is to distinguish three ways in which "the good" is used:

1. of the cause of preservation of all the things that are;
2. of whatever is predicated of every good;
3. of what is choiceworthy for itself.

This is not a classification, into coordinate groups, of things that are good; nor is it an exhaustive classification of the ways in which "good" is used (we also speak of instrumental things as good). It is a distinction made with a particular purpose; and the purpose is stated, although very obscurely, in the first line: "since happiness is the greatest good *for us.*" The distinction is to introduce a discussion of the good *for us:* i.e., the subject matter of ethics.

The objective of this first move becomes clear only when the passage is placed beside a fleshed-out discussion such as the first chapter of the *Magna Moralia,* where we have something recognizable as the same threefold distinction. [The relevant passages are reproduced in translation as an appendix to this note.] This time the point is brought out explicitly: it is that the first two ways in which the good is spoken of are irrelevant to ethics, and therefore to be eliminated from the present discussion.

The first rejected use in *MM* is "the good of gods"; in Arius [A 1] we have "the cause of preservation of all things that are," and later "the first god," if the manuscript reading is correct, or "first, the divine," if the text is emended as in Wachsmuth's edition (see Sharples, n. 80). More on that subject shortly. The second rejected use in *MM* (actually the third use mentioned) is first taken to be the Platonic Idea of the Good, but after some discussion that is put on one side in favour of "the common [good], as definition or induction." This is to be compared with Arius' [A 2], "what is predicated of every good" or "the genus of all good things." The accepted use, mentioned second in order in *MM,* is "what is best for each of the things that are, and that is what is choiceworthy for its own sake.'' In Arius' list we have [A 3] "what is choiceworthy for itself" and "the end, to which we refer everything, which is *eudaimonia*.''

It seems fairly clear that Arius' division [A] is nothing but a derivative of this section of *MM*. The *MM* discussion starts by establishing that politics or ethics, being the best, must have the *best* as its goal. Arius picks up this point in his otherwise pointless first sentence, "Since happiness is the *greatest* good for us, we must distinguish . . ..'' And his first description of the subject matter of ethics [A 3] is very close to the phrasing of the equivalent in *MM*. The two rejected items need some further clarification, however, before it can be seen how close the resemblance is.

What *MM*'s expression "the good of gods'' (b 4) means is not at once clear. It is presumably not what is good *for* gods, but rather the good that belongs to gods or the good that is characteristic of gods. Arius interprets this in the spirit of *Metaph*. Lambda 10, or more exactly in the spirit of the pseudo-Aristotelian *De mundo* (chapters 5–6), where the notion of the divine as the source of preservation for all the different beings in the cosmos is set out more explicitly than in the *Metaphysics*. The parallel structure of *MM* and Arius makes this interpretation of Arius more likely than that of von Arnim, who claims that we have here not "a later bowdlerization (*Verballhornung*) of Aristotelian theology, but rather a return to an earlier form closer in expression to Plato.'' Von Arnim was persuaded that there should be something Platonic about [A 1] because in a similar division of the good in *EE* 1.8 the Idea of the Good stands in the first place, with the common good and the human good following. The wording of Arius, however, makes it difficult to detect any Platonic tone in [A 1] and the comparison with *MM* shows that we need no longer try to do so, since it shows that the Idea of the Good, if Arius had wanted to mention it, would have been subsumed under [A 2] rather than [A 1].

Now, what is the relation of [B] to [A]? The third division of [A] is described as what is choiceworthy for itself, and it is this that is divided into three in [B]. In [A] it is identified as "the end, to which we refer everything, which is *eudaimonia*.'' Of course, *eudaimonia* is only one of the items in the class "choiceworthy for itself,'' and it is this larger class that is divided, not *eudaimonia* by itself. To understand how this happened, we have to go back to the *MM* again.

The author of *MM*, as we have seen, distinguishes the relevant kind of good as "what is best for each of the things that are, and that is what is choiceworthy because of its own nature (1182b7). This is at the level of generality appropriate to this stage of the argument in *MM*. After the argument that leads to the rejection of the Idea of the Good and the universal good, the author repeats the relevant kind of good, but this time, instead of the general formula "what is best for each of the things that are,'' he inserts "what is best—and best in the sense of best *for us*'' (1183a6). We already know, of course, that ethics is about the *human* good. But there is no mention of *eudaimonia* yet, nor of the *telos*. These concepts are introduced only after some further divisions.

Arius has confused the proper sequence of his divisions [A] and [B] by mentioning the *telos* and *eudaimonia* prematurely. What is divided in [B] is indeed a subsection of [A], namely [A 3], but under its proper, general description "what is choiceworthy for itself."

Arius' divisions [B] and [C] make sense as parts of a continuing attempt to classify *eudaimonia*. It gives point to the division in [B] if we see it as leading towards a claim that *eudaimonia* falls into subsection [B 2] "the ultimate for the sake of which we do all things," as opposed to [B 1] "the ultimate for the sake of which we do some things" and [B 3] "whatever is a part of these." And (as Mr. Sharples notes) there is a trace, however faint, in these phrases of a division that we find in *MM* just before the first emergence of *eudaimonia*. Arius prefers "ultimate" (*eschaton*) to "perfect" (*teleion*) in *MM*: "Again, of ends themselves the perfect is always better than the imperfect. *Perfect* is one in the presence of which we need nothing further, imperfect is one in the presence of which we need something further: e.g., in the presence of justice we need many further things, but in the presence of *eudaimonia* we need nothing further" (1184a8–12). The author of *MM* then goes straight to his conclusion (without anything corresponding to Arius' [C]): "So *this* (sc. *eudaimonia*) is that best-for-us that we seek, which is a perfect end."

Arius' division [C] does not divide [B 2], as we might have expected, but offers a new division of "things choiceworthy in themselves," i.e., of all things so called in any of the ways distinguished in [B]. [C] uses two technical terms (*prohegoumenos, hylikos*) that are probably borrowed from Stoics and are certainly not Aristotelian; so we shall not expect to find a close parallel in *MM*.

MM Book 1, Chapter 2, continues the discussion that leads up to the correct classification of *eudaimonia*, after what corresponds to Arius' division [A], with divisions that are recognizably similar to [D] [G] and [F] in Arius, in that order; but I have nothing to add to Mr. Sharples' discussion of these sections.

In conclusion, then—and the point of this note is—it is plausible that behind the apparently unmotivated and confused series of divisions at the beginning of this section of Arius we can detect a coherent argumentative structure, in which we are led from a very general notion of the good to the proper subject matter for ethics. We find such a structure in the *Magna Moralia*, and either this book itself, or less probably some unknown source used by its author, is likely to have been the source of this part of Arius' list.

APPENDIX: *Magna Moralia*, Book 1.1–2

The following is a translation or summary of parts of the first two chapters of the *Magna Moralia* that are especially relevant to Arius' list of divisions of goods. In the left hand margin are both Bekker's page numbers and the letters and numbers allocated by Dr. Sharples to those divisions in Arius' list that appear to correspond.

Chapter 1

[The book opens by declaring that ethics is a branch of politics, and that its first subject must be the nature and origin of virtue. It continues with a succinct account of the treatment of virtue by the Pythagoreans, Socrates, and Plato. The author then introduces his own discussion.]

1182a32   First, then, we must observe that every science and every potentiality has a goal; and this goal is good, since no science or potentiality is for the sake of a bad thing. So if the goal of every potentiality is good, clearly the goal
1182b1   of the best will be best. But the political potentiality is the best one; consequently its goal will be ⟨the best?⟩ good.

[A1]   Hence we must obviously speak about the good—not about the good unqualified, but about the good *for us*. For we need not speak about the good
b 5   of gods—about that there is another account and a different inquiry. So we must discuss the political good.

[A3]   But this must be divided again. About good in what sense? For it is not simple. Good is spoken of either as what is best for each of the things that are,[1] and that is what is choiceworthy because of its own nature; or as what
[A2]   makes other things good when they share in it, and that is the Idea of the Good.

b10   Now, should we speak of the Idea of the Good, or not, but rather about good as what is common to all [good] things; for that would appear to be different from the Idea. The Idea is separable, and by itself, but the common is present in all [good] things, and so is not the same as the Idea, since what
b15   is separable and naturally self-subsistent will not be present in all [good] things. So, are we to speak of the good that is present in things?

Or rather not, for the following reasons? [The author distinguishes two ways of interpreting the "common" good, according to whether it is arrived at by definition or by induction, and argues that in either case it does not fall in the domain of any science, and so not within that of ethics.]

1183a6   It is clear, then, that it is of the *best* good that we must speak, and best as the best *for us*.
           [No one science deals with all the good because the good falls in all of the categories.]

a23   So [it is the function of ethics to speak] of the good, and of the best, and of the best for us.
           [Further criticism of the Idea of the Good, and of Socrates' claim that virtue is a kind of knowledge.]

Chapter 2

1183b19   Now that those things have been settled, let us try to say in how many ways the good is spoken of. Of goods, some are honorable, some praiseworthy,
[D1]   some potentialities. I mean by *honorable* such as the divine, the better, such as soul, mind, the older, the principle, and so on; for the honorable is what occasions honor, and all such are associated with honor. So virtue is hon-
b25   orable, when a good man develops from it, for he then takes on the form
[D2]   of virtue. Some goods are *praiseworthy,* such as virtues, for praise arises

[D3]   from virtuous deeds. Some goods are *potentialities,* such as position, wealth, strength, beauty: for these may be used well by the good man and badly by

b30   the bad; hence such goods are called potentialities. Indeed they *are* goods (for each of them is assessed on its use by the good man, not the bad); but these same goods can be brought about by chance, since from chance come

b35   wealth and position, and generally whatever falls into the class of poten-

[D4]   tiality. A final, fourth group of goods is what preserves or creates a good, as exercize does health, and so on.

1184a1 [G1]   But goods have a further division: of goods some are in every respect and every way choiceworthy, some not. Justice, for example, and the other

[G2]   virtues, are in every respect and in every way choiceworthy; strength, wealth, power, and such are not in every respect nor in every way.

[F1][F2]   Again, in another way: of goods, some are ends, some are not ends. E.g.,

a5   health is an end, the means to health are not ends. And in these cases the end is always better, as health is better than healthful things, and in general terms something is better if other things are means to it.

[B2?]   Again, of ends themselves the perfect is always better than the imperfect. Perfect is that in the presence of which we need nothing further, imperfect

a10[B1?]   is that in the presence of which we do need something further; e.g., in the presence of justice we need further things, but in the presence of *eudaimonia* we need nothing further.

So this is the best-for-us that we seek, which is a perfect end: indeed the perfect end is the good and the end of goods.

NOTE

1. The participle *on,* not the preposition *en,* is to be read in 1182b8: cf. *EE* 1218a31, "each thing seeks its own proper good."

CHAPTER 9

Oikeiōsis in Arius Didymus

Herwig Görgemanns

Most histories of ancient philosophy mention the fact that the concept of *oikeiōsis* was essential for Stoic ethics. *Oikeiōsis* is something which a human being has from birth. It is primarily a relation to oneself (*oikeiōsis pros heauton*), starting with self-awareness, and then implying an active desire (*hormē*) to support and protect oneself. With the growing maturity of the rational element in the individual this primary *oikeiōsis* is transferred from the physical or biological self to the rational self, and its cultivation and perfection become the proper goal or *telos* of human life. There is a third application of *oikeiōsis,* which appears in various forms and contexts in our sources. This is a relation to other persons and things which are felt to belong to oneself, and at this point social relations and duties come into the theory.

I do not want to go into the details of the Stoic theory, but shall rather turn to Arius Didymus. Strangely enough, he sets out the theory of *oikeiōsis* not in his discussion of Stoic ethics, but as a part of his section on Peripatetic ethics. This section falls into two distinct parts (pp. 116.21–128.9; pp. 128.11–147.25[1]), which are generally regarded as separate treatises. We can restrict our attention to the first part. It has been analysed in detail by von Arnim, Dirlmeier, Pohlenz and most recently in a well balanced study by P. Moraux.[2] There is no need to discuss all the points which have been raised. One fact which has become sufficiently clear is that this part is a coherent treatise, not a collection of doxographical notes. In spite of some irregularities there is a philosophical argument carried through from beginning to end, and we can hear an author defending his position and trying to convince the reader with all kinds of arguments: proofs, examples taken from life and from poetry, and sometimes with rhetorical devices.[3] The *oikeiōsis* concept is at the basis of the treatise, although the word (in verbal form) occurs only occasionally (pp. 118.12; 122.3; 123.9,25; 125.23; 126.2).

The obvious problem is how a theory which is regarded as typically Stoic can be presented by a doxographical author as Peripatetic. One might almost suspect that Arius by mistake took a Stoic author for a Peripatetic. But this cannot be true, because the *oikeiōsis* theory is made to serve as a basis for a doctrine of values pointedly Peripatetic, in which goods outside of virtue are acknowledged. Arius must have followed a Peripatetic source which had the *oikeiōsis* concept built in.

These facts pose some far-reaching questions concerning the interrelations of the philosophical schools during the late Hellenistic period, including the vexed Antiochus problem. In this paper, however, I propose to discuss only two questions of limited scope. First, can we, by analyzing the text, find out something about the nature and origin of the anonymous Peripatetic essay which Arius used and to which he seems to refer by the word *hypographē* ("sketch, outline")?[4] (It will be assumed that we have in Stobaeus the text of Arius in an essentially unadulterated, although perhaps abridged, form.) I want to study some passages in detail, but I shall not try to make comparisons with other texts such as Cicero, *De finibus*. Parallels of this kind are only occasionally used to support an argument. As a consequence, we shall not be able to discuss the place of the treatise in the history of the Peripatos, nor its possible relations to philosophers like Antiochus and Xenarchus. But it may be of interest to see how far the analysis of the text itself leads. The second question is the origin of the notion of *oikeiōsis*. I want to approach this question with the help of a semantic study of the history of the word, assuming that for understanding a philosophical term it is useful to study also its nonterminological uses and connotations. The discussion of these two topics will make up Sections III and IV of my paper. At the beginning I shall give a brief survey of earlier research on the *oikeiōsis* section in Arius Didymus (Section I of this paper). In addition I shall offer (in Section II) a translation of the Greek text (pp. 116.19–128.9), for there is no available English translation, and translation is often useful for sharpening issues of interpretation.

I. HISTORY OF THE SCHOLARLY DISCUSSION

J. N. Madvig in his commentary on Cicero's *De finibus*[5] made the first important observations. He pointed out the similarity between the Peripatetic ethics in Arius and the ethics of Antiochus of Ascalon as represented by Cicero in *De finibus* book 5. Antiochus, being an Academic philosopher, but maintaining the fundamental identity of Academic and Peripatetic doctrine, had also worked the *oikeiōsis* theory into his own system, and the resulting similarity with Arius is sometimes striking. Madvig concluded that Antiochus was Arius's main source. This was accepted, among others, by Hermann Diels in his *Doxographi Graeci*,[6] at least for the section we are concerned with. The passages in Cicero and Arius Didymus appeared to be very characteristic for Antiochus, who was viewed as a thoroughgoing eclectic, or rather syncretist, combining not only Plato and Aristotle, but also the Stoa. Diels's description has become famous: "*Stoicae disciplinae non guttae sed flumina immissa sunt, vix ut Aristotelea subinde adgnoscantur.*" ("Not just drops, but floods of Stoic doctrine have been poured in, so that the Aristotelian element is sometimes almost unrecognizable.") This line of argument was continued by Hans Strache in his work on Antiochus.[7]

The matter can be approached, however, from a different angle. Peripatetic ethics in Arius is certainly different from Aristotelian ethics; but is it necessary or even probable that Arius used a late and syncretistic source for his doxography? Might he not have used an author from the early Peripatos, who had introduced some innovations into Aristotelian ethics? The name of Theophrastus was suggested by Leonhard Spengel,[8] who pointed out that Theophrastus is quoted by name in a later section of Arius (p. 140.8). Generalizing and developing this aspect, Hans von Arnim came to the conclusion[9] that we find here the *oikeiōsis* theory as originally devised by Theophrastus, and that the early Stoics borrowed the theory from him for their own purposes. The analogy with Antiochus in *De fin.* 5 is then to be explained not by dependence of one from the other but by common derivation from Theophrastus. All this amounted to a reversal of the conventional picture; moreover, Stoicism lost its claim to originality in the matter of *oikeiōsis*. Von Arnim also pointed out some Theophrastean texts preserved by Porphyrius in which he speaks of natural relationship to a widening circle of beings, and took these fragments as a confirmation of his thesis.

The next important contribution came from Franz Dirlmeier.[10] He accepted neither Antiochus nor Theophrastus as a direct source. It had already been observed that certain details stand against these assumptions. Arius Didymus (p. 118.16) names pleasure among the objects of first *oikeiōsis*. Antiochus (*De fin.* 5.45) denies it this status. Arius's final definition of the *telos* (p. 126.12 ff.) is carefully distinguished from another, which can be identified as that of Critolaus. Therefore the text cannot go as far back as the time of Theophrastus. It remained to assume as source a late Peripatetic writing, the author of which we cannot identify. But apart from the question of a direct source, Dirlmeier found much truth in von Arnim's analysis. For much of the vocabulary that had passed for Stoic he could quote Peripatetic parallels. Above all he traced the biological way of thinking that seems to lie behind the *oikeiōsis* theory back to Theophrastus. Two examples may be mentioned: the expression *ta kata physin* as a description of goods, which is quite common in the context of the *oikeiōsis* theory, turned out to be Theophrastean, and secondly it seemed significant that Theophrastus had given particular attention to animals and child development in ethical discussions.

The views of von Arnim and Dirlmeier did not hold the field for long. Max Pohlenz studied *oikeiōsis* in its Stoic setting,[11] and as far as Arius Didymus was concerned he illustrated Diels's "*flumina*" with a wealth of parallels from Stoic sources. These parallels proved more convincing than the Peripatetic ones which Dirlmeier had given, because they concerned the line of thought, whereas Dirlmeier had based his argument chiefly on vocabulary. But Pohlenz did not just fall back on the position of Diels and Strache. He dropped the Antiochus theory and voted for Dirlmeier's unknown late Peripatetic. He acknowledged also that there was a biological trend in the ethics of Theophrastus and that natural affinity (*oikeiotēs*) was important for him. But he distinguished natural affinity from Stoic *oikeiōsis*. Theophrastus might have paved the way but he had certainly not developed the theory itself. Pohlenz turned his attention also to the question of how Antiochus, as well as our anonymous Peripatetic, could with a good conscience present the *oikeiōsis* theory as Peripatetic, and he showed that since Carneades there had been a tendency to regard those Stoic doctrines which seemed universally acceptable as borrowings from Platonic or Aristotelian sources. Antiochus, it seems, presented his philosophy as a return to the ancients, but his idea of their philosophy was partly an unhistorical construct. Our anonymus Peripatetic might have had a similar attitude.

The solution which Pohlenz gave was widely recognized, and later research tended to confirm its general outlines. I refer to the studies of Brink, Pembroke and Moraux.[12] C. O. Brink modified the picture by admitting that one motif in the developed *oikeiōsis* theory—the widening circles of relationships—is too similar to the Theophrastus fragments to be independent, and argued that the Stoic *oikeiōsis* theory, which had been a fresh and independent departure in the field of ethics, was later supplemented by this idea of Peripatetic origin.

Finally, I must mention the work of Michelangelo Giusta,[13] who tends to revive certain notions of the Arnim-Dirlmeier school. Giusta minimizes the influence of Antiochus and sees the common source of Arius Didymus and Cicero (*De fin.* 5) in a major doxographic work which he calls the "*Vetusta Placita*" and attributes conjecturally to Arius Didymus himself. *Oikeiōsis* theories, in his view, were developed by the early Peripatos (probably Theophrastus) as well as by Stoics and Epicureans. This fact is to be explained by a common background: a desire, going back in the last instance to the sophistic concepts of *nomos* and *physis,* to base ethics on the natural needs and urges observed in children.

II. TRANSLATION

This translation presents the text contained in Johannes Stobaeus, *Anthologium* 2, 7.13–14 (in the edition of C. Wachsmuth vol. 2, pp. 116.19–128.9). In general I translate the text as it was printed by Wachsmuth without marking his additions, omissions and emendations. In those cases, where I depart from his text, I give an explanation in square brackets. In round brackets I add some supplements necessary to make the text readable and understandable in English. In the left margin I give my own division into chapters and paragraphs, in order to make reference easier. In addition I give the traditional page numbers of Wachsmuth's edition.

ARISTOTLE AND THE OTHER PERIPATETICS ON ETHICS

1.1   Character (*ēthos*), he says, has its name from habit (*ethos*). For (those characteristics) of which we have the beginnings and seeds from nature,

p. 117   attain perfection by habit and right upbringing, and therefore the study of character is a study of habit and concerns only the animals, and above all

.2   man. For in the other (animals) habits are shaped not by reason but by force, and this is how they acquire their characteristic qualities; man, however, acquires them by being formed by reason as a result of habituation, insofar as the irrational part of the soul is in a condition which accords with reason.

.3 What is called "irrational part of the soul" is not that which is absolutely irrational, but that which is capable of being influenced by reason, as is the case with the emotional (part of the soul). So this part is open to receive

.4 virtue. One part of the soul is rational, the other irrational: rational that which judges, irrational that which impells. Of the rational part that which contemplates the eternal and divine things is called scientific, and that which is about acts in human and temporal matters is called deliberative. And of the irrational part that which strives for things that are in our power is called desirous, that which is, so to speak, on the defense against other people, is

.5 called irascible. Therefore the class of virtues also falls into two parts, a

p.118 rational and an irrational one, because this is the respect under which the nature of contemplation and of acting (is to be distinguished). It follows, furthermore, that virtue of character (which is irrational and related to acting) does not consist in knowledge, but in an habitual condition of deciding what is the noble thing (to do).

2.1 Now it is characteristic of virtue that it is brought to perfection by three

.2 things, nature, habit, and reason. For man, who is distinguished in body and soul from the other living beings, since he is in between immortal and mortal things, and has bonds of community with both, with the rational beings by the divine element in his soul, with the irrational beings by the mortal element in his body, accordingly reaches out for perfection of both

.3 these elements. And first of all he strives for existence, because he is by nature well-disposed towards himself. It is also a natural and fitting consequence of this fact that he feels happy with conditions (or things) according

.4 to nature unhappy about conditions (or things) contrary to nature. Thus, he is eager to take care of his health, he reaches out for pleasure, and he struggles to preserve his life, because these things are according to nature and for their own sake choiceworthy and good. On the other hand, he wards off and avoids illness and pain and perishing, since these things are contrary

.5 to nature and for their own sake to be avoided and bad. For dear to us is

p. 119 our body, dear our soul, dear their parts and their faculties and their activities, and by provident care to protect these things [reading "*hōn*," not Usener's

.6 "⟨*di*'⟩ *hōn*"] the beginnings of drive, duty and virtue arise. Now, if in regard to choosing and avoiding the above-mentioned things no error at all occurred, if rather we continually enjoyed the good things and were free from the bad things, then we would never have searched for correct and errorless selection in these matters. But after we had frequently erred out of ignorance about choosing and avoiding, and neglected the good things and approached the bad things like good ones, we were forced to go in search of firm knowledge of these judgements, and when we found that this knowledge is in harmony with nature, we gave it the name "virtue" in view of the overwhelming importance of its function (*aretē* from *aristos,* "the best"), and we gave it superhuman admiration and honour above all other things. For actions have their basis essentially in the selection of things according to nature and the nonselection of things contrary to nature, and as well the so-called duties; and therefore also the ethically right acts and ethically wrong acts occur in and about these things.

3.1 Almost the whole outline of (the ethical system of) this school is developed

.2 from this starting point, as I am going to show in a short (survey).—That children are for their procreators not only choiceworthy because of their usefulness but also for their own sake, is clear from the evidence. For there

p. 120   is nobody of so savage and brutish a nature that he would not be eager to provide for his children to live in happiness and to fare well after his death, rather than the opposite. It is in consequence of this parental love that those who are going to die make testaments and provide (even) for those who are still in the mother's womb, leave guardians and protectors (for them), entrust them to those closest to them and implore these to help them, and in some

.3   cases when children die the parents die with them. But if children are loved so much because of being choiceworthy for their own sake, it follows necessarily that also parents and brothers and the woman who shares one's bed and relatives and the other members of a household and fellow citizens are treated as friends for their own sake, for we have by nature certain (different) kinds of affinity to them also. For man is an animal that is friendly

.4   and lives in community with other men. If among these friendly relations some happen to be remote, and some close, this doesn't make any difference for our argument, for in each case they are choiceworthy for their own sake

.5   and not only for their usefulness. Now if a friendly relation to fellow citizens is choiceworthy for its own sake, it follows necessarily that the same is the case about friendly relations toward persons of the same ethnic group and of the same race, and so also about human beings in general. In fact all

p. 121   those who save another person have this attitude to him: they mostly act not with a view to the merit (of the other person), but because he (or the act)

.6   is choiceworthy for his own sake. For who would not rescue a man, when he sees him being overcome by a beast, assuming he could do so? Who would not show the way to (a stranger) who has lost his way? Who would not assist a man perishing through lack (of food)? Who would not if he discovered a trickle of water in a waterless desert, put up a sign to draw the attention of other travellers to it? Who does not value highly a good reputation after death? Who does not abominate utterances of the following kind as being contrary to human nature: ''When I am dead, may the earth go up in flames—I don't care, for I am all right'' (from an unknown tragedy,

.7   *TrGF, Adespota* F 513)? All this leads to the conclusion that we have natural good-will and friendliness toward everybody, and these attitudes evidently have the character of being choiceworthy for their own sake and of being according to reason; for ''there is one race of men and one race of gods, and we both have our breath from one mother'' (Pindar, *Nemeans* 6.1–2),

.8   which is nature. But although there exists a general love of mankind in us, the character of being choiceworthy for its own sake is still much more evident in the relation to friends, with whom we have regular contact. And if a friend is choiceworthy for his own sake, (this predicate applies) also

p. 122   (to) friendship and good will, not only from all those who share our life but also from the majority of mankind; and therefore praise is also choiceworthy for its own sake, because we are well disposed towards those who praise us. And if praise is choiceworthy for its own sake, this applies also to good reputation; because we take it from the outline (of Peripatetic ethics) that good reputation is nothing else but praise from the general public.

4.1   By these arguments it is clearly established that those goods which come from outside are by their nature choiceworthy for their own sake; and isn't this therefore much more true about those goods which are about us and in

.2   us: I mean those concerning body and soul?—If man is choiceworthy for his own sake, it follows that the parts of man are also choiceworthy for their own sake. Now the most general division of man is into body and soul. Therefore the body must also be choiceworthy for its own sake. For how can it be that for us the body of a fellow man should be choiceworthy for its own sake, but not our own? Or that a fellow man should be choiceworthy for his own sake, but not each of us for himself should be choiceworthy for his own sake? Or that this might be the case, but the parts of the body and the excellences of the parts and of the whole body should not be choiceworthy? It follows that health, strength, beauty, swiftness of foot, good (bodily) condition, keenness of the senses, and in general all excellences of the body, to say it in one word, are choiceworthy for their own sake. Another general argument is that nobody who has his wits about him would choose to be ugly and deformed in shape, even provided that such a repulsive appearance did not entail any practical disadvantage. So it appears that avoidance of ugliness is reasonable even without a practical disadvantage. If, however, ugliness is to be avoided for its own sake, beauty is choiceworthy not only for its usefulness but also for its own sake. For it is clear that beauty has by itself some attraction, and everybody feels naturally drawn towards beautiful people, even without any (consideration of) usefulness: one is willing to do good and to benefit them, and so (beauty) is seen to produce good will. The result of this argument is again that beauty belongs to those things that are choiceworthy for their own sake and ugliness to those that are to be avoided for their own sake. The same argument can be applied also to health and illness, strength and weakness, swiftness of foot and slowness, soundness and defects of the senses.

Therefore now, if it is proved that the bodily kind of goods are also choiceworthy for their own sake and the ills, that are opposite to them, to be avoided for their own sake, then it follows with necessity that also the parts of the soul are choiceworthy for their own sake, and also their virtues and those of the whole soul. For virtue, after making its entrance, as we have indicated, starting from the bodily and external goods, and then turning toward herself and contemplating that she herself belongs also to the things according to nature, even in a much higher degree than the virtues of the body, became well-disposed toward herself as toward something choiceworthy for its own sake, and even more toward herself than toward the bodily virtues. Therefore the virtues of the soul have a far surpassing value. However, this may be concluded also from what we discussed earlier. If health of body is choiceworthy for its own sake, the same is much more true about health of the soul; and health of the soul is temperance, which rids us from the excess of emotions. And if bodily strength belongs to the good things, strength of the soul will be in a much higher degree choiceworthy for itself and good; and strength of the soul is courage and endurance, which brings the soul into a good and strong condition; and therefore courage and endurance will also be choiceworthy for their own sake. In a corresponding way, if bodily beauty is choiceworthy for its own sake, beauty of the soul will also be choiceworthy for its own sake, and it is justice that is beauty of the the the soul; for "doing no wrong makes us beautiful as well" (Menander frg.790 Koerte). [The heading which occurs here in the text: "That the three kinds of goods, those about the body, the soul and the external ones, correspond with each other, although they are different," must be regarded as a later addition.] A similar relation exists also in the

.3 p. 123

.4

.5

5.1

.2

.3 p. 124

.4

p. 125

.5

.6

case of the virtues, since it appears that the three kinds of goods, in spite of their enormous difference, yet have some correspondence [I do not translate the words *pros ton logon,* which appear to be due to an interpolation], and I shall now try to explain this correspondence clearly. The same thing which we call health in the body, is called temperance in the soul, and in the external (goods) wealth; for wealth takes care of most mistakes (we make), as well (as health takes care of bodily disorders and temperance of excessive emotions). And the same thing which (is called) strength in the body, (is called) courage in the soul, and power in the external (goods); and what (is called) keeness of the senses in the body, (is called) reason in the soul, and good luck in the external goods; and what (is called) beauty in the body, (is called) justice in the soul, and friendship in the external (goods). So there exist three kinds of goods which are choiceworthy for their own sake, those which concern the soul and those which concern the body and the external ones, and those which concern the soul are much more choiceworthy than the others, since the soul has a more leading position and is more choiceworthy than the body.

6.1

.2

p. 126

.3

It is clear, then, that the virtues of the soul are more choiceworthy than those of the body and the external (goods), as they (all) in the same way win the first rank (in a comparison with the other two classes). But the others are taken as aims as well; in the first instance as things choiceworthy for their own sake, and secondly as being useful for public and social life, and also for contemplative life. For an assessment of the life (one leads) is made on the basis of public and social acts and of contemplative acts. Virtue is not selfish according to this school of thought, but it is social and public; and since virtue is, as we said before, above all well-disposed toward herself, it follows that she must also by her very nature be well-disposed toward the knowledge of truth. A consequence of this is also that (decisions about) going on living are assessed on the basis of social and public and contemplative acts, and (decisions about) departing (from life) from the opposite. Thus one can come to the conclusion that even [reading *kai* with the mss., not Wachsmuth's conjecture *kakōs*] for a wise man there may be reasons to take his own life, and for an inferior man there may be reasons to go on living, since for those who are able to perform social and public acts and contemplative acts, whether they are valuable or inferior individuals, there are reasons to go on living, but for those who are unable to do so, there is reason to take their own lives.

7.1

.2

Since now virtue is much superior to bodily and external goods, with regard to its (practical) effects as well as with regard to (its character of) being choiceworthy for its own sake, it is logical to regard the purpose (of life) not as ''an accumulation made up from (the goods of the soul as well as) the bodily and external goods,'' nor as ''the successful obtaining of these goods'' [reading *autōn* with the mss., not Usener's conjecture *hapantōn*], but rather as ''a life in accordance with virtue in (enjoyment of) the goods which concern the body and the external ones, either all or the most and most important of them.'' Therefore happiness is ''activity in accordance with virtue consisting in actions under normal [reading *proēgoumenais* with the mss., not Wachsmuth's conjecture *chorēgoumenais*] conditions, as you would wish them''; and the goods which concern the body and the external ones are (rightly) called ''productive of happiness,'' since by their presence they contribute something (to it). Those who say that they "make happiness complete" (implying that they form an essential part of it) do not understand that happiness is a (kind of) life and life is made up of actions; but none of the bodily or external goods is in itself an action or, speaking more generally, an activity. Now, since these things are related in this way, there can come into existence beneficence and gratitude and thankfulness and love of mankind and of children and of brothers, and further the patriot and the lover of parents and family [reading *ho te philopatris kai philopatōr kai philoikeios* with the mss., not Wachsmuth's conjecture *to te philopatri kai philopator kai philoikeion*], and accordingly sociability and good-will and friendship and equality and justice, and the whole divine chorus of the virtues. Whosoever does not care for them can be seen making mistakes in the choice of things which are good and the avoidance of things which are bad, and in the acquisition and in the use of things which are good; and he will be generally judged to fail in the choice because of (faulty) judgement, in the acquisition because of (wrong) ways and means, in the use because of ignorance. They fail in choice, if they choose what is not good at all, or what is less intensely (good) than it should be. This happens to most people, when they prefer the enjoyable to the useful and the useful to the noble and overstep proper measure in their impulses. (They fail) in acquisition, if they do not make it clear (to themselves) beforehand, wherefrom and how and to what extent they should provide these things for themselves. (They fail) in use—considering that all use has reference either to itself [or "oneself," reading *hauton* with the mss., not Heeren's conjecture *hautēn*] or to others— in reference to itself [or "oneself"] if they do not approach things in due measure; in reference to others, if they do not observe the relation to merit which an appropriate (act) must have. Whereas inferior people fail in these respects, valuable people act rightly by doing the opposite in every way, having virtue as a guide for their actions. All virtues, in fact, have in common (the elements of) judging and deciding and acting. For virtue cannot be without judgement and decision and action; but reason goes at their head, having as it were a (general) leadership both over things falling into her department and over those falling into the departments of the others: over choiceworthy things and those to be avoided, over actions to be performed and not performed, and over those that involve a more or less; but each of the other (virtues) restricts itself to its own department alone.

p. 127

.3

.4

.5

p. 128

III. ANALYSIS

Chapter 1 sets out the Peripatetic concept of *aretē*, emphasizing the three elements which are necessary for it: nature, habituation and reason. There is no mention of *oikeiōsis*.

Chapter 2 opens with the statement that three things are essential[14] for perfect virtue, and the three elements explained in chapter 1 are listed (§ 1). This looks like a summary of chapter 1; but the particle *de* suggests that a new start is being made, and the continuation with *gar* (§ 2) implies that the initial statement needs a confirmation or explanation. These formal elements all point forwards, and it seems awkward that the relation to chapter 1 is given no formal recognition, for example, by beginning with *dē* instead of *de*.

But is the forward connection of 2.1 quite in order? There is obviously a correspondence between *teleiousthai* in § 1 and *teleiotēs* in § 2. This "perfection" is in § 1 related to *aretē*, in § 2 to body and soul; but this is not an important divergence, since *aretē* appears again in § 6 and is indeed the end of a process of perfection. But difficulties arise about the three elements named in § 1. Nature, in fact, is mentioned in § 3, and again in § 6 and 7 (p. 119.13, 16, 17). Reason is introduced in § 6 under the name of *eidēsis* and its harmony with nature is emphasized. But of habituation there is no trace at all.[15] This fact should not be taken lightly, because habituation is a distinctive feature of the Aristotelian theory of *aretē*, and it is quite justified that chapter 1 lays so much stress upon it. On the other hand, its absence from 2.2–8 is not due to oversight. The duality of nature and reason is essential for the chapter, and it is carefully prepared for in § 2 by reference to the dual nature of man. In § 5 *oikeiōsis* is shown to concern body as well as soul. The dual concept is, of course, not un-Peripatetic,[16] but it is essentially different from the three-element concept, and that should be sufficient to throw doubt upon the original coherence of chapters 1 and 2. The sentence 2.1 seems to be not the introduction to chapter 2, but the summing-up of chapter 1, and the compilator—presumably Arius—must have reformulated it superficially in order to provide a transition to chapter 2, which actually starts a new and different treatise.[17]

§ 3 and 4 introduce the *oikeiōsis* toward onself, which is based on nature and guided by the distinction of things according to and contrary to nature. Its primary object is "being," which seems to mean the physical existence and well-being of the individual. The three points mentioned in § 4—health, pleasure and life—are to be taken as illustrations of "being."[18] The inclusion of pleasure has a particular point, because the Stoics in general rejected this notion (Diog. Laert. 7.85–6).[19] Finally, § 4 mentions two new concepts, "choiceworthy for its own sake" and "good" (and the opposites), which are attached to "according to nature" as if being synonyms or expansions of this term. This may be unsatisfactory,[20] but as a short statement of what would require a careful terminological analysis in a more technical treatise it is quite understandable. The use of "*agatha*" has again an anti-Stoic point, because a Stoic would call these objects "*ta prōta kata physin*" and would reserve the word "*agatha*" for the virtues, which come at a later stage.

§ 5 takes a further step. The first clause sums up what has been said in § 3–4 about *oikeiōsis*-relation to the body, modified by the term "*philos*" (which is quite common elsewhere within the *oikeiōsis* theory). Then soul is added in accordance with the dual concept of human nature (§ 2). Mention of the parts, powers and functions of both indicates that more might be said on this point. However, the shortness of this paragraph, especially the absence of examples concerning the soul (as they were given for the body in § 4), makes it difficult to understand its import precisely. Finally we are told that in order to attain the two categories of goods, *hormē, kathēkon,* and *aretē* appear. With them, it seems, ethics in its full sense is established, and the short sketch has come to an end.

But in § 6 there follows a supplementary passage (connected by *gar*), which gives details about the conditions and processes that lead to *aretē*. This must be taken as an explanation of the final step in § 5. At the origin are mistakes[21] made in choices "concerning the above mentioned things"—which must mean those things about body and soul, toward which the individual has an *oikeiōsis*. Difficulty in making the right choice makes a certain kind of knowledge necessary, which is to ensure the right choices. It is called *aretē* and awarded the highest value. It is not said to belong to *physis,* but to be found "in harmony with nature" (*synōidos tēi physei*). This seems to indicate that we have left the sphere of *oikeiōsis* in the proper sense, which is directed towards things *kata physin,* and that *aretē* is connected with it only indirectly.[22]

At this point two observations should be made. First, virtue is described in purely intellectual terms. This contradicts an assertion in 1.5 which denies that ethical virtue is knowledge. We may take this as a confirmation of the heterogeneity of chapter 1. Secondly, virtue is certainly a matter of the soul. But it must be different from those faculties and functions of the soul mentioned in § 5, because it has to direct the processes of choice among them. So it seems that the faculties of the soul are split up into more elementary and "natural" ones, which are the direct object of *oikeiōsis,* and virtue, which is above them and only indirectly a matter of nature. The "natural" faculties and functions of the soul may be imagined to be like those *prōta kata physin* which Arius lists on pp. 47.20–48.2: intelligence, ingeniousness, industry, persistence, memory.[23]

§ 7 confirms the importance of *aretē* as defined in § 6, but it does not add a new motif. The content of § 5 and 6 is loosely summarized and put into different terms. These terms are definitely Stoic[24] (*eklogē–apeklogē, kathēkonta, katorthōseis*), and the expression "*ta legomena kathēkonta*" suggests that the author is conscious of using a somehow unfamiliar terminology (although he used the word already in § 5)—perhaps because it is not at home in his school. We may speculate that his intention was to show by reformulating his argument that the Peripatetic doctrine is universally acceptable, even in the framework of the dominant Stoic school.

The next sentence (3.1) is obviously added by the compiling doxographer, presumably Arius Didymus, who interrupts his source, the *hypographē.*[25] He regards the part he has transcribed before as a basis of Peripatetic ethics, from which all the rest can easily be developed. With "as I am going to show briefly" he indicates that from now on he is going to abbreviate. Does this imply that up to here the transcript was fairly complete? We may doubt that. On the contrary, some lines of thought in chapter 2 remain obscure and must be supplemented by the reader, whereas the following chapters abound in examples and repetitions. The only point where a real excision seems to be made is just where the interrupting remark occurs, that is, at the beginning of chapter 3; 3.2 does not smoothly continue 2.1–7, and if it is to be taken as a fresh start, we miss an introductory remark about the subject and aim of the new section.[26]

In fact the beginning of chapter 3 can mislead the reader. He may think that the picture of development presented in chapter 2 is to be continued and a new element added, namely, relations to fellow men. But this cannot be the right interpretation, because it soon becomes clear that the author no longer uses the genetic or developmental approach. Chapters 3–7 have a subject of their own, which is the Peripatetic doctrine of three classes of goods: external goods (ch. 3), goods of the body (ch. 4) and of the soul (ch. 5), continued by reflection on the uses of these goods in life (ch. 6) and a discussion on the purpose of life (*telos,* ch. 7).[27] The order in which the classes of goods are treated is not the same in which they are usually enumerated, but the reason is obvious: it is an ascending order of value, and this is pointed out in repeated comparisons. Chapter 7 makes it clear that the aim of the treatise is to prove the overwhelming superiority of the goods of the soul, which must be taken account of in the definition of the *telos.*

We see that there is no unbroken continuity between chapter 2 and chapters 3–7. There is the awkward joining between 2.7 and 3.2, the difference between development and comparative approach, and we can add the observation that chapter 2 seems to have only two classes of goods: the external goods are not given a place in the developmental framework.[28] On the other hand, there are common features also. The set of ideas connected with *oikeiōsis* permeates both parts, and no real difference of philosophical standpoint or interest is perceptible. Moreover, there is a backward reference in 5.2 to 2.6, which we must examine in detail later on. At this moment it may suffice to point out the problems.

Chapter 3, on external goods,[29] starts with the relation to one's children, then passes on to parents, relatives, members of the same *polis* and of the same *ethnos* and race, and finally to all human beings. This is the pattern of widening circles of relationship which is connected with *oikeiōsis* in Cicero, *De fin.* and other sources, and even some of the examples recur elsewhere. I want to mention only one particular point. There is obviously a strong tradition to start the series with one's children. The oldest example is provided by Chrysippus (SVF 3.179), who is quoted as saying repeatedly: "We become well disposed to ourselves immediately after birth, and to our offspring." It is rather awkward to mention one's offspring immediately after one's birth. Arius Didymus escapes this criticism, because he mentions offspring not at the beginning of the developmental treatise, but as the first item of a systematic survey of external goods.[30]

Another interesting point concerns terminology. Here (and throughout the rest of the treatise) the main qualification of the goods is *di' hauto haireton,* "choiceworthy for its own sake," as distinguished from "useful for something else." The term was first introduced in 2.4 in the context of *oikeiōsis.* Now it becomes the main terminological instrument, stressed by frequent and stylistically somewhat pedantic repetition. *Oikeiōsis,* on the other hand, recurs only five times, and not in key positions, but rather in side remarks.[31] It may be suggested that the author has preferred to place the term "choiceworthy for its own sake" in the foreground, because it has specifically Peripatetic overtones.

It has been noted since von Arnim (140) that chapter 3 mentions only social relations, although in 4.1 it is suggested that the whole ground of external goods has been covered. Pohlenz (31) found this in agreement with the Stoic idea of external goods, which did not include things like wealth and power (SVF 3.96–7). Now the situation in Arius is complicated by the fact[32] that in 5.5 wealth, power and good luck are mentioned among the external goods. The inconsistency can be resolved if we assume with Moraux (325–27) that the latter passage is an interpolation. We shall soon have a closer look at it.

On chapter 4 I want to make only one comment. In § 2 bodily goods are named, and the list is in close agreement with the list of *prōta kata physin* which Arius gives on p. 47.20–3: health, strength, good condition, keenness of senses, beauty, swiftness, wholeness. This list stands in the introductory section and is therefore not assigned to one particular school, but similarity with the shorter Stoic lists (p. 79.20–80.1) and Plutarch, *De comm. not.* 4 (1060C) speaks for Stoic origin. This, then, would be another example of Stoic material being used in our treatise.

Now we pass on to chapter 5. Virtue, according to 5.2, "makes her entrance starting from the bodily and external goods, as we have indicated," and as a second step she turns to herself and appreciates her own value. The reference to 2.6 is beyond doubt.[33] It seems that the developmental approach of chapter 2 is now resumed. We can in fact find in 2.6 a concept of two phases in the genesis of virtue, the first of which is outward-directed and concerns the correct choice of other things, whereas the second one concerns the appreciation of virtue itself. The first phase, in which virtue has a selective function, may be what is meant in 5.2 by "enter from." But then we come up against a contradiction: the objects of selection in 2.6 are the goods of body and soul (external goods not occurring in the whole chapter); in 5.2, bodily and external goods. This is quite in keeping with the conceptual structure of chapters 3–5, and therefore the contradiction cannot be due to a slip of a careless writer, but it points to a structural fault.

In the second phase of 5.2 virtue turns toward herself and finds that she belongs to the things according to nature, even more than the virtues of the body. (No mention of the external goods.) This process is also described as an *oikeiōsis* of virtue toward herself, a concept that does not occur elsewhere in *oikeiōsis* theories and is certainly a transposition of the primitive *oikeiōsis* of the individual toward itself to a higher level.[34] The outcome of this *oikeiōsis*-process must be, according to the context of chapter 5, the goods of the soul quite generally, and "virtue" is obviously to be taken in the general sense of "virtues or excellences of the soul" (p. 123.27), which are not all of an intellectual nature, as the examples in the following paragraph go to show. We may see this comprehensive virtue of the soul in the first phase as well, where it has to cope with the problems of the external and bodily goods. Intellectual as well as emotional powers come into play when man endeavours to provide himself with these goods. This is a consistent picture, but it differs from the intellectual concept of virtue as a judging power in 2.6. On the other hand, the second phase has aspects that are closer to 2.6. We find an intellectual term: *theasamenē,* and the result of reflecting upon herself is a comparative value judgement, quite similar to the function of virtue in 2.6. Thus the virtue concept of chapter 2 comes into play, although it does not quite fit the tendency of chapter 5 to equate virtue with the goods of the soul generally.

Another point of comparison is the function of *physis.* In 5.2 virtue (of the soul) is seen to be "according to nature" just like the other kinds of goods, only in a higher degree. This is in agreement with a rather broad concept of virtue. In 2.6 virtue as a kind of knowledge is "in harmony with nature." This corresponds with a purely intellectual concept of virtue. The difference is clear. This observation fits in with another one concerning the term *oikeiōsis.* In 5.2 it is mentioned, although in an unusual way. In 2.6 the word is absent, and we saw reasons for suspecting that this is no accident, because virtue as a capacity of judgement is not directly "according to nature."

Can we draw any conclusions from our observations on 2.6 and 5.2? In addition to the contradiction concerning the objects of the first phase there seems to be a basic disagreement about the concept of virtue. It is only the developmental point of view and the two-phase structure that is the same in 2.6 and 5.2. This confusing situation can be explained if we assume that the backward reference in 5.2 has been added by somebody who wanted to link chapters 2 and 5, but did not succeed to reconcile their differences.[35] If this is right, it follows that chapters 2 and 5 (or the whole block of chapters 3–7) did not originally belong to the same treatise, but to separate Peripatetic essays. A third person must have put them together because they seemed to supplement each other, without paying much attention to their conceptual divergences. In 5.2 he inserted the back reference to link the heterogeneous parts. For the identity of the compiler we have only one clue. By saying "*kathaper hypedeixamen*" he identifies with the Peripatetic doctrine he is expounding. A doxographer like Arius Didymus who is reporting the doctrine of another school would hardly have chosen this personal way of speaking. It can be concluded that the joining was made by a Peripatetic and that Arius already found the composite treatise as a whole.

An alternative which might be suggested is that the absence of external goods from chapter 2 is due to an abridgement[36] and that the original shape of the chapter should be reconstructed on the basis of 5.2. But such an attempt will hardly lead to a satisfactory result, and it would not solve the difficulties concerning the concept of virtue and its relation to the goods of the soul. Chapter 2 itself seems to be basically complete, although several points are reduced to mere catchwords. There is only one difficulty about it which remains. Could any Peripatetic treatise on ethics completely disregard the external goods? If speculation is permitted, we might imagine that they were to be introduced as a supplement after the basic structure of ethics was established.[37] The treatise as we have it breaks off at this point. After the interruption of 3.1, however, we find just what we expected, only in a different argumentative context. But this is not very difficult to understand, if we assume the following procedure of the compiler: he found that the first treatise ended with the same subject (external goods) with which the second one began. In order to avoid a doublet he left out what we described as a ''supplement'' and still could feel satisfied that he had not omitted this important point of Peripatetic ethics. This procedure would, of course, betray a lack of sense for argumentative coherence. But this is not surprising after our analysis of the reference in § 5.2.

We can now pass on to the second part of chapter 5, which returns to the method dominating the whole account of the three classes of goods: systematic comparison. In 5.3 it takes the shape of a list of pairs of virtues of the body and the soul, each one accompanied by an *a fortiori* argument for the value of the latter. The pairs are:

body	—	soul
health	—	temperance
strength	—	courage and endurance
beauty	—	justice

The series health–strength–beauty coincides with the beginning of the list in 4.2, which I mentioned before. So the coherence with chapter 4 is good. But it seems also possible to suggest a source for the table of pairs outside the treatise. Arius mentions in his section on Stoic ethics (pp. 62.15–63.5) certain qualities of the soul which are not virtues but additional capabilities acquired by training. They are called health of the soul, strength of the soul and beauty of the soul,[38] and their characteristics are explained by analogy to the bodily qualities, from which their name is derived. Since all this is Stoic textbook material, it is very probable that the Peripatetic author made use of this list in order to organise his comparison. The changes he made are easy to understand. He identified these qualities of the soul with the virtues of temperance, courage, and justice, quite contrary to the Stoic definitions. This raised their status, which was necessary, because it would not do to illustrate the class of ''goods of the soul'' with certain secondary mental qualities. The explanations had to be changed accordingly. There is one indication that the author is upholding a Peripatetic position, although using Stoic material: he says that temperance rids us from the excess (literally ''intensity,'' *sphodrotēs*) of the passions, pointing to *metriopatheia,* not *apatheia.*

5.4–5 continues or rather repeats the argument of 5.3. The introductory sentence, ''A similar *logos* (argument? relation or proportion?) exists also in the case of the virtues,'' is not very appropriate, because there is no transition to virtue from something else. We are again given a comparative list, which this time includes a third class, the external goods. The terms are:

body		soul		external
health	—	temperance	—	wealth
strength	—	courage	—	power
keenness of the senses	—	reason	—	good luck
beauty	—	justice	—	friendship

The awkwardness of this passage has called forth some attempts at explanation and justification, but Moraux (325–27) is certainly right to doubt its authenticity. Under the categories of textual criticism it can be described as a doublet: somebody found a fuller version of the comparative table in § 3, and instead of replacing § 3 he added the new text on. We can at least suspect where the larger list came from. The *Aristotelian Divisions* (ch. 56) contain the following table of goods:[39]

soul		body		external
reason	—	good condition	—	good reputation
justice	—	good looks	—	good luck
courage	—	strength	—	friends
temperance	—	beauty	—	wealth

The structure is the same as in 5.4–5. The descending order soul-body-external is more natural than body-soul-external; the latter can be explained by the interpolator sticking to the order in § 3 and just adding the third category. He also took over the entries from § 3 and their arrangement, which differs from the *Divisions;* he only added a fourth row with "keenness of the senses" (which occurs in 4.2, but not in the Divisions) and "reason." This is understandable, because it makes up the number of the four virtues, although it is not clear why this entry is given the third place. The external goods may have been added from the *Divisions.* "Power" is not to be found there, but this is not very far removed from "good reputation" in the *Divisions,* which is explained as a means to do what one wants. There is, however, no simple explanation for the assignment of the external goods to the rows, which is quite different from the *Divisions.*

Certainly there is always a great amount of arbitrariness in the analogies of these tables, and it may be that the interpolator, seeing that his first two columns, which he had based on § 3, had a different arrangement from the table in the *Divisions,* and that it would not be possible to assign the external goods to exactly the same pairs of body-and-soul goods, freely redistributed them. This seems to be the easiest solution, but other possibilities remain, for example that the table that served as a model was not identical with but only similar to chapter 56 of the *Divisions.* Can we guess who made the interpolation? It might be a doublet due to the author himself, a note made for later replacement of § 3, which by some accident was incorporated after this paragraph. But it might as well be the work of Arius Didymus.

It would be characteristic of doxographical procedure that he supplemented his text from a Peripatetic schoolbook, whereas the Peripatetic author himself had drawn upon Stoic material.

At this point we might try to draw some general conclusions. Arius Didymus seems to have placed at the beginning of his section of Peripatetic ethics an excerpt on basic concepts (ch. 1). Then he continued with a Peripatetic treatise which used the *oikeiōsis* concept and led up to a discussion of *telos* (chs. 2–7). This treatise was itself composite, one part being based on the body-soul duality and using a developmental approach (ch. 2), the other based on the classification of goods and using a comparative approach (chs. 3–7). In 5.2 we observe a not very successful attempt of this author to link the two parts. We cannot say anything about the joining itself, because at 3.1 Didymus interposes and probably leaves out a transitional passage. The rhetorical, almost passionate presentation seems to be characteristic for the author of the composite treatise chapters 2–7. In 5.4–5 we have an interpolation which is perhaps due to Arius Didymus supplementing the treatise from a Peripatetic source with a fuller table of goods. So it seems possible to identify three strata of the text. But none of them can be shown to go back to the early Hellenistic period, and the Peripatetic authors seem to be in free contact with Stoic philosophy. If our observations on 5.3 can be taken as characteristic, these Peripatetics do not hesitate to adapt conceptual material from Stoic sources to their purposes. Taken as a whole, our study tends to support the general view of Pohlenz and his followers: This is basically a late Hellenistic text, written by one or more Peripatetic authors who freely used Stoic concepts without giving up what they regarded as Peripatetic essentials. The adoption of a Stoic *oikeiōsis* concept can very well be a part of this pattern.

IV. A SEMANTIC APPROACH TO *OIKEIŌSIS*

If we want to look at the early stages of the *oikeiōsis* theory, we cannot expect much help from Arius Didymus; we must study the relevant texts from early Hellenistic times, scant as they are. Let us begin with the Theophrastus fragments.

The first of these fragments, from the second book of Porphyrius *De abstinentia,* chapters 20–32, is probably taken from Theophrastus *Peri eusebeias*. On the subject of animal sacrifice Theophrastus said (ch. 22) that originally man did not kill any living beings, because friendship and the sense of kinship (*to syggenes*) were generally very strong, and even animals were regarded as belonging to us by kinship (*oikeia einai nomizōn*). Another argument, perhaps from another context, follows: In case a man proves to be harmful by his natural instinct (and is, therefore, incorrigible), it is regarded as just (*dikaion*) to kill him, in spite of *oikeiotēs;* in other cases as unjust (*adikon*). This pattern also applies to our relation to animals, and consequences can be drawn concerning sacrifices. Without going into details we may note that *oikeiotēs* appears here as a condition for justice, and this seems to apply not only to the relation to men, but also to animals. Comparing this with the *oikeiōsis* theory we find a certain similarity, since moral relations are derived from a belonging-together, for which the Greek word *oikeios* stands. Some Stoics did in fact connect justice with *oikeiōsis*.[40] But the differences are marked. The word form is different: *oikeiotēs*, not *oikeiōsis*. *Oikeiotēs* is not used for a relation to oneself, which is the pivotal point of the *oikeiōsis* theory. *Oikeiotēs* extends to animals, which is not the case in the *oikeiōsis* theory.[41]

The second fragment is preserved in the third book of Porphyrius, chapter 25. It is a matter of dispute how far it extends. The general theme of this book is justice. Theophrastus is quoted as arguing that men are *oikeioi kai syggeneis* to each other and even to animals; then it is concluded that there must be justice even between men and animals. Perhaps this conclusion no longer belongs to the quotation and is added by Porphyrius. But he seems to have used Theophrastean material in this passage also, and the similarity to the first fragment is striking. For us it is important that the meaning of *oikeios kai syggenēs* is defined more carefully than in the first fragment. It refers not only to blood relationship, but also to a community of life, of culture, and even of biological and mental structure. By these criteria widening circles of *oikeiotēs* can be constructed: family, members of a polis, Greeks and barbarians separately, mankind in general, and as a last step, animals are included. The flexible interpretation of *oikeiotēs* and the idea of widening circles bring this passage closer to Stoic *oikeiōsis*. Still, the essence remains different. Theophrastus does not have a developmental approach, starting with a child's first impulses.[42] He is concerned with observable facts, objective bonds between beings. The *oikeiōsis* of the Stoics is built upon elementary experiences of the individual, its consciousness and its primal urges. So far as these texts appeal to observable facts, these are facts of human behaviour, e.g., the general fact of parents loving their offspring and caring for them. If both sides appeal to *physis* (the term is not, however, in the Theophrastus texts), they mean different things. Theophrastus goes back to the systematic order of the natural groups of living beings, the Stoics to the basics of human behavior.[43]

The contrast seems to be clear, but shall we completely put aside the similarities? In particular the picture of widening social circles in the second Theophrastus fragment seems to be close to some Stoic *oikeiōsis* texts and also to Arius Didymus. C. O. Brink suggested that this is in fact a Theophrastean element which was adopted by the Stoics since Chrysippus in order to fill a gap in their own theory. This would, in a way, justify later Peripatetics in claiming the Stoic combination of the two theories as their own. The gap to which Brink (137) refers can be described as follows: Stoic *oikeiōsis* was fundamentally egocentric, it is "the moral principal of self" (140). On the other hand, the social ideas of the Stoics were tied up with the concept of the world state, but this belonged, strictly speaking, to wise men only, and the majority of fools were nothing but a disturbing element. Obviously there was no basis for a realistic social ethics, and the Theophrastean *oikeiotēs* groups were helpful to overcome this defect. The first trace of their adoption would be, according to Brink, the mention of the love of children in Chrysippus's *oikeiōsis* fragment. To this extent Brink accepted von Arnim's and Dirlmeier's position.

I think this is a very interesting construction, which has the merit of avoiding an "all-or-nothing" attitude and of doing justice to the points of contact between *oikeiotēs* and *oikeiōsis*. It rests, however, on the assumption of an essential incompatibility between the two, which permits only an addition of one to the other, not an organic relation. The matter is, of course, highly conjectural, because we have full expositions of the *oikeiōsis* theory only in authors like Arius Didymus and Cicero *De finibus*, where far-reaching contamination is possible. I want to suggest, nevertheless, that there is a kinship between the Theophrastean and the Stoic ideas due to a common background in thought and language of the late 4th century. The name of Aristotle may stand for this background, but we should not restrict our attention to him. The claim I am making can, I think, best be supported by some reflections on the word *oikeiōsis* and its antecedents.

A valuable study on this subject is contained in an article by Professor Kerferd[44] and I can only venture a few steps beyond his results. *Oikeiōsis* in the reflexive use, the *oikeiōsis pros heauton*, does not occur before the Stoics. But the reflexive phrase is certainly secondary and even paradoxical. The word *oikeios* and its derivatives refer primarily to a relation between two things, etymologically to their belonging together as members of the same household (*oikos*). The transformation of relational concepts into reflexive concepts is not infrequent in Greek philosophical language. The earliest example is the famous *gnōthi sauton* "know thyself." The expression *hauton kratein* appears first in Antiphon the Sophist and gave rise to several other expressions referring to self-discipline. Xenophon has *epimeleisthai hautou* and *andrapodizesthai heautōn* ("to take care of oneself" and "enslavers of themselves," both perhaps from Antisthenes), Democritus *heauton aischynesthai* or *aideisthai* ("to be ashamed of oneself"); Gorgias *prodidonai heauton* ("to betray oneself"). Most important for us is *heauton philein*, "to be one's own friend," which is known to Sophocles and Euripides, obviously from ethical discussions of their time. The idea of *kratein heautou*, having power over oneself, can be seen as the nucleus of Plato's theory of the parts of the soul, and Aristotle was led by *philein heauton* to the theory of *philautia* (*EN* 9.4). The antecedents of *philautia* were studied by Kajetan Gantar in an article entitled "Amicus sibi," from which I have taken most of my examples.[45] Gantar did not forget to mention *oikeiōsis* in this context. The Stoics, it seems, followed a well-established linguistic pattern when they wanted to build up an ethical theory of the autonomous, self-sufficient individual. They took a concept describing the outward relations of a human being and projected the pattern into his interior. Therefore it is not very probable that outward-directed *oikeiōsis* is a later addition to their system; it is rather the prototype, which served as a model for self-*oikeiōsis* and only occasionally faded into the background. A comparison with Aristotle's *philautia* has sometimes been made.[46] *Philautia* is a side issue in Aristotle's *philia* discussion, but one could imagine some philosopher lifting *philautia* out of its original context and using it for an introductory discussion on ethics, leading up to the concept of *eudaimonia.*

But we must return from speculation to facts. If we want to go back beyond the Stoics, we must take into account the verb *oikeioō,* from which the noun is derived. The verb has two usages. In the active or middle voice it is construed with *tina* or *ti,* meaning "to claim ownership, to appropriate, to win over to one's own side." Professor Kerferd has pointed out that usually an existing relationship or kinship which might be called *oikeiotēs* is presupposed for the action of *oikeioun.* A very clear example can be found in Plato's third epistle, 317E. Dionysius is requested to enter into friendship with Dion (*Diōna oikeiōsamenon*), motivated by their kinship (*oikeiotēs*). The act of *oikeioun* is generally a friendly and peaceful one. In the *Laws,* book 8, 843E, Plato speaks of the illegal trick of a farmer who appropriates (*spheterizein*) a swarm of bees issuing from the beehive of a neighbor. He "goes along with the pleasure of the bees" (*tēi tōn melittōn hēdonēi synepomenos*) which, according to an old belief, like loud noises, and by making a great racket he "wins them over to himself" (expressed by the middle voice: *oikeiousthai*), obviously inducing them to settle down on his own grounds. The connection with pleasure is interesting, and perhaps there is a play on the etymology: he makes the bees select the place for their future *home.*

The noun *oikeiōsis* is not derived from this usage, as the construction shows (the accusative object would be converted into a genitive), but from another one: *oikeiousthai* as a passive (clearly recognizable in the aorist *ōikeiōthēn*), which is used with *tini* or *pros tina,* a construction shared by the noun. The general meaning is "to become *oikeios* (related) to somebody or something." It is noteworthy that there is no instance where the agent is expressed by *hypo tinos,* as would be expected with a passive verb. The reason is not difficult to see. The person (or thing) whose *oikeios* one becomes is not an agent who aims at "appropriating" the partner. Instead this is a spontaneous process which is directed at, but not caused by a partner.[47] Only in very rare cases is an agent brought in, and in these cases the verb is converted into the active voice and *physis* is the subject: nature makes us well disposed toward something.[48]

In order to find out if there are characteristic connotations of the word which link it with the philosophical term I want to discuss three instances. (1) Pseudo-Demosthenes 61 (*Erotikos*) 4 says that lovers, *erastai,* are a kind of people in whose nature it is to become friendly not with everybody, but only with the beautiful and well-behaved boys (*ouch hapasin alla tois kalois kai sōphrosin oikeiousthai pephyken*). We are here in the semantic field of love, friendship, sympathy, and *oikeiousthai* functions as a selective act; it gives a definite direction to the impulse, and it is understood that this is the right and legitimate direction. As a determining factor, nature is mentioned (implied in *pephyken*). (2) Aristotle has (except for *Pol.* 1336b30) only the composite verb *synoikeiousthai,* but I suppose that the preposition *syn* does not make much difference. In *EN* 8.14/12, in the context of friendship, he notes (1161b21) that parents love their children more than children their parents, and that quite generally the being that produces is more attached (*synōikeiōtai*) to its product than conversely because what has sprung from a thing, belongs (is *oikeion*) to its source, for example, teeth and hair to their owner, but not the other way round, or, anyway, in a lesser degree. Aristotle goes on to explain that children are loved like parts of oneself. The passage suggests that *oikeiōsis* is essentially an unsymmetrical relationship,[49] and this seems to be an important difference from *philia* (at least in its normal form). The overtones are not so much those of feeling attracted but of valuing something highly, of cherishing, caring, taking an active interest. This would suit children as well as teeth and hair. (3) *EN* 10.5 (1175a29–30). Pleasures are a crowning fulfilment of activities, and there are different kinds of pleasure belonging to different activities. "This can also be seen from the fact that each pleasure is attached to the activity which it crowns" (*ek tou synōikeiōsthai . . . tēi energeiāi hēn teleioi*). What exactly this *synōikeiōtai* means must be gathered from the following text. Without going into the details I want to suggest the interpretation "it is specifically coordinated and adapted," with a stress on the specific or selective character of *oikeiōsis*. Aristotle makes this clear by the observation that each pleasure *synauxei* (furthers, supports, helps to develop) the activity to which it belongs; *ta de synauxonta oikeia*, "and whatever supports or is helpful, is *oikeion*." What was not central before, "caring and being helpful," is here the focus of meaning. This explains the very unusual way in which Aristotle expresses himself. Normally the grammatical subject of *oikeiousthai* is the primary thing, and a statement is made about its relation or behavior toward secondary things, which only become important by this relation. It would be quite natural to regard "activity" as primary and to say that each activity has its *oikeia hēdonē*, which is its result and fulfilment. Aristotle, however, makes the reverse statement and presents *hēdonē* as a subject to which an activity is *oikeia*. This way of speaking avoids the misunderstanding that the *oikeia hēdonē* is a result of an activity, in which one takes an active interest, which is cherished and aimed at. This kind of relation exists rather in the opposite direction, although pleasure can only metaphorically be regarded as an agent.

I think that this brief survey has shown certain aspects in the use of *oikeiousthai* in the second half of the fourth century which made the word useful for the Stoics. Because of the unsymmetrical nature of the relationship it was more suitable than *philia* as a basis for an individualistic ethics. Also, it had a dynamic potential, because it implied caring for, active interest in, and, potentially, responsibility for something or someone. This could provide a basis for the ideas of *hormē* and *kathēkonta*. Even the reflexive use has its antecedents in the Aristotelian text which mentions teeth and hair, just as the Stoics mentioned the parts of the body. Aristotelian *philautia* may have provided still another model. The texts surveyed also shed some light on two particular problems. We mentioned before that parental love is a standard example of outward directed *oikeiōsis* and that its combination with the developmental view in the Chrysippus fragment *SVF* 3.179 presents a logical difficulty.[50] It might seem more to the point to mention love of a child toward his parents as the starting point of a development.[51] Aristotle shows why parental love follows quite logically upon self-*oikeiōsis:* children may be regarded as parts of oneself, and a child's relation to its parent is a much less convincing example of *oikeiōsis.* Under this aspect it seems that Chrysippus did not intend a developmental explanation at all, but a logical expansion of self-*oikeiōsis.*[52] The other point is pleasure. Aristotle says twice that pleasure has an *oikeiōsis*-relation to man or his actions.[53]. The Stoics used to discuss whether man has an *oikeiōsis* toward pleasure, Chrysippus denied it, Posidonius accepted it, and we found the statement in Arius Didymus.[54] The problem is usually seen as a piece of controversy with Epicureanism, but obviously it refers to an element inherent in the word before it became a philosophical term which comes to the surface in Plato[55] and Aristotle.

Let us now turn to Theophrastus. Although *oikeiōsis* as a noun occurs once in a Theophrastus fragment (fr. 190 Wimmer), the verb is not attested in any of his writings. The fragment was thought to be important by Dirlmeier, but less so by recent critics. It comes from Photius, *Bibl.* cod. 278 and is an excerpt from Theophrastus's treatise on kinds of honey (*Peri melitōn*). There is one kind, honey-dew, which is found on leaves, especially leaves of oaks and linden trees. At the end of his excerpt Photius adds the remark: "And somehow the bee has a certain *oikeiōsis* toward the oak" (*echei de pōs hē melitta oikeiōsin tina pros tēn drȳn*). Theophrastus obviously referred to the well-known preference of bees for hollow oaks to build their hives in,[56] and this habit was mentioned in connection with the honey on the leaves. We may think that there is again a play on the derivation from *oikos:* bees are specially attracted to oaks and feel literally at home there. There is no reason to doubt the authenticity of the word, but it does not imply more than Plato's *oikeiousthai* in connection with the beekeeper. It is not a general expression for friendly relations between living beings. Theophrastus did study these relations in his botanical and zoological writings, including *Historia Animalium,* Book 9 (assuming the book is by Theophrastus), but the word occurs nowhere in this context.[57]

The Theophrastus fragments we discussed earlier have more relevance. They show an awareness that ethics (more specifically justice) depends on the nature of relations within a group or community. This is in keeping with Aristotelian thought about *philia*[58] and can certainly be regarded as a development from this basis. Here is a common ground with the Stoics. The main innovation is an application of classificatory procedures, which results in an unusually comprehensive view of moral relations, including animals. *Oikeiotēs* is the word for the natural basis of these relations. It is a very general word directly relating to *oikeios* and not sharing the special overtones we found in *oikeiousthai* and *oikeiōsis,* especially its unsymmetrical nature, its emotional aspects and its implication of an active interest. Nevertheless, the fundamental idea of "belonging together" as represented by the word *oikeios* is common to both.

Looking back, we find that this semantic study has not provided us with a new clue for understanding the development of the theory and for analyzing the extant texts. But it may help to explain why the Stoics chose the word *oikeiōsis* to express their idea of the origin of moral obligation, and to suggest that Theophrastean *oikeiotēs* and Stoic *oikeiōsis* have developed independently from similar antecedents. If a cross-fertilization took place—either in the way described by Brink or by late Hellenistic syncretism, of which Arius Didymus would be an example—this is a convergence of ideas which from their origins were not very far from each other.

NOTES

1. Page and line numbers refer to Johannes Stobaeus, *Anthologium*, ed. C. Wachsmuth and O. Hense; vol. 2 ed. C. Wachsmuth (Berlin 1884).
2. For bibliography, see n.9–12.
3. I just mention p. 118.15–20: a strict parallelism, relieved by skilful variation.
4. P. 119.20 *tēn holēn tēs haireseōs hypographēn;* p. 122.6 *kata tēn hypographēn;* p. 129.5 *hypographontes.*
5. Cicero, *De finibus* ed. J. N. Madvig (Kopenhagen 1839, 3rd ed. 1876) Excursus 7.
6. H. Diels, *Doxographi Graeci* (Berlin 1879) p. 71f.
7. H. Strache, *De Arii Didymi in morali philosophia auctoribus,* Diss. Göttingen 1909. Id., *Der Eklektizismus des Antiochos von Askalon* Berlin 1921 (Philol. Unt. 26).
8. L. Spengel, *Über die unter dem Namen des Aristoteles erhaltenen ethischen Schriften* (München 1841) (Abh. d. philos.-philol. Cl. d. kön. bay. Ak. d. Wiss. 3.2) p. 495n.
9. H. v. Arnim, *Arius Didymus' Abriss der peripatetischen Ethik* (Wien-Leipzig 1926) (Ak. d. Wiss. Wien, phil.-hist. Kl., Sitzungsber. 204.3).
10. F. Dirlmeier, *Die Oikeiosis-Lehre Theophrasts* (Leipzig 1937) (Philologus Suppl. 30.1).
11. M. Pohlenz, *Grundfragen der stoischen Philosophie* (Göttingen 1940) (Abh. d. Ges. d. Wiss. Gött., phil.-hist. Kl. 3.26).
12. C. O. Brink, "*Oikeiōsis* and *Oikeiotēs:* Theophrastus and Zeno on Nature in moral theory," *Phronesis* 1 (1956) 123–45; S. G. Pembroke, "Oikeiōsis," in: A. A. Long (ed.), *Problems in Stoicism* (London 1971) 114–49; P. Moraux, *Der Aristotelismus bei den Griechen von Andronikos bis Alexander von Aphrosidias* 1: *Die Renaissance des Aristotelismus im 1. Jh. v. Chr.* (Berlin-New York 1973) (Peripatoi 5) 316–444.
13. M. Giusta, *I dossografi di etica,* 2 vols. (Torino 1964–67).
14. *Symbebēkenai* can indicate either a logical inference ("it follows that . . .," but one would expect the present tense) or a necessary attribute ("it is characteristic that . . .") or a contingent attribute ("it is by chance that . . .," but this does not fit the content of the proposition). There is a similar expression in § 7. For a survey of these meanings, see Bonitz,*Index Aristotelicus* s.v. *symbainein.*
15. Pohlenz, 27, noted that Arius had attached *oikeiōsis* loosely to a single point of ch. 1, to which he did not come back later. (It appears that the "single point" means the three elements.) Moraux 320 sees no difficulty at all and finds not only nature, but also habituation and reason in 2.2–8.
16. Pohlenz, 27, n.2 quotes Aristotle,*Protrepticus* fr. 10c W.
17. Pohlenz, 27, seems to have suspected this, but without really spelling out the problem. He points out that the *oikeiōsis* theory is usually placed at the very beginning of an ethical discourse.
18. Pohlenz (27f.) points out that normally life appears as the first object of *oikeiōsis,* from which the others are derived, and calls the coordination of life with health and pleasure "illogical." This argument is not very strong, since Stoic texts do not have the same terminology (the first aim is "*hē hautou systasis,*" and the first impulse is "*to tērein heauto,*" Diog. Laert. 7.85), and the required logical order is there, if the term "being"

is not left out of account. The order of the three terms, which also displeased Pohlenz (life coming last!) can be explained as a climax from more everyday impulses and activities to the supreme crisis of fighting for one's life.

19. Posidonius dissented (F 169 E.-K.; cf. Pohlenz 17 on some other Stoic sources), but this does not seem of importance here.
20. Pohlenz, 28, again calls this "illogical."
21. Pohlenz, 29, argued plausibly that these mistakes presuppose the Stoic doctrine of *diastrophē*.
22. In order to show that it is possible to make a terminological distinction which restricts the *physis* character to the lower classes of goods I refer to the *physei agatha* of *EE* 8.3 (1248b26–30, 40), also 37a4, b31, 38a17, 49a25, b17.
23. Cf. also p. 81.1–4. In Cicero, *De fin*. 3.5.17 we find cognition (*katalēpseis*) and arts in this function, similarly in *De fin*. 5.18.48–19.54.
24. This is Dirlmeier's observation (86).
25. See n.4.
26. A gap has generally been recognized since von Arnim 139.
27. The new approach was well described by Pohlenz 30–32.
28. This was first pointed out by von Arnim (148f.) and recently stressed by Giusta (1.71, 97f.).
29. The heading is given in the summary (4.1).
30. This was correctly observed by Pembroke 125, although with a different valuation.
31. Only in 5.2 *oikeiōsis* is directly linked with virtue, but we shall see that this passage has a doubtful standing.
32. Observed by von Arnim 1.c, but ignored by Pohlenz.
33. It is not possible to take the phrase as referring to chapters 3 and 4 only, meaning: we have seen that there are virtues in the field of bodily and external goods, and now a transition is made to the goods of the soul. There may be virtues of the body, but not of external goods.
34. Cf. Dirlmeier, 96. There is an approach to this notion in the phrase "*sola enim sapientia in se conversa est*" (Cic. *De fin*. 3.7.24).
35. Already Dirlmeier 95f. noticed that 5.2 is not quite in keeping with its environment and can be detached easily, and so included it in the Theophrastean material.—With 5.2 goes 6.2, which refers back to 5.2. It may be mentioned that there is another incorrect reference to our chapter 2 on p. 143.11–14, probably inserted by Arius. Here he replaced love of offspring by love of parents.
36. As Moraux (324 n.19) seems to suggest.
37. This assumption can be supported by a parallel: The Stoic *oikeiōsis* treatise in Cicero *De fin*. 3 is structured in just this way. First (3.5.16–19) the *prōta kata physin* are introduced; they concern body and soul, but not external objects. Then (3.6.20–22) the problem of choice is explained, and when choice becomes stable (*constans consentaneaque naturae*, cf. Arius 2.6 *bebaion eidēsin* and *synōidon tēi physei*), in its very intellectual consistency lies the beginning of the real and final good, which is above all the forementioned things. This is the way leading to wisdom and virtue. It is much later (3.19.62–20.68) that natural relations to external objects are discussed, to children first, then to mankind in general. Obviously, social ethics constitutes a separate and later chapter. The structure of *De fin*. 5 is more complicated, but here as well the external objects come later and as a supplement (5.23.65–8). In 68 the *bona aut animi aut corporis* are grouped separately from those *quae sunt extrinsecus*.
38. The word "*artiotēs*" ("wholeness," "not being crippled"), which follows upon "health" in the list on p. 62.19, can be taken as a mere expansion of "health" (although in other lists it has a separate standing); it is not picked up in the following explanation.

39. Noted by Wachsmuth, ad 1, but not discussed by later scholars.
40. Details: Pohlenz, 10f.; Pembroke, 122f.
41. *Oikeiōsis* to animals is expressly denied by Chrysippus (Cic. *De fin.* 3.20.67). There may be a polemical reference to Theophrastus.
42. Dirlmeier (50–60) found a developmental approach in many Peripatetic texts, including Theophrastus. But there is no evidence that it was combined with *oikeiōsis* or *oikeiotēs*.
43. For studies of the contrast, see Pohlenz 12f. and Brink 140f.
44. G. B. Kerferd, "The Search for Personal Identity in Stoic Thought," *Bull. of the John Rylands Univ. Libr. of Manchester,* 55 (1972), 177–96.
45. K. Gantar, "Amicus sibi", *Živa antika* 16 (1966), 135–75; 17 (1967), 49–80. Some passages referred to (a small selection only) are: Antipho, *VS* 87 B 58; Xenophon, *Mem.* 1.2.2 and 6; Democritus, *VS* 68 B 84, 244, 264; Gorgias, *Palamedes* (*VS* 82 B 11a) 19; Sophocles, *Aias* 1364–7; Euripides, *Medea* 85–7.
46. It occurs already in Alexander of Aphrodisias, *De an.* p. 151.3 ff.
47. Lingistically, *oikeiousthai* must therefore be classed as a "*deponens passivum*" like *hēdesthai* ("to feel pleasure"), *pheresthai* ("to be in motion"), *peithesthai* ("to obey"), which have the forms of the passive, but the meaning of the middle voice.
48. Pembroke 116 (and n.7) has rightly drawn attention to these instances: Chrysippus *SVF* 2.178 (= Diog. Laert. 7.85); *SVF* 3. 146 (= Plut. *De comm. not.* 4, 1060C); Alex. Aphr. *De an.* p. 163.24–31. Cicero *De fin.* 3.7.23 says "*primo nos sapientiae commendari ab initiis naturae,*" where *ta prōta kata physin* appear as an agent. This is a variation upon the expression of Chrysippus.
49. Cf. Pembroke, 116: "not bilateral."
50. See above, p. 176
51. Brink (140 n.96) thinks that the mention of offspring might be an "afterthought"; Pembroke (123–25) speculates that parental love might function as a stimulus for the child's love and so start off the development of *oikeiōsis* in the child.
52. My remarks here have benefited from discussion at the Rutgers conference on Arius Didymus.
53. *EN* 10.5 (1175a29–30, quoted above) and 10.1 (1172a20).
54. See above, p. 174 with n. 19.
55. Cf. the mention of pleasure in Plato's passage on bee-swarms. More Peripatetic material: Dirlmeier 50 n.1.
56. References in *RE* 3.1.450.
57. He has, however, *oikeios* with the overtone "beneficial": *CP* 3.1.2 (*chōran oikeian*); 3.1.3 (connected with *prosphoron*); 5.15.2 (*enia . . . tōn oikeiōn kai synergountōn*).
58. The correspondence has been studied in detail by Brink 133f.

Comments on Professor Görgemanns' Paper
The Two Forms of Oikeiōsis *in Arius and the Stoa*

Brad Inwood

In Section III of his paper, Professor Görgemanns examines Arius' main discussion of *oikeiōsis* and aligns himself roughly with current orthodoxy: Arius draws on late Hellenistic sources for his synopsis of Peripatetic ethics; his attribution of the doctrine of *oikeiōsis* to one school or the other tells us nothing about its ultimate origins. On this section of Professor Görgemanns' paper I shall make only a few comments (Section I of my remarks), dealing with points of emphasis or suggesting alternative views in a field where few theories can be firmly excluded. I shall, however, have more to say (my Section II) about Professor Görgemanns' novel hypothesis concerning the ultimate inspiration for the doctrine of *oikeiōsis* (his Section IV) since here, I think, there is more room for debate.[1] Along the way I want to draw attention to the nature of the relationship between affinity to others (social *oikeiōsis*) and being well-disposed to oneself (personal *oikeiōsis*). This is an important issue and one which merits close examination, for clarity on this point is fundamental to many of the problems raised by discussions of *oikeiōsis*.

I

Professor Görgemanns has convincingly argued for a stratification of our text and supposes that Arius as the final compiler (Stobaeus being a mere copier or abbreviator) is responsible for welding these various sources into whatever unity they have. The strata are (using Professor Görgemanns' division of the text into chapters): chapter 1; chapters 2–7. The latter, however, is itself a composite text. Its author has combined chapter 2 with chapters 3–7 which employ a different approach. Allowance must be made for some vagueness at transitional points, as at chapter 2.1. An additional stratum is identified as well: chapter 5.4–5 which Professor Görgemanns regards as an interpolation, perhaps by Arius himself.

There can be little doubt that our text does break into these sections. In comment, I raise some doubts about their combination, their character and Arius' role in the production of the final result.

Professor Görgemanns follows Paul Moraux's recent analysis of this text (in volume 1 of *Der Aristotelismus bei den Griechen*) on many points and subscribes, he says, in broad outline to the view that "this part is a coherent treatise, not a collection of doxographical notes.'' In fact, Professor Görgemanns' own discussion shows that the irregularities in the text are not minor enough to justify such a generous evaluation. In our text we find (in addition to other substantial differences between chapter 1 and chapter 2) conflicting conceptions of virtue in chapter 1.5 and chapter 2.6. We find several conflicts between chapter 2 and chapters 3–7, including a ''flat contradiction'' between chapter 5.2 and chapter 2.6, which are linked by an explicit cross reference. There is, moreover, inconsistency in the classification of the so-called external goods, which are apparently restricted to social relationships in chapters 3–4 but extended to include the more traditional Peripatetic external goods in chapter 5.4–5.

This point requires more than a mere mention. If Arius is the ''interpolator'' of chapter 5.4–5, then Arius has not fully grasped the coherent argument he is trying to create out of diverse Peripatetic components. If the source for chapters 3–7 made the clumsy addition, then Arius had at hand an incoherent text and failed to rectify it by simple excision. In either case the coherence of the treatise is impugned on a significant point. The most generous assumption would be that someone after Arius made the blunder, but this seems unlikely.[2]

More puzzles are raised by chapter 5.4–5. It does not seem profitable to posit a particular chapter of the *Aristotelian Divisions* (ch. 56) as a source for our text and then to attempt an explanation of the rather substantial divergences between them. The simplest solution is surely the one Professor Görgemanns mentions in passing, to suppose that the model for the interpolation was of the same type as chapter 56 of the *Divisions* but not dependent on it.

Another problem is whether we can be sure that chapter 3.1 is Arius' work and that the *hypographē* referred to here (p. 119.20–21) is the source Arius is following. Is this Arius interjecting a remark of his own into a coherent text before him? The texts cited by Professor Görgemanns in n.4 are not decisive. Page 129.5 is different in sense and drawn from a different source. The reference made to a *hypographē* at p. 122.6 is inconclusive. Here Arius may well be referring to a text he is not following, but one used to supplement his principal source. In fact, the wording seems to suggest this. We are left then with chapter 3.1 (p. 119. 20–21) which must be interpreted by its context alone. This is notoriously difficult to do, because the text to which it refers does not correspond to this announcement. The connection of the ethical system as a whole with the *oikeiōsis* to oneself and the related topics of chapter 2 is nowhere made clear, and the author's treatment of the next topic is fuller, not more condensed, than his handling of chapter 2.

Far from it being certain that it is Arius who says ''as I am going to show'' (p. 119.21), we are in doubt as to who is making the promise. But one might suppose that the speaker of *kathaper epideixō* here is the same as the speaker of *kathaper hypedeixamen* at p. 123.21–22 (ch. 5.2). The promise of chapter 3.1 would, then, be made by the same person who wrote chapter 5.2 and chapter 2.6. Is this Arius or his source? The answer would affect our picture of Arius as a doxographer. But we cannot, I think, determine whether he, or his source, conflated the various strata of our text.

Returning to the problem of the coherence of the treatise, we should observe that a large part of the treatise is organized around a duality of body and soul. This is in contrast with the three elements of virtue in chapter 1 as well as with the threefold analysis of goods in the interpolation. Where does this dualistic approach come from? We must begin to think of Antiochus here, for the similarities are too striking to be overlooked.

The treatments of *oikeiōsis* which have come down to us from Arius and Antiochus are similar in several respects which distinguish them from Stoic versions. First, both treat *oikeiōsis* as part of a Peripatetic ethical system. Second, both free the theory from the technical psychological underpinnings which the Stoics characteristically gave it.[3] Third, both treat *oikeiōsis* to oneself as a duality, not a unity. There are distinct dispositions to one's body and to one's soul and the two can be compared or contrasted. Stoic sources for the doctrine do not do this.

It is, moreover, generally recognized that chapter 2 shows a higher than normal level of Stoic language. This, too, reinforces ties to the Stoicizing Antiochus. So too does Arius' use of *di' hauto haireton* as an equivalent for *agathon*. In Cicero's version of Antiochus this appears as the equivalence of *per se expetendum* and *bonum*.

Nevertheless, it is the body-soul dichotomy in the doctrine of *oikeiōsis* which points most definitely to Antiochus. This is familiar as the main difference between the version in *De finibus* 3[4] and the Antiochean attack on it in Book 4. Use of the body-soul dichotomy is not just a Peripatetic alteration of the Stoic version; it is also the main weapon in Antiochus' powerful criticism of the Stoic doctrine. This criticism was quite pointed, as a little background will show.

According to Alexander of Aphrodisias[5] the first object of *oikeiōsis* was for some Stoics the animal itself, but later and more sophisticated Stoics replaced this formulation with a reference to the animal's *systasis*. Both versions appear at Diogenes Laertius 7.85, drawn from Chrysippus' *On Ends,* although the *systasis* formulation is given pride of place. This is also the formulation reflected in the Latin versions of Cicero (*status* in *De finibus* 3) and Seneca (*constitutio* in *Ep.* 121). It is tempting to suppose that Chrysippus refined the earlier version by replacing "oneself" with "one's own constitution" as the *prōton oikeion.*[6]

Seneca tells us (*Ep.* 121.10) that this constitution is defined by the Stoics as *principale animi quodam modo se habens erga corpus,* i.e., *hēgemonikon pōs echon pros to sōma.* It is hard to believe that this is not Chrysippus' definition. He thought, then, that what a man is well-disposed to is the intimate relationship of soul to body which constitutes the self. The critics, represented by Antiochus, separated this compound self and set up independent relationships of being well-disposed to the two parts. Then they charged the Stoics with misrepresenting the nature of our relationship to these two parts of ourself by reducing our *oikeiōsis* to the body to insignificance and by elevating our *oikeiōsis* to the soul to an unreasonable level.

For the Stoics, however, the self had to remain unified; so, therefore, did the *oikeiōsis*.

The importance of this attack on Chrysippus' doctrine was great, for not only is Antiochus' "Peripatetic" theory in *De finibus* 5 based on his anti-Stoic attack in Book 4, but the dichotomy reappears in the theory of the *prōton oikeion* found in Arius Didymus at pp. 47–48, in Alexander *De anima mantissa* pp. 162–163 and in Arius' Peripatetic account here (ch. 2).[7]

Thus when the doctrine of the *tria genera bonorum* intrudes in chapter 5 of our text, in conflict with this simple body-soul dualism, we may interpret it not as a conflation of two strata of Peripatetic origin, but as a rather abrupt juxtaposition of Antiochean and more strictly Peripatetic material.[8] This, of course, leaves unanswered the question of whether Arius made the conflation or whether he accepted it, perhaps unwittingly, from his source.

II

In Stoic ethics two distinct ideas go under the label "*oikeiōsis*": social *oikeiōsis* and personal *oikeiōsis*. The former is very similar to the notion of *oikeiotēs,* while the latter is, as Brink and Pohlenz argued, quite different. The problem I wish to raise now concerns the relation between the two. The evidence invoked will have relevance to the discussion of the structure of chapters 2–7 and to Professor Görgemanns' thesis (in Part IV of his paper) that personal *oikeiōsis* was derived from social relationships denoted by "*oikeios*" and related terms by turning them inward towards oneself.

At chapter 3.2 the doctrine of a natural affinity to others, *oikeiotēs* or social *oikeiōsis,* is introduced. Arius has promised to show how the doctrine of personal *oikeiōsis* and the dependent material in chapter 2 form the basis of the rest of his account of Peripatetic ethics. But this appears not to happen, and some sort of discontinuity has long been suspected here.[9] Moraux is, of course, something of an exception,[10] and his reluctance to acknowledge discontinuity seems to be based on consideration that Arius is arguing that social *oikeiōsis,* the basis of the intrinsic "choiceworthiness" of our fellow men, is rooted in deeply ingrained natural tendencies, just as is the personal *oikeiōsis* of chapter 2. But in chapter 3.1 we are promised a demonstration of how the rest of the Peripatetic ethical system is based on personal *oikeiōsis* and associated concepts (*apo toutōn hormēsthai*), not how it rests on social *oikeiōsis.* It is only by assuming that the two are rooted in what is more or less the same fact of human nature that the program announced in chapter 3.1 can appear to be fulfilled. But such an assumption is unwarranted, for there is no obvious reason why an apparently egoistic trait of human nature should be linked to the altruistic trait of natural social affinity. Their very compatibility seems to demand defense.

Pohlenz (*Grundfragen* p. 30) supposed that the sharpness of the transition here was the result of a simple omission of a statement that *oikeiōsis* is directed at one's offspring as well as at oneself. This, he thought, would make the transition to the new theme (the *di' hauto haireton,* announced already at p. 118.17) clear. But is Pohlenz right to suppose that the social *oikeiōsis* is so straightforwardly linked to the personal *oikeiōsis*? As we shall see, the evidence for this connection is scanty and difficult to interpret. This may well be, as Brink suggested, because the social *oikeiōsis* was grafted onto the Stoic doctrine of personal *oikeiōsis* from Peripatetic sources and because the Stoics accordingly had at most a somewhat *ad hoc* theory to account for their connection. Most of the time our Stoic sources treat the two kinds of *oikeiōsis* quite independently of each other, as for example in *De finibus* 3. Is it just an accident, then, that there is so rough a transition between them in Arius' synopsis of Peripatetic ethics?

If the connection between the two kinds of *oikeiōsis* was nowhere made clear, is it right to suppose with Pohlenz that the thematic awkwardness is a sign of a simple omission? Or with Professor Görgemanns that this is an indication of a composite text? If the compiler of chapters 2–7, either Arius or his source, were trying to connect the two *oikeiōseis* but had no clear model for doing so, might this not produce the result we have? It will not do, however, to suppose a simple shift at this point from an "Antiochean" to a Peripatetic source, since the body-soul dichotomy remains prominent in most of chapters 3–7 despite the change from a developmental to a comparative approach.

What can be suggested, though, is that the thematic gap between chapter 2 and chapter 3 is the result of an inadequacy in the compiler's sources and his own failure to compensate for this. Whether the compiler in question is Arius or an anonymous Peripatetic, he was unable to make good on his promise to connnect the two forms of *oikeiōsis* in a philosophically coherent way. He did, however, try. Chapter 4.1–2 contains an awkward *a fortiori* argument for a form of personal *oikeiōsis.*[11] "For how can it be that . . . a fellow man should be choiceworthy for his own sake, but not each of us for himself should be choiceworthy for his own sake?" The compiler is arguing for personal *oikeiōsis* on the basis of a social *oikeiōsis.* This connects the two, but it does so in the opposite way to that promised in chapter 3.1, where the rest of the system of ethics was to follow from the contents of chapter 2.

Is it Arius—or his source—who sets himself the goal of bridging this gap in his sources? The attempt is unsuccessful, producing neither philosophical coherence nor a smooth textual transition. But it is an original attempt to do a job that still needed to be done.[12]

That the connection still needed to be explored is a point which must yet be demonstrated. First, however, I would like to recall the thesis of Brink. In addition to hypothesizing that social *oikeiōsis* was borrowed by the Stoics from the Peripatetic *oikeiotēs,* he suggested that a sort of "reflexivization" could account for the link between the two *oikeiōseis* in the Stoa: "*oikeiotēs* can be thought to move inward, as it were, so as to include the individual's relation to himself as a moral agent; and it will be noted that the two principles are brought into a logical connection of sorts in Arius Didymus's summary'' (p. 140). Professor Görgemanns pushes this suggestion one step further, arguing that personal *oikeiōsis* was in fact derived by transferring a social relationship indicated by *"oikeios"* and related words from its external object to the self, turning it inward and thus making an originally external relationship into a reflexive relationship. Let us call this the reflexivization thesis and note that if this thesis explains the origin of the Stoic doctrine of personal *oikeiōsis*, then Brink's theory that the Peripatetic *oikeiotēs* was grafted onto an independently developed, originally Stoic *oikeiōsis* is unlikely to be true. Professor Görgemanns has found support for his thesis in a study of the linguistic background of the word *oikeiōsis*. This factor is important and I shall not challenge it. Instead, I shall try to counterbalance his argument with others of a different character which I believe are of greater weight.

One consideration is that the arguments used by the Stoics themselves to support personal *oikeiōsis* show no trace of reflexivization. Chrysippus did not argue, as Arius did (ch. 4.2), that it would be unreasonable for a man to be concerned for others but not for himself. Rather, his argument[13] was that Nature, which is rational, would not create an animal and then fail to make it inclined to preserve itself; that would not be *eikos*. Similarly Antiochus argues not from the natural love we feel for others, but from the alleged internal contradiction in any act of self-hate.[14]

Another consideration is that personal *oikeiōsis* can be plausibly dated to the time of Zeno,[15] but social *oikeiōsis* cannot be dated so early in the development of Stoic ethics. However, the main argument against the reflexivization thesis is this.Our evidence shows that Chrysippus and the later Stoics made only a weak connection between the two *oikeiōseis*. But the connection for which we do have evidence is an extension from the relationship one has to oneself and one's parts, to one's offspring, and thence to all other humans. If the reflexivization thesis were true, the relation of derivation would have run in the opposite direction.

Our best texts dealing explicitly with the Stoic theory of *oikeiōsis* do not make an effort to connect personal *oikeiōsis* (which is used primarily in discussions of the *telos*) with a social relationship. Thus the version taken from Chrysippus' *On Ends* at Diogenes Laertius 7.85–86 ignores social *oikeiōsis*.[16] Similarly, Seneca's version of *oikeiōsis,* in *Ep.* 121, and the version earlier in Arius Didymus (pp. 47–48), which is contaminated with non-Stoic sources, are both restricted to personal *oikeiōsis*. The same is true of *De finibus* 3.16ff. Here Cicero relates a middle Stoic account of personal *oikeiōsis* as it is used to ground the doctrine of the *telos* in basic facts of human nature. When, later in the book (62ff.), the naturalistic roots of the virtue of justice are explored, social *oikeiōsis* is introduced. It is derived from the love parents feel for their children, not the love children feel for their parents. This makes difficult a connection to personal *oikeiōsis* rooted in the first instincts of a child, and in fact no effort is made here to link the two.

Hierocles, in the papyrus text *Ethikē stoicheiōsis* (col. 1–8), deals only with personal *oikeiōsis*. Characteristically, it is based on an elaborate Stoic psychology. He may have tried to link it to social *oikeiōsis* in col. 9 and 11, but a gap in the text makes it impossible to tell. In fact it is most unlikely that Hierocles here supplied a method of basing social *oikeiōsis* on the personal variety. For col. 9 treats personal *oikeiōsis*, called *eunoētikē;* the social or familial, called *sterktikē;* and a novel form of *oikeiōsis*, directed to external things, called *hairetikē*, as being parallel and analogous. There is no clear sign of derivation.[17]

Pembroke[18] has observed that the social *oikeiōsis* at *De finibus* 3.62ff. is supported by characteristically Stoic arguments. These include an argument from the rational and teleological character of Providence, which is analogous to the argument used to support personal *oikeiōsis* at Diogenes Laertius 7.85. It would make no sense for Nature to create an animal and not make it inclined to preserve itself; similarly, it would make no sense for Nature to arrange for offspring to be born and to allow them not to be cared for. This is the reason why parents naturally love their offspring, and this feeling is in turn the basis for the social *oikeiōsis* and ultimately for justice. Pohlenz[19] points to similar material at *De natura deorum* 2.128–29, and the parallelism between the roots of personal and social *oikeiōseis* is confirmed at *De finibus* 3.62 by reference to our avoidance of pain and at *De officiis* 1.11–12, where the same power of Nature is made responsible for both instincts.[20] But what we are looking for and what Arius needs is not mere similarity of origin but a relationship of derivation.

The only Stoic text which provides a link is found in chapter 12 of Plutarch's *De stoicorum repugnantiis*:[21]

> Why then again in every book of physics, yes and of ethics too, does he keep writing ad nauseam that from the moment of birth we have a natural affinity to ourselves, to our parts and to our own offspring (*SVF* 3.179)? In the first book concerning Justice he says that even the beasts have been endowed with affinity to their offspring in proportion to its need, except in the case of fishes, for their spawn is nourished of itself . . . (*SVF* 2.724).

The second half of this text (*SVF* 2.724) confirms that Chrysippus' starting point for the social *oikeiōsis* and the derivation of Justice from human nature was a parental concern for offspring, as at *De finibus* 3.62 and *De natura deorum* 2.128–29. The first half (*SVF* 3.179), a loose paraphrase of the gist of the introductions to various of Chrysippus' books,[22] clearly suggests the same thing, i.e., that Chrysippus saw love *for* offspring as the basis for further social *oikeiōsis*. Thus Chrysippus is in a dilemma: how to base a social *oikeiōsis* first appearing in a parent on instincts supposedly present from birth.[23] But more important, this text provides our only useful information about how the two kinds of *oikeiōsis* were related to each other by Chrysippus; we shall return to it presently.

First, our review of possible links between the two should be completed. Since we are trying to explain the linkage on p. 119 of Arius' Peripatetic synopsis, the brief[24] reference back to it at p. 143.11–14 is important. Like an intriguing text of Antiochus dealing with the "seeds of virtue" (*De finibus* 5.41ff.), this text links the personal *oikeiōsis* to the social by making the child's affection for others the basis of human social bonding.[25] Arius singles out, as no Stoic does, a child's love for its parents; Antiochus mentions a child's recognition of its nurses and its fondness for its playmates. This is undoubtedly an interesting way to connect the two *oikeiōseis*. But it is not Chrysippus' way, as far as we know,[26] nor is it implied on p. 119 of our text. One curious thing about Antiochus' account is that, when he leaves the topic of the "seeds of virtue" to discuss the roots of social bonding (*De finibus* 5.65ff., parallel to 3.62ff.), he reverts to the Stoic version: *a procreatoribus nati diliguntur*. This is remarkable, because it involves him in the same difficulty Chrysippus seems to be caught in: how to connect a parent's love with an instinct allegedly found in the newborn. In *SVF* 3.179 the words *euthus genomenoi* reveal Chrysippus' embarrassment and the phrase *nata a primo satu* in *De finibus* 5.65 puts Antiochus in the same position. Why did he stay with the Chrysippean dilemma when his own child-centered derivation at 5.41ff. could have helped him escape?[27]

Two additional Stoic sources may appear to offer clues to the derivation of the social *oikeiōsis* from the personal. Hierocles, in a text preserved by Stobaeus,[28] gives a detailed summary of how one should behave to other people, based on the image of a man standing at the centre of a series of concentric circles representing his various social relationships. Much could be said about this text. But for our purposes one need only note that although a man's relationship to himself is put on the same scale, as it were, with his social relationships, we learn nothing about the connection between these two kinds of relationship. For the purposes of practical moral advice Hierocles has taken for granted the facts about human nature which we would like to have explained.

More interesting is a text of Epictetus (*Diss.* 1.19.11–15). Starting from the dilemma of how to reconcile the egoism of the personal *oikeiōsis* with the altruism of the social, he links the two by flatly asserting that this altruism is part of what it means to be a rational man. Thus the *oikeiōsis* to one's rational constitution, as Seneca puts it (*Ep.* 121.14), involves altruism because of the very fact of rationality. Epictetus implies that Nature, rational and teleological as always, has arranged things such that the two principles never conflict if both are properly understood. But this intriguing and truncated argument would, if fleshed out, yield a reconciliation of the conflict which might be expected to arise between the two *oikeiōseis*, not a derivation of one from the other.

If we set aside Antiochus' child-centered derivation of the social *oikeiōsis* from the personal, which turns up oddly in Arius and which, like Arius, he did not consistently hold, we are left with only the Chrysippean derivation at *SVF* 3.179. This, if anything, indicates the Stoics' own way of dealing with the problem. Attention has been drawn to the conflict here: how can a parent's affinity for his offspring be connected directly to his affinity to himself, which has existed since birth? Since the Stoic version of the *oikeiōsis* theory was, we may believe, the source for later Hellenistic versions, Chrysippus' failure to forge a firm and plausible link can be seen as the cause for the confusion seen in later discussions. Perhaps, then, the prevailing embarrassment on this point is the reason for the discontinuity between chapter 2 and chapter 3 of Arius, for the odd Antiochean theory at p. 143, and for the inverse derivation in chapter 4.2. Arius or his source probably did not have a satisfactory doctrine with which to bridge the gap, so he turned to the new topic at chapter 3.2 leaving discontinuity as a mark of his difficulty.

But what of the link implied in *SVF* 3.179? Professor Fortenbaugh suggested in discussion that one's offspring could be regarded as "parts" of oneself, since at conception the father and mother contribute parts (*merê, apospasmata*) of their own souls to produce the offspring.[29] Chrysippus may have used this notion of offspring as parts of their parents to explain how the egoistic personal *oikeiōsis* could be the basis of a natural affinity to others. It is hard to see how else this alleged fact of human nature could be explained by the Stoics.

This suggestion is reinforced by the existence of a close parallel in earlier philosophy. I refer to the *Nicomachean Ethics* 8.12 1161b16ff., where Aristotle deals with the topic of family love (*sungenikê philia*) and its origin. The parallels to the theory of social *oikeiōsis* are close. Once the basic family relationships are established there is an extension of them to our other kin and to social relations, just as in so many Stoic texts. But it is the similarity in the derivation of the basic relationship of *philia* which matters for present purposes: it is the love parents feel for their children that is basic, not vice versa. Aristotle acknowledges that children love their parents, because they are born from them (*ap' ekeinōn ti onta* 1161b19), but the parental feeling is stronger since the offspring are like parts of themselves (*heautôn ti onta* 1161b18). For, Aristotle says, "the thing produced is *oikeion* to its source, e.g., a tooth or hair or whatever to the one who has it; but to the product the source is nothing, or less important." There are other reasons for the superior strength of parental love, but this is the one Aristotle returns to (1161b27ff.): "parents, then, love their children as themselves; for the children they produce are like second selves (*heteroi autoi*) by virtue of being separated (sc. from them) . . . ."[30]

If Chrysippus knew this text or one like it, it could certainly have suggested to him the sort of solution to his problem which Professor Fortenbaugh has suggested on the basis of *SVF* 3.179. The use of this or some similar text to bridge the gap is all the more likely if Brink is right and the social *oikeiōsis* had its origins in the Peripatetic *oikeiotēs*. And if Chrysippus found the link between personal and social *oikeiōsis* in a text like this, that would partially explain the awkwardness of his own theory. The notion of natural love for one's offspring as parts of oneself was not originally intended to connect a fact about newborn animals (personal *oikeiōsis*) to a fact about adults (social *oikeiōsis*), but Chrysippus made it do that service.[31] The observation in Aristotle does all it is meant to do; the Stoic adaptation does not.[32]

If this is the correct account of the connection between the two *oikeiōseis* made by Chrysippus when he integrated *oikeiotēs* into the school's doctrine, then it follows that the reflexivization thesis is false. For if the original personal *oikeiōsis* were derived from the social *oikeiōsis* or from *oikeiotēs* by a form of inward-turning, then the connection between the two would have been easy and clear. Chrysippus would not have been in the position of having to grope for expedients to help graft the new *oikeiōsis* onto the old. But this he seems to have done. Further, insofar as we have evidence for the Stoic theory, the derivation runs in the opposite direction to that suggested by the reflexivization thesis. Third, if the reflexivization thesis were true and the Stoics had from the beginning had a unified doctrine of the two forms of *oikeiōsis*, we would almost certainly not see in the later discussions of the topic the embarrassing silences, the confusion, and the experimentation which we do in fact see.

If, as I believe, Brink is closer to the truth when he suggests that the social *oikeiōsis* was a later graft onto the Stoic doctrine of personal *oikeiōsis*, then there is at least one consequence for our text of Arius Didymus. The thematic gap between chapter 2 and chapter 3 need not be explained by a lacuna, a mere textual misfortune. It can be explained as a result of the compiler's overambitious attempt to join two themes which had not been satisfactorily connected before. If the Stoics themselves had only an *ad hoc* explanation for the relation of the two *oikeiōseis*, it is less puzzling that this late Hellenistic text failed to produce a philosophically coherent doctrine from them. The compiler saw the need to do so, but his reach clearly exceeded his grasp. We are, perhaps, no more certain than before whether this attempt was made by Arius or by his source, but the absence of thematic unity at this point in the text can be seen in a different light.

NOTES

1. While the topic of the inspiration for the theory is on the agenda, attention should be drawn to J. M. Rist's recent reminder that the Cynics as well as Peripatetics and Academics are to be considered: "Zeno and Stoic Consistency," *Phronesis* 22 (1977) 161–74.
2. That the interpolator was a man of some wit, not merely a misguided scribe, is suggested by the apparent purpose of the interpolation. The point, according to chapters 5.6–6.1, is to prove that goods of the soul are more valuable than all other goods. A Peripatetic would want to deal with external goods too, although the basic source was organized around the body-soul dichotomy. The interpolator of chapter 5.4–5 had a notion of the comparative method used to structure the rest of this section, but lacked either the skill or the interest to integrate his new material to the context.
3. Near the end of chapter 2 Arius introduces some technical terms of Stoic psychology and ethics as being dependent on the doctrine of *oikeiōsis*. But for most Stoic accounts the psychological concepts *sunaisthēsis* and *hormē* are fundamental for the doctrine (Diogenes Laertius 7.85 for one example, but Hierocles shows the same pattern). At p. 47 Arius uses some of the psychological terms of the Stoic theory, but not in the Stoic fashion.
4. Such a dichotomy is hinted at in 3.17–18 with the contrast between the body and *cognitiones*. Even this, however, is not a clear contrast of bodily to psychic goods.
5. *De anima mantissa*, p. 150 Bruns. I assume undogmatically that Alexander is the author of the relevant portions of the *Mantissa*.
6. So Pohlenz *Grundfragen* p. 9 and R. Philippson "Das erste Naturgemässe" *Philologus* 87 (1931–32) p. 455. Pembroke (*Problems in Stoicism* p. 145 n.77) disagreed. Whether

the earlier version was Zeno's or Cleanthes' (whose views on *oikeiōsis* were known to Hierocles, col. 8.11) or both is not vital here. For bibliographical details see Professor Görgemanns' notes.

7. Interestingly, though, this dichotomy of the self is absent from Alexander's essay on the Aristotelian *prōton oikeion* (*Mantissa* pp. 150–53).

8. Confirmation for this is available. Professor Görgemanns has noted the conflict between the normal Peripatetic list of external goods in chapter 5 and the limitation of external goods to social relationships in chapters 3–4. Antiochus, in *De finibus* 5.68, contrasts the goods of body and soul with external goods; and his list of external goods is restricted to familial and social relationships just as the earlier list in Arius is. It would be just like Antiochus to graft the Stoic notion of external goods onto his own body-soul dichotomy.

9. Moraux, *Der Aristotelismus* pp. 320–21 nn. 11–13 for the views of von Arnim, Dirlmeier, and others.

10. Moraux pp. 320–21.

11. Arius is immediately concerned to show that bodily goods are choiceworthy *per se,* but he does so by arguing that our own self as a whole is choiceworthy *per se* and consequently that its components are too. This is supported by the *a fortiori* argument that the self is choiceworthy *per se.*

12. See below for another and conflicting attempt to derive one kind of *oikeiōsis* from the other at p. 143.

13. Diogenes Laertius 7.85, paralleled by Hierocles col. 6.40–44 and Seneca *Ep.* 121.18 and 24.

14. *De finibus* 5.28ff. Like Chrysippus, Antiochus also excludes the possibility of indifference to oneself (5.30).

15. Rist, op. cit.

16. If the latter turns up in Diogenes Laertius 7 at all, it is only at 7.120 where love for one's offspring in its true sense is restricted to sages; ordinary men are excluded. This would be a poor basis for a general theory of social bonding.

17. Similarly at *Mantissa* p. 162.18ff. the two kinds are paralleled with no hint of their precise relationship to one another. This is also true of the discussion in the anonymous commentary on the *Theaetetus* (col. 7.44–8.1). There the *eunoētikē* and the *sterktikē* are grouped together as a *kēdemonikē oikeiōsis* in contrast to the *hairetikē*. This shows that these two forms of *oikeiōsis* were thought to be similar and compatible; it does not shed light on the derivation of one from another.

18. *Problems in Stoicism* pp. 121–22.

19. *Grundfragen* p. 45ff.

20. Seneca uses this argument to support the doctrine of personal *oikeiōsis* (*Ep.* 121.18).

21. 1038B, tr. after Cherniss. Von Arnim puts the indirect speech of *SVF* 3.179 in quotation marks. Cherniss is right to regard it as a paraphrase, for no single text is indicated as a source.

22. We are giving the benefit of the doubt to Chrysippus by allowing that Plutarch's polemical paraphrase is a reliable representation of something Chrysippus did say, rather than an amalgam of statements about the two *oikeiōseis* drawn from different works. If it is not, then we have no evidence at all that Chrysippus saw the need to connect them.

23. *SVF* 3.492 glosses over the fact that Cicero's treatment of *oikeiōsis* falls into the same dilemma; so too does Kerferd in his comment on the passage ("Search for Personal Identity" p. 195).

24. And inaccurate; see Pohlenz *Grundfragen* pp. 37–38.

25. *De finibus* 2.45 speaks of family affection generally, with no distinction between the version stressing a parent's love and that stressing a child's.

26. Rist, op. cit. p. 173, is wrong to say that the child's love for its parents played a key role for the Stoics in effecting the transition from the personal to the social *oikeiōsis*.
27. For someone keen to avoid the dilemma, there is the option of interpreting *euthus genomenoi* and *nata a primo satu* figuratively, as indications of the naturalness of the social instinct. But the developmental approach leads us to expect literal use of temporal terms; and the phrase *euthus genomena* in the relevant text of Aristotle (*EN* 1161b25, see n.31) is literal.
28. Pages 61–62 of von Arnim's edition (Berlin 1906) of Hierocles.
29. *SVF* 1.128; cf. 2.749, 756.
30. On children as parts or products of their parents, cf. *EE* 7.8 and *EN* 9.7 1167b28–1168a9, 19–27; also 4.1 1120b13–14 and Plato *Rep.* 1.330C.
31. Hence the embarrassment with *euthus genomenoi* in *SVF* 3.179. In Aristotle children are loved from the moment of *their* birth (*euthus genomena*, line 25). The verbal similarity emphasizes the awkwardness of Chrysippus' use of the idea.
32. Professor Görgemanns acknowledges this problem briefly. But it weighs more heavily against the reflexivization thesis than he concedes. One thing we can be sure of in the midst of this unavoidably speculative discussion is that for Chrysippus the developmental approach (and so personal *oikeiōsis*) is central. If the "logical" derivation of social *oikeiōsis* from personal *oikeiōsis* is not consistent with this approach, that is a strong argument that social *oikeiōsis* is not integral to the Stoic doctrine, as it would naturally be according to the reflexivization thesis.

One further remark. Professor Görgemanns argues that *philia* differs from *oikeiōsis* since it is symmetrical while the latter is not. But in the relevant text (*EN* 8.12) Aristotle argues 1) that love for one's children is basic to other forms of *philia* and 2) that love for one's own parts and products explains why one's children are loved. 2) is necessary in view of the primacy of self-love. Aristotle seems to take self-love as a starting point and explains love for others as a derivation from it, an egoism also apparent in the notion that a friend is a second self (*EN* 9.4 and 8). The *philia* we see here is just as egoistic as the Stoic *oikeiōsis* and just as asymmetrical.

CHAPTER 10

Arius, Theophrastus, and the *Eudemian Ethics*

William W. Fortenbaugh

In his survey of Peripatetic ethics (2.7.13 p. 116.19–2.7.25 p. 147.25 W.), Arius names Theophrastus within an account of moral virtue (2.7.20 p. 137.13–142.13). The naming occurs roughly in the middle of this account (p. 140.8) and has caused considerable speculation, for no other philosopher is named in Arius' survey of Peripatetic ethics.[1] Boldest is the claim of Arnim that Arius has drawn his material from a school compendium, whose primary source was Theophrastus.[2] This position has been subject to considerable criticism and, I think, adequately refuted by various scholars, who point to the presence of post-Theophrastean material within Arius' survey.[3] Nevertheless, the occurrence of material explicitly attributed to Theophrastus is important, as is the possibility of identifying passages which can be called Theophrastean in that they incorporate views which were previously advanced and defended by Theophrastus. I plan, therefore, to discuss both that text in which Theophrastus is named (parts I and II of this paper) and also two other passages, which I believe reflect the thinking of Theophrastus (parts III and IV of this paper). Along the way I hope to show that Theophrastus was doing interesting work in the field of ethics and that this work is closely related to Aristotle's *Eudemian Ethics*.

I

The following is a translation of Stobaeus' *Anthology* 2.7.20 (p. 140.7–142.13 W.). The section numbers are mine and are intended only to facilitate discussion within this paper.

p. 140.7   1. Therefore the mean relative to us is best. For example, Theophrastus says, during meetings[4] one man goes through many things and chatters at length, another says little and not what is essential, but a third says only
.10   what is necessary and so lays hold upon due measure.[5] This is the mean relative to us,[6] for it is determined by us by means of reason. Wherefore virtue is "a disposition to choose, being in the mean which is relative to us, determined by reason and such as the practically wise man would determine it."

.15   2. Then setting out several coordinates (and) investigating (the matter) in conformity with his teacher, he next tried to adduce individual cases in the

.20

following manner.[7] For the sake of examples the following were chosen: (i) temperance, intemperance, insensitiveness; (ii) gentleness, irascibility, lack of feeling; (iii) courage, rashness, cowardice; (iv) justice [* * *] (v) liberality, prodigality, meanness; (vi) greatness of soul, smallness of soul, vanity; (vii) magnificence, shabbiness, extravagance.

p.141.1

.5

.10

.15

.20

p.142.1

3. Of these dispositions some are bad on account of excess or deficiency in regard to emotions; others are good, obviously on account of being mean-dispositions. For (he says) (i) that neither the man entirely lacking in appetite nor the man given to appetite is temperate. For the one, like a stone, does not even desire things which accord with nature, and the other is intemperate on account of excessive appetites. But the man between these two, having an appetite for the right things, at the right time and to the extent he ought, and using reason like a rule(r) to make determinations in accordance with propriety, is both called temperate and is in accordance with nature. (ii) Neither the man who lacks feeling and never becomes angry at anyone[8] is gentle, nor the man who becomes angry at every provocation, even if it is very small, but rather the man who has the middle disposition. (iii) Neither the man who is frightened of nothing, even if it be a god which approaches, nor the man who is frightened of everything and the proverbial shadow is courageous [* * *] (iv) Neither the man who distributes the larger portion to himself nor the man who distributes the lesser is just, but the man who distributes the equal portion. And the equal is the proportionate, not the arithmetically equal. (v) Neither the man who lavishes sums at random nor the man who does not lavish sums is liberal [* * *] (vi) Neither the man who deems himself worthy of all great things nor the man who deems himself worthy of nothing at all is great of soul, but the man who accepts what is due (to him) from each individual[9] and to the extent that is appropriate. (vii) Neither the man who is splendid on all occasions, even when it is not right, nor the man who never is, is magnificent, but the man who in accordance with opportunity[10] adapts himself to the individual case.

.5

.10

4. Such is the form of the moral virtues, being concerned with emotion and viewed as a mean-disposition. It enjoys a reciprocal implication with practical wisdom, though not in the same way. Rather practical wisdom follows upon the virtues on account of their peculiar character, while the virtues follow upon practical wisdom *per accidens*. The just man is also practically wise, because such reason (i.e., practical wisdom) gives him his special form. The practically wise man, however, is also just, not on account of his peculiar character, but rather because he, too, does what is noble and good, and nothing bad.

This portion of Stobaeus' *Anthology* divides into four sections. In the first (p. 140.7–14) we are told that the mean relative to us is best and then offered some illustrative remarks concerning this mean. In the second section (p. 140.15–141.2) we are given a list of coordinate dispositions: seven virtues are listed in conjunction with related vices. In the third section (p. 141.3–142.5) the seven virtues or, more accurately, the seven corresponding persons are discussed individually. Finally there is a fourth section (p. 142.6–13), dealing with the relationship between moral virtue and practical wisdom. Although this section has been claimed for Theophrastus,[11] it is quite independent of the other three sections. It involves terms of Stoic origin (*antakolouthia* p. 142.7–8, *eidopoiein* p. 142.11)[12] and also a shift to direct discourse. While in the third section Arius (or his source) summarizes Theophrastean material in indirect discourse, in the fourth he shifts to direct discourse and reports a Peripatetic argument which is post-Theophrastean and influenced by developments within the Stoa.[13] We may, therefore, leave aside this fourth section and concentrate on the preceding three sections.

Even these three sections cannot be attributed to Theophrastus without considerable qualification. Arius' hand is unmistakable at the beginning of the second section: "Then setting out several coordinates (and) investigating (the matter) in conformity with his teacher . . ." (p. 140.15ff), and also in the third section, which is marked by both considerable compression and the epitomator's penchant for indirect discourse. Further, the repeated use of the "neither-nor" (*oute-oute*, p. 141.5–142.1) formula may be due to Arius, though that is by no means certain.[14] Finally, the first section may involve several non-Theophrastean elements. If the opening "therefore" (*oun*, p. 140.7) is intended to provide a tie with what has gone before in the compendium, then perhaps the entire first sentence (i.e., the words, "Therefore the mean relative to us is best") should be assigned to Arius. The subsequent example concerning conversation is certainly Theophrastean, but the inclusion of a definition of moral virtue, taken verbatim from Aristotle's *Nicomachean Ethics* 1106b36—1107a2 is problematic. This inclusion might be thought to support the view that Theophrastus' work often took the form of a commentary on existing Aristotelian material.[15] But even if some of Theophrastus' work was of this sort, it seems to me far more likely that the *EN* definition of moral virtue has been introduced by Arius (or his source). For Arius' compendium is marked by a willingness to combine material from different sources. The section on moral virtue (2.7.20) is no exception.[16] Arius begins by following the *MM*, sometimes quoting verbatim and sometimes writing freely. Then at 139.19 he shifts to the *EE*, because this treatise has what the *MM* lacks—namely, a discussion of the mean relative to us (1220b21–33). At p. 140.7 he makes another shift, this time to Theophrastus, who offers what is missing in the *EE*—namely, a listing in conjunction with discussion of the several moral virtues.[17] If the Theophrastean text in front of Arius lacked a definition of moral virtue as a mean relative to us, Arius may well have shifted source once again and introduced a verbatim quote from the *EN*, after which he returned to his Theophrastean text.[18]

Assuming that the above remarks are sufficient to warn us against treating the Theophrastean excerpt as though it were a verbatim quote, I now want to focus on those features which suggest a close tie between Theophrastus and Aristotle's *Eudemian Ethics*. First the sentence, "For the sake of examples the following were chosen" (p. 140.17–18) all but reproduces *EE* 1220b35. Whether this sentence should be attributed to Theophrastus or Arius (or his source) is a much discussed question. Since the preceding sentence ends in such a way as to suggest the immediate introduction of Theophrastean material, certain scholars have held that the sentence reminiscent of *EE* 1220b35 was written by Theophrastus, who was either reporting what Aristotle said in lecture[19] or commenting on the table of virtues and vices in the *EE*.[20] In either case Theophrastus would be telling us that the upcoming list of virtues and vices was selected by Aristotle. Nevertheless, the sentence in question may be thought to pick up the earlier phrase, "setting out several coordinates" (140.15). In this case we would have a statement by Arius, who is telling us that the soon-to-be-listed virtues and vices were chosen by Theophrastus.[21] Here two possibilities suggest themselves. Arius (or his source) may have found words reminiscent of *EE* 1220b35 in the text of Theophrastus and chosen to preserve the reminiscence in his statement concerning Theophrastus' selection of virtues and vices. Alternatively Arius (or his source) may have been influenced by his own reading of the *EE*. This is not improbable, for Arius had been working with the *EE* (as stated, 139.19–140.6 is based upon *EE* 1220b21–33), and he will have read *EE* 1220b34–1221b3 carefully before deciding to shift sources at p. 140.7. On this hypothesis, the sentence under consideration will indeed relate to the *EE*, but it will not be evidence for a close tie between Theophrastus and the *EE*.[22]

Rather than try to force a decision between these several interpretations, I want to address myself to a detail. It is the suggestion that our Theophrastean text is excerpted from a commentary on the table of virtues and vices in the *EE*. This seems to me most unlikely, for the Theophrastean table of virtues and vices departs significantly from the order of the Eudemian table. In particular, temperance (*sōphrosynē*) is treated first instead of fourth. This ordering is striking (it is without parallel not only in the *EE* but also in the *EN* and *MM*) and prompted Arnim to postulate a fourth Aristotelian course of lectures on ethics.[23] However, a much simpler explanation suggests itself, the moment we recall that Theophrastus wrote a work which circulated under three different titles: *On Education, On Virtues,* and *On Temperance* (Diogenes Laertius 5.50). In a work focusing on education (hence the Arabic title *Kitab al-adab* recorded by Ibn al-Nadīm, al-Fihrist 252 [Flügel][24]) not only is a discussion of virtues fully in order, but also a discussion in which temperance is given pride of place (hence the title *On Temperance* found both in Diogenes and in a papyrus list dating from the third century A.D., Pack[2] 2089). I suggest, therefore, that our text derives from a work with an educational orientation. It is not part of a commentary on the *EE*, but, as we shall immediately see, it does contain features which unquestionably relate it closely to the *EE* and not to the *EN*.

Among these features are the use of *salakōnia* ("extravagance") to name the excessive disposition coordinate with magnificence and shabbiness (p. 141.2) and the use of *analgēsia* ("lack of feeling") to name the deficient disposition coordinate with gentleness and irascibility (p. 140.19). In both cases the Theophrastean text exhibits affinity to the *EE* and not to the *EN*. In the latter treatise *salakōnia* does not occur at all and *analgēsia* is used only in a general way to signify insensitivity to pain (1100b32). It is never used for a vice coordinate with gentleness and irascibility. (The adjective *analgētos* occurs at *EN* 1115b26, but in this passage it is used to characterize the man who lacks fear.) In the *EE*, however, the adjective *salakōn* is used to refer to the extravagant man (1221a35, 1233b1); the substantive *analgēsia* and the adjective *analgētos* are used for lack of feeling and for the man who lacks feeling, respectively (1220b38, 1221a16). The usage of *salakōn* is of especial interest for the lexicographer. Hesychius actually cites Theophrastus to document *salakōn* in the sense of "misguided spender" (*Lexicon*, vol. 4 p. 5 no. 100 Schmidt). The word does occur in Aristotle's *Rhetoric* 1391a2–4, but here it is used in conjunction with *soloikos* to describe the vulgar individual who lacks good manners. This usage is the earlier one and in Book 3 of the *EE* 1233a38–b1 Aristotle remarks that the excessive spender is nameless but has a certain affinity to the tasteless (*apeirokalos*) and vulgar (*salakōn*) individual. Apparently Aristotle felt some misgivings about a new usage which Theophrastus either introduced or helped to establish. Later the author of the *MM* was to use both the adjective *salakōn* and the noun *salakōneia* without hesitation (1192a37, b2). Like Hesychius, he could have cited Theophrastus to justify his usage, but felt no need to do so.[25]

It should perhaps be mentioned that our Theophrastean text does not characterize any vice as unnamed. Since both the *EE* 1221a3, 40 and the *EN* 1107b2, 1108a17 expressly recognize unnamed dispositions, and since the *MM* recognizes none, we may be tempted to argue that, all things considered, our Theophrastean text is more closely related to the *MM* than to either the *EE* or the *EN*. Here, however, some caution is in order, for in the Theophrastean text only the list of coordinates is complete in regard to vices. The subsequent analysis concentrates itself on the virtuous individual (even with Spengel's addition,[26] only the man who lacks feeling, the *analgētos* p. 141.12, and the intemperate man, the *akolastos* p. 141.8, are named; the insensitive man is merely described as one who lacks appetite, *anepithymētos* p. 141.6) and is clearly a very concise resumé of what was once a far more detailed discussion. This allows the possibility that Theophrastus originally raised some doubts concerning the names of certain vices.[27] Furthermore and perhaps more importantly, Theophrastus may have found it unnecessary to mention in all contexts the problem of nameless dispositions. In his treatise *On Education* (D.L. 5.50), from which our text is likely to be an excerpt, Theophrastus may have deliberately passed over any discussion of unnamed dispositions, in order to take up the subject in more theoretical (linguistic) works such as the *Kinds of Virtue* (D.L. 5.42) or the book *On Virtue* (D.L. 5.46). Certainly we should not demand that Theophrastus say everything all of the time.

There are three further details which closely relate our Theophrastean passage to the *EE*. First, the insensitive man (*anaisthētos*) is compared with a stone (p. 141.7). This comparison is found in the *EE* 1221a23, but it is absent in both the *EN* and the *MM*.[28] Second, while ambition (*philotimia*) and lack of ambition (*aphilotimia*) occur in the *EN* as vices coordinate with an unnamed virtue (1107b24–1108a1, 1125b1–25), they are absent from the *EE*, the *MM* and our Theophrastean text. Third, both the *EE* 1221a4, 23–24 and the Theophrastean text (p. 140.20, 141.16–18) include justice in the list and in the subsequent exposition of coordinate dispositions. There are, of course, certain differences between the Eudemian and the Theophrastean treatments of justice: the Eudemian list has the word *dikaion*

(1221a4) instead of *dikaiosynē* (p. 140.20);[29] no coordinate vices are named in the Theophrastean text (but this is to be explained by textual corruption); the clarification of the equal (*to ison*) as proportionate equality occurs only in the Theophrastean text (p. 141.18). Nevertheless, the agreement between the *EE* and the Theophrastean text seems to me significant, for both do what the *EN* fails to do. They treat justice as a regular mean-disposition coordinate not only with an excessive disposition but also with a deficiency—namely, the disposition of one who seldom seeks gain (*EE* 1221a23–24), who assigns himself too little (p. 141.17).[30]

Still another feature of our Theophrastean text may be called upon to strengthen the connection with the *EE*. This is the complete absence of social dispositions in both the list of coordinates and the subsequent treatment of virtuous individuals. The absence is particularly striking, for the Theophrastean text begins with an example drawn from the sphere of social interaction: to illustrate the mean in regard to us, the chatterer and the overly silent man are distinguished from the person whose conversation suits the situation. Perhaps this initial mention of social behavior can be explained away by reference to the epitomator's scissors and paste technique. Anyone who can slip an Aristotelian definition of virtue into a Theophrastean excerpt is certainly capable of combining Theophrastean material from two different contexts: e.g., from a discussion of the mean, in which conversation serves as an example, and a more or less independent analysis of ethical dispositions, in which social habits are not included. But whatever we think of the relationship between the several sections of our text, it remains true that the absence of social dispositions in both the list of coordinates and in the subsequent discussion of virtuous men suggests a connection with the *EE*, for in this treatise mean-dispositions within the sphere of social interaction are explicitly refused the status of moral virtue (1234a24). We know that Theophrastus had an especial interest in social dispositions (e.g., the *Characters*)[31] and can, I think, reasonably speculate that he was so impressed by the special status of these dispositions, that he deliberately excluded them from the treatment of virtue and vice preserved in our text.

II

In this part I want to call attention to the sentence with which Arius begins the third section of his Theophrastean excerpt: "Of these dispositions some are bad on account of excess or deficiency in regard to emotions (*pathē*), others are good, obviously on account of being mean-dispositions" (p. 141.3–5). This sentence is in direct discourse and may be a verbatim quote from Theophrastus.[32] Alternatively it may be a transitional remark by Arius (or his source), who immediately shifts to indirect discourse, in order to report Theophrastus' handling of the several virtues and vices.[33] If the latter is correct, it still may be the case that Arius' remark was prompted by a Theophrastean text. For our purposes the important point is that virtue and vice are referred only to emotion or *pathos*. There is no mention of action or *praxis*. At risk of making too much of a single sentence, I want to suggest that the absence of any reference to *praxis* is another case of closer relationship to the *EE* than to the *EN*.

Let me develop this point, beginning with a brief look at Book 2 of the *EN*. Here Aristotle first focuses on moral virtue as habit. He tells us that by repeating a particular kind of behavior, say, steadfast endurance in the face of danger, one becomes a courageous individual who regularly exhibits steadfast endurance (1103b2, 16–17, 1104a35–b3). Next Aristotle considers the pleasures and pains, which follow upon tasks (*erga* 1104b5). He says that such pleasures and pains are indications of moral character, and then after a reference to Plato's *Laws,* he argues that since the virtues are concerned with *praxeis* and *pathē,* and since every *pathos* and every *praxis* is accompanied by pleasure and pain, it follows that virtue is concerned with pleasures and pains (1104b13–16). The idea that moral virtue is related to (both) *pathos* and *praxis* does not immediately reappear. This is most striking when Aristotle draws a threefold distinction between emotion (*pathos*), capacity (*dynamis*) and disposition (*hexis*) and then argues that moral virtue is neither an emotion nor a capacity, but rather a disposition in regard to emotion—no mention being made of action or *praxis* (1105b19–1106a13). Later, however, when Aristotle comes to discuss moral virtue *qua* mean, he distinguishes between *pathē* and *praxeis,* mentions several kinds of *pathē,* and then passes over the class of *praxeis* without giving a single example (1106b16–24). A little later Aristotle tells us that not every *praxis* and not every *pathos* admit of a mean. To illustrate the case of *pathos* he mentions spite, shamefulness and envy. As *praxeis* he names adultery, theft and murder (1107a8–12). Still later when the several virtues and vices are discussed individually, Aristotle picks out a class concerned with *logoi* and *praxeis* (1108a11). This division may be based upon the *pathos-praxis* distinction, but the distinction is not explicitly introduced. It does, however, recur later in a discussion of the relationship between the mean and its extremes (1108b18–19) and then again in a summary passage (1109a20–24), after which Aristotle states that it is difficult to achieve the mean and then illustrates his point by reference to being angry and giving money (1109a24–30). The two examples may be intended to reflect the distinction between *pathos* and *praxis,* but it is hard to be certain.[34]

The corresponding portion of the *EE* is different. While the threefold distinction between emotion, capacity and disposition is again introduced to elucidate the notion of moral virtue (1220b6–20, cf. 1221b34–37), the distinction between *pathos* and *praxis* does not recur. The relationship between moral virtue and pleasure and pain is discussed without the *pathos-praxis* distinction (1220a34–39, 1221b37–1222a5). The same holds for Aristotle's remarks concerning the mean (1220b21–35) and modes of behavior which do not admit of a mean (1221b18–26). There is no exact parallel to the *EN* passage concerning difficulties in hitting the mean, so perhaps one cannot fairly claim a difference at this point. But certainly one should note that the *EE* fails to repeat the *EN* classification of dispositions concerned with *logoi* and *praxeis*. In fact, the *EE* mixes up the listing of the *EN* by placing truthfulness and friendliness in front of greatness of spirit and magnificence (1221a6–11).

The significance of these differences is, of course, a matter of scholarly discussion.[35] Here I want only to suggest that the differences may be connected with Peripatetic investigations of *pathos* and in particular with the investigation of *pathē* like kindness (*charis*) and faultfinding (*mempsis*). In Aristotle's *Rhetoric* kindness is defined as service (*hypourgia* 1358a18) rendered to someone in need. A similar definition is found in Arius' compendium of Peripatetic ethics (p. 143.18–19). Faultfinding was discussed by Theophrastus in his work *On Emotions* (Simplicius, *In Cat.* 235.8) and although this work and any definitions contained therein are now lost, it is, I think, significant that in the *Characters* Theophrastus defines *mempsimoiria* as inappropriate complaint (*epitimēsis*) concerning one's lot (17.1). What these cases tell us is that for Aristotle, Theophrastus and other Peripatetics doing something (rendering service, complaining) can be a *pathos*. Perhaps then Peripatetic investigation of *pathē*, like kindness and faultfinding, led to the realization that the distinction between *pathos* and *praxis* is not always sharp. Anger may be different from giving money, but that the former should be classified as a *pathos* and the latter as a *praxis* (cf. *EN* 1109a24–30) is not immediately clear.[36] For when giving money is a response to need, it can be thought of as a *pathos;* and when anger manifests itself in vengeful action, it would seem to be a *praxis*. We can, of course, imagine a context in which the *pathos-praxis* distinction is useful. In a legal context, for example, crimes like adultery, theft and murder (*EN* 1107a11–12) might be classified together as *praxeis* to be punished. But in an ethical context—especially within a theory of virtue—the utility of this classification is not at all obvious, and certainly open to the objection that an act of adultery is just as much emotional behavior as seeking safety or taking revenge. My guess is that Aristotle saw this when he wrote the *EE*, for in this work adultery is not labeled a *praxis*. As in the *EN* 1107a8–17, so in the *EE* 1221b18–26 adultery is introduced to illustrate the idea of behavior which does not admit of a mean, but now in the *EE* the distinction between *pathos* and *praxis* is quietly dropped, as it also is later in the *MM* (1186a36–b3).

In concluding this section, I want to anticipate a possible objection and to state clearly that it would be a mistake to explain (and to attempt to rescue) the *pathos-praxis* distinction by construing *pathos* as a mode of suffering. For while we could develop a theory in which "feeling" is opposed to action,[37] it is, I think, quite clear that Aristotle is not working with such a dichotomy, when he investigates moral virtue. He begins Book 2 of the *EN* by focusing on what a man does, not on what he feels. By repeatedly doing what is right, Aristotle argues, a man becomes virtuous and thereafter habitually does what is right (1103a14–1104b3). The application of this general principle to, say, courage (1103b16–17, 1104a20–2, b1–3) is straightforward, for courage is a disposition in regard to fright and confidence, both of which are practical emotions—that is to say *pathē* whose very essence involves doing something.[38] Of course, a practical emotion like fright is more than doing something (seeking safety). It also involves thinking danger imminent and experiencing certain feelings. Aristotle is fully aware of this, and in regard to feeling he states explicitly that *pathē* are accompanied by pleasure and pain (*EN* 1105b23).

In other words, Aristotle would never deny the occurrence of feelings, which can be quite intense and which encourage us to speak of feeling frightened and the like. Still, it is one thing to acknowledge the importance of feelings, and another to assert that they are the primary ingredient in those *pathē* which are the province of moral virtue.[39] Aristotle does not hold the latter view, and indeed he may have come to doubt whether pleasant and painful feelings always accompany emotional response. At least in the *EE* he does on one occasion qualify the connection between *pathos* and pleasure and pain. He speaks of *pathē* as phenomena which are in themselves accompanied for the most part by sensory pleasure and pain (1220b13–14). The qualifier "for the most part" is not present in the corresponding portion of the *EN*, and may be a mark of sophistication. Aristotle may be telling us that while feelings are connected with emotional response *per se* (i.e., they follow directly upon emotion and are not due to some additional factor external to emotion), the connection is nevertheless defeasible.[40] Most people who are angry or frightened experience painful feelings, but on occasion men seek revenge or safety and do not experience anything that can be properly called painful feeling (sensation or disturbance).

In offering the preceding interpretation of *EE* 1220b13–14, I do not wish to suggest that the importance of pleasure and pain is minimized in the *EE*. On the contrary, Aristotle recognizes that pleasure and pain have a corrupting influence (1222a1–2, 1227a38–39) and states repeatedly that moral virtue concerns pleasure and pain or things pleasant and painful (1220a34–39, 1221b38–39, 1222a10–14, b9–12, 1227b1–2, 6). Nevertheless, Aristotle never says that moral virtue is entirely concerned with pleasure and pain,[41] nor does he neglect the relationship between moral virtue and *praxis*. When developing the doctrine of the mean, he mentions *praxis* (1220b27), and later he states clearly that as a result of moral virtue men are disposed to do the best actions (1222a6–7, cf. 1220a23–4). The same is true of the detailed account of virtues and vices in Book 3. The account of courage, for example, begins by relating the courageous man to the emotion of fear (1228a27) and then goes on to characterize this man as one who endures (*hypomenein*) things which are extremely fearsome (1228b8). To be sure, Aristotle does not ignore pleasure and pain. He points out that the fearsome things, with which courage is concerned, are those which cause destructive pain (1229a32–b12). He also notes that endurance motivated by pleasure, such as that involved in *thymos*, is not courageous behavior (1229b27–34). But if Aristotle recognizes the importance of pleasure and pain, he does not make them the exclusive sphere or even primary concern of courage. Significantly he concludes his account by restating the connection between courage and endurance: courage, being a moral virtue, will make a man endure things fearsome for some end (1230a29–30). This end is said to be nobility; pleasure is mentioned only as one kind of improper motivation (1230a30–33).

It would, of course, be wrong to suggest that the Eudemian analysis of individual virtues never varies in its emphasis. Clearly it does. Within the account of gentleness, for example, pain is central. Aristotle tells us that we call *thymos* a pain

(1231b15) and that we see that the gentle individual is related to the pain which arises from *thymos* (1231b6–7). The account of magnificence is, however, quite different. Here the emphasis is placed firmly upon action, while pleasure is mentioned only once. Aristotle begins with the statement that magnificence is not concerned with any chance action and choice, but with expenditure (1233a31–32). He states that there is no magnificence without expenditure (1233a33–34) and characterizes the magnificent individual as one who is disposed to choose the appropriate magnitude in great expenditure and to desire this sort of mean even with a view to this sort of pleasure (1233a36–38). The reference to pleasure has worried scholars and prompted conjecture,[42] but for us the important point is that this reference is not repeated; suitable expenditure remains the focus of Aristotle's analysis. Something similar can be said regarding greatness of soul. Pleasure receives some notice (1232a34, b12–14), but the emphasis is upon proper action and correct judgment (assessment). Greatness of soul is referred to taking and employing honor (1233a4–5). The great souled man is presented as one who disdains (correctly assesses) trivial honors (1232a38–b25) and lays claim to (acts appropriately in regard to) great honors (1232b31–1233a30).[43]

Such an inclusive analysis of the individual moral virtues does not result from indecision concerning the proper sphere of moral virtue. It is rather a direct consequence of Aristotle's view of moral virtue. He thinks of moral virtue as a perfection in regard to certain complex *pathē* (namely, those emotions like anger and fear, which involve action, judgment, and feeling) and so adopts a complex or inclusive view of moral virtue.[44]

III

Ten pages before the naming of Theophrastus occur three definitions of happiness (p. 130.18–21). The second of these definitions: "The activity of a complete life (lived) in accordance with virtue," is also found in the *EE* 1219a38–39.[45] The first definition: "The first-rate practice of perfect virtue in a complete lifetime," and the third: "The unimpeded practice of virtue in conditions which accord with nature," do not have an exact parallel in the Aristotelian treatises, but in substance they are not incompatible with Aristotelian doctrine.[46] That these two definitions derive from Theophrastus and that the epitomator's source here is Theophrastus' work *On Happiness* are suggestions already advanced in the scholarly literature.[47] I doubt that either of these suggestions can be proven beyond doubt but I am prepared to say that both the first and third definitions are Theophrastean at least in so far as they make explicit the importance of favorable conditions. The first does this by introducing the qualifier "first-rate,"[48] the third by mentioning "unimpeded" activity in conditions "which accord with nature." This is not a new point,[49] but it bears repeating for it may throw some light on the relationship between Theophrastus and the *EE*.

Let me develop this point by quoting a passage from Cicero's *Tusculan Disputations:* "(Theophrastus) is, however, abused by everyone, first for the book which he wrote *On the Happy Life,* in which he treats at length, why the man, who is put on the rack, who is being tortured, cannot be happy. In this book he is even thought to say that the happy life does not mount the wheel. Nowhere, indeed, does he say this explicitly, but what he does say, has the same force'' (5.24). Here we learn that Theophrastus was roundly criticized for maintaining the incompatibility of torture and happiness. Further, we are told that in his book *On Happiness* Theophrastus never said, ''The happy life does not mount the wheel,'' but rather something which amounted to the same thing. It would be idle to speculate what words Theophrastus actually used, but not, I think, to mention an Aristotelian passage which occurs in the third of the books common to the *EN* and *EE*. The passage runs as follows: ''When people say that the man on the rack or the man caught up in great misfortunes is happy, providing he is good, they are talking nonsense, either willingly or unwillingly'' (1153b19–21). This is certainly the kind of sentiment which Cicero says was to be found in Theophrastus' work *On Happiness*. Since it occurs in a context which is almost certainly Eudemian in origin (it occurs in the discussion of pleasure which concludes the common books), I am tempted to claim another point at which the *EE* exhibits closeness to Theophrastean ethics.

Whether there is an identifiable contrast with the *EN* is another matter and one concerning which I am frankly puzzled. The crucial passage is *EN* 1.10, where Aristotle asks whether we should call a man happy while still alive and subject to changes of fortune. In support of a positive answer Aristotle asserts that living well depends upon action in conformity with virtue (1100b8–11), that the good man bears fortune most nobly (1100b20) and even in extreme adversity does not become wretched, for he will not do what is hateful and base (1100b34–35). These remarks are indeed striking and have been seen as an anticipation of Stoic *autarkeia*[50] and of Antiochus' distinction between the happy and most happy life.[51] For our purpose the important point is that they are without parallel in the *EE*. This may be chance, but it may equally reflect an increased awareness of fortune's role in determining the quality of human life. In other words, it may reflect a new outlook, which later generations associated with the name of Theophrastus and which is prominent in Arius' account of happiness (p. 129.18–134.6). This account begins with the statement that happiness results from noble actions performed under first-rate conditions (p. 129.19–20) and contains repeated assertions concerning the importance of favorable conditions (p. 130.18–21, 132.8–18, 133.20–22, 134.2–4). There are, of course, passages which almost certainly reflect developments after Theophrastus (e.g., p. 129.20–130.4 seems to involve a response to Stoic criticism and p. 130.4–12 a rejection of Critolaus' handling of bodily and external goods), but that in itself does not rule out important ties to Theophrastus. The explicit recognition that virtue (p. 132.21–133.2) can be lost is Theophrastean as well as Aristotelian (Simplicius, *In Cat.* 402.20–22).[52] So also may be the third definition of happiness: ''The unimpeded practice of virtue in conditions which accord with nature'' (p. 130.20–21). The adjective ''unimpeded'' (*anempodistos*) recalls a passage within the common books (1153b11)[53]—again the discussion of pleasure, which is almost certainly *Eudemian*—and may well be another reflection of the fact that Theophrastus along with other members of the early Peripatos gave special attention to the *EE*. At least, I find it plausible that Theophrastus took over the idea of unimpeded activity and then went on to explain it by reference to conditions which accord with nature (p. 130.20).[54]

IV

Within the elucidation of terms present in the first definition of happiness, Arius (or his source) states that first-rate practice is activity in goods which accord with nature (p. 132.8–10). He then goes on to explain that a good man can act nobly in bad conditions, but he cannot be happy, for happiness is not a matter of enduring what is terrible, but rather of enjoying what is good in addition to preserving justice within the community and depriving oneself neither of what is fine in contemplation nor of necessities which are in accordance with life (p. 132.15–18). What interests me here is not only the insistence upon favorable conditions but also the recognition that happiness is more than contemplation. The preservation of justice involves political and social activities, which are part of human happiness.

The composite nature of human happiness is given even clearer recognition in a later section dealing with different modes of life: "Indeed (the good man) will choose both to do and to contemplate fine things. When he is prevented by circumstances from becoming involved in both, he will engage in one of the two, preferring the life of contemplation, but pursuing political activities on account of his social instinct. Wherefore he will marry and beget children and engage in political activity and love temperately and become intoxicated as circumstances dictate, though not on principle" (p. 144.4–11). Here the ideal of a life which makes room for both contemplation and political-social activity is quite pronounced, but since the passage is awkwardly related to what precedes (p. 143.24–144.4) and since it is followed immediately by remarks which introduce the topics of suicide and funeral preparations and therefore suggest a response to Stoic and Epicurean doctrines (p. 144.11–15),[55] one is tempted to argue that the entire section is the work of a late compiler and so cannot be related directly to Theophrastus. After all, this Peripatetic eschewed marriage and championed the life of contemplation over that of political activity, so that a passage, in which an inclusive view of happiness is emphatically advanced, cannot be plausibly associated with Theophrastus.[56]

I want to concede straightway that there are Theophrastean texts which encourage such an argument. First there is the famous excerpt from Theophrastus' work *On Marriage*. Here the wise man is advised against marriage and women are described in a most unattractive manner (Jerome, *Against Iovinianus* 1.47, p. 388–90 Bickel). Second, there are texts in which Theophrastus appears to opt for the life of contemplation to the exclusion (as far as possible) of political-social activity. Best known is Cicero's *Letter to Atticus* 2.16.3, in which Theophrastus' preference for contemplation is contrasted with Dicaearchus' commitment to practical activity.

Also well known is a passage in Cicero's work *On Ends* 5.11, in which both Theophrastus and Aristotle are said to have assigned preeminence to quiet contemplation—a style of life most similar to that enjoyed by the gods and therefore most worthy of the wise man. Similarly in the address of Julian to the uneducated Cynics (*Orations* 6.185A–B) we are told that Pythagoras and his followers, including Theophrastus and Aristotle, advised likening oneself as far as possible to God, for what we are sometimes, he is always. The passage invites comparison with the tenth book of the *EN* 1177b33–34: "but we ought as far as possible to be immortal and to do everything to live in accordance with what is best in us," and might be thought to rule out associating Theophrastus with an inclusive view of the best life, such as Arius records on p. 144.4–11.[57]

This is, however, not the end of the matter, for there are Theophrastean texts which do suggest an inclusive view. The most important of these is found in Stobaeus' *Anthology* 3.3.42 (p. 207–08 Hense): "Therefore the man who is going to be admired for his relationship to the divinity must be one who likes to sacrifice, not by offering large sacrifices but by honoring the divinity frequently, for the former is a sign of wealth, the latter of holiness. Then he must take good care of his parents in their old age and arrange his own life in a way which is obedient to their wishes, for when a man is not of this character, but rather disdainful of the laws of nature and of the city, he has transgressed both kinds of justice. Furthermore, he ought to take good and benevolent care of his wife and children, for the latter return the service as their father grows old, while the former will give back the kindness in times of sickness and in the daily management of the household. [* * *] If it is necessary to loan money to someone, try to do so on a solid basis, for it is characteristic of the wiser man to put out money wisely and regain it on friendly terms, rather than to contract with benevolence and then recover the loan with hostility."

The importance of this text for us is that it connects the service of God (or the gods) with a string of everyday good works. The man who is going to be admired must not only sacrifice regularly but also see to the well being of his parents, wife and children. The end of the text seems to involve a lacuna and therefore is difficult to interpret with confidence, but perhaps we can say that Theophrastus seems to have extended his discussion from family to business relationships and so to have offered a quite inclusive picture of admirable behavior. I do not want to overlook the fact that our text is the conclusion of an argument (it begins with "therefore") and so may have occurred in some special context, which, if known, would straightway undo my interpretation. But admitting this danger, I still want to suggest that this Stobaeus text offers an important counter to those texts which encourage us to dissociate Theophrastus from an inclusive view of the best life. This is most clear in regard to Jerome's excerpt from the work *On Marriage*. For while Jerome's excerpt would have us believe that wives are little or no help during sickness (p. 389 Bickel), our Stobaeus text states explicitly that wives return kindness in times of sickness. That this is Theophrastus' considered opinion and that he had a positive attitude toward marriage seems to me most likely, for quite apart from doubts about Jerome as a source,[58] we know that Aristotle considered Theophrastus a possible husband for his daughter Pythias (Diogenes Laertius 5.12–13). At least this is what Diogenes' version of Aristotle's will seems to say. In the Arabic version(s), Theophrastus appears to be called upon to act as trustee.[59] But either way Theophrastus' involvement would be quite odd, were Theophrastus a philosophic misogynist, who on principle rejected marriage and the security which comes with family.

Our Stobaeus text also offers something of a correction to the texts of Cicero[60] and Julian,[61] for while these texts emphasize a god-like life of quiet contemplation, the Stobaeus text finds admirable both the service of God and everyday helpfulness at home. This suggests an inclusive view of the best life—a view, which invites comparison with the *EE*. For in this treatise the exclusive view of *EN* 10 is not advanced.[62] The *EE* defines happiness as the activity of a complete life (lived) in accordance with complete virtue (1219a38–39), recognizes that there are both moral and intellectual virtues (1219b26–1220a4) but avoids any suggestion that happiness is activity in accordance with some one best virtue (cf. *EN* 1098a17–18). Instead the *EE* connects happiness with virtue in its entirety (1219a37, 39) and turns our attention to the fine-and-good man, who is marked by complete virtue (1248b8–13, 1249a16–17) and who engages in social-political activities, though for different reasons than, say, a civic individual of Spartan stamp (1248b37–1249a16). In regard to our Stobaeus text it is of especial interest that the service and contemplation of God are said to be the standard according to which man should choose external and bodily goods (1249b16–21). This service may well include not only prayer and sacrifice but also acts of justice and moral virtue.[63] This is, of course, an interpretation that needs separate treatment, but on the general issue of inclusive vs. exclusive life I am prepared to say that the *EE* combines worship with practical activity and that this combination was picked up and perhaps emphasized by Theophrastus. For not only did he write works *On Piety* and *On Divine Happiness* (Diogenes Laertius 5.50 and 49), but as our Stobaeus text makes clear, he also combined (at least on occasion) divine service with social responsibility. In which treatises and in which contexts Theophrastus developed this combination can no longer be determined,[64] but we can, I think, conclude that when Arius reports a composite view of the best life (p. 144.4–11, cf. 144.19–21), he is not recording a view which is incompatible with the ethical thinking of Theophrastus. This is not to say that the Arius text in question is excerpted directly from some Theophrastean work such as the book *On Happiness,* but it is to say that the text is Theophrastean in spirit and may reflect the way in which Theophrastus responded to and built upon the *EE*.

NOTES

A first version of this paper was read at Cornell University on May 3, 1979. I wish to thank Professors Richard Sorabji and Elizabeth Asmis for the helpful comments they offered at that time. A second version was read at the Rutgers conference on Arius Didymus, March 28, 1981. The participants in the conference, and especially my commentator Allan Gotthelf, are to be thanked warmly for pointing out deficiencies and offering criticisms, which led me to make several changes in this final version.

N.B. The following abbreviations are used throughout the notes:

Arnim (1) = H. v. Arnim, *Die drei aristotelischen Ethiken* SB Wien 202.2 (1924);

Arnim (2) = H. v. Arnim, *Arius Didymus' Abriss der peripatetischen Ethik* SB Wien 204.3 (1926);

Dirlmeier = F. Dirlmeier, *Die Oikeiosis-Lehre Theophrasts, Philologus Supplementband* 30 (1937);

Fortenbaugh (1) = W. W. Fortenbaugh, *Aristotle on Emotion* (London 1975);

Fortenbaugh (2) = W. W. Fortenbaugh, "Die Charaktere Theophrasts, Verhaltensregelmässigkeiten und aristotelische Laster," *Rheinisches Museum* 118 (1975) 62–82;

Kapp = E. Kapp, review of Arnim (1) *Gnomon* 3 (1927) 73–81;

Kenny = A. Kenny, *The Aristotelian Ethics* (Oxford 1978);

Moraux = P. Moraux, *Der Aristotelismus bei den Griechen*, vol. I (Berlin 1973);

Regenbogen = O. Regenbogen, "Theophrastos," PW Suppl. 7, 1354–1562;

Walzer = R. Walzer, *Magna Moralia und aristotelische Ethik, Neue philol. Untersuchungen* 7 (1929);

Zeller = *Die Philosophie der Griechen in ihrer geschichtlichen Entwicklung* 3rd. ed. (Leipzig 1879) Bd. 2.2, p. 806–69.

All other references are given in full.

1. The heading "Aristotle and the other Peripatetics on Ethical Subjects" (p. 116.19–20) does include the name of Aristotle and the immediately following "he says" (p. 116.21) seems to introduce Aristotle as subject of the opening sentence. But allowing this, it remains true that throughout the survey proper names are avoided. Arius speaks of the old Peripatetics (*archaioi* p. 129.4, 131.2) and often uses the third person plural to indicate (give the impression) that he is presenting the views of Peripatetics in general. At the beginning of the account of moral virtue, Arius does this twice (p. 137.16, 137.24), while presenting material closely related to the *MM* (p. 137.13–23 = *MM* 1185b1–8, p. 137.24–138.20 = *MM* 1185b13–22).

2. Arnim (2) 8–9, 31, 67, 135, 157–58.

3. For example, p. 126.12–127.2 is directed against Critolaus (cf. p. 46.10–15) and therefore post-Theophrastean. See Dirlmeier 77–78 and Regenbogen 1493–94.

4. The phrase "during meetings" translates *en tais entychiais*. Since *entychia* is found neither in Aristotle nor elsewhere in Theophrastus, one might doubt the Greek text. Heeren proposed reading *en tois peri eutychias*, but that idea finds no supporters today. Dirlmeier 6–7 is probably correct to compare the use of the verb *entygchanō* in *Characters* 1.3 and to explain *entychia* as a formal (business) meeting. Cf. Plutarch, *Adul. et am.* 67C.

5. The words "due measure" translate *ton kairon*. Although *kairos* is often used with special reference to the critical moment or season, here it seems to be used for fitness or due measure. See L.S.J. *s.v.*

6. Here the translation is based upon the reading of the manuscripts and not upon Wachsmuth's emended text.

7. The Greek text here is quite problematic. My translation is based upon the text of Wachsmuth, which incorporates two conjectures by Spengel. However, Moraux 380 n.204 defends the reading of the manuscripts, and if one prefers this reading, then a translation of the following sort is in order: "Then setting out several coordinates in conformity with his teacher, next adducing individual cases, he tried to investigate (the matter) in the following manner."

8. The words "Neither . . . at anyone" translate Spengel's addition to the Greek text. The addition is printed by Wachsmuth.

9. The phrase "from each individual" translates the reading of manuscript P: *aph' hekastou.* Wachsmuth follows F and prints *eph' hekastou.*

10. Or possibly "in accordance with due measure." See n.5.

11. Arnim (2) 68.

12. The noun *antakolouthia* is translated by "reciprocal implication"; the verb *eidopoiein* by "give(s) . . . (his) special form". Aristotle has the adjective *eidopoios, (Top.* 143b7–8, *EN* 1174b5) but not the verb *eidopoiein,* whose Stoic use is well attested (*SVF* 2.378, 393, 449, 1044).

13. Moraux 386 suggests a Peripatetic counterpart to the Stoic doctrine of the reciprocal implication of all virtues.

14. Cf. Moraux 389.

15. I do not wish to deny that some of Theophrastus' work was equivalent to a commentary on the teachings of Aristotle, but I am hesitant to follow scholars like Zeller 813, 816 and H. C. Baldry, *The Unity of Mankind* (Cambridge 1965) 144, who so exaggerate this aspect of Theophrastus' work that he becomes little more than an interpreter of Aristotelian doctrine.

16. The fact is well known. See, for example, Moraux 379–82.

17. Whether or not the *EE* list (1220b38–1221a12) originally included the moral virtues (see n.27), the subsequent discussion (1221a13–b3) is restricted to vice or, more accurately, to vicious individuals.

18. Moraux 383 n.213 thinks that the *EN* definition contains elements: namely, the mention of choice and determination by the practically wise man, which are irrelevant to the Theophrastean context. Arnim (1) 133 sees a combination of different sources, but he thinks Theophrastus responsible for the mix. Theophrastus, Arnim suggests, found the *EN* definition in a collection of definitions and combined it with material from an imagined fourth course of lectures on ethics.

19. Arnim (1) 133–37; (2) 64–65.

20. Kenny 14, n.2.

21. Kapp 73, Dirlmeier 5, Moraux 388.

22. I am indebted to Allan Gotthelf for some very helpful criticism.

23. Arnim (1) 134–37.

24. The Arabic title has been translated in more than one way. Bayard Dodge offers "Morals" and then explains with "Theophrasti de Moribus" (*The Fihrist of al-Nadīm* [New York 1970] 2.607). N. Wilson, too, adopts "de moribus," and on the basis of this translation allows that the work in question may be the *Characters.* Nevertheless, F. Rosenthal seems to be correct when he translates "*Uber die Bildung*" (*Das Fortleben der Antike in Islam* [Zurich 1965] 49). My colleague, Professor Fadlou Shehadi, suggests "Moral Education."

25. The noun *salakōneia* occurs in Arius' compendium at p. 146.6–7, where the epitomator seems to be drawing on the *MM.* See Wachsmuth's note *ad loc.* and the discussion of Moraux 393–94.

   Arnim, (1), 137 is much impressed by the usage of *salakōnia* and thinks it supports his thesis concerning four Aristotelian lecture-courses: *MM,* the version followed by Theophrastus, *EE,* and *EN.* While all speculation involves uncertainty, I find it much more likely that Theophrastus' use of *salakōnia* (Arius' text and Hesychius) has influenced the *MM* which is post-Aristotelian.

26. See n.8.

27. I agree with Moraux 389 that the original Theophrastean text was much fuller and therefore may have included a caveat concerning the name of one or more virtues. I

am, however, less happy with Moraux's claim that Theophrastus found it especially difficult to mark off the individual virtues from each other. At least, I do not think Moraux proves his point by citing Alexander, *Mantissa* 156.25–7: "For according to Theophrastus it is not easy to conceive of the different kinds of virtue in such a way that they have nothing in common with each other, but they acquire their names according to what predominates." The common element mentioned in this passage is practical wisdom (*phronēsis*). We are told (1) that Theophrastus recognized a conceptual tie between each of the moral virtues and practical wisdom (cf. Arius p. 142.6–13) and (2) that he believed that each of the moral virtues could be marked off and assigned its own name in accordance with some dominant characteristic. No mention is made of any special difficulty in distinguishing between the several moral virtues; if anything, the *Mantissa* passage suggests the opposite.

28. It should at least be noted that in both the *EE* and our Theophrastean passage the comparison with a stone is coupled with the recognition that the insensitive man lacks desires which are in accordance with nature: *kata physin* (p. 141.7); *kata tēn physin* (*EE* 1221a21–2).

29. Certain scholars have suggested deleting the column of virtues from the Eudemian list. See D. J. Allan reviewing Dirlmeier, *Aristoteles, Eudemische Ethik* in *Gnomon* 38 (1966) 148 and M. J. Mills, "The Discussion of *andreia* in the Eudemian and Nicomachean Ethics," *Phronesis* 25 (1980) 216–17, n.6. The deletion would resolve certain difficulties and also remove the word *dikaion*. But the deletion would necessitate further surgery (1222b6–8 would have to go) and is a procedure which I prefer to use as little as possible.

30. Moraux 385 says that the Theophrastean account of the just man as one who distributes to himself whatever is proportionately equal (p. 141.16–18) involves a different conception of justice than that found in the *EE* 1221a23–4, where proportionate equality receives no mention. It is certainly correct that the *EE* makes no mention of proportionate equality, but whether this justifies speaking of a different conception of justice seems to me doubtful. The *EE* offers only the briefest remarks and these are restricted to the two extreme cases: the man who seeks gain everywhere and the man who rarely does so. The reader (or auditor) understands that the just individual falls somewhere in the middle, but further hints concerning his character are simply not given.

   Arnim (1) 138–41 focuses on the fact that both our Arius text and the *EE* 1221a23–4 associate justice exclusively with personal gain. This is important, but I do not see why it must be pre-Nicomachean. Aristotle's mature ethical thought may well have taken notice of both a just disposition in regard to personal gain (*EE* 1221a6, 23–4) and also a just disposition in regard to distributions, whether to oneself or to others (*EN/EE* 1134a1–3).

31. For a philosophical discussion of the kinds of disposition which interest Theophrastus in the *Characters,* see Fortenbaugh (2).

32. Arnim (1) 134, 136 thinks the direct discourse is to be assigned to Theophrastus, who then shifts into indirect discourse to report Aristotelian material.

33. Kapp 73.

34. Cf. the discussion of the relationship between mean and extremes. Here Aristotle introduces the *pathos-praxis* distinction (1108b18–19) and then gives three examples. The generous man, who gives money properly, is listed togehter with the courageous and temperate man (1108b19–23). Perhaps the generous man is to be associated with *praxis* as against *pathos*, but that is no more clear than at 1109a20–30.

35. See, for example, E. Kapp, *Das Verhältnis der eudemischen zur nikomachischen Ethik,* Diss. (Freiburg 1912) 42–48; W. Theiler, "Die grosse Ethik und die Ethiken des

Aristoteles," *Hermes* 69 (1934) 362–64; F. Dirlmeier *Aristoteles, Magna Moralia* (Berlin 1958) 216.

36. See my "A Note on Aspasius, in *EN* 44.20–21," *Proceedings of the World Congress on Aristotle,* Vol. I (Athens 1981) 175–78.

37. See now A. Kosman, "Being Properly Affected: Virtues and Feelings in Aristotle's Ethics," in *Essays on Aristotle's Ethics,* ed. by A. Rorty (Berkeley 1980) 103–16.

38. On practical emotions, see Fortenbaugh (1) 79–83.

39. The qualifying phrase "which are the province of moral virtue" is of some importance, for the word *pathos* is quite ambiguous and can be used to refer to pleasant and painful feelings. See, e.g., *EN* 1105a3, where *pathos* refers to the pleasure which grown men share with babies (1105a2) and animals (1104b34–5).

40. I want to thank Professor Harold Cherniss for discussing this point with me. My choice of words is intended to recall the language of Kosman, who writes as follows: "Fearing is related to fleeing, desiring to reaching for, anger to striking out at, in no accidental way. In each of these cases, a certain action or range of actions is connected to a *pathos* in some important logical sense. The connection is defeasible, but it is not a merely accidental connection." As a statement about Aristotle I cannot accept Kosman's position, for Aristotle is quite clear that in the case of emotions like fright and anger the connection is not defeasible. In his *Rhetoric* Aristotle tells us that for a man to be frightened there must be some hope of safety, for fear makes men deliberate, and no one deliberates concerning things considered hopeless (1383a5–8). In other words, fright always involves some action directed toward safety. When a man is convinced that safety is impossible and therefore does not even deliberate about ways to escape, then he is not frightened. He may well be upset and pained by what he foresees, but is not frightened. For the case of anger, see Fortenbaugh (1) 80.

41. Despite Solomon (Oxford translation), Rackham (Loeb) and Dirlmeier (Akademie translation), *EE* 1227b6 does not say that moral virtue is "wholly" ("entirely," "ganz") concerned with pleasures and pains. It says rather that all moral virtue is concerned with pleasure and pain (cf. 1221b38–39, and 1222b9–10). The position of *pasa* is emphatic and may be compared with similar cases at 1223a36 and 1223b21.

42. Richards proposed reading "expenditure" instead of "pleasure." Rackham in a note to the Loeb edition calls the conjecture probable. Dirlmeier (Akademie translation) defends the received text in notes to 1232a34 and 1233a38.

43. In our Arius text the great-souled man is characterized as one who does not lay claim to everything but rather takes what is right (p. 141.20–142.3). Similarly the just man and the liberal man are described in terms of action: The former distributes what is fair (p. 141.17); the latter neither lavishes nor fails to lavish sums (p. 141.19–20). The magnificient man (p. 142.3–5) is also a doer. His splendor is not something private like feelings, but rather those great expenditures which attract attention and embellish a man's life.

44. See my "Aristotle: Emotion and Moral Virtue," *Arethusa* 2 (1969) 166–69.

45. There is one difference between Arius and the *EE:* the former has "virtue" (p. 130.18), the latter "perfect virtue" (1219a39).

46. In Arius' introduction to ethical theory, prior to his surveys of Stoic and Peripatetic ethics, the first definition is attributed to Aristotle (p. 51.12, and once the text has been corrected, then also on p. 50.11–12). In accordance with this attribution Arius or his source employs the third singular, "he says" (p. 51.13). This usage contrasts with the later survey of Peripatetic ethics, for here in the corresponding part (in both cases it is a matter of elucidating the phrase "in a complete lifetime") we have the third plural "they added" (p. 131.20; cf. "they said", "they used to say" p. 131.14, 15), which refers generally to the older Peripatetics (cf. p. 129.4, 131.2). It is quite certain that the general reference is preferable. The specific attribution to Aristotle is due to Arius

or rather his source, and reflects the tendency of later generations to credit the founder of a school with subsequent developments. See Dirlmeier 19 and Moraux 308–12. The latter is certainly correct when he says that Arius has drawn his material from two different sources.

47. The first suggestion is advanced by Dirlmeier 19; the second by Arnim (2) 31.

48. I use "first-rate" to translate *proēgoumenēn* (p. 130.19). On p. 132.8–10 Arius explains first-rate activity as that which occurs among goods which are in accordance with nature (cf. p. 51.14–15). For literature on the usage of *proēgoumenos* see Moraux 353 n.17.

49. Moraux 356.

50. A. A. Long, "Aristotle's Legacy to Stoic Ethics," *Bulletin of the Institute of Classical Studies* 15 (1968), 74–76.

51. Dirlmeier 18 n.1 and O. Gigon, *Marcus Tullius Cicero, Gespräche in Tusculum*, 3rd ed. (München 1976) 560.

52. Both Arnim (2) 33–34 and Moraux 357 n.133 want to alter Wachsmuth's text on p. 132.22, so that it is not virtue but rather happiness which can be lost. I am not persuaded by their arguments, for although Wachsmuth's text is hardly a paradigm of well-stated argumentation, it is intelligible. When we keep in mind that happiness depends upon virtue, then the fact that human virtue is not unloseable (p. 132.22) can be cited to justify the claim that divine and human happiness are not the same (p. 132.21). It can also serve as a lead-in to the thesis that one should not be counted happy until dead (p. 133.2–6). Matters of fortune are unclear (p. 133.3–4), and as Theophrastus argued by reference to Pericles, misfortune can affect one's character (Plutarch, *Per.* 38.1–2). When a person is so affected as to lose his virtuous character, then he is no longer happy, for happiness requires virtue.

53. Cf. *Politics* 1295a35–37, where Aristotle makes explicit reference to his *Ethics*. See Kenny 7.

54. There seem to have been Academic precedents for this move. Especially interesting is Speusippus' definition of happiness: "a perfect disposition in conditions which accord with nature" (Clement of Alexandria, *Stromata* 2.22.133 = fr. 57 Lang). Concerning the meaning of the phrase *en tois kata physin echousin* Dirlmeier 38 is properly cautious, but he is also correct to emphasize a connection between Theophrastus and the Academy.

The idea that nature functions as a standard is also present in the excerpt, which Arius explicitly attributes to Theophrastus. The temperate man is said to be in accordance with nature (p. 141.11), the insensitive man to be one who fails to desire those things which are in accordance with nature (p. 141.7). See further the scholium on Plato's *Laws* 631C, p. 303–4 Greene.

55. See Moraux 403–6, 412–14, who thinks a compiler has combined materials that were originally quite independent. It seems to me also quite possible that an epitomator has excerpted material from a single source but done so in such a manner as to create the impression of inconsistency and awkwardness. Without attempting to argue the case, I would suggest: (1) That the life of a teacher is called *meson* (p. 144.4) not because it occupies a place between political and private life (so Moraux 404), but because it falls between (shares features with) the life of common men and philosophers. (2) The particle *gar* is not always used to introduce an explanation. It may be so used on p. 144.5 (Moraux 404), but it also may have an assertive force: "*Indeed* (the good man) will choose both to do and to contemplate fine things." Cf. Plutarch, *Agis*. 2.1, where *gar* is assertive and combined with *men*. But whichever interpretation is correct, the sentence on p. 144.4–5 is intelligible enough, for it follows upon the mention of the teacher's life, and this life involves both doing and contemplating. (3) The listing of marriage, begetting children etc. (p. 144.8–11) is not inappropriate in its place, for one wants to know the full range of behavior to which man's social instinct leads. (Moraux 406 argues that from the standpoint of content, p. 144.8–11 does not belong together with p. 144.7–8.)

56. This is the position of Walzer 191–92. Cf. Moraux, "L'exposé de la philosophie d'Aristote chez Diogène Laërce," *Revue Philosophique de Louvain* 47 (1949) 29, n. 104.

57. I am assuming that *EN* 10 advances an exclusive view of happiness, according to which theoretical activity is the sole component of the best life for man. While this assumption is also the opinion of most modern scholars, it has on occasion been challenged and most recently by D. Keyt, "Intellectualism in Aristotle," *Paideia,* Second Special Issue: Aristotle (1978) 138–57. A footnote is not the place for lengthy criticism, but five considerations may at least be touched upon.

(1) Throughout 10.7–8 (1177a12–1179a32) Aristotle works with a twofold distinction between contemplation and practical activity. The life of contemplation is said to be divine (1177b30–31) and perfect happiness is called a form of contemplative activity (1178b7–8). In contrast, the life given over to practical pursuits is labeled human and second best (1178a9–10). Nowhere in 10.7–8 does Aristotle explicitly mention, let alone develop, a third alternative, in which both contemplation and (some minimum of) practical activity are essential components.

(2) The idea that each of us has two sides or aspects: a divine intellect and a composite human nature (1177b27–28, 1178b5) can be used to develop a third notion of happiness, in which both contemplation and practical activity are essential components (Keyt 145–46). We should, however, be clear that Aristotle does not do so in *EN* 10.7–8. Instead he uses the two aspects to develop two exclusive notions of happiness: a strictly intellectual life and one devoted to practical pursuits. Of course, Aristotle does acknowledge that an individual (even one who engages in contemplation) will *qua* man choose to do (morally) virtuous deeds (1178b5–6), but he does not say or even suggest that such deeds are essential ingredients in some third mode of happiness. Rather he is nodding to the human condition without abandoning his dichotomy and the related injunction to be immortal as far as possible, to do everything to live in accordance with one's intellectual (contemplative) capacity (1177b33–34). In other words he recognizes that human frailty is a constraint upon contemplation, but he does not develop a third kind of happiness, which requires mixing contemplation with practical activity.

(3) Aristotle speaks of an intellect which contemplates things noble and divine (1177a13–21). He identifies each of us with this psychic element (1178a2) and argues that it would be odd not to choose the corresponding life (1178a3–4)—namely, that of contemplation. One may object to the psychology and point out that elsewhere Aristotle advances a different notion of the self (Keyt 150), but that does not undo what is said in 10.7–8. Nor does the fact that Aristotle expresses himself with some caution: "It would seem that each (of us) is this" (1178a2). Aristotle is fully aware that he is advancing a controversial psychology, but he does work with the psychology, in order to develop an exclusive view of perfect (divine) happiness.

(4) Aristotle claims that contemplative activity alone is loved for its own sake (1177b1). This may be a mistaken claim (Keyt 151) but it is part of the argument in 10.7–8, and once accepted it does support an exclusive notion of happiness. We may, of course, wish that Aristotle had not made such a claim, but wishing cannot rewrite 10.7–8.

(5) After repeatedly contrasting contemplation with practical activity (1177a30–b16), Aristotle states that contemplative activity constitutes perfect happiness, providing it be granted a complete life time (1177b24–25). Here Aristotle shows a clear interest in precise statement. He recognizes that a single act or even several acts of contemplation are not sufficient for happiness and therefore adds that the contemplation must persist over a life time. That Aristotle chose to express himself any less accurately (explicitly) in regard to such an important matter as the relationship between contemplation and practical activity, is of course possible but, in my opinion, unlikely.

My conclusion is that we should take *EN* 10.7–8 at face value. It is an interesting statement of strict intellectualism, which Aristotle quietly drops in the *EE* and in the *Politics* 7–8. He may have been well advised to do so, but that is not an adequate reason for forcing an inclusive view of happiness on *EN* 10.7–8.

58. It is most probable that Jerome's knowledge of the Classical Greek philosophers including Theophrastus was derived from later sources. Whether Jerome found the excerpt from Theophrastus' work *On Marriage* in Seneca's *De Matrimonio* (F. Haase actually printed the text of Jerome in his edition of the fragments of Seneca, Vol. 3 [Leipzig 1872] 428–30) or in Tertullian's *De Nuptiarum Angustiis* (F. Bock, *Aristoteles, Theophrastus, Seneca de matrimonio* [Leipzig 1899] 11) or in some work of Porphyrius (E. Bickel, *Diatribe in Senecae Philosophi Fragmenta* vol. 1 [Leipzig 1915] 17–20, 213–14) or in still some other lost work, is quite uncertain.

59. See I. Düring, *Aristotle in the Ancient Biographical Tradition* (Göteborg 1957) 219,238.

60. A later text in Cicero's *On Ends* is also instructive: "From this (account of the highest good given by Peripatetics) others tried to appropriate small portions; each wanted to appear to advance his own view. The knowledge of things was often marvelously praised for itself by Aristotle [and] by Theophrastus. Captivated by this alone, Erillus maintained that knowledge is the highest good and that no other thing is to be sought for itself" (5.72–73). Here Theophrastus is clearly dissociated from the unorthodox Stoic Erillus, who advanced a narrow view of the good for man. Cf. Diogenes Laertius 7.165. In contrast, Theophrastus will have offered a more inclusive view and presumably one that made room for practical-political activity. See *On Ends* 5.58–64.

61. The Julian passage is a typical example of later harmonizing. In the preceding sections of his speech, Julian has argued that the goal of likening oneself to God is identical with the goal of the Delphic exhortation to know oneself (183A–184C) and that an investigation of the leading philosophers will show that all their doctrines are in agreement (184C–185A). Then comes the passage in question: "Therefore the god at Delphi proclaims, 'Know yourself,' and Heraclitus says, 'I searched myself,' and further Pythagoras and his followers down to Theophrastus speak of likening oneself as far as possible to God, and indeed Aristotle, too. For what we are sometimes, God is always" (6.185A–B). Clearly the Platonic formula: "likening oneself as far as possible to God" (*Republic* 613A, *Theaetetus* 176B, *Laws* 716C–D), is attributed to Theophrastus in accordance with Julian's aim to demonstrate unity among the philosophic schools (see Regenbogen 1482). This does not mean that Theophrastus would not have endorsed some version of the formula. He may well have discussed it in his works *On Happiness* and *On Divine Happiness* (Diogenes Laertius 5.43, 49) and even offered an historical survey beginning with Pythagoras. But how he interpreted and advocated likening oneself to God is not immediately clear. Contemplation will not have been overlooked, but as the seventh book of Aristotle's *Politics* makes clear, comparison with God is possible, when one is advocating an inclusive goal of life (1323b21–26, 1325b23–30).

62. This difference between the *EN* and *EE* has been discussed often. See, for example, G. Verbeke, "L'idéal de la perfection humaine chez Aristote et l'évolution de sa noétique," *Fontes Ambrosiani* 25 (1951) 83–84 and 92–93, J. Cooper, *Reason and Human Good in Aristotle* (Cambridge 1975) 89–143, D. Devereux, "Aristotle on the Active and Contemplative Lives," *Philosophical Research Archives* 3 (1977) no. 1138 and Kenny 190–214. The difference is curiously not recognized by Moraux 411–18, in what is otherwise a fine discussion of the *vita contemplativa* and *vita activa* in the doxographic tradition.

63. Kenny 178.

64. It is not even certain from which work the Stobaeus text is excerpted. Among the candidates are *On Piety* (J. Bernays, *Theophrastos' Schrift über Frömmigkeit* [Breslau 1866] 74), *On Friendship* (Zeller 863 n.4) and *Kinds of Virtue* (Regenbogen 1481).

Comments on Professor Fortenbaugh's Paper With Special Attention to *Pathos*

Allan Gotthelf

Professor Fortenbaugh's aim in this impressive examining of the Arius Didymus passage in which Theophrastus is named, and surrounding and related ones as well, is not only to see what words and views we can safely attribute to Theophrastus himself, but also to show (i) that "Theophrastus was doing interesting work in the field of ethics," and (ii) "that this work is closely related to Aristotle's *Eudemian Ethics*"—more closely, that is, than to the *Nicomachean Ethics*. The bulk of his paper consists of discussion of, by my count, eleven "features which, taken together, suggest a close tie between Theophrastus and Aristotle's *Eudemian Ethics*." While I am inclined to think that Professor Fortenbaugh is right in both of his claims, I want to explore the method of demonstration and to consider whether the evidence is in fact as strong as he suggests it is.

Professor Fortenbaugh begins by raising some healthy doubts about the extent to which the section on moral virtue (p. 137.13–142.13) can be attributed to Theophrastus, properly focusing discussion first on the paragraph containing the philosopher's name (p. 140.7ff). He makes some preliminary remarks about these lines and then begins his list of *Eudemian*-influenced features. I shall follow him through that list, and return to p. 140.7ff. and the question of attribution as these lines come up in the list.[1]

1. *Page 140.17–18 all but reproduces* EE *1220b35* (F.pt.I). That it certainly does. Professor Fortenbaugh reviews several interpretations of the source and role of this line in Arius, and reserves judgment on the matter. He has already rejected the interpretation under which Theophrastus would be commenting on an Aristotelian list of virtues and vices, and he gives some good reason for thinking that the line is Arius' own.[2] So, either Arius, as Professor Fortenbaugh says, "found words reminiscent of *EE* 1220b35 in the text of Theophrastus" or the line was "the unprompted doing of Arius (or his source)." I want to make two small points. First, the latter seems quite likely, since immediately prior to quoting Theophrastus, in the lines from p. 139.19 to 140.6, Arius had been making close use of the *Eudemian* lines which immediately precede 1220b35, and we can thus expect 1220b35 to have been fresh in his mind. This is especially so, since he must have made a conscious decision that the *Eudemian* exposition which he had been fol-

lowing was incomplete without an example of the mean relative to us, without an argument for preferring this mean to the mean *pros allēla* in the definition of moral virtue (or whatever 140.10–12 is arguing for), and without a definition of moral virtue, all at this point; so, he would have read and digested 1220b35 before making that decision.

On this hypothesis, however—and this is my second point—the similarity between 140.17–18 and *EE* 1220b35 is *not* evidence of a Theophrastean use of *EE*. Professor Fortenbaugh acknowledges this point, but the wording of his conclusion does not sufficiently reflect it. He writes, ''I suggest, therefore, that our text derives from a work with an educational orientation. It is not part of a commentary on the *EE*, but as we shall immediately see, it does contain features which unquestionably relate it closely to the *EE* and not to the *EN*.'' Even with the forward reference this still reads to me like a conclusion from the foregoing, and as such is not warranted.

Incidentally, the suggestion that our text derives from a work with an educational orientation seems to me an attractive possibility, but Professor Fortenbaugh's argument seems to establish it only as a possibility, not as something one is ready to suggest as so. One can imagine any number of other reasons for the ordering of the list of vices and virtues we find in Arius. For instance, perhaps its author went down a list of *pathē* in order to identify the corresponding *hexeis,* and started with bodily pleasures or *epithumia,* before going on to anger and fear. The list of *pathē* at *EN* 1105b21–23 starts off in just that way. I am not suggesting that this explanation would be any better than Professor Fortenbaugh's, I just think his suggestion is made too confidently.

2. *The occurrence of* salakōnia *and* analgēsia *in the list of vices* (F.pt.I). The evidence seems clear, and does suggest a *Eudemian* rather than a *Nicomachean* influence. I do think we should be wary, though, about accepting any hypothesis to explain these occurrences which rests, as Professor Fortenbaugh's does, on the assumption that *EE* is later than *EN.* Other explanations of the differences between *EE* and *EN* terminologies are surely possible, and the assumption of *EE* lateness requires for its own support chronological claims, about just such differences, that are established independently of that assumption. What we can say here is that Professor Fortenbaugh has offered some terminological data compatible with a late *EE,* and that proponents of a later *EN* will have to account for them.[3]

3. *The explainability of the absence of unnamed dispositions in Arius' table* (F.pt.I). Professor Fortenbaugh anticipates an objection to his thesis, and I count the defeat of the objection as a third pro-*Eudemian* feature. Arius has no unnamed dispositions in his list, while *EE* has several—but that is not to count against *Eudemian* influence: Arius' passage ''is clearly a very concise resume of what was once a far more detailed discussion.'' So perhaps Theophrastus did express some doubts about disposition names, or maybe he left his doubts for a more theoretical treatise.

Now, either is certainly possible. But, so too is the possibility that Theophrastus never himself shared Aristotle's doubts, but from his very first exposure to them thought them wrong—thought, that is, that in fact the Greek language had very good names for the dispositions in question. On *this* possibility, Theophrastus will have come to the writing of his ethical treatises with terminology already firmly established in mind, and will *not* have been influenced by *EE*. As far as I can see, this possibility is at least as likely as the two proposed by Professor Fortenbaugh, perhaps even more likely, and this fact points to a general question I want to raise about the methodology in this part of his paper.

Professor Fortenbaugh has already warned us against the picture of Theophrastus as slavish commentator; let us accept that warning. The more interesting and original, then, we take him to be, the less we should expect Aristotle's wordings to be the primary influence on him, and the more we should entertain hypotheses involving independence and originality on Theophrastus' part. Consider, for instance, the previous matter about *salakōnia*. Maybe Theophrastus had *EN* in front of him, and not *EE*, but remembered an earlier lecture or discussion in which Aristotle had proposed the term, or maybe he had no Aristotelian proposal in mind at all but had the fresh thought himself that *salakōnia* was the disposition in question; or maybe (as the evidence does seem to suggest) he *had EE* in front of him but was not *influenced* by its use of *salakōnia*, which is to say that maybe the presence of that term in *EE* was no part of his ground for (and no part of the cause of his) choosing to use the term. The more original a thinker one thinks Theophrastus to be, the more probable this becomes.

What this all comes to is in part a general question about the meaning of Professor Fortenbaugh's claim of a *Eudemian* influence on Theophrastus (what exactly does ''influence'' come to in this context?), and in part a claim that, for certain features of Arius' text, the real possibility of Theophrastean originality weakens Professor Fortenbaugh's claim of probability for the thesis of *Eudemian* influence.

4. *The* anaisthētos *is likened to a stone in* EE *as in Arius, but not in* EN *or in* MM (F.pt.I). This is true—but I am not clear how much weight to put on this. If comparison to a stone was a standard joke in the school, I can easily imagine it left out of the *Nicomachean* lecture notes, as something Aristotle knows he will remember. Professor Fortenbaugh's hypothesis of *Eudemian* borrowing is I suppose more likely, given other evidence of *Eudemian* influence, though surely Theophrastus heard both courses several times and could recall the comparison whether or not *EE* was in his sight or mind.

5. Philotimia *and* aphilotimia *appear in* EN *as vices coordinate with an unnamed virtue, but are absent in Arius, as well as in* EE *and* MM (F.pt.I). As I am inclined to see the division of concern-for-honors into two types as significant,[4] there is a case for *Eudemian* (though also for *Magna Moralia*) influence here. This case, and all arguments from omissions in Arius, are weakened however by Professor Fortenbaugh's very plausible claim, already quoted, that what we have here ''is clearly a very concise resume of what was once a far more detailed discussion.''

6. *The treatment of* dikaiosunē *(Arius) and* to dikaion (EE) *as a mean-disposition, with extremes* (F.pt.I). *EN,* on the contrary, does not list justice in its own catalogue of ordinary virtues. *EE* and Arius do, treating it "as a regular mean-disposition coordinate not only with an excessive disposition but also with a deficiency— namely, the disposition of one who seldom seeks gain (*EE* 1221a23–4), who assigns himself too little (p. 141.17)." This is true, and counts to some extent for Professor Fortenbaugh's thesis. How much it counts is not clear to me, since the terminology on p. 141.16—17 seems more different from *EE* 1221a23–24 than someone with his thesis would hope. And Moraux's minimal point, that *EE* makes no *mention* of proportionate equality (above, F.note 30), puts yet additional distance between *EE* and Theophrastus.[5]

7. *The absence of the social dispositions in Arius* (F.pt.I). Arius' table of virtues and review of the virtuous individuals includes no mention of the social dispositions. This suggests to Professor Fortenbaugh a connection with *EE,* "for in this treatise mean-dispositions within the sphere of social interaction are explicitly refused the status of moral virtue."

This explanation for the absence is certainly a possible one. Alternatively, of course, Arius' "very concise resume" may have omitted these dispositions, which do come last in both *EN* and *EE,* in the name of conciseness, though I imagine Professor Fortenbaugh's explanation is the more likely one.

On his explanation, however, it is puzzling that the example of a mean relative to us, given at the beginning of the paragraph and explicitly attributed to Theophrastus, is drawn precisely from the social sphere. He recognizes this, and to account for it suggests a tendency on Arius' part to scissors and paste. This tendency is evidenced for instance by the "slipping" of an Aristotelian definition of virtue into a Theophrastean excerpt. (That this inclusion of the *Nicomachean* definition was not Theophrastus' doing is suggested in Professor Fortenbaugh's paper and n.18 mentions Moraux's observation that the definition contains elements, namely the mention of choice and of determination by the practically wise man, which are irrelevant to their new context.)

This gives us an opportunity to reflect on what is really the prior question: how much of p. 140.7*ff.* is Theophrastus? I make a few schematic remarks:

(1) On p. 138 and 139 Arius is following *MM;* on p. 139.19 he switches to *EE* which he follows until p. 140.7 where Theophrastus is introduced. The switches are motivated: as I suggested above, one can understand how Arius might have felt the need for the example, the argument, and the formal definition he gives before proceeding to the list of virtues. (Those who come to *EE* already familiar with *EN* typically expect a definition at this point in *EE*'s argument and are initially surprised that they have to wait for the full one until the end of Book II). So, the *oun* at 140.7 is surely, as Professor Fortenbaugh suggests it might be, Arius'. Whether the first part of the sentence is also Theophrastus seems still an open question, though.

(2) The argument in 10–12 seems also difficult to assign, and the problem is compounded because, as Professor Fortenbaugh notes, there is disagreement about the text. With Wachsmuth's emendation, we have a (rather peculiar) argument for the thesis that the mean relative to us is best. Nothing corresponds to this argument in *EE* or *EN* or *MM,* and its conclusion has already been argued for on p. 139.23–24, following *EE* 1220b27–28. On Wachsmuth's reading we can state, however, that whoever wrote 10–12 also followed it with the *Nicomachean* definition, since those lines continue a case already in progress for that definition. If the mean relative to us is best, then (perhaps for the reason given at *EE* 1220a29–30 [cf. 22–23], but not reproduced by Arius) moral virtue is to be defined in terms of *it* (rather than in terms of the mean *pros allēla*). And, if it is best because it is defined by means of *logos* (p. 139.23–24, *EE* 1220b27–28), then it is *hōrismenē logōi.*[6] On Professor Fortenbaugh's translation of the unemended text we get an argument that some mean (perhaps the one in the Theophrastean example) is relative to us (rather than perhaps *pros allēla*) on the ground that it is determined *by us* (i.e., by our reason), which is a bad enough argument that one might be inclined towards accepting Wachsmuth's emendation. But even on Professor Fortenbaugh's reading there is a clear linguistic, if not logical, progression via *hōrismenē logōi* to the *Nicomachean* definition.

As for Moraux's claim that the mention of choice and of determination by the *phronimos* are irrelevant in this context, much the same could be said for the definition in its original, *Nicomachean* context: though *prohairetikē* is foreshadowed at 1106a3–4, neither of the remaining clauses of the definition is anticipated by anything already said in that context. But, if one thinks the exposition calls for a definition at that point, and one has a formal definition at hand, one gives it whole, and talks about *prohairesis* or the *phronimos* later.

(3) The *eita* in line 15 makes it natural for me to see the preceding lines just discussed—the argument in 10–12 and the *Nicomachean* definition—as Theophrastean. I suppose what I am suggesting is that the entire long paragraph from p. 140.7 to 142.5 is from Theophrastus (except possibly for p. 140.7, and of course for p. 140.7–8 and 140.15), but I prefer to leave the matter undecided.

8. *141.3–5 and EE refer virtue to* pathos *only, not to* pathos *and* praxis (F.pt.II). This contrast between *EE* and *EN* is well documented by Professor Fortenbaugh, and represents an important and deliberate difference between the two treatises. If p. 141.3–5 is typical of Theophrastus' treatment of virtue, we have one of the stronger pieces of evidence for a *Eudemian* influence.

What I must take issue with, however, is the explanation Professor Fortenbaugh offers of this difference. The explanation involves (i) a thesis about the Peripatetic understanding of *pathos,* (ii) an interpretation of the *EE* account of virtue, and (iii) an assumption of a late *EE.* There is an important element of truth in the first of these I think, but the issues need some sorting out, and when sorted out they do not, I shall argue, support Professor Fortenbaugh on (ii) or (iii). This is a digression we are both taking from the main thesis of his paper, but its importance for Aristotelian studies makes it well worth doing.

(i) The restriction of moral virtue to *pathē*, Professor Fortenbaugh suggests, reflects a growing Peripatetic awareness that the distinction between *pathos* and *praxis* "is not always sharp." All *pathē* to which a moral virtue corresponds are "*pathē* whose very essence involves doing something," and in some cases (e.g., *charis, mempsis*) "doing something" is fundamental. In support of the latter, Professor Fortenbaugh offers the *Rhet.* 2.7 definition of *charis*, and Simplicius' report that *mempsis* was mentioned as a *pathos* in Theophrastus' *Peri pathōn*. In support of the former, we are referred to Professor Fortenbaugh's earlier work on emotions, some of which is reviewed in notes, and to some important texts in *EE*. It will be worth summarizing the evidence he offers and I do so, lettering each item separately.

(a) The insistence at *Rhet.* 1383a5–8 that where there is no hope of safety one does not experience fright shows that "fright always involves some action directed toward safety" (n.40). The same is said for anger and its goal of revenge at 1370b13, and we can generalize: all *pathē* to which a moral virtue corresponds involve essentially a goal. Such practical emotions have three dimensions: they involve assessment, feeling, and action. Some may involve more feeling and less action, others more action and less feeling, but all essentially involve at least some action, some doing.

(b) *EE* 1220b13–14 shows that, though feelings of pleasure and/or pain are often involved in those *pathē* which are the province of moral virtue, they are not their "primary ingredients," and accompany them only "for the most part." This qualification does not occur in the *EN* account, "and may be a mark of sophistication."

(c) Though *EE* describes moral virtue as a mean in regard to certain *pathē*, the review of individual virtues in *EE* 3 makes frequent reference to ways of acting (as well as of assessing and feeling), showing too that action has become an essential dimension of those *pathē*. The same is true of Arius' review of the virtuous and vicious individuals on p. 141.5–142.5.

(ii) On this account of *pathos* we find *EE* and *EN* offering essentially the same account of moral virtue and its actualization: moral virtue is a disposition to act as well as feel in certain ways. But with this more complex and sophisticated notion of *pathos* as itself embodying action along with assessment and feeling, this same notion of moral virtue can be described as a mean in regard to *pathos* alone, without the *EN* mention of *praxis* that would imply an easy and sharp distinction between *pathos* and *praxis*.

(iii) The natural hypothesis to explain the presence in *EE* of a more sophisticated notion of *pathos*, which was apparently adopted by Theophrastus, is that *EE* was the later of Aristotle's two works, and that the historical progression was *EN, EE,* Theophrastus.[7]

Response to (i): Much of Professor Fortenbaugh's discussion in this section is stimulated by his concern to reject the thesis that *pathos* is fundamentally "a mode of suffering,'' a ''being acted upon,'' as its root in *paschein* might suggest (and does suggest to Aryeh Kosman, whose view Professor Fortenbaugh quotes and criticizes in n.40). I want here to argue that in the last analysis Kosman's view of a *pathos* and its relationship to its corresponding *praxis* is essentially correct, and I take myself here to be elaborating on his claim that the *pathos/praxis* connection is ''logical but defeasible.''[8] Let us review the evidence.

(a) The *Rhetoric* passage on the connection between fear and deliberation makes clear that fear (and by implication the other *pathē*) involve a goal. But we need to see in what way this is the case, for having a goal and acting toward that goal are not the same thing. Professor Fortenbaugh himself makes this clear in his book, *Aristotle on Emotion:* ''When men become frightened, they think safety possible and *in the absence of any restraining influence* act for the sake of safety. Their emotion is practical in the sense that it involves a particular kind of goal and *normally manifests itself* in a particular kind of goal-directed behavior'' (p.80, emphasis added). All sorts of restraints are possible, for instance: ''The continent man, knowing that his appetites are bad, refuses on account of his rational principle to follow them'' (*EE* 6 = *EN* 7 1145b13–14).

Now, the possibility of restraining influences is, I take it, precisely what Kosman had in mind in calling the connection between emotion and action ''defeasible,'' and surely he and the earlier Fortenbaugh are right against the current paper's n.40.[9]

The key to sorting this all out, I suggest, is that while a *pathos* does not essentially incorporate an action, it does essentially incorporate a *desire*. The goal of a *pathos* is the goal—or, more precisely, object—of its desire. Professor Fortenbaugh himself recognized this in *Aristotle on Emotion,* when he wrote: ''Anger is a practical emotion aiming at revenge. Aristotle makes this clear in the *Rhetoric* when he defines anger as a desire for revenge (1378a30) . . .'' (p.80). An appetite (*epithumia*) is of course a desire for a certain type of bodily sensation; love is a certain wish for another's good; fear, while primarily a painful feeling accompanying the expectation of evil, includes a desire for safety; etc.

The connection between *pathos* and *orexis* in Aristotle has not, to my knowledge, been explored in any depth, and the constraints of space prevent my trying to do so. I do not know of anywhere that Aristotle explicitly states that all *pathē* that are the concern of moral virtue essentially involve desire, but I do not believe it would be hard to piece together Aristotelian propositions that would entail this. For one thing, everywhere Aristotle discusses the causes of animal motion he insists on the central role of desire, so if *pathē* are to be intimately connected with action, they must somehow embody desire.[10] And if that is granted, we can turn to the practical syllogism, and in general to the role of desire in the causation of action, for guidance on the question of the relationship between *pathos* and action.[11]

(b) *EE* 1220b13–4 is admittedly difficult to interpret, and it is worth noting that Professor Fortenbaugh does not argue for his own interpretation. An alternative interpretation of ''for the most part'' is to see in the exceptions it implies, not action present when feeling is not, but *assessment*—the very assessment Professor Fortenbaugh discussed so well in *Aristotle on Emotion*. This is equally possible, and even more so once *pathos* is logically dislodged from action. Interestingly, as Aristotle observes at *EN* 1115a9, "people even define fear as expectation of evil." One could imagine someone saying, "I was so frightened, I didn't have time to feel anything." His attention would be directed to the action desired in the fear, but that would not entail that the action was itself the fear or some part of it: the action was rather the object of the *desire* for safety, and it was this desire, and not the action it was a desire for, that was logically part of the fear.

(c) I think that a careful review of the survey of the virtues in *EE* 3 would reveal a significant and consistent restriction of the definitions of the virtues to ways of assessing and feeling. Regrettably, I cannot demonstrate this here. I thus restrict myself to two observations:

First of all, even on the view I am suggesting, that a moral virtue is actualized primarily in a certain way of assessing and feeling, an action would normally result. After all, the desire that is inherent in any (practical) *pathos* is a desire *to act* in some way, and the function of a moral virtue is to enable us consistently to *act* well. Thus it is no surprise that much of the discussion of any virtue will be concerned with the actions it issues in. It does not follow from that that the *pathos* one is rightly disposed in regard to is itself, even in part, the action that follows from it.

Secondly, in the case of something like "the giving and taking of money," the issue between virtue and vice seems to be how much one *cares* about one's wealth as against other considerations, say, the welfare of one's friend or neighbor—and that seems clearly to be a *pathos*. It seems that there are different sorts of carings most people will have—a person will care about his wealth, about esteem (*timē*) from himself and others, about being candid concerning his accomplishments, etc.— and in each case it will be possible to care too much or too little or to the right extent and at the right time, and so on. An account of moral virtue in terms of *pathos* alone, I suspect, is focused on these carings, rather than on the actions that naturally issue from them. But while caring about safety has a name of its own— i.e., fear—as does caring about revenge—i.e., anger—other carings do not have names of their own. They, therefore must be described in terms of the objects cared about—giving and taking of money, esteem, candor about one's accomplishments, etc. My suspicion then, though admittedly I have not argued for it, is that something like this is the explanation of the mixture of *pathē* and *praxeis* in the list of concerns of moral virtue—and that this and the previous point together go a long way towards explaining the passages Professor Fortenbaugh cites in support of his thesis.

Response to (ii): If the preceding is correct, one will have to look elsewhere for an explanation of the difference between *EE* and *EN* on the sphere of moral virtue. As mentioned above, on Professor Fortenbaugh's interpretation we have the same account of moral virtue and its actualization in both *EE* and *EN,* but a more sophisticated notion of *pathos* in *EE,* and the latter leads to the different formulation of that account: now that *pathos* includes action, moral virtue can be characterized in terms of *pathos* alone. My discussion of *pathos* suggests that the notion of *pathos* has not essentially changed from one work to the other, but rather it is the account of moral virtue that has changed. That is to say, in *EE* moral virtue is actualized in a series of assessments and feelings (and only secondarily in actions), while in *EN* it is actualized sometimes in assessments and feelings and sometimes in actions (if some moral virtues pertain to *pathē* and others to *praxeis,* as one interpretation has it), or always in action as well as in feeling and assessment (if every moral virtue concerns both a *pathos* and a *praxis,* as the other interpretation has it).

The explanation for this (admittedly subtle) difference in conceptions of moral virtue is by no means clear. Perhaps, though, Aristotle came to realize in the later *EN* that justice does not involve any single *pathos;* or perhaps at the time of writing *EE* Aristotle was, as Professor Fortenbaugh suggests, more concerned about the role of fortune in life and the way it might interfere with the realization in action of even a morally virtuous person's desires and, wanting moral virtue and its actualization to be something fully under an agent's control, restricted it to desire, and thus *pathos.*[12]

Response to (iii): Here we can be very brief. On my account of *pathos* and moral virtue, there is nothing in the *EE/EN* difference to support a later *EE,* and perhaps even some grounds for a development from *EE* to *EN.*

Finally I want to comment briefly on *charis* and *mempsis.* The former is defined in *Rhet.* 2.7 as service rendered.[13] There is a question about the seriousness with which we should take the definitions in the *Rhetoric.* Professor Fortenbaugh has some sound remarks about this matter in the opening pages of his "Aristotle's *Rhetoric* on Emotions."[14] Here I do not want to dispute his insistence that these definitions deserve more respect than they have been given in the past, but merely to underscore his observation that many of the definitions are tailored to some extent to the purposes of the work. *Pathos* itself, for instance, is at 1378a19–21 defined nonessentially in terms of its effect on judgment, surely because of the relevance of this feature to the orator's concerns (cf. 1356a14–19). Similarly, in view of the close general connection between *pathos* and *praxis* (see my n.11), and the fact that *charis* surely sometimes designates some such feeling-tinged emotional attitude as benevolence, we should not be surprised by a discussion in the *Rhetoric* that fails in one case to distinguish clearly the emotion from the action.[15] As for *mempsis,* which does not appear as a *pathos* in Aristotle himself, it is interesting that Simplicius, in the passage Professor Fortenbaugh has directed our attention to, quotes Theophrastus as saying that *mempsis* differs from *orgē* and *thumos* in "the more and the less." Since on my reading all of Aristotle's accounts of these *pathē* put the emphasis on feeling and desire, I find it hard to believe that for Theophrastus in this context *mempsis* is fundamentally a case of doing something.[16]

9,10. *The stress on the role of fortune in the first and third definitions of happiness at p. 130.18–21* (F.pt.III).[17] Professor Fortenbaugh is properly cautious about the implications that can be drawn from the likelihood that these definitions are Theophrastean together with the greater space given to the issue of fortune in *EE* than in *EN,* and I want not so much to dispute the implications as to underscore the caution, particularly again as it bears on the case for a late *EE.*

The bearing of fortune on happiness does of course get more space in *EE* than in *EN,* and is probably of greater concern in the former, but it is worth noting that this concern is not reflected in *EE*'s formal definition of happiness at 1219a38–39. At the same time, it *is* a strong concern in *EN* (see especially the formulation at 1101a4f.), even if not as great a concern as in *EE.*

The use of *anempodistos* does recall 1153b11, most certainly *Eudemian* in origin, as Professor Fortenbaugh says, though we must not rule out the evident possibility that *EE* 4–6 was revised for use as *EN* 5–7, and that any item of language might have been added during revision.[18] Of course, the tie between the unimpeded and the natural can be found in *Physics* 2.8 (probably early), but admittedly that does not say anything for *EN.* While *anempodistos* does not appear in connection with happiness in the undisputedly *Nicomachean* books as it does at 1153b11, we do get something like the same thought expressed with *empodizei* at 1100b29, in connection with a discussion of the impact of fortune on happiness. (Admittedly it's *to makarion* there, but a similar point seems made about *eudaimonia* at 1101a9.)

But even if we grant that there is a smoothly increasing concern with fortune when we read in order *EN, EE,* Theophrastus, and also that Theophrastus gave special attention to *EE,* I think we want to be very cautious about counting this towards showing that *EE* was later than *EN:* on this or any other ethical issue, Theophrastus could certainly have found himself more in agreement with an earlier than a later work of Aristotle's. In fact, I suspect that on any issue, all other things being equal, the latter hypothesis will be at least as likely as the hypothesis that *EE* is the later work.

11. *Theophrastus and* EE *put forth an inclusive view of happiness,* EN *an exclusive view* (F.pt.IV). This is a large and complex issue, and there is not space to argue it all here, so I restrict myself to a word of caution.

First of all, as John Cooper has shown, even if *EN* 10 is "exclusivist" or intellectualist, *EN* 1–9 surely is not.[19] Cooper himself reads the *EN* 1.7 definition of happiness as pointing towards an intellectualist view, but Terence Irwin, John Ackrill, and now David Keyt, have together made a very strong case for taking it the other way.[20] I want particularly to bring Keyt's rather obscurely located paper to wider attention, for it presents a very strong case in favor of an inclusivist reading even of *EN* 10. If this can be made out, the case for a Theophrastean tie to *EE* on grounds of circularity is severely weakened, and, unless it can be shown that Theophrastus himself read *EN* 10 as intellectualist, in fact fails.[21]

In sum, while I find myself in agreement with Professor Fortenbaugh on the Theophrastean provenance of most of Arius p. 140.7–142.5, I find the evidence he presents for a *Eudemian*-influenced Theophrastus less convincing than he does, but not entirely unconvincing, though I am not extremely confident in these judgments. I am more confident however, on the negative side, in my disagreement with Professor Fortenbaugh about his thesis of a late *EE,* and on the positive side, in my agreement with him on the interesting—and stimulating—character of the work Theophrastus was doing in ethics.

NOTES

1. The citations in parentheses immediately after each feature is numbered and summarized in italics are those of the relevant parts of Professor Fortenbaugh's paper.
2. As became the custom at the conference, I use ''Arius'' throughout as equivalent to ''Arius (or his source).''
3. We ought to move more cautiously, I also think, in rejecting *Magna Moralia*—or, more precisely, its source—if John Cooper's thesis about that work has any plausibility. See his ''The *Magna Moralia* and Aristotle's Moral Philosophy,'' *AJPh* 94 (1973) 327–49; for a contrary view, see Christopher Rowe, ''A Reply to John Cooper on the *Magna Moralia,*'' *AJPh* 96 (1975), 160–72.
4. See C. J. Rowe *The Eudemian and Nicomachean Ethics: A Study in the Development of Aristotle's Thought,* Proc. Cambridge Philol. Soc. Supplement No. 3, 1971, 50–51, and Kevin P. Osborne *Aristotle's Conception of Megalopsychia,* unpublished dissertation, City University of New York, 1979, ch. II.
5. It is interesting that *EN* 5 = *EE* 4 does not speak of the deficiency characteristic of the *zēmiōdēs* or ''waster'' in *EE* 2. The passing reference to justice at the end of *EN* 2.7 (1108b7–9) actually seems better fitted to that common book than does the *EE* 2 (1221a23–24) passage. And if my checking of 1134b11ff. and chapter 2 in the book on justice has not missed something, there is in that book no place for the sort of injustice toward self that the ''waster'' is supposed in *EE* 2 to commit. I am not sure what that means for the common claim that the book on justice has its real home in *EE.* (I do not find any evidence in that book of the sort of ''mature'' theory, incorporating both views, which Professor Fortenbaugh describes at the end of his n.30.)
6. On this reading, the argument of these lines, which, as I mentioned, corresponds to nothing in *EE, EN,* or *MM,* seems to be an attempt to combine the *EE* argument for its doctrine of the mean with the *EN* definition of moral virtue by constructing an argument from that doctrine to the additional two clauses in that definition (or at least to the next to last one). While I am by no means certain that my account of that argument is correct, I do think it is a thoughtful attempt to combine the *EE* and *EN* materials, and not just the work of a passive copier. This does not, however, allow us to conclude Theophrastean authorship, since one outcome of the Rutgers conference on Arius Didymus was—at least for most of us—an increased respect for Arius' philosophical capacities.
    It is too bad that p. 140.7–12 does not discuss which mean the ''mean relative to us'' is better than. If it had, and if we could show it to be Theophrastean in origin, we would have another test for *Eudemian* vs. *Nicomachean* affinity: *EE* describes that (arithmetical) mean as the mean *pros allēla* (1220b23; cf. b30–32), *EN* as the mean *tou pragmatos* (1106a29, b7; cf. *kata to pragma* at a28 and 34, and *kata tēn arithmetikēn analogian* at 35). *MM,* interestingly, makes no attempt to characterize or distinguish the type of mean that moral virtue is supposed to be (unless there is a lacuna at 1190b8, as Ramsauer and Susemihl thought, and something was said there about the type of mean involved).
7. Professor Fortenbaugh's wording of his thesis (F.pt.II) does not rule out (and perhaps encourages our considering the possibility of) a Theophrastean discovery of the com-

plexity of *pathos,* subsequently adopted by Aristotle in a late *EE.* Such a notion—that Theophrastus developed important notions and taught them to Aristotle—would wreak havoc with claims of *Eudemian influence* on Theophrastus, though not, of course, with claims of *Eudemian affinity,* and perhaps that is the ultimate claim of Professor Fortenbaugh's paper.

8. "Fearing is related to fleeing, desiring to reaching for, anger to striking out, in no incidental way. In each of these cases a certain action or range of actions is connected to a *pathos* in some important logical sense. The connection is defeasible, but it is not a merely accidental connection." (Kosman, *loc. cit. supra* n.40.) Kosman should not, however be held responsible for anything I say here, as we have never discussed this matter.

9. Professor Fortenbaugh has suggested in conversation that with the deliberation the *Rhetoric* passage insists on, we have at least a mental action, and, one might add, also the beginning of an action proper. These, I shall suggest shortly, are not logically parts of the *pathos* either.

10. I have observed some people speaking, and have myself fallen into speaking, of the moral virtues as concerned with "the nonrational desires," and I think this language and the interpretation it suggests is very insightful. In several places Aristotle, apparently following *Republic* 4, divides *orexis* into three types, *epithumia, thumos,* and *boulēsis* (Bonitz *Index,* 423a6–8), and at *DA* 432b5–8 (a passage not cited by Bonitz) states that *boulēsis* is *en tōi logistikōi,* while the former two are *en tōi alogōi* (cf. *Rhet.* 1369a4). At *EE* 1227a3–5 (cf. 1226b19–20) Aristotle seems to be understanding *boulēsis* to be desire that results from deliberation. (*Boulēsis* is a difficult notion that received insufficient attention because of misunderstandings about Aristotle's conception of practical reasoning. There are helpful recent discussions in two papers by Terence Irwin, "First Principles in Aristotle's Ethics," *Midwest Studies in Philosophy* 3 [1978] 256f. and "Reason and Responsibility in Aristotle" in *Essays on Aristotle's Ethics,* ed. A. O. Rorty, 128ff.) The implication seems to be that all desire which is not the result of deliberation is nonrational and to be located somewhere under *epithumia* or *thumos* (which Aristotle says at *DA* 433b3–4 are not very different). It seems clear that the desires which must be associated with the practical *pathē* if they are to cause action are in this sense nonrational desires.

11. There are valuable recent studies on these matters by John Cooper in the first chapter of his *Reason and Human Good in Aristotle* (Cambridge 1975) and by Martha Nussbaum in Essay 4 of her *Aristotle's De Motu Animalium* (Princeton 1978). Professor Nussbaum's "The Common Explanation of Animal Motion", a paper read to the ninth Symposium Aristotelicum, expands on and revises the doctrine of that essay, and is very helpful on the defeasibility issue.

Two further observations on the *pathos-praxis* connection: (1) it is worth remembering that in most cases restraints to the translation of a *pathos* into action are absent and action normally does follow; because of this we can expect that when Aristotle's focus is not on the possibility of restraint, he will ignore them in his formulations. This may well be the case for texts like the *Rhetoric,* for instance, where his focus *is* elsewhere. (2) A clearer explanation than we now have of the relationship between *pathos* and desire, and thereby *pathos* and action, is necessary I think before we can say much that is useful about the precise logical relationship between the *pathos* of fear and the deliberation which *Rhet.* 1383a7 says fear makes (*poiei*) men engage in, though it might be noted now that the verb Aristotle uses suggests that even this connection may be defeasible.

12. Both suggestions are, I believe, due to John Cooper. The first appears in his "The *Magna Moralia* and Aristotle's Moral Philosophy," 346; the second arose, as I recall,

at his Spring 1981 seminar on *EE* at Princeton University. I have Professor Cooper to thank for first bringing *EE*'s restriction of moral virtue to *pathē,* and much else about *EE,* to my attention, in this seminar. He should not be held responsible, however, for the use I have made of whatever I have learned from him.

13. There is some question about the text at 1385a18, and earlier editors (e.g., Cope and Freese) read it in such a way that *charis* came out as that feature of us *in virtue of which* we rendered the appropriate service, and they translated it "benevolence." Professor Fortenbaugh is probably right, though, in citing the text of Roemer, Ross, and Kassel who follow Spengel.

14. *AGPh* 52 (1970), 42–53; repr. in *Articles on Aristotle,* v. 4, ed. J. Barnes *et al.,* 134–40.

15. Perhaps in a more careful analysis Aristotle would have made all this clear. Cf. Aspasius, *CIAG* v. 19, 46.26–28.

16. Material throughout this paper, but especially in this section, has been added during revision for publication. Silence on any of my points in Professor Fortenbaugh's paper should not be construed as inability to reply. He expanded his remarks on *pathos* in response to my comments on the original paper, and graciously permitted me to expand considerably on mine. His silence on my points is doubly noble, since he is not only the subject of my comments, but their editor.

17. I count the stress in the first definition as feature #9, and that in the third as feature #10.

18. This possibility reveals a serious problem for claims to locate the common books which are based on stylometric studies, as Terence Irwin suggests in his review of Anthony Kenny's *The Aristotelian Ethics* (Oxford 1978) in *The Journal of Philosophy* 78 (1980) 342, and others have stressed more strongly.

19. *Reason and Human Good in Aristotle* (Cambridge 1975), chapter 2. Cooper's account does not, though I think it could, deal with the Book 6 text discussed by Thomas Nagel in "Aristotle on *Eudaimonia,*" *Phronesis* 17 (1972), repr. in A. O. Rorty, ed., *Essays on Aristotle's Ethics* (Berkeley 1980).

20. The issue, as far as the definition in 1.7 is concerned is, of course, in the interpretation of *teliotatēn* (*aretēn*). Irwin's suggestion is cited, and criticized, by Cooper in *RHGA* 100 n.10; Ackrill's view is presented in his 1974 Dawes Hicks Lecture, repr. A. O. Rorty, *op. cit.,* 28–29. David Keyt's view is presented in his "Intellectualism in Aristotle," *Paideia* Special Aristotle Number (1978) 138–57.

21. While I have some important reservations about Keyt's account of the second happiest life in 10.8, I am inclined to agree with the bulk of his argument. In a long note (n.57), Professor Fortenbaugh outlines some criticism of Keyt's position. All I can do here is indicate the direction of a response; part of our disagreement hinges, I think, on precisely how the terms "inclusive" and "exclusive" are defined, but I will not be able to get into that here. I follow Professor Fortenbaugh's numbering of his five points: (1) Keyt shows that the first life, which F. calls "the life of contemplation," is itself inclusivist in the relevant sense; he does not claim a third alternative; (2) Keyt shows that the best life is not "a strictly intellectual life" in any way that implies a failure (*pace* Cooper, *RHGA* 164) to possess as well as to practice fully all the moral virtues; he shows further that there is no reason to think that exercises of the moral virtues are, in 10.7, no longer ends, no longer constituents of happiness; and, as Cooper demonstrates (*RHGA* ch. 3), there is no evidence in 10 that morally virtuous actions have value only as means to contemplation; (3) Keyt's argument for his reading of 1178a2 seems to me convincing; (4) Keyt admits problems with 1171b1, but goes with the weight of the evidence; (5) Keyt's account of the "superstructure" view gives a perfectly natural explanation of this point. I don't find him to be "forcing" his interpretation on 10 at all.

Index of Ancient Sources